The Open Space District's Mission is to enhance the quality of life in Marin through the acquisition, protection, and responsible stewardship of ridgelands, baylands, and environmentally sensitive lands targeted for preservation in the Marin Countywide Plan.

OPEN SPACES

Lands of the Marin County
Open Space District

Barry Spitz

Marin County Open Space District
3501 Civic Center Drive, #415
Marin County Civic Center
San Rafael, CA 94903
(415) 499-6387
http://marin2.marin.org/mc/pos

ISBN 0-9620715-6-0

First edition

Cover painting, *Mt. Burdell* by Patricia Wallis
Back cover illustration by Ginger Berryman, age 8
Title page photo by Rand Knox, MCOSD
Facing page photo, hikers on White Hill by David Hansen
Photographs from collection of Marin County Open Space District, unless noted

Design and maps by Dewey Livingston

Printed and bound in Canada by Friesens

PREFACE

ON NOVEMBER 7, 1972, sixty-five percent of the voters of Marin County voted yes on Measure A, "Shall the Marin County Regional Park District be created and established?" The Marin County Open Space District (MCOSD) was born December 31, 1972, and the first acquisition funds became available in December, 1973. In the years since, the District has acquired hundreds of undeveloped parcels, totaling more than 13,000 acres. The lands are now grouped into 32 Open Space Preserves, which are open to all visitors, at all times, free of charge.

When I first considered writing a trail guidebook of the District's lands, I thought I already knew them reasonably well. After all, I had been hiking and running long distances over Marin trails for nearly 30 years (including more than 2,500 visits to Terra Linda/Sleepy Hollow Divide Preserve!). But I was astonished by what I found.

The Preserves are larger, lovelier, and richer than I had ever suspected, and contain many trails and hidden beauties previously unknown to me. They are as lustrous a jewel as any in the crown that is Marin County's protected open spaces. Discovering and exploring—and the prospect of sharing—the Preserves' many treasures made working on this book a pleasure.

This is the first guidebook ever written about District lands. Indeed, very little has been published on any of the Preserves (Ring Mountain an exception). Part of this paucity stems from a long-time guiding philosophy of the MCOSD, which is to acquire and protect open space lands, then to leave them unchanged save for environmental and safety concerns. For this reason, the District does not ordinarily provide such visitor amenities as trailhead parking, bathrooms, water fountains, or trash cans. And publicity regarding Preserves has always deliberately been kept to a minimum.

This philosophy remains unchanged. But the defeat of a 1996 tax measure to augment the District's land acquisition fund in the face of sharply escalating real estate prices—in a County renown for its love and support of open space—was pause for reflection by those who manage and love the District. Perhaps if more voters knew what stunning lands their monies had bought and saved from development, the ballot outcome may have been different. Hopefully, this book will increase public awareness of the Preserves, enhance the pleasures of the thousands who already visit regularly, and make Marin residents even more proud of what they have achieved.

This guidebook is intended for all users—hikers, bicyclists, equestrians, runners, dog walkers, first-time and regular visitors, families, those interested in natural and cultural history, etc. Every trail and fire road recognized by the MCOSD (see "Criteria" chapter) is described in detail. By using the accurately measured distances between trailheads and intersections—I walked every route with a surveyor's wheel—the descriptions, and the accompanying, all-new maps, readers will be able to devise hundreds of different trip options.

But first, a few personal comments regarding two issues that have troubled the District in recent years; access to trailheads and conflicts among user groups.

Preserves have always been recognized as County-wide resources that will nonetheless be used primarily by neighborhood residents. Those living adjacent to trailheads, or on narrow streets leading to them, have, justifiably, been concerned about the potential for excessive traffic. While I certainly hope readers of this guidebook will wish to explore unfamiliar Preserves, the impact on any one of the more than 200 trailheads will be negligible.

Still, the book addresses neighbors' concerns in several ways. No individual trailheads are given preference over others. Only signed trailheads are cited. Private property is noted and scrupulously avoided, and nothing in this book is intended to in any way invite or encourage passage onto or across privately owned lands. Sensitive local access issues are mentioned in notes at the start of each relevant trail description. Reminders of courteous behavior, such as refraining from loud talk at residential trailheads, picking up after dogs, minimizing engine idling, parking well clear of driveways, etc., are sprinkled throughout.

Since we come to open space for the serenity it offers, to escape the cares of everyday life, conflicts between user groups are particularly unwelcome. Ironically, much of the rhetoric is directed at the District itself, which saved the lands from development and opened them to the public in the first place. Any set of user rules will dismay some. To get along in open space lands, we must rely on time-tested verities; consideration, tolerance, courtesy, respect for laws. I hope this guidebook makes a contribution.

The book opens with chapters on the setting, geology, climate, flora, and fauna common to all the District's lands. Next are two chapters on history, one relating to Marin County in general, the second to the first owners (the original Mexican land grantees) of each of the Preserves. Then come chapters, in alphabetical order, on the 32 Preserves themselves. Each is introduced by an Open Space Ranger. Within each Preserve chapter are maps and descriptions of all District-recognized trails

*Big Rock Ridge,
separating Novato
from central Marin,
remains one of the
wildest, most scenic
areas of the county.
There are six
MCOSD Preserves—
Ignacio, Indian Tree,
Indian Valley, Loma
Verde, Lucas Valley
and Pacheco Valle—
on Big Rock Ridge.
(David Hansen)*

and fire roads. Note that the distances cited in each heading refer only to the segment within the Preserve.

Nothing in this book supersedes, or is intended to supersede, approved District plans, policies, and rules.

Many people were involved in preparation of this guidebook, and I wish to acknowledge some of them:
• Dewey Livingston, a dear friend, drew the maps, designed the book, set the text, imparted much knowledge, and came on long research walks.
• Ron Miska, the District's Planning and Acquisition Manager, helped guide the project over hurdles, and wrote the several "boxes" sprinkled though the book.
• Chris Bramham, Chief Open Space Ranger, meticulously reviewed text and maps.
• John Aranson, the District's master trail builder, shared his love of those trails.
• Brian Sanford, Supervising Ranger, was unstinting of his time and knowledge.
• David Herlocker, District Naturalist, the "small animal" descriptions.
• Pamela, Sally, Lily—my family—for their patience and understanding throughout.

Despite great care taken in research, and the gracious help I have received from those reading various stages and sections of manuscripts, errors certainly remain among the literally tens of thousands of facts gathered here. I accept responsibility for all such errors, and apologize to anyone inconvenienced by them. Corrections, additions (I'm sure long-time visitors are aware of many more treasures and anecdotes than I have uncovered), and other comments are welcomed. Please direct them to: Ron Miska, Planning and Acquisition Manager, Marin County Open Space District, 3501 Civic Center Drive, #415, San Rafael, CA 94903.

Explore and enjoy!

TABLE OF CONTENTS

The Preserves

WORDS FROM THE GENERAL MANAGER

WELCOME to the lands of the Marin County Open Space District.

The District was formed in 1972 by vote of the people of Marin. Established under provisions of the State Public Resources Code (section 5500), the Open Space District is a separate, special district governed by the County Board of Supervisors, acting as its Board of Directors. The sole purposes of the Open Space District are to acquire special natural lands and to manage them for natural resource protection and compatible public use. The District is now the owner and steward of more than 13,000 acres of publicly accessible open space located throughout the County.

The Open Space District's budget is separate from the County of Marin and is derived largely from local property taxes. Funds not spent in one year carry over to the next year, allowing for accumulation of dollars for costly land acquisitions. Funds can only be spent for open space-related purposes.

WHY THIS GUIDE?

It's Saturday morning and you want to get out into Nature. Do you know where to go?

For years, the Open Space District has not "advertised" its Preserves, nor marketed them. Preserve maps have been available only by request. This was done not so much to hide public open space lands, but rather to be sensitive to those who live next to them. The Open Space District works to be a good neighbor in many ways, including not inviting large numbers of people to limited entrances and encouraging visitors to be respectful of adjacent private lands and residents.

Although use of the Preserves has not been promoted by the District, as with all good things, these open space areas have become increasingly popular. One of the biggest issues facing the Open Space District as we move into the new millennium is how to manage increasing numbers of visitors while preserving natural resource values and meeting the needs of local neighborhoods.

Another development has been coverage of these same Preserves over the Internet, and in newspapers, magazines, and privately produced trail guides. Some of the information given to the public is correct, some isn't. The District cannot control who publishes what about Open Space Preserves. We can, however, provide our own guide to properties, with personal tips for their enjoyment. We are fortunate, indeed, to have the committed interest of Mr. Barry Spitz, author of the extremely popular and meticulously researched *Tamalpais Trails*. We believe the time for our own guidebook is right.

Mr. Spitz has compiled this guidebook to Open Space District properties. Through it, you will learn more about the District, its history and philosophy, its practices and its vision, and most specifically, the many Preserves and the trails and natural and cultural history to be found within them.

ON OPEN SPACE USES AND AMENITIES

The District's open space system now includes 32 Preserves, representing some of the best of Marin tidal wetlands, oak-bay woodlands, chaparral, redwood groves, and natural grasslands. Once acquired by the public, these lands are managed for what is termed "passive recreation," activities which have minimal impact on their natural environment. Because preservation of this natural environment is paramount, you won't find park-like improvements in Open Space Preserves such as restrooms, picnic tables, trash cans, and parking lots. You will find trails, fences only where needed, controlled access gates to limit unauthorized vehicle entry, spring restoration for wildlife purposes, etc.

You can walk, run, skip, or ride (horses or mountain bikes) on open space lands. Or sit down to do a painting, watch birds, take a nap. You are guaranteed to leave open space in a better frame of mind than when you entered.

EMPHASIS ON LOCAL/COUNTY-SIGNIFICANT OPEN SPACE

The Open Space District is one among several public agencies (federal, state, water districts, and cities) managing major public lands in Marin. Each public agency has its own style, purpose, and direction for its properties. With some exceptions, most District open space is located within the eastern third of the County, near or adjacent to residential areas. It is intentional that these lands are so close to home. They are meant to be your public open spaces, easily reached without getting into your car and driving for an hour. They are where you can take a walk in the evening and still make it back in time for dinner. These open space areas are the day-to-day breathing room of our communities. Chances are that there is an Open Space Preserve near you.

ON ACCESS. PARKING LOTS, AND NEIGHBORHOOD NEEDS

Open Space Preserves typically have multiple access points rather than one controlled entry. A few people accessing open space off a street in a residential area pose little problem if those people are mindful where they park. There are no parking lots to invite, say, evening tailgate parties or other noise and annoyance to immediate neighbors. Users who drive to open space must find parking where they can without blocking neighbors' driveways or Preserve entrance gates. Parking at a gate may mean that a fire truck or medic responding to an emergency (maybe yours!) can't get in. Whenever possible, walk or ride your bike or horse to open space.

INTERPRETIVE, VOLUNTEER AND COOPERATIVE PROGRAMS

While District staff does much of the work to keep open space lands and programs going, it is really the dedication of users and volunteers who make the Preserves the gems they are. Through the "Volunteers in Environmental Work" program, groups and individuals nurture Preserve biota and develop close ties between people and "their" lands. Ranger-led interpretive walks help neighborhoods connect directly with the open space behind their homes. The District's Naturalist program expands participants' knowledge of the natural world through hands-on experiences.

A nurturing valley oak, Mt. Burdell Preserve.

The District is also a full partner in regional efforts for open space protection and trail development through cooperative work with, among others, the Bay Area Open Space Council, the Bay Area Ridge Trail, and the Bay Trail. The Open Space District also works cooperatively with the Marin Agricultural Land Trust in their efforts to preserve the agricultural landscape and way of life in Marin.

HEADED OUT? BEFORE YOU GO

Before you head into open space, we ask you to note the following.

1. Tell someone where you are going and when you expect to be back.

2. Wear sturdy shoes and carry water. Bring a jacket if cool weather (or night) is expected, and a map.

3. Be aware of natural conditions on open space that can cause harm. Some of these lands are really wild. There are rattlesnakes, steep drop-offs, poison oak. You can get lost. Be alert and use your good common sense. Keep an eye on your kids.

4. At open space entry gates in residential areas, keep your noise level down and your dog under control.

5. Complaints about dogs off leash are the ones most frequently received by Open Space Rangers. Though your dog may be cute, letting him/her chase wildlife or run and jump on other people is not. Bring a six-foot leash and use it. Dogs are allowed off-leash on fire roads only, with you and under your command. Dogs are not allowed in designated Wildlife Protection Areas. If you want to let your dog run free, consider using one of the increasing number of dog parks in Marin. You are responsible for the conduct of your dog and can be cited for violations.

6. Illegally-ridden bikes are the second most common complaint received by Open Space Rangers. When riding a bike, be sure to bring equipment for minor repairs. Please obey speed limits and ride only where permitted. Use a headlamp at night. Bikes are not allowed on single-track trails unless specifically designated and signed for such use. If you are found in violation of trail access rules, you can be cited.

7. Be aware that you are not the only one out on open space (although sometimes it may seem like it). Be courteous. Bicyclists yield to equestrians and hikers, hikers yield to equestrians. Go the extra mile—let the other guy go first.

8. During summer, be aware that Preserves may be closed occasionally during extreme fire conditions. Please honor these closures. We and the County Fire Department don't want to have to come find you should a wildfire break out. Red Flag closure information is available on a daily basis at 499-7191. If you see a fire on open space, call 911.

9. Most importantly, enjoy yourself!

May your open space visit bring you health, clarity of mind, and true recreation.

The Marin County Open Space wishes to gratefully acknowledge financial contributions from Connie Berto and the Trails Preservation Council toward the preparation and production of this book. Thanks are also due to the following individuals for reviewing draft portions of the book: Beverly Bastian, Connie Berto, Jonathan Braun, Ralph Camiccia, Eleanor Capers, Carol Colbert, Rick Fraites, Stanley Gobbin, Nancy Helmers, Dick Liebes, Bill Long, Caroline McFadden, Michael More, Phillip Paisley, Beth Pollard, Jean Starkweather, and Chuck Taylor.

Frances Brigmann
General Manager, Marin County Open Space District
September, 1999

GEOLOGY

MARIN COUNTY is a triangle-shaped, 520-square-mile peninsula on the central California coast. Immediately south is the Golden Gate, the one great breach in the Coastal Range, through which all Central Valley rivers complete their journey to the ocean. The east side of Marin is edged by water; San Francisco Bay south of San Pedro Peninsula and San Pablo Bay north. Sonoma County forms the entire northern border of Marin (save for Point Reyes). To the west is the Pacific Ocean.

Complex forces have shaped, and continue to shape, the soils and underlying rocks of Marin. The earth's outer crust (lithosphere) is composed of huge plates, to 60 miles thick. These plates move over the molten asthenosphere, another 200 miles thick. Such movements join and break up continents, raise mountain ranges, create volcanoes (Mt. Burdell is of volcanic origin), and ultimately explain many of the earth's major features.

Marin is a particularly active and complex area geologically as it straddles the intersection of two such plates, the Pacific to the west and the North American, upon which the rest of the mainland rests. The divide between the two is the San Andreas Fault, which runs some 600 miles north-south across California. The Pacific Plate is sliding north in relation to the North American plate—Point Reyes was once adjacent to today's Los Angeles—at an average rate of one-two inches a year. Sometimes the movement is more violent, 20 feet in seconds during the violent 1906 San Francisco earthquake.

The Pacific Plate rode over another plate, the Farallon, scraping off, shearing, grinding, and otherwise jumbling much of the rockbed that is now Marin (and most of the Bay Area). This tangled mixture of rocks is called the Franciscan Complex. Its main components are sedimentary rocks—sandstones, mudstones, and shales—much of which was washed down from the Sierra. The sandstone graywacke is dominant in Marin. Chert is another local sedimentary rock. It is very hard so resists erosion and is prominent in outcroppings. Greenstone (of which Bald Hill is an example) is an igneous rock of volcanic origin. Highly distinctive serpentine (the state rock of California), found in several Preserves, is a metamorphic rock formed deep within the earth. Serpentine soils are high in the heavy metals magnesium, iron, chromium, and nickel, and deficient in plant nutrients calcium, potassium, and sodium, so support a unique flora.

Also shaping Marin are the Earth's periodic global swings in temperature. Some 12,000 years ago, when the most recent Ice Age was at its coldest, so much surface water was frozen as polar icecaps that sea level was considerably lower. It was apparently possible to walk to the Farallon Islands, now more than 20 miles offshore. Melting glaciers have been raising sea level since. Waters first began entering the Golden Gate about 10,000 years ago. They reached Richardson Bay some 8,700 years ago and have since covered Marin's earliest Native American settlements. Rising waters also flooded the San Andreas Fault, creating Tomales Bay and Bolinas Lagoon.

Mt. Tamalpais' East Peak is the highest point in the County, elevation 2,571 feet. (West Peak was once higher, at 2,604 feet, but its top was bulldozed during construction of a military base in 1950.) The next nine tallest Marin peaks are Big Rock Ridge (1,887'), Pine Mountain (1,762'), Loma Alta (1,592'), Mt. Burdell (1,558'), Hicks Mountain (1,532'), Barnabe Peak (1,466'), Shroyer Mountain (1,458'), White Hill (1,430'), and Green Hill (1,418'). The summits of White Hill and Green Hill are on MCOSD lands, and District Preserves cover parts of Mt. Tamalpais, Big Rock Ridge, Loma Alta, and Mt. Burdell—the latter two within a few feet of the summit.

Associated with the tallest peaks are long, prominent ridges, defining features of the Marin landscape and barriers to travel. Most District preserves are on these ridgetops or their slopes, as they were generally the County's last, remaining undeveloped lands. For example, there are six Preserves—Ignacio Valley, Indian Tree, Indian Valley, Loma Verde, Lucas Valley, and Pacheco Valle—on Big Rock Ridge alone.

The major stream of Marin is Lagunitas Creek, which flows from the north face of Mt. Tamalpais to Tomales Bay. The headwaters and watersheds of dozens of smaller creeks are found within the Preserves.

One of many glorious waterfalls throughout District lands.
This one is on Cascade Creek, Cascade Canyon Preserve. (Brad Rippe)

WEATHER

MARIN COUNTY, with the rest of the central California coast, enjoys a Mediterranean climate, characterized by wet, mild winters and dry, hot summers. Only four other areas in the world—the coast of Chile, the west coasts of South Africa and Australia, and the Mediterranean basin itself—have such a climate. (These five regions thus also share a similar flora, and many of Marin's invasive plants came from other Mediterranean areas.)

Virtually all rainfall occurs in the months of October through April. January is historically the wettest month, followed, in roughly equal pairs, by December/February, November/March, and October/April. Rainfall amounts vary within the County, generally highest on northern slopes inland (which are therefore more wooded). Winter temperatures in coastal areas almost never drop below freezing and in inland valleys only occasionally, and not by much. Daily highs rarely fail to reach 45 or 50 degrees (all temperatures Fahrenheit). Although the top of Mt. Tamalpais may be dusted with snow once or twice a year, snowfall elsewhere in Marin is highly unusual.

Summers are generally rainless, with rarely more than one or two brief showers over a four, five, or even six month period. Summer temperatures may vary tremendously; it is not unusual for a fog-covered Bolinas Lagoon Preserve to be 30, 40, even 50 degrees, cooler than inland, south-facing Mt. Burdell Preserve, little more than ten miles away. Daily highs regularly reach 80 or 90 degrees, occasionally 100, in northern, inland valleys. Evenings are cool throughout Marin, often dipping below 60 degrees.

Fog plays a role in the weather in both winter and summer. In winter, air near the wet ground absorbs moisture, which then condenses as "radiation" (or "ground" or "tule") fog on cold mornings. Hilltops may remain sunny and considerably warmer. In summer, fog forms above the cold current along the Pacific coast. This fog then penetrates through breaks in the hills, such as to Bothin Marsh via Tennessee Valley.

Every few years, a weather pattern known as *El Niño* produces exceptionally wet (but relatively mild) winters. A record storm in January 1982 caused serious flood damage, much still evident. The winter of 1997-98 was the most recent *El Niño* year, and parts of Baltimore Canyon Preserve received more than 80 inches of rain. Another weather pattern, called *La Niña*, is associated with cooler than usual temperatures. Marin also experiences droughts, the most recent severe one in the mid-1970's. Water shortages result as Marin relies largely on watersheds inside the County.

FLORA

MARIN COUNTY, with its mild climate, varied habitats, and extensive open space, harbors an exceptionally rich flora. More than 1,000 native higher plants (ferns and flowering plants), plus several hundred naturalized aliens, have been identified within the County's 529 square miles. The District's 32 Preserves reflect this diversity of habitat.

While a detailed presentation of the Preserve's flora is beyond the scope of this book, the more common native plants are introduced below. Less abundant species are introduced where appropriate within individual trail descriptions.

Readers interested in learning more should contact the Marin chapter of the California Native Plant Society at 1 Harrison Avenue, Sausalito, CA 94965. The chapter has compiled thorough lists of plant species for just about all the Preserves; copies are available at the District's Civic Center headquarters. Chapter members are also updating the late John Thomas Howell's definitive *Marin Flora*, first published by the University of California Press in 1949 (supplements issued in 1970 and '80). The current authoritative work on the State's flora is *The Jepson Manual of Higher Plants of California*, published in 1993, also by the University of California Press.

FERNS
Ferns are more primitive than the flowering plants, reproducing through spores rather than seeds. Nearly 20 fern species grow within the District. They are generally found in cool, moist forests, where they carpet the understory.

Bracken *(Pteridium aquilinum var. pubescens)*
Found the world over, bracken is also likely the most abundant fern across District preserves. It grows in grassland, brushy canyons, and light woodland. Some ethnic groups harvest the unfolding, young fronds, or fiddlenecks, as food. But the *Jepson Manual* describes bracken as "TOXIC in quantity to livestock and humans" and it also contains carcinogens.

California maidenhair *(Adiantum jordanii)*
Maidenhairs are a great favorite, and commonly cultivated in gardens. The lobed leaves are distinctive. Maidenhairs grow in wetter woodlands. The genus name comes from the Greek "unwettable," as they shed water.

California polypody *(Polypodium californicum)*
This fern grows in shaded areas, such as north-facing slopes, wooded canyons, and rock crevices. Unlike most other common local ferns, the tips of its leaves are somewhat rounded. It is also summer deciduous.

Coastal wood fern *(Dryopteris arguta)*
An abundant fern in wooded areas, except for redwood forests. Generally one-two

feet in height and about six inches across at its widest (also lowest) leaves. The sori containing the sporangia, on the underside of the fronds, are round.

Giant chain (*Woodwardia fimbriata*)

These are much the largest ferns within the District, or anywhere in California. Fronds can reach up to nine feet, although six-seven feet are more common local limits. Chain ferns only grow beside streams and springs. There is a luxuriant cluster at Two Bricks Spring beside Middle Burdell Fire Road.

Goldback (*Pentagramma triangularis*)

Goldbacks grow in partially shaded canyons and light woodlands. Youngsters enjoy pressing the fern's underside (it need not, and should not, be picked) onto dark clothing as the golden-green spores leave a detailed imprint. The leaves dry and curl in summer.

Western sword (*Polystichum munitum*)

Sword ferns are abundant in redwood and Douglas-fir forests. There are woodlands, such as that of Nature Trail (Roy's Redwoods), where sword ferns completely dominate. They are large ferns, reaching five feet.

TREES

While several million trees grow on District lands, fewer than a dozen species account for almost all the total. References to trees are found extensively throughout the text as they are landmarks, and constant companions, along District trails and fire roads.

California Bay (*Umbellularia californica*)

California bay, also referred to in this book as "laurel" and "bay laurel," is the most abundant tree within lands of the Marin County Open Space District.

Most visitors are familiar with bay's long, slender leaves, which produce a pleasing, pungent odor when rubbed, cut, or crushed. The oils are more concentrated than in leaves traditionally sold for cooking (*Laurus nobilis*) and the *Jepson Manual* says they "may produce TOXIC effects in some people."

Laurels display great variability depending on growing conditions. They may be shrubs at the edge of chaparral or rise to more than 100 feet when competing with redwoods for sunlight, such as in Roy's Redwoods. They can be components of mixed woodlands, form dense, all-laurel forests, or stand isolated, sculpted by the wind, high on grassy slopes. They can grow out of seemingly inhospitable rocks, and even attain massive girth in multiple trunks there, such as on Ring Mountain. They often live on despite a downed main trunk, sending up ramrod straight vertical shoots.

The Miwoks had many uses for the bay. For example, hunters rubbed laurel leaves over themselves; the scent helped gain them closer access to deer, elk, and other prey.

Umbellularia is the only native California member of the essentially tropical Laurel family, which includes some 2,200 species worldwide.

Coast Live Oak (*Quercus agrifolia*)

Coast live oak rivals the laurel in numbers across the District; surely a million or more grow within the 32 Preserves. Huge sections of MCOSD land, such as the three tall slopes bordering Pacheco Valle, are dominated by live oak.

Coast live oak's evergreen leaves vary even on a single tree, apparently depending on position in relation to sunlight. Identification is further hampered because oaks hybridize and some trees clearly represent crosses. Also, coast live oaks vary greatly in size. On Mt. Burdell, there are specimens 75 feet tall with huge trunks and broad, round-topped crowns 100 feet across. On the upper reaches of Old St. Hilary's, coast live oaks grow as prostrate mats. Generally, any local oak tree (as opposed to a shrub oak) having leaves with a convex upper surface is a coast live oak.

Coast live oaks can live 250 years or more, the bark furrowing and browning over the decades. Their acorns (and those of valley oaks) were the primary food source for Marin's Miwoks, who consumed several hundred pounds annually per person. The old Spanish name for the coast live oak is "encina."

Valley Oak (*Quercus lobata*)

To many, valley oak rivals the redwood as the quintessential tree of California. Unique to California, they are also the largest of North American oaks; the record is 9.3 feet in diameter. Some reach ages of up to 600 years, becoming, in the words of *Oaks of California,* "The absolute monarchs, steadfast lords of the countryside, governing the landscapes in which they reside."

Valley oaks are deciduous, so can usually be distinguished in winter from the more numerous coast live oaks. The bluntly lobed leaves usually don't arrive until April. An old name, dating from Spanish days, is "roble."

Other oaks and oak relatives

California black oak (*Quercus kelloggii*) has large leaves, up to eight inches, which

---

Oak Woodland Restoration

OAKS PROVIDE VALUABLE HABITAT for many native animals and are a majestic symbol of northern California's wildlands. Yet where are the young oaks that will replace the aging giants? The paucity of young oaks can be attributed largely to overgrazing that began more than a century ago, and continues to this day. You will find young oaks in several Preserves, though, because the District plants hundreds of them every year to reestablish wildlife corridors. Such corridors allow birds and small animals to pass between separate woodlands without becoming dinner for predators in open grasslands.

are usually deeply 6-lobed and bristle-tipped. The leaves yellow in late fall, adding bright color to oak woodlands, then drop in winter. Fresh green (and reddish) leaves return in March.

Also in modest numbers within the Preserves are blue oak (*Q. douglasii*), canyon oak (*Q. chrysolepis*), interior live oak (*Q. wislizenii*), which is shrubby in Marin County, and Oregon oak (*Q. garryana*).

Two other local trees are in the oak family (Fagaceae) but not true oaks (genus *Quercus*). Tan (tanbark) oak (*Lithocarpus densiflorus*) grows in several Preserves at the edge of redwood forests, and can reach 100 feet or more. Many have been dying on Mt. Tam in recent years from a fungus infection spread by beetles. At press-time, this beetle incursion appears to be spreading to coast live oaks. Tanoak bark was once commercially for tanning hides. The tree has hairy, evergreeen leaves, and an acorn fruit.

The nut of chinquapin (*Chrysopsis chrysophylla*) is surrounded by a spiny bur-like casing, nasty to the touch. Chinquapin is rarely tall within the Preserves, and often appears shrubby in chaparral.

Redwood (*Sequoia sempervirens*)

Redwood groves are found within at least 20 District Preserves. Some of the tallest redwoods in Marin County grow in Roy's Redwoods.

Redwoods, the tallest trees in North America, are in the same Bald Cypress family as giant sequoias (*Sequoiadendron giganteum*) of the Sierra, North America's most massive trees. Redwoods once ranged widely over the Pacific Rim but now cling only to the central and northern California coast (and just over the Oregon border).

Redwoods have a thick, tannin-rich bark which keeps them protected from insects and other invaders, as well as from fire. Indeed, they can live for 1,000 years or more. Roots are surprisingly shallow, but interlock in mature groves for greater strength.

Redwoods require huge amounts of water, year-round. That restricts them to creek canyons and moist northern slopes in coastal areas, where fog drip gets them through dry summers.

Redwood seeds are tiny; weighing some 1/8000th of an ounce. Only a negligible percentage grow to mature trees. More common is vegetative sprouting from roots or burls. Recent research indicates these "offspring" are not all identical genetic clones.

Virtually all of Marin's sizable virgin redwood stands—other than in Muir Woods— were logged in the building boom following the Gold Rush. The size of the felled giants can often be gauged by the ring of redwoods that have since sprouted from their roots.

Douglas-fir (*Pseudotsuga menziesii*)

Only two species of trees within the District exceed 150 (sometimes 200) feet— redwood and Douglas-fir. Douglas-fir bark is grayer and more furrowed than redwood's. Its cones have distinctive three-pointed bracts. Needles, which may ex-

ceed 60 million on monarchs in the Pacific Northwest, have two whitish bands on
the lower surface.

Douglas-fir has been expanding its range on District Preserves and throughout Marin this century. The ending of grazing and the suppression of wildfires are
two factors. Indeed, there are those who now even consider Douglas-firs as "weeds"
when they successfully invade traditional oak habitat.

Douglas-fir is the most important timber tree of the Pacific Northwest. They
are not true firs, hence the scientific name *pseudotsuga*, "false hemlock."

Pacific madrone (*Arbutus menziesii*)

This well-known tree inspires adulation. Willis Jepson, dean of California botanists, said of it, "None other in the western woods is more marked by sylvan beauty."
John Thomas Howell wrote in his *Marin Flora*, "[Madrone's] flowers and fruits
[are] beyond compare—the former like sculptured ivory urns, the latter like etched
carnelian globes."

Most distinctive is the tree's bark, which peels back each year to reveal the
cool, red/orange/brown wood beneath. The peeling may be a defense mechanism
against potential insect and fungal invaders. Madrone produces juicy but bland-
tasting orange-red berries, which Miwoks ate both heated and raw. Indeed, its botanic
name "arbutus" derives from the Latin "strawberry tree."

Along several Preserve trails, such as Woodoaks in San Pedro and Wildcat in
Indian Valley, madrones mingle with the closely related, and similar looking, manzanita *(Arctostaphylos manzanita)*. The larger leaves of the madrone, to six inches,
are a distinguishing feature.

California buckeye (*Aesculus californica*)

Most of the common trees within the Preserve retain their foliage year-round. The
buckeye, however, is deciduous and its appearance varies greatly over the year. One
cannot improve on the description found in Howell's *Marin Flora*: "In several as-
pects and at all seasons the buckeye is attractive, whether it is the tracery of bare
branches etched against the winter sky, or the vernal opulence of leaf and flower
conformed into a huge bouquet, or the dull rich tone of colored foliage bronzing
the autumn canyonside."

The *Jepson Manual* labels all parts of the buckeye as poisonous. Native Miwoks
leached the toxin from the big, brown seeds, using the residue for flour. The toxin
was put into shallow, dammed ponds, stupefying fish to make them easier to catch.

Big-leaf maple (*Acer macrophyllum*)

The blade of this maple's leaf can reach almost 10 inches across, earning its common and botanic names ("macrophyllum" means "big leaf" in Latin). Indeed, its
lobed leaves are the largest of some 118 maple species worldwide. These leaves color
in fall, producing Marin's best "New England-type" foliage display. They then fall
and carpet adjacent trails. The tree is found only along streambanks or in adjacent
moist canyons.

California toyon (*Heteromeles arbutifolia*)

Toyon, in the rose family, borders the hazy edge between shrub and tree, and can be placed within either group. Fifteen feet is its usual height limit.

Although toyon is commonly called Christmas berry, its red fruits are actually pomes, like apples and pears, and not berries. "Heteromeles" is from the Greek, "different apple." The berries are abundant in December, accounting for the name. (Another name is California holly, the origin of "Hollywood.")

Arroyo willow (*Salix lasiolepis*)

This is the most common of several Marin County willow species. The arroyo willow is invariably associated with wet soils, such as along stream banks and springs. Although it can reach 30 feet in height, it is often shrubby.

SHRUBS

Shrubs are woody plants that are generally shorter than trees, although there is overlap. They are also multi-branched from the base, compared to the single, large trunk of most trees. Shrubs can be found in all District habitats—within deep and light woodland, dotting grassland, or dominating chaparral.

Coyote brush (*Baccharis pilularis*), Sunflower family

Coyote brush—also called baccharis, coyote bush, and chaparral broom—is abundant, and spreading, in most every Preserve. Coyote brush grows in several habitats but is most conspicuous when expanding into formerly grazed lands, where it may be the only shrub.

Coyote brush is an evergreen with separate female and male plants. In December, the fruiting female bushes are covered with fine, white pappus, ready to carry seeds away in the wind. This gives the shrub yet another name, "fuzzy-wuzzy."

Chamise (*Adenostoma fasciculatum*), Rose family

Chamise and manzanita are Marin's dominant chaparral shrubs. Chamise crown-sprouts vigorously after fires so fire-suppression in recent decades may be reducing its range. Chamise, sometimes called greasewood, grows in dense mats out of root burls. The leaves are needle-like to conserve water. Chamise's evergreen leaves take on a purplish hue in fall, producing a corresponding annual tinge to the upper, southern face of Mt. Tamalpais.

Manzanita (Genus *Arctostaphylos*), Heath family

Most people recognize manzanita, a quintessential component of Marin's chaparral. There are dozens of species and subspecies of manzanita in California; they hybridize and classification has been difficult.

Several species grow within the Preserves. The most abundant is *A. glandulosa*. It is the only local species with a burl (stump-like root crown) base. Alice Eastwood, the grand lady of Marin botany, first described the species. They are hearty survivors of fires, and Eastwood noted some "may be as old as the giant redwoods themselves."

The largest manzanita, attaining a tree-like height of nearly 25 feet within Indian Valley Preserve, is *A. manzanita* (sometimes called Parry's manzanita). It is generally found in open wooded hills, often adjacent to the similar-appearing madrone.

"Manzanita" means "little apple," referring to the appearance of its fruits, which were eaten by Marin's native Americans.

California hazel (*Corylus cornuta* var. *californica*), Birch family

Hazel, also called hazelnut and filbert, can be classified as a small tree. It is abundant in the District's moist, shaded canyons, such as along the trail to Cascade Falls (Cascade Canyon). The leaves are covered with velvety hairs, making them soft to the touch. The fruit, enclosed within a papery circle of bracts, is a delicacy and the tree is cultivated elsewhere. Finding a ripe hazelnut, however, is a frustrating affair; birds arrive first. Hazel's flexible stems were used in basket-masking by several California tribes.

Huckleberry (*Vaccinium ovatum*), Heath family

Huckleberry is abundant on moist, shaded slopes. There is even a Huckleberry Trail in Blithedale Summit Preserve. The serrated, evergreen leaves are distinctive all year. The dark berries ripen in August; they are tasty but small. Howell says of them, "The berries are of two kinds, a rarer form with a bloom and one more common, without a bloom. Both are delicious but there is a discernible difference in flavor even when the two kinds are on bushes growing side by side, as is often the case."

Poison oak (*Toxicodendron diversilobum*), Sumac family

(Discussed in the "Some Cautions" section)

Sticky monkeyflower (*Mimulus aurantiacus*), Figwort family

Sticky, or bush, monkeyflower is common along many District trails, often at the edges of chaparral and scrubby woodland. The evergreen leaves have a sticky feel, thus the name. The flower, with unequal lobes, is usually an orange/yellow. The flowers on some plants persist well into winter.

Ceanothus, California-Lilac (genus *Ceanothus*), Buckthorn family

Several Ceanothus species grow on District lands. Perhaps most spectacular is *C. thyrsiflorus*, known as blue blossom and as wild or mountain lilac. It can be prostrate, or tree-like to 20 feet or more in height. In March through May, the light blue blossoms emit a pervasive, pleasant fragrance.

San Geronimo Ridge is the type locality (meaning where the specimen first described for science was collected) for *C. jepsonii*, or musk brush. It has spiny leaves, large violet-blue flowers, and reddish-tinged fruits; in Howell's words, "One of the most interesting and attractive [plants] on the Marin County serpentine barrens."

Yerba santa (*Eriodictyon californicum*), Waterleaf family

Common in chaparral and brushy woodland, often alongside sticky monkeyflower. Yerba santa has dark green leaves, lanceolate in shape with serrated edges. They are frequently mottled black by a mold. The funnel-shaped, white flowers are usually at their peak in May. The name is Spanish for "blessed grass."

WILDFLOWERS

At least 600 species of wildflowers have been identified on District lands. (A more botanically precise name is "herbs," non-woody, flowering plants—annual, biennial, or perennial—whose above-ground parts last less than one year or growing season.) A sampling of the showiest and most abundant native flowers is presented here.

The list below is by floral color, which is only a guide as nature's palette resists easy classification. The heart of Marin's wildflower season is usually mid-March through mid-May. Plants whose peak bloom is normally early (before March) or late (after May) are so noted. Annuals depend solely on seeds to carry on their lives; biennials and perennials last more than one year. Grasses, whose flowering parts are inconspicuous, are treated separately at the end of the section.

Please do not pick any wildflowers within the District; it is illegal, the blossoms fade quickly, and it deprives other visitors of their enjoyment. Also, some

---

Habitat Restoration

MORE OFTEN THAN NOT, habitat restoration translates to removing non-native (exotic) plants that have invaded MCOSD lands. Without the natural controls found in lands of their origins, exotics can quickly outcompete native plants and become the dominant plant species. Native animals cannot use them for food, and their stands can become so dense that they cannot even be used for cover by the larger animals.

French (*Genista monspessulana*) and Scotch (*Cytisus scoparius*) broom, in the Pea family, are primary culprits, though there are many others. Both are natives of the Mediterranean Basin that escaped the residential landscapes for which they were imported. French is the more common broom in Marin. Scotch broom is generally leafless and has larger yellow flowers than French broom. Individual plants of both species can produce thousands of seeds, and these seeds have proved viable for 80 years and longer.

Another highly successful invader is yellow star-thistle (*Centaurea solstitialis*), in the Sunflower family. Introduced from the Mediterranean Basin during Gold Rush days, it is now widespread in grasslands throughout California. Yellow star-thistle crowds out other wildflowers, has sharp spines that plague visitors, and is toxic to horses. The deep taproot, to eight feet, makes it very hard to pull.

MCOSD staff and volunteers have expended countless thousands of hours eradicating exotic species, so that native flora and fauna may return to their former locales. But the effort must be continuous due to the effective survival strategies of these tenacious plants.

plants within the District are formally listed, or are candidates for listing, as endangered or threatened.

White

Milk Maids (*Cardamine californica*), Mustard Family
Always among the year's very first bloomers, often appearing in January, abundant by February, and in flower for several months after. Often tinged deep rose. Prefers partial shade but widespread. Perennial.

Miners lettuce (*Claytonia perfoliata*), Purslane family
The large, disk-like leaves have long been gathered as a salad green. Small white flowers in center. Widespread. Annual.

Soap plant (*Chlorogalum pomeridianum*), Lily family
While the spider-like flowers are not often seen—they open in evening to attract vespertine insects and are closed by morning—the long, wavy leaves are seemingly everywhere but in deep forest. The bulb has been used as a soap since Miwok days.

Star lily (*Zigadenus fremontii*), Lily family
Rivals milkmaids as first spring bloomer. Tall stems (to three feet) covered with creamy flowers. Grassland, brush, light woodland. Quick to sprout after chaparral burns. Bulb.

Red/Pink

Indian paintbrush (genus *Castilleja*), Figwort family
Paintbrush's striking red flowers stand out in chaparral and other rocky places. Several species of this taxonomically difficult genus grow within the District, and some three dozen throughout California. Domingo Castillejo was a Spanish botanist. Perennial.

Indian warrior (*Pedicularis densiflora*), Figwort family
Grows in crimson clusters in chaparral and light woodland. A partial root parasite, it gains nourishment from other plants. Perennial.

Shooting stars (*Dodecatheon hendersonii*), Primrose family
The color of Marin's shooting stars is hard to classify; *Jepson* says "magenta to deep lavender." But the reflexed corolla (petals), with white, yellow, and black bands is distinctive. Very early bloomer, in light woodland. Perennial.

Red larkspur (*Delphinium nudicaule*), Buttercup family
Grows on rocky, shaded slopes, where its bright red, spurred flowers stand out. Also common is the western, or coast, larkspur (*D. hesperium*), which has dark blue-purple flowers. Legend has it that lupine was misidentified as larkspur when the Marin town was named. Perennial.

California fuchsia (*Epilobium canum*), Evening primrose family
Not particularly common in any of the Preserves, but distinctive for the scarlet red flowers that stand out so late in the year, even into November and December. Clings to shallow soils on dry rock faces. Sometimes called Zauschneria, for its former genus. Perennial.

Clarkia (*Clarkia* genus), Evening primrose family
There are some four dozen clarkia species in California. The red petals of farewell-to-spring (*C. amoena*) have darker red spots near their center. Red ribbons (*C. concinna*), or lovely clarkia, has thin, deeply lobed petals that resemble ribbons. Elegant clarkia (*C. unguiculata,* formerly *C. elegans*) is found in wooded areas. *C. rubicunda* is profuse on Ring Mountain. *C. purpurea* grows abundantly within several Preserves, particularly Mt. Burdell. The genus is named for Captain William Clark of the Lewis & Clark Expedition. Annual.

Starflower (*Trientalis latifolia*), Primrose family
Sometimes abundant in deep shade. The 5-7 rosy petals rest atop the slenderest of pedicels. Perennial

Blue/Purple
Hound's tongue (*Cynoglossum grande*), Borage family
A very early bloomer, occasionally flowering as early as December and with some plants fruiting by February. The "tongue" part is the leaf. Found in light woodland. In the same family, and with similar-looking flowers, as non-native, but widely naturalized, forget-me-nots (genus *Myosotis*). Perennial

Shooting Star (*Dodecatheon hendersonii*), Primrose family
Begins to brighten grassland and light woodland by early February, and can still be found well into April. The corolla is reflexed, and colored magenta to deep lavender, with a white and black band. Perennial

Baby blue-eyes (*Nemophila menziesii*), Waterleaf family
Howell is accurate in saying "this is one of the most beautiful and best-loved wildflowers of the spring, a high favorite with everyone." The bright blue flowers have white centers, blue veins, and black dots. "Nemophila" is Greek for "woodland-loving. Annual.

Blue-eyed grass (*Sisyrinchium bellum*), Iris family
Abundant in Preserve grasslands from late winter into late summer. The leaves are grass-like. The species name, "bellum" (beautiful) is most appropriate, but "blue-eyed" is not as the centers are yellow. Perennial.

Iris (*Iris douglasiana*), Iris family
Often blue but also commonly a pale cream, deep purple, and many shades in between; "iris" is Greek for rainbow. Generally begin flowering in March. The plant is

Tiburon mariposa lily (Calochortus tiburonensis), perhaps the most celebrated flower in Marin County. It grows only on Ring Mountain, and nowhere else in the world. Its discovery by Dr. Robert West in 1972 helped galvanize the effort that led to today's Preserve. (Larry Serpa)

very bitter, making it unwelcome in pastures. The pale variety, *major*, was once recognized as the "Marin iris." Two other iris species grow within the District; one, ground iris (*I. macrosiphon*), has a fragrance. Perennial

Blue dicks (*Dichelostemma capitatum*), Lily family
Long stems raise the bell-shaped flowers above grasses throughout the District. First-blooming among several similar plants, some white, in the *Dichelostemma*, *Brodiaea*, and *Tritelia* genera that botanists have been reclassifying for years. Perennial.

Sky lupine (*Lupinus nanus*), Pea family
Some 10 lupine species, some shrubby and not all blue, grow in the District. One of the more common of the annuals is sky lupine (*L. nanus*). Howell wrote: "It is this lupine which in the spring obscures the green of grassy hills and valleys with mantles and sheets of blue. And yet again it mingles with buttercups, poppies, popcorn-flowers, or tidy-tips to form flower gardens of surpassing beauty." Annual.

Yellow
California buttercup (*Ranunculus californicus*), Buttercup family
Abundant in a variety of habitats, particularly grassland at wood's edge. Shiny, bright yellow flowers. Can have 7-23 petals, usually in middle of that range. "Ranunculus" is Latin for "little frog," as it prefers wet soils. Perennial.

Suncups (*Camissonia ovata*), Evening primrose family
Four-petaled, and low-lying. Often found together in grassland with taller butter-cups. Genus named for L.A. von Chamisso, a French-born German botanist who collected in the San Francisco area in 1816 on a Russian expedition. Perennial.

Tarweed (*Madia* and *Hemizonia* genera), Sunflower family

Tarweed is a name applied to species in both the Madia and Hemizonia genera, and botanists have several times reclassified plants. Some tarweeds are late bloomers, in their glory in September and October, when they are the most colorful and abundant flower in Preserve grasslands. One species can grow to eight feet tall. They also have a pleasing fragrance that pervade grassland on still, late summer afternoons.

Orange

California Poppy (*Eschscholzia californica*), Poppy family

The poppy needs no introduction. Here is Howell's paean: "No poet has yet sung the full beauty of our poppy, no painter has successfully portrayed the satiny sheen of its lustrous petals, no scientist has satsfactorily diagnosed the vagaries of its variations and adaptability. In its abundance, this colorful plant should not be slighted: cherish it and be ever thankful that so rare a flower is common!"

Named by its European discoverer, Chamisso, for Johann Eschscholtz, a fellow traveler on the 1816 Russian expedition to the Bay Area. So the type specimen for California's state flower is in the St. Petersburg (Russia) Academy of Sciences! Annual, sometimes perennial.

GRASSES

Sizable areas in many of the Preserves are dominated by grasses, containing few shrubs or trees. Grassland is an important habitat for many other flowers and for numerous animals. Grasses also grow in wooded areas, serpentine, and in every other environmental niche.

While non-native plants are found within all Preserves, nowhere are they as extensive as within grasslands. It has been said that not a single square meter of grassland in California is without an alien species. The successful invasion of California's grasslands by Eurasian species was one of the swiftest and most spectacular biotic transformations ever recorded.

The invasion has traditionally been dated from 1769, with the first Spanish mission and livestock herd, in San Diego. Recent research on pollen grains of the very successful invader red-stem filaree (*Erodium cicutarium*) found in mission walls suggests the transformation likely began decades earlier, perhaps spreading north from missions established in Baja California. The significant rise of livestock numbers early in the 19th century accelerated the process. The newcomer grasses, generally hearty annuals in the oat, barley, and other tribes, outcompeted native flora, particularly in overgrazed areas.

Identifying individual grass species is difficult. There are some 10,000 members worldwide of the grass family (*Poaceae*, the most economically important plant family) and many require microscopic examination of their tiny flowering parts (florets, arranged in spikelets) for identification. Even the state grass of California, purple needlegrass, found in many Preserves, was reclassified, to *Nassella pulchra* (formerly *Stipa p.*) in the new *Jepson Manual*. Perhaps the best-known and easiest to identify species is rattlesnake grass (*Briza major*); it too was introduced from Europe.

FAUNA

*Before I came to work as the Open Space In-
terpretive Naturalist, I thought that the natural scenic areas of Marin were all under the
administration of the National Park Service
or State Park system. I was amazed to discover
that so many acres of incredible wild land are
actually located right in the backyards of communities along the eastern side of the county,
and are managed by the Open Space District.*
     *While hiking these trails of the various Preserves one is
constantly impressed with the amazing diversity of plant and
animal life found here. Every turn of the trail seems to reward the
hiker with a glimpse of a new landscape, from fern shrouded
forests to serpentine chaparral. Even the smallest Preserves can
offer a glimpse into a variety of fascinating habitats.*
     *My advice to all Open Space hikers is stop! Pause for at least
a moment every now and then to let your ears be filled with the
mystifying sound of the Swainsons Thrush or the chatter of
Bushtits. Stoop low and admire the subtle beauty of the less
obvious wildflowers. You may find that the most memorable
moments of a hike happen when you are standing still!*
                                    — *David Herlocker, District Naturalist*

THE DIVERSE FLORA of the District's Preserves provides habitat for a rich variety of
animal life. Of thousands of animal species (mostly insects) to be found on District
lands, a handful are introduced below. They give a hint of the joys of animal obser-
vation available to patient Preserve visitors. The District offers an ongoing program of Naturalist's walks. Call 499-3647 to learn more.

INSECTS
Monarch Butterfly (*Danaus plexippus*)
This well-known, large, orange and black butterfly can be seen in Marin year-round.
Thousands of them congregate in a grove north of Bolinas to wait out the winter.
These adults disperse east to seek out milkweed plants (genus *Asclepias*) on which
to lay their eggs. The caterpillars eat the milkweed, acquiring a toxin that makes
them unpalatable to bird predators. Stands of *A. fascicularis* on Mt. Burdell Preserve are presently being monitored by monarch researchers. The caterpillars in
turn become adults that travel further east to produce the next brood. The adults
that emerge in the Sierra foothills and northern Central Valley are the ones that
make the return flight to overwintering trees on the coast.
     There are many other butterfly species within the Preserves. Look for them
feeding on favorite nectar sources such as buckwheats, coyote mint, and thistles.

SPIDERS

The most common of the local, large orb-weaving spiders is the golden garden (*Argiope aurantia*). This species is most noticeable in the fall when females build huge webs, as much as three feet across. These large spiders look formidable but they are not aggressive and do not have a venom that is dangerous to humans.

FISH

Salmon (*Oncorhynchus kisutch* and *O. mykiss*)

Two species of salmon still perilously cling to their ancient spawning runs in the County—coho (*Oncorhynchus kisutch*, also called silver salmon) and steelhead (*O. mykiss*). Marin was once famous for its salmon, yielding both the largest coho ever taken in California (22 pounds, in 1959) and the largest steelhead anywhere (30 pounds, in 1906). Dams and other environmental changes have sharply reduced those runs throughout the west. The MCOSD, along with other public and private agencies, works to maintain and augment remaining salmon populations in Cascade Creek, San Geronimo Creek, Miller Creek, and elsewhere.

Both salmon species (steelhead were reclassified from trout to salmon in 1989) enter Marin creeks from the Pacific after the first heavy rainfalls of winter. They swim upstream to the sites where they were born. Females deposit thousands of tiny eggs each in shallow depressions in the bottom gravel at creek's edge. Males, often fighting for the privilege, fertilize the eggs. All adult cohos then die while some of the adult steelhead survive to make another ocean-creek roundtrip.

The young feed on insect larvae and small aquatic animals. But only a tiny fraction of them survive to swim out to the Pacific when the rainy season returns. The salmon make the adjustment to salt water, then spend two to four years in the ocean before returning to begin the cycle anew.

MOLLUSKS

Banana slug (*Ariolomax columbianus*)

All species of banana slugs are hermaphroditic (having both male and female reproductive organs). Their penises, longer than the bodies, sometimes become stuck during copulation, in which case the slug may resort to chewing off its own in order to disengage! Slugs are important members of the woodland ecosystem, helping to recycle decaying plant and animal material.

AMPHIBIANS

Frogs

The most common local frog is the Pacific treefrog (*Hyla regilla*). This species ranges in color from yellow to green, brown or black, but may be distinguished by dark stripes that pass through the eye. Adult males migrate to breeding sites (usually ponds, but sometimes streams or even large puddles) with first winter rains. Here they sing the breeding chorus which may be deafening at times (particularly at Hidden Lake on Mt. Burdell). During late spring, tadpoles emerge as tiny (1/2-3/4") froglets, which may form a living carpet of hopping bodies around breeding pools.

The western toad (*Bufo boreas*) is one of the species of amphibians that appears to be declining in some areas where it used to be common. Biologists are not sure what might be causing this worldwide decline in certain amphibian popula-tions but it is nice to know that, at least for now, western toads are fairly common at Mt. Burdell and Indian Valley Preserves.

Salamanders

Open Space Preserves are home to both the rough skinned newt (*Taricha granu-losa*) and the California newt (*T. torosa*). Rough skinned newts are most commonly encountered in streams that pass through redwood forests, while the California newt usually inhabits the pools and streams found in oak savanna habitats. Adult newts travel to breeding sites during winter rains, where they mate, lay eggs, and then leave. The larvae live underwater and grow to a length of about 2 inches. They then transform into adults and leave the aquatic environment to take up terrestrial life in burrows or rotting logs. Anyone that handles adult newts should wash their hands before eating, and should avoid touching their eyes, as the skin secretions of these salamanders are highly toxic. (Some accounts describe tarichatoxin as the most poisonous non-protein substance known.)

Other common salamanders of Marin are encountered under objects on the ground, usually during winter and spring. The most numerous are the California slender salamander (*Batrachoseps attenuatus*), which often looks more like a worm than a salamander. Close inspection reveals four tiny legs and large dark eyes. Also common is the arboreal salamander (*Aniedes lugubris*), which may be found in large colonies in hollow oak trees.

REPTILES

Lizards

The western fence lizard (*Sceloporus occidentalis*) is frequently seen darting among rocks and, of course, along fences. Children enjoy catching them; be sure to release quickly. This lizard is also known as "Blue belly" for its underside; usually the males are brighter and also show blue on their throats and sides. Recent research suggests that a substance in the blood protein of western fence lizards, a prime host for ticks, kills Lyme-disease bearing bacteria. Fence lizards thus make the outdoors safer for us!

Two species of alligator lizard are found in the Preserves. The southern alliga-tor lizard (*Elgaria multicarinata*) is more common, in oak savanna and drier habi-tats. The northern alligator lizard (*E. coeruleus*) is found in coastal locations and in redwood/Douglas fir forests.

Snakes

Some ten snake species reside in District lands. The common garter snake (*Thamnophis sirtalis*) is the widest-ranging North American reptile, living in many habitats from the Everglades to farther north into Canada than any other reptile. Our local subspecie has red bars along its sides. A second common garter snake is the western terrestrial (*T. elegans*), with a clear mid-dorsal stripe the full length of its 2-3 foot body.

The gopher snake (*Pituophis melanoleucus*) is our largest snake, sometimes to six feet or longer. It is light-colored with generally brownish, square-shaped blotches across the back. Like the rattlesnake, which it resembles, it may hiss and vibrate its tail when threatened, but is not venomous.

The western yellow-bellied racer (*Coluber constrictor mormon*) is a greenish-brown snake that is common in grassland, particularly near wet meadows and springs. A typical encounter with a racer is to barely glimpse the disappearing tail as you look to identify the cause of a faint sound slipping through the grass.

The California kingsnake (*Lampropeltis getulus*) is actually rare locally but a treat to spot. It is black and patterned with narrow white bands over its usually four to five foot body. In its diet are other snakes, including the rattler.

The Northern Pacific rattlesnake (*Crotalus viridis oreganus*) is in the "Some Cautions" section.

BIRDS

More than 300 species of birds live on, or visit, Preserve lands each year. Numbers are highest during winter, particularly in wetland Preserves, when migrating water-fowl pass through or spend the season. Scores of bird species, from eagle to hummingbird, breed within the Preserves.

By preserving habitat, District lands have greatly aided most local bird species. But public access to formerly off-limits lands has come with a price for others. For example, California quail (*Callipepla californica*), once abundant in Indian Valley when it was private and fenced off, is now all but gone there, severely disturbed by off-leash dogs, feral cats, and humans. The problem is so widespread that California quail, the State bird, is now considered a candidate for protection as an endangered species.

Below is a sampling of a few of the more common and easily identifiable birds to be found on or above MCOSD lands, in standard American Ornithologists Union checklist order. To learn more, contact the Audubon Society of Marin (383-1770), or visit Richardson Bay Audubon Center at 376 Greenwood Beach Road in Tiburon.

Great blue heron (*Ardea herodias*)
The stately great blue heron is the longest-legged and tallest (four feet) of Marin's

---

Environmental Education

MCOSD offers two ways to learn more about the plants and critters on open space. You can become a subscriber to the MCOSD naturalist program, or you can attend one of the ranger walks held monthly on various Preserves. Naturalist outings offer an in-depth look at open space subjects, whereas ranger walks cover a variety of general topics. Either way, you'll gain a greater appreciation of MCOSD Preserves and the bounty of open space resources in Marin County. For schedules, contact the MCOSD Field Office at 499-6405.

birds. Great blues have a wingspread of six feet when in their characteristic slow, folded neck, flight. But they are most often seen standing motionless in shallow water, head erect, waiting for prey to spear. Great blue herons nest in trees at Audubon Canyon Ranch, adjacent to the rich feeding grounds of Bolinas Lagoon Preserve.

Great egret (*Ardea albus*) and Snowy egret (*Egretta thula*)

Marin's two egrets are long-legged, all-white birds. Great egrets, nearly the size of great blue herons, have yellow bills and black legs and feet. The smaller snowy egrets have slenderer black bills and yellow feet. Both hunt by wading in shallow water. Both breed at Audubon Canyon Ranch, adjacent to Bolinas Lagoon. The Ranch is open to the public in spring. The great egret was long the symbol of the National Audubon Society—it was the killing of a warden by hunters gathering egret plumes (*aigrettes*) for women's hats that triggered the Society's growth.

Turkey vulture (*Cathartes aura*)

It would be unusual to visit a Preserve and not see turkey vultures soaring on the thermals. They are among the largest birds in Marin, with a wingspread of nearly six feet. Turkey vultures remain abundant despite their large size, seemingly decreasing numbers of their dietary staples (dead animals), and the near extinction of their cousins, the California condor, which once ranged into Marin as well.

Turkey vultures can be distinguished from other large raptors by the shallow "V" (dihedral) shape of their wings in flight, the infrequent, slow wing flaps, the black and white wing undersides, and, up close, the featherless red head. They virtually never call. If a vulture flies up when approached, there is likely a carcass nearby.

Red-tailed hawk (*Buteo jamaicensis*)

Red-tailed hawks soar in wide circles, then make swift dives (called stoops) onto their prey, usually rodents. Red-tails are smaller than turkey vultures, with a wingspread of some four feet, but larger than other local hawks. In the right light, the red of the tail is dramatic, but at other times may not be apparent. The red-tailed's wild, piercing call is sometimes mimicked by jays.

Mallard (*Anas platyrhynchos*)

In winter, it is common to find five to ten species of ducks feeding in wetland Preserves. The abundant mallard, by far the most common duck in America, is one of the few ducks to remain all year and breed here. Spotting a family of ducklings is always a joy. Only male mallards have characteristic green heads and white collars.

Great horned owl (*Bubo virginianus*)

There are not large numbers of great horned owls within the Preserves—they require sizable hunting territories—and they are not often seen. But their deep hoots are regular treats for visitors around sunrise and sunset. Great horneds are much the largest of several owl species in Marin, and the only large ones with tufts. They are powerful birds, capable of taking prey as heavy as skunks.

Several pairs of northern spotted owls (*Strix occidentalis*), which are on the

Federal list of threatened species, also breed in District woodlands.

Northern flicker (*Colaptes auratus*)
The flicker may be the most abundant woodpecker in District Preserves. Atypical of woodpeckers, they feed mostly on the ground, and are often seen when flushed upwards by approaching visitors. In flight, flickers display a conspicuous white rump. Other common Marin woodpeckers are the acorn (*Melanerpes formicivorus*), with its clown-like facial markings, and the downy (*Picoides pubescens*) and similar but larger hairy (*P. villosus*). Less common, but spectacular, is the pileated (*Dryocopus pileatus*), Marin's largest woodpecker.

Western scrub jay (*Aphelocoma californica*)
Scrub jays seem ubiquitous in chaparral and light woodland sections of all Preserves, checking out visitors for a meal opportunity. They are blue, but a separate species from the blue jay (*Cyanocitta cristata*) of the eastern states. Steller's jays (*C. stelleri*), which have a dark crest, are also common in well-wooded Preserves.

Common raven (*Corvus corax*) and American crow (*C. brachyrhynchos*)
Crows and ravens are unmistakable as our only large, all-black birds. Ravens are some six inches larger than crows, and have a thicker bill and wedge-shaped tail. Crows and ravens are revered in Native American lore and some ornithologists have proclaimed them the smartest of all birds.

American robin (*Turdus migratorius*)
Everyone knows the robin. They are much more abundant locally in winter, when northern breeders augment the permanent residents, but total numbers vary markedly year to year. Also arriving in winter in wooded Preserves are varied thrushes (*Ixoreus naevius*). They are in the same thrush family as robins and similar in size and appearance, but have a black breastband and orange eyebrows and wingbars.

California towhee (*Pipilo crissalis*)
California (formerly called Brown) towhees are very common in chaparral and light woods. They scrape the duff, both feet together, turning up meals. A more conspicuously colored towhee, also common, is the spotted (*P. maculatus*), formerly called the rufous-sided. Males have a striking pattern of black on top, chestnut sides, and white underparts and wing patches.

Dark-eyed junco (*Junco hyemalis*)
The small (about six inches) juncos are abundant in woodland Preserves. They are commonly found feeding, alone or in small flocks, on or near forest floors. Juncos have white outer tail feathers that are conspicuous in flight.

White-crowned sparrow (*Zonotrichia albicollis*)
White-crowned sparrows are found in greatest numbers in colder months, when many overwinter here. Males have a black and white striped head. The songs and

calls of white-crowneds have been studied extensively and experts can distinguish dialects, identifying where a sparrow was born. Also common locally are the aptly named song sparrow (*Melospiza melodia*) and, in winter, the golden-crowned sparrow (*Zonotrichia atricapilla*).

Red-winged blackbird (*Agelaius phoeniceus*)

Red-winged blackbirds are among the most abundant birds in America. Males have striking red shoulder patches, or epaulets, which stand out both in flight and when the bird is clinging to a reed in the marshy areas it favors. Females and immatures are brownish with black striping. They form huge flocks in winter. Also abundant locally are Brewer's blackbirds (*Euphagus cyanocephalus*), which have yellow eyes. Males are all-black, with a purplish tinge on the head, and females are dull brown.

MAMMALS

More than 35 mammal species live on District lands. While it is the smallest among them—bats, shrews, voles, moles, and mice—that are most abundant, larger mammals tend to capture attention. So below are introductions (in alphabetical order) to some of the District's bigger, native, land mammals, just about all of whom may be seen in all of the Preserves. Note that Marin's three largest mammals during Miwok days—grizzly bear, black bear, and elk—were all extirpated shortly after the Gold Rush. (Elk have since been reintroduced at Point Reyes National Seashore.)

Black-tailed deer (*Odocoileus hemionus*)

The black-tailed (also called the mule deer, particularly in the Sierra) is the only deer species native to Marin. They are most active in morning and evening. Dietary staples include acorns and leaves of various shrubs and trees.

The males grow antlers, which are first covered with velvet. This velvet is rubbed off by the fall mating season, when the antlers may be used in jousting contests for breeding privileges. The antlers are then shed.Spotted fawns, one or two in a brood, are born in spring. They are able to walk within minutes of birth.

Deer can live 10-15 years in the wild. As former predators—mountain lion, bears, bobcats—have been reduced or eradicated, deer are likely more abundant now than they were in Miwok days. Some believe this increase has been a detriment to oak tree reproduction, as deer browse newly fallen acorns.

Blacktail jackrabbit (*Lepus californicus*)
Brush rabbit (*Sylvilagus bachmani*)

One hare, the blacktail jackrabbit, and one rabbit, the brush rabbit, are native within the District. Hares and rabbits are in the same order (Leporidae). Hares are distinguished by their divided upper lip and long hind legs, and their young are born open-eyed and furred. The jackrabbit relies on its long ears to detect enemies and its long legs to escape.

The smaller brush rabbit, wih a white "cotton" tail, relies on concealment.

Rabbits are prolific breeders—they may do so at any season in Marin, where food is always available.

Bobcat (*Lynx rufus*)

Bobcats roam in most Preserves but are secretive, so seen only by lucky, sharp-eyed observers. Bobcats hunt rabbits, squirrels, small reptiles, and birds. They have never been a threat to Preserve visitors.

Bobcats are 25-30 inches across and weigh 15-35 pounds. They can be confused with a feral cat, but the short, "bobbed" tail, black at the tip, is usually a key.

Coyote (*Canis latrans*) and Mountain lion (*Felis concolor*)

See "Some Cautions" section

Gray fox (*Urocyon cinereoargenteus*)

The gray is Marin's only native fox, although the red fox (*Vulpes fulva*), which has a white tip to its tail, has been introduced. The omnivorous gray fox eats small mammals such as mice, along with insects, fruits, acorns, and birds and their eggs. Unlike most other foxes, they can climb trees to hunt and escape predators.

Foxes are mostly nocturnal so be wary of any seen during the day, as it may be rabid or otherwise ill (advice also applying to raccoons and skunks).

Raccoon (*Procyon lotor*)

Although raccoons are found in all Preserves, they are nocturnal, so not frequently seen. But their tracks are easily spotted in mud. They resemble a human handprint, with five well-formed toes and the claws appearing as dots.

Raccoons are omnivorous, as every suburban dweller who has had a garbage can overturned knows. In the wild, they take mice, small birds and bird eggs, frogs, insects, fruits and berries, invertebrates, and more. They generally hunt near water. The species name "lotor" means "one who washes," as raccoons, for reasons unknown, wash their food before ingesting it.

Striped skunk (*Mephitis mephitis*) and spotted skunk (*Spilogale putorius*)

There are two skunk species in Marin County, the striped and the spotted. The striped has two white stripes along its back and one on its head. The spotted skunk is about half the size of the striped and has a broken white/black pattern. Skunks appear fearless or tame for good reason, as no animal wishes to be sprayed. Another reason to keep children away is the danger of rabies; skunks' incidence of rabies exceeds that of domestic dogs.

Western gray squirrel (*Sciurus griseus*)
California ground squirrel (*Citellus beechyi*)

The western gray is large, up to a foot in body-length. Its bushy tail and white belly distinguish it from the brownish California ground squirrel. Western gray squirrels spend much of their time in trees but also forage on the ground. They make a rapid barking sound. Acorns, other seeds, and certain fungi are dietary staples for both these diurnal squirrel species. A third local squirrel is the golden-mantled (*C. lateralis*). Fellow members of the order Rodentia are the chipmunks, of which the Sonoma chipmunk (*Eutamias sonomae*) may be the most common within the Preserves.

EARLY MARIN HISTORY

THE COAST MIWOKS call themselves "The First People." Evidence has been found dating their presence in Marin back some 8,000 years at Olompali (Mt. Burdell), one of the oldest continuously occupied native sites in California. Marin's Miwoks were linguistically related to other Miwok groups in California.

Temperate Marin offered abundant food sources and Miwoks hunted elk, deer, rabbits, ducks, and other birds. They fished in the inland bays on boats made of tied bundles of tule rushes. At water's edge, they gathered shellfish. There was trading with nearby tribes, such as for obsidian with the Pomos in Sonoma County. Grassland was burned to encourage the growth of oaks, source of their dietary staple, acorns.

Coast Miwoks lived in villages near the bay or in seasonal camps inland. Men gathered in communal sweat lodges for social, health, and ceremonial purposes. Families lived in conical redwood structures lined with grasses. Miwok villages have been recreated in Point Reyes National Seashore and at Olompali State Historic Park. The Marin Museum of the American Indian, at Miwok Park in Novato, has a collection of local artifacts, other displays, and records of village sites and archeological digs. Some Miwok names, possibly including Tamalpais ("west" or "coast" "hill"), have been handed down.

The first Miwok contact with Europeans was in 1579 when Francis Drake put his ship *Golden Hinde* ashore for repairs. Drake's chaplain, Francis Fletcher, wrote, "They are a people of tractable, free, and loving nature without guile or treachery."

In 1593, Sebastian Cermenho, a captain on Spain's lucrative Philippines to Mexico trade route, was shipwrecked off Point Reyes and met Miwoks as well. (A search and recovery effort for his galleon, the *San Agustin*, is being undertaken.) In 1603, Sebastian Vizcaino may have put in along Tomales Bay. Although the galleons making the yearly roundtrip between Manila and Acapulco passed the Marin coast, there is no record of another European visit until 1775.

All of today's California had been claimed by Spain from the 16th century. It was part of their Mexican empire, and called Alta California. But Spain made no effort to settle, or even explore, Alta California until threats to her dominion began developing in the middle of the 18th century. Russians were approaching by land from the north, and the British, French, and upstart Americans by sea.

Spain responded by setting up a chain of religious establishments (missions), aimed at baptizing and "civilizing" the native Americans, plus associated towns (pueblos) and forts (presidios) along the coast. The first mission was in San Diego in 1769; twenty more followed to the north. San Francisco's mission and presidio were established in 1776, a year after Spain's Juan Ayala became the first European to sail into San Francisco Bay. Members of Ayala's party visited Marin.

There was a high death rate among the native Americans at the San Francisco site, which was blamed on the cold, foggy weather. So, on December 14, 1817, an asistencia (hospital mission) was dedicated in Marin, 20th in the chain. It was named San Rafael Arcangel, for the angel of bodily healing. Actual construction began in 1818. The location was that of today's mission although the present re-creation dates only from 1949. (The original mission building, in disrepair, was sold for lumber in the 1860's.) The asistencia was upgraded to full mission status in 1825.

Despite sunnier skies, and the benevolence of some of the padres attached to the mission, Marin's estimated 3,000 Miwoks at the time suffered terribly. Their way of life was disrupted as they were forced to abandon old beliefs and to work and live at the mission. But deadliest were introduced European diseases, notably measles, smallpox, and syphilis, for which the Miwoks had no immunity. The high death rate, plus intermarriage and flight to remoter lands, reduced Marin's Miwok population some ninety percent by 1840, a single generation.

There were a couple of unsuccessful attempts at rebellion, most notably in 1823. One Miwok "chief" who managed to long elude the Spanish was dubbed "El Marinero" for his skill on the waterways. He was finally captured, and died in captivity in 1834, but his name became attached to the County.

In 1821, Mexico won independence from Spain (although news did not reach Marin until the following year). In 1834, Mexico secularized the Alta California missions and their vast land holdings. The future Marin County, unsettled except at the mission, suddenly was literally up for grabs and Mexico was eager to oblige.

Mexico wanted to populate Alta California to ward off increasing foreign encroachments—ships of several nationalities now called regularly and overland travel to California opened with Jedediah Smith in 1826. (James Miller, later a Marin land baron, co-led the first overland party of settlers, which arrived in 1844.) Mexican authorities accelerated a practice begun decades earlier by Spain; the granting of huge ranchos.

Grants were made by the Mexican governors. Grantees had to be Mexican citizens, Catholic, and male. Several European-born, non-Catholic residents qualified by applying for citizenship and converting. Friends, soldiers, and others performing services for the government were given preference although there was so much land, and so few living in the province, that a rather large percentage of petitioners were successful.

Grants were measured in leagues, one league being 4,428 acres. Boundaries were drawn on rough maps called *diseños* and marked in an ancient ceremonial with neighbors as witnesses. Grants were free and carried only nominal conditions relating to living on the land and improving it. Between 1834 and the last days of their rule in 1846, Mexican authorities carved all Marin into 21 grants covering nearly 320,000 acres.

It is now easy to view this short period as a "golden" era in Marin. A handful of landowners ran vast ranches in an abundant country so wild and open that black, even grizzly, bears still roamed. Herds of cattle wandered freely, rounded up by *vaqueros*. The meat, hides, and tallow, were the *ranchero's* main source of food, trade, and income. There was also hunting, logging, farming, and sheep raising. *Californios* exhibited a gracious hospitality to one another and to the occasional visitors. But there were downsides. For example, travelers describe the impossibility of sleep due to fleas and Marin's first land grantee, John Thomas Reed, died from what may have been a simple injury when there was no doctor to stem the bleeding.

Control of California effectively passed from Mexico in the Bear Flag Revolt of 1846, in which the only fatality occurred at Olompali in Marin. California was formally handed over to the United States in 1848 by the treaty of Guadalupe-Hidalgo ending the U.S.-Mexican War. The discovery of gold that year, with the first flood of fortune-seekers arriving in '49, quickly changed everything. California was admitted as a state in 1850 with Marin one of the original 27 counties.

In 1852, a United States Land Commission convened in San Francisco to rule on the validity of each of the Mexican grants. The pre-1846 *Californios* who filed claims faced years of legal expenses, as all decisions were appealed and cases often wound up in the United States Supreme Court. Titles (patent) were not issued until decades later. Many grantees with good claims still lost all or much of their land to agents and lawyers.

These ranchos have a direct relation to the Marin County Open Space District Preserves of today; the stories behind them helping to explain why such sizable tracts so close to San Francisco remained undeveloped for so long. Half of today's Preserves have boundaries that exactly match lines drawn for the Mexican land grants. Twenty of the District's Preserves are clustered on just four of the original ranchos, all 32 on just nine grants. Background on these nine grants follow. More recent elements of local history are incorporated into individual Preserve and trail descriptions.

But first, a general note on dairying within the County. When the Gold Rush produced a large and eager nearby market in San Francisco and the Sierra foothills, Marin's ranchos began shifting from cattle raising to dairying. (Hogs were also an integral part of each ranch.) Throughout the second half of the 19th century, Marin was the number one dairy county in California. Munro-Fraser, in his 1880 *History of Marin*, writes, "There is probably no better dairy country in the world than Sonoma and Marin counties." He records that Marin produced more than half the State's butter in the 1860's, with "an average of a pound of butter a day to each cow." Marin was also the leading producer of cheese. During the 19th century, cows were hand-milked, the milk then strained and separated. Southern Marin dairies rushed their milk to San Francisco in the days before pasteurization.

An unfortunate side effect of livestock grazing was that the County's (and almost all of California's) native grasses were to a large extent outcompeted and replaced by Eurasian annuals. The annuals were brought in both deliberately and accidentally, for example, as seeds on the hooves of imported livestock, then spread. Unlike native bunchgrasses, which can retain a green color year-round, annuals die back each spring to produce the golden hillsides that give extra meaning to "The Golden State."

It was Marin's dairying past that left large acreages undeveloped into the post World War II-period. It is these ranches that are the core of today's Marin County Open Space District Preserves.

THE MEXICAN LAND GRANTS

RANCHO CAÑADA DE HERRERA (6,600 acres)
Preserves: Bald Hill, Cascade Canyon, Loma Alta, Terra Linda/Sleepy Hollow Divide (parts), White Hill

JUSTO AND MARIA Sais came to Monterey with the first wave of northern California settlers in the 1770's. A son, Juan Sais, was born in Monterey in 1779. Juan served in the military for at least 15 years, stationed in Yerba Buena (San Francisco). He married Dominga Massa and the couple had 13 children.

Sais family members began living in today's San Anselmo around 1837. Bears roamed the hills and there was an Indian rancheria at the foot of Red Hill. In 1839, Juan Sais sent son Domingo to the Mexican governor in Monterey to petition for the San Anselmo land, called Cañada de Herrera (Valley of the Blacksmiths), in the family's behalf. Domingo (b. 1806) had been a soldier at Yerba Buena since 1826.

Acting Governor Jimeno agreed with the request, but made the grant—upper Ross Valley (San Anselmo and Fairfax)—in Domingo's name only. The parents were furious. A family story is that mother Dominga took Domingo over her knee and spanked him. Juan moved out, to Rancho Sausalito, where he died in 1846.

Domingo and wife Manuella had six children. They, and other members of the extended family, lived in an adobe called La Pavidion on a knoll south of present Sir Francis Drake Boulevard. In Marin historian Jack Mason's words, "The Sais family was an oasis of hospitality in the wilderness." They began a small ranching operation.

Domingo's grant was confirmed by the U.S. Land Commission on October 20, 1853, the first in Marin. But Domingo died 27 days later, apparently from injuries suffered in falling off a horse. He left debts and no will, plunging the family into years of financial crisis. There were also legal battles, including with Domingo's brother Nasario, who claimed to have lived on the rancho before Domingo. Pedro, Domingo's oldest son, ended up with 3,193 acres and Manuella with 1,539, including today's downtown San Anselmo and the Cascade area of Fairfax.

In 1873, Pedro, short of cash, sold his entire holdings for $60,000 to Peter Austin and Ebenezer Wormouth. Manuella held onto most of her acreage. She provided the right-of-way through which both the railroad and future Sir Francis Drake Boulevard passed through the Ross Valley. Manuella died in 1891, Pedro in '92.

Mason says, "Through intermarriage with the Pachecos, the Peraltas, the Blacks and other early families the Sais *genre* survived; today no blood strain runs as deep and strong in the county's bloodstream as theirs."

RANCHO CORTE MADERA DEL PRESIDIO (7,845 acres)
Preserves: Alto Bowl/Horse Hill, Blithedale Summit, Bothin Marsh, Camino Alto, Old St. Hilary's, Ring Mountain, Tiburon Ridge

John Thomas Reed was born in Dublin in 1805. He came to Mexico in 1820, to Los

Angeles in 1825, the Bay Area a year later. Reed proceeded to erect a "shack" in Sausalito, becoming the first native English speaker, and the first European not directly associated with Mission San Rafael, to live in Marin. He also started the first ferry service on San Francisco Bay.

In 1834, Reed petitioned to become a Mexican citizen and, a few months later, applied for Rancho Corte Madera del Presdio ("cut wood for the Presdio," as redwood was shipped to San Francisco). It was awarded October 2, 1834, the first land grant in Marin and first north of San Francisco Bay.

Reed built a house on a small hill at the corner of today's La Goma Street and Locke Lane, which was then at water's edge. This house, and two subsequent ones, are gone but three almond trees planted by Reed survive. He also began work on the sawmill—still standing, completely rebuilt, in Old Mill Park—that gave Mill Valley its name.

In 1836, Reed married Hilaria Sanchez (1813-1868) of a prominent Bay Area Mexican family. Reed had first met her when she was nine. She spoke no English.

They had four children. Eldest was John Joseph (1837-1899), among the first non-natives born in Marin. To celebrate, the proud father climbed to the top of Tamalpais and planted a wooden cross. (This was the first documented ascent of the peak, although others surely preceded him.) Ricardo (1839-51), Hilarita (1840-1908), and Maria Inez (1841-83) followed.

John Thomas Reed was sole owner of land that is now valued (with the buildings upon it) in the trillions of dollars. But his chance to enjoy it was brief. In 1843, Reed suffered an accident, possibly falling from a horse. A phlebotomy was performed but no one could then stop the subsequent bleeding; there were as yet no doctors in Marin. Reed died June 29, 1843, age 38.

Decades of court fights lay ahead and the Reed family title patent was not issued until 1885. By then, half the land had already been sold off to pay legal fees.

John Joseph ended up with more than 2,000 acres, the Reed Rancho covering the northern part of the Tiburon peninsula. He lived there with wife Carlota and son John Paul, keeping up old *Californio* ways. Hilarita received more than 1,000 acres on the southern end of Tiburon, plus Strawberry. She married Dr. Benjamin Lyford, who managed dairy ranches on the lands. The Lyford family house on Strawberry Point, built in 1878, was transported across Richardson Bay in 1957 and now stands on the Audubon property off Greenwood Beach Road. Maria Inez inherited 646 acres in Mill Valley, upon which her husband Thomas Deffebach also ran a dairy ranch. Carmelita Garcia, a daughter of Hilaria Reed by a second marriage, received 325 acres.

Reed heirs held onto sizable parcels for decades, and still retain some land.

RANCHO NICASIO (56,616 acres)
Preserves: Indian Tree, Little Mountain, Verissimo Hills

The story behind Rancho Nicasio is complex, perhaps now beyond full unraveling. According to the dean of Marin historians, Jack Mason, it involved a swindle perpetrated by Mexican Governor Juan Alvarado and military commander General Mariano Vallejo.

In 1835, following secularization of California's missions, the baptized natives attached to San Rafael were to be given their own land. They chose Nicasio, site of a sizable earlier Miwok settlement, and Vallejo supposedly set aside 80,000 acres for them. But apparently no deed was issued.

This lack of formal evidence led the natives to appeal to Governor Alvarado. In 1839, he granted them one league (4,428 acres) of Tincasia, at the southern edge of Nicasio Valley, where they were living, but no more. Then Alvarado, with Vallejo in collusion, employed a complicated ruse to try to gain the balance of the grant lands for himself. In effect, he offered the natives just $1,000, and didn't even deliver that.

The next Governor, Manuel Micheltorena, turned Alvarado down and instead awarded Nicasio's 56,600 acres, largest of Marin's land grants, jointly to Juan Cooper and Pablo De la Guerra. Cooper had also previously been granted Rancho Punta de Quentin (which see). Alvarado did not relinquish his claim, and fought an ultimately losing legal battle in Mexican, then U.S. courts, for years.

De la Guerra was a Spanish-born aristocrat who had been educated in England. He defied American authority during the takeover from Mexico in 1846 but later served four terms as a State senator.

In 1849, Cooper and De la Guerra hired Jasper O'Farrell (who first laid out San Francisco's streets, one bearing his name) to survey their holdings. O'Farrell divided Nicasio into five lots, awarding two (totaling 16,293 acres) to Cooper, two (30,844 acres) to de la Guerra, and one (9,479 acres) to himself as payment.

All three landowners then sold out: Cooper to Benjamin Buckelew for $10,000; De la Guerra to Henry Halleck for $30,000; O'Farrell to James Black for $2,000 (and presumably a land trade). President Lincoln signed the land patents in 1861.

Buckelew, overextended financially having also bought the Corte Madera del Presidio and San Quentin grants, went bankrupt within a few years and lost his lands.

Halleck was more successful. He had arrived in California as a lieutenant in 1847, built San Francisco's famous Montgomery Block and founded the west's largest law firm, which had a hand in more than half of all the 1,400 grant claims that went before the Land Commission. Later, he was Lincoln's chief-of-staff during the Civil War.

Halleck spent time hunting and fishing at Nicasio and had a house on what is now called Halleck Creek. He sold numerous parcels, including more than 4,000 acres to Black. And he gave 30 acres, plus support money, to the Indians of Nicasio, upon which several of the last full-blooded survivors spent their final days.

More on James Black's story is found in the Mt. Burdell Preserve section.

Note that while the Little Mountain-Verissimo Hills-Indian Tree area was just within Rancho Nicasio, the subsequent history of these three Preserves is tied to Rancho de Novato.

RANCHO DE NOVATO (8,870 acres)
Preserves: Deer Island, Mt. Burdell, Rush Creek

Rancho de Novato was awarded to Fernando Feliz in 1839 for years of service to Mexico. (Note that there was a separate Rancho Corte Madera de Novato immediately west.) William Brewer, here in 1862 with the California Geological Survey, called the Novato area, "the finest grazing district in the state."

Feliz had already built fences, corrals, and two houses on the land when he decided to leave Marin and move north. He was granted an eight-square-league rancho in Mendocino and, in 1844, sold Rancho de Novato to Jacob Leese. The price was 110 cows, 50 bulls, 25 calves, and a stallion. Feliz reportedly felt overcompensated.

Leese, a native of Ohio, had arrived in California in 1833 and became a successful merchant. He married a sister (Rosalia) of the powerful General Vallejo. Leese also built the first solid house in San Francisco, on the site of today's St. Francis Hotel.

In 1846, Leese sold the Rancho to Captain Bezar Simmons for $6,000. Simmons, from Vermont, had come to California as captain of a whaler and then invested in real estate. In 1849, Simmons returned to Vermont to bring his wife out west. She died a month after reaching San Francisco of a fever caught crossing Panama. Simmons took her remains back to Vermont. When he returned, his financial affairs were in disarray. He transferred 2,000 acres of the northwest section to his son Benjamin but the rest of Novato fell into the hands of trustees. Simmons died in 1850, at age 40.

The trustees included Henry Halleck, soon to own much of Rancho Nicasio, and Simmons brother-in-law Frederick Billings. They leased the Rancho to Dr. Reuben Knox. In 1851, Knox drowned, along with four others, in a boating accident in San Pablo Bay near Novato. Archibald Peachy, law partner of Halleck and Billings, bought the Rancho in 1852 and secured its clear title before the Land Commission.

Peachy promptly sold the Rancho, half each to Andrew McCabe and James Johnson. By 1857, the Rancho passed to partners Joseph Sweetser, originally of Maine, and the widower Francis DeLong, from Vermont. It was Sweetser and DeLong who are most associated with Novato's early development.

To satisfy San Francisco's demand for fresh fruit, Sweetser and DeLong began a huge orchard—some 44,000 fruit trees and 8,000 grape vines—just northwest of downtown. The 20,000 apple trees were said to comprise the first or second largest apple orchard in the world. Many of the apples were crushed for cider and vinegar. The rancho was also expanded through reclaiming some 2,000 acres of marshland.

In 1879, Sweetser sold out to DeLong, but retained one square mile, which would become downtown Novato. He moved to Florida, where he died in 1886, but his body was returned for burial in Novato.

DeLong died in 1885, age 87, at his Novato home. The Rancho went to his son Frank, who had crossed the Isthmus of Panama with him in Gold Rush days.

The younger DeLong (1837-1910) was well-liked and served eight years in

the California Senate. But he also spent lavishly. By 1893, a year of economic tur-
moil in America, DeLong was bankrupt. In 1894, heavily mortgaged Rancho Novato
was auctioned to satisfy the many creditors. The new owners were a syndicate, mostly
former creditors, called the Novato Land Company. The new manager, who moved
into DeLong's mansion, was Point Reyes rancher Robert Hatch. In 1905, Hatch was
succeeded by Robert Trumbull, later a much-respected Marin County supervisor.

Most of the land grant was divided into seven dairy ranches, labeled A through
H (there was no G, as it looked similar to C as a cattle brand), plus the Home Ranch
around the DeLong house. Each ranch was leased to tenants, some of whom then
became owners when the Novato Land Company began selling the properties in
1909.

RANCHO PUNTA DE QUENTIN (8,895 acres)
Preserves: Baltimore Canyon, King Mountain

Juan (born John) B.R. Cooper arrived in Monterey in 1823 at age 31 aboard his
own ship, *The Rover*. He later sold the vessel to Governor Luis Arguello, one of
many actions that put Mexican authorities in his debt. Cooper was involved in the
quasi-legal trade of otters for silk with China, with the Hawaii (Sandwich Islands)
trade, and other activities, and became quite wealthy. In 1827, he married
Encarnacion Vallejo, sister of General Vallejo, military ruler of the North Bay. The
couple had two children, Anna Marie and John Henry.

In 1840, to pay off a $5,250 debt, Governor Juan Alvarado awarded Cooper
Rancho Punta de Quentin. It covered the lower Ross Valley to San Anselmo, plus
the San Quentin peninsula. It was named for a Miwok, Quintin (or Quentin), who
was captured by the point that now bears his name. Four years later, Cooper was
also granted a 16,293-acre portion of Rancho Nicasio. He also owned ranchos in
Sonoma and Monterey.

Cooper spent little time on his ranchos, hiring others to work them. In 1850,
he sold both his Marin ranchos to real estate speculator and developer Benjamin
Rush Buckelew. Cooper became harbor master of Monterey. He died in San Francisco in 1872.

Buckelew got over his head financially, was enmeshed in lawsuits, and his
ranchos slipped away. He died, almost landless and penniless, in 1859 at age 37.

James Ross, for whom Ross and Ross Valley are named, acquired most of the
Rancho in 1857. A provision in his will called for giving each of his two daughters a
$10,000 dowry. Ross died in 1862 and the provision then bankrupted the cash-
strapped family when the daughters married. The rancho was mortgaged.

But George Worn (of Worn Spring Fire Road, bordering Bald Hill Preserve),
who married Ross' daughter Anne, untangled the finances and redeemed the rancho.
Portions were sold off, including 1,233 acres of the future Kentfield and Larkspur
to William Murray and Patrick King (of King Mountain Preserve).

RANCHO SAN GERONIMO (8,723 acres)
Preserves: Giacomini, Maurice Thorner Memorial, Roy's Redwoods

Rancho San Geronimo (named for Saint Jerome) was originally granted to Rafael Cacho in 1844. Two years later, it was bought by Joseph Warren Revere, a naval officer who had arrived in the Bay Area a few months earlier. He was the grandson of Paul Revere, the Revolutionary War figure. Revere ran cattle to the gold fields and inspected lumber for the U.S. government.

In 1850, Revere sold half his interest to Rodman Price, a future governor of New Jersey, and, three years later, the other half to Rodman's brother, Francis Price. The Prices mortgaged the property to the Ward family of Boston, who later foreclosed.

Adolph Mailliard had joined the Ward family by marrying Annie Ward in 1846. (Annie's older sister, Julia Ward Howe, wrote *The Battle Hymn of the Republic*.) Mailliard, though born in New Jersey, was related by blood to Napoleon Bonaparte. Napoleon's older brother, King Joseph of Spain, had an illegitimate son, Louis Mailliard, with a lady-in-waiting to his wife. Louis was raised with the legitimate children. He came with Joseph to the latter's 1,800-acre estate, Point Breeze, in Bordentown, New Jersey, after the Bonapartes were overthrown, serving as Joseph's secretary. Louis' wife died a few days after giving birth to Adolph, who was then raised in France.

In 1867, Adolph bought Rancho San Geronimo, sight unseen, from his wife's family. The couple sailed to Marin from New York the following year.

Before settling in San Geronimo, the Mailliards also bought 113 acres in San Rafael and lived there for several years in a mansion they built, Fairhills. Once in San Geronimo Valley, Mailliard raised champion racehorses. The family also began a long tradition of service to the community. One example was selling, for a nominal price, the water rights to Lagunitas Creek, still the County's primary source of drinking water. Adolph's great-grandson, William Mailliard, served 20 years as a U.S. congressman representing Marin.

The family suffered financial setbacks when Adolph's New York brokerage business failed. In 1869, Mailliard sold land to the Dickson brothers, John (630 acres) and William (500 acres). He also borrowed $20,000 from the brothers James and Thomas Roy, later repaid with land, part of which is now Roy's Redwoods Preserve.

The Mailliard financial situation worsened after they literally sunk a fortune into a money-losing gold mine just south of today's Maurice Thorner Memorial Preserve. The rancho was mortgaged to Prince Napoleon Charles Bonaparte, another grandson of King Joseph. But an additional Ward inheritance in 1886 enabled the family to retain most of their land. Anne died in 1895, Adolph a year later. Their family house, later the Woodacre Improvement Club, burned to the ground in 1958.

Mailliard's three children—John, Joseph, and Louise—began subdividing the property in 1904. In 1912, they sold much of the remaining land to the Lagunitas Development Company, which then laid out tracts across the valley.

RANCHO SAN JOSE (6,600 acres)

Preserves: Ignacio Valley, Indian Valley, Loma Verde, Pacheco Valle

Ignacio Pacheco was the original grantee of 6,600-acre Rancho de San Jose, and two Preserves bear his name. The first Pacheco family member to the New World had been recruited in Spain by Aztec conqueror Hernan Cortes. Ignacio's grandfather arrived in California with the pioneering 1776 DeAnza expedition. His father was *alcalde* (mayor) of the San Jose pueblo, where Ignacio, the only son, was born in 1808.

Ignacio, a soldier, was based at the Presidio in the future San Francisco. He married Josefa Higuera in 1833; they would have one surviving child, Salvador.

For his service, Ignacio was granted Rancho Agua Caliente in Sonoma County. In 1834, Ignacio visited Marin and thought the land richer, so asked to trade his Sonoma grant. Mexican authorities honored his request. The rancho was named for Ignacio's birthplace.

Josefa died in 1838. Around 1840, Pacheco married Maria Guadalupe Duarte and had two more children, Jose Ramon and Maria Antonia. Maria Guadalupe died young and Ignacio then married her sister, Maria Loreto, at Mission San Rafael in 1851. They would have six more children.

Pacheco ran a prosperous rancho and held several government positions. Education was another priority. His children (and those of his few neighbors) were well-schooled at Pacheco's expense on the grounds of his hacienda. Ignacio died in 1864. The 1880 *History of Marin* says of him, "All old settlers will remember Mr. Pacheco as one of Natures' noblemen, a man with a kindly face and an open heart and hand for the needy." In 1865, his widow married a neighbor, James Black (see Mt. Burdell Preserve).

Pacheco children Catalina and Gumesindo continued to live on the property. Both served as original (1883) trustees of the San Jose School District and Gumesindo was also a County supervisor (1902-1916). The 12-room home built by Gumesindo around 1881, called "The Big House," still stands, off Alameda del Prado and visible from Highway 101. Pacheco descendants (the Rowland family, Gumesindo's daughter Abigail having eloped with Clarence Rowland) still live there. The house is the centerpiece of the family's Pacheco Ranch Winery. Growing several tons of cabernet grapes on their 75-acre property, the Pacheco/Rowlands are now the oldest family in the State still involved in agriculture on their original grant lands. The winery—the wine is made and bottled on the site—borders Loma Verde and Pacheco Valle preserves.

RANCHO SAN PEDRO, SANTA MARGARITA Y LAS GALLINAS (21,680 acres)

Preserves: Lucas Valley, San Pedro Ridge, Santa Margarita Island, Santa Venetia Marsh, Terra Linda/Sleepy Hollow Divide (parts)

Timothy Murphy was born in County Wexford, Ireland, in 1800. He worked in

London in the meatpacking house of Hartnell and Company. The company sent him to Peru in 1826, then, in 1828, to their new plant in Monterey, California.

After the plant failed, Murphy set out on his own and made a fortune in the otter trade. Her served the Mexican government in various positions and in 1837 was named administrator for Mission San Rafael and agent for Marin's 1,400 remaining Miwoks. Don Timoteo, as he was called, was judged an able administrator

John Lucas was born in County Wexford, Ireland, and arrived in Marin in 1852, age 26. He soon after made the long trip back to Ireland (he was away nearly two years) to bring over his fiancee, Maria Sweetman. When Lucas returned, he was owner of 7,600 acres (including today's Terra Linda/Sleepy Hollow Divide and Lucas Valley Preserves), inherited after the death of his uncle Timothy Murphy.

The couple had six children and adopted another. Their first home was by what is now Highway 101, in the valley that came to bear his name. In 1863, they moved to a larger house on a 2,340-acre parcel called Lucas' Home Ranch, now Terra Linda. John Lucas died in 1900, Maria in 1910. Both are buried in Mt. Olivet Cemetery, on land they donated to the Catholic Church. (Courtesy, Marin County Historical Society) for the Miwoks, learning their language and doing what he could to help save their culture.

For his service, Murphy was awarded three parcels in 1844—San Pedro, Santa Margarita, and Las Gallinas—as a single grant. He built San Rafael's first private home at the future corner of Fourth and C streets, a structure that later served, until 1873, as Marin County's first courthouse. (There is a plaque at the site.) Murphy also became *alcalde* (mayor) and *juez de paz* (justice of the peace) for the nascent town. His hospitality was legendary and he started the tradition of a rodeo and banquet on St. Raphael's Day (October 24) that long continued as San Rafael Day. Murphy, six feet six inches and 300 pounds, survived a wrestling match with a bear in the San Anselmo valley and had a witness (Domingo Sais) and claw marks on his jacket to prove it.

Murphy was a fast friend of General Vallejo, the most powerful figure in the North Bay in the Mexican era, and proposed marriage to his sister Rosalia. Rejected, he never married, a factor in the future division of his enormous estate. Instead, Murphy brought over his brother, Matthew, and nephew, John Lucas, to help him manage the land.

Timothy Murphy died in 1853. Matthew Murphy inherited virtually all the San Pedro Peninsula, including today's San Pedro Ridge Preserve. But Matthew died within months, of wounds suffered after he was accidentally shot by a guard while riding near newly opened San Quentin Prison. Much of the grant lands, less what was sold to settle debts, went to young John Lucas.

RANCHO LAS BAULINES (8,920 acres)
Preserve: Bolinas Lagoon

Rancho Las Baulines was awarded in 1836, to Rafael Garcia. He was one of the first non-natives to live in Marin, a corporal attached to Mission San Rafael. He helped quell a sizable Indian attack at the Mission in 1823; the grant was his reward.

But Garcia, under a murky arrangement that produced years of court battles, then moved north into the Olema Valley (Rancho Tomales y Baulines). Garcia was apparently opening the original Baulines grant for his brother-in-law, Gregorio Briones.

Briones was born in 1791; his father had traveled with Father Junipero Serra in establishing Mission Dolores (San Francisco) in 1776. Gregorio served the standard 10-year term as a soldier, then was an administrator, under several Mexican governors, including stints as *juez de pas* and *alcalde* at San Rafael. In 1822, he married Ramona Garcia at Mission Dolores.

Briones lived on Garcia's original grant land and was finally awarded 8,920 acres on February 11, 1846, in the last days of Mexican rule. Despite the murky background, Briones' grant was confirmed by the Land Commission and upon appeal. Briones, however, had to give 500 acres of Bolinas Mesa to his attorney, Volney Howard, and sell thousands of other acres to cover additional legal costs. He left some 3,000 acres, divided equally, to his five children upon his death in 1863.

CRITERIA
FOR INCLUDING TRAILS AND FIRE ROADS

THERE ARE WELL OVER 1,000 regularly-traveled routes—ranging from deer paths to well-maintained fire roads—across the District's 32 Preserves. It was a challenge to decide which to include and describe.

To narrow the list, only routes that run at least one-tenth of a mile wholly within a Preserve and are accessible without crossing private property (unless over a public easement) were considered. Among these, the following were chosen:

1. *All fire roads.* These are broad routes specifically maintained by the District for emergency and other official vehicle access. Many are old ranch roads. A few are old railroad beds. Several were cut to access water tanks. Some were carved as breaks to protect against fires; protection road and fire protection road are alternate names.

2. *All trails that are signed, or are planned to be signed.* These are routes maintained and cleared by the District. Many (but not all) meet District standards regarding width, steepness, and other factors. Some are former roads no longer used by vehicles and now narrowed by advancing vegetation. Some have been worn in "socially" by users before or after public acquisition. Some were built by the District, as new routes or replacements for old ones. Trails shorter than .1 mile are sometimes referred to as "connectors," and not separately described. Note that the District has not completed signing all Preserves.

3. *Selected unsigned trails that are either heavily used or particularly important as links.* Some of these "gray area" routes may become officially designated trails, while others may some day be marked as closed.

The District realizes that not all travel is done on designated trails or fire roads, but discourages such use. Some unofficial routes cross environmentally sensitive areas. For example, an illegally carved route in Cascade Canyon Preserve passed right through the only Marin locale of a rare and endangered wildflower, the mallow *Sidalcea hickmanii*. Some of these routes create excessive erosion. Some pass through private property. Some expose visitors to unavoidable poison oak.

All routes labeled as fire roads (or as "roads" if they are paved) in this book are open to all user groups; pedestrians, cyclists, and equestrians. Routes designated as trails are open to hikers and (unless posted otherwise) equestrians, and closed to bikers. There are, at press time, three trails open to bicycles: Wagon Wheel in White Hill Preserve, Fox Hollow in Loma Alta, and Windy Ridge in Blithedale Summit.

"Paths" are unofficial routes. There are hundreds of them but only a few are cited in the text, where they might cause confusion. Also noted but not separately described are several public easements the District owns across private lands as access to Preserves.

Only the portions of trails and fire roads within MCOSD Preserves are described in detail and measured although continuations onto adjacent public open space are noted. Routes are generally described in the uphill direction unless there are access problems with the lower end or if the route is commonly used to complete an up-and-down loop.

The following abbreviations are used throughout the book:

• Marin County Open Space District—MCOSD, OSD, the District
• Fire Road—F.R.
• mile—m (as .56m or 1.22m)
• Golden Gate National Recreation Area—GGNRA
• Marin Municipal Water District—MMWD
• North Marin Water District—NMWD
• The stand-alone words "trail" or "fire road" are capitalized when referring to the specific route of the chapter heading.
• References to a creek's "left bank" and "right bank" are based on looking downstream.
• Telephone numbers are area code 415 unless otherwise stated.

Key to Maps

• All maps are oriented with north at top of map
• Elevations marked are approximate, based on USGS topo map contours
• Trail alignments and Preserve boundaries subject to change
• Because of the small scale in this book, Preserve boundaries are approximate; if needed, check with the MCOSD office for more details
• Please respect private property

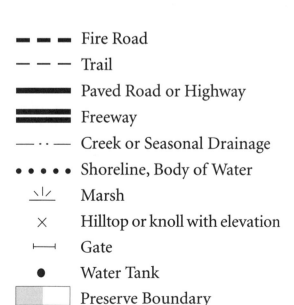

▬ ▬ ▬	Fire Road
— — —	Trail
▬▬▬▬	Paved Road or Highway
▬▬▬▬	Freeway
— ·· —	Creek or Seasonal Drainage
• • • • •	Shoreline, Body of Water
⅄⅂	Marsh
×	Hilltop or knoll with elevation
⊢—⊣	Gate
●	Water Tank
▭	Preserve Boundary

The Preserves

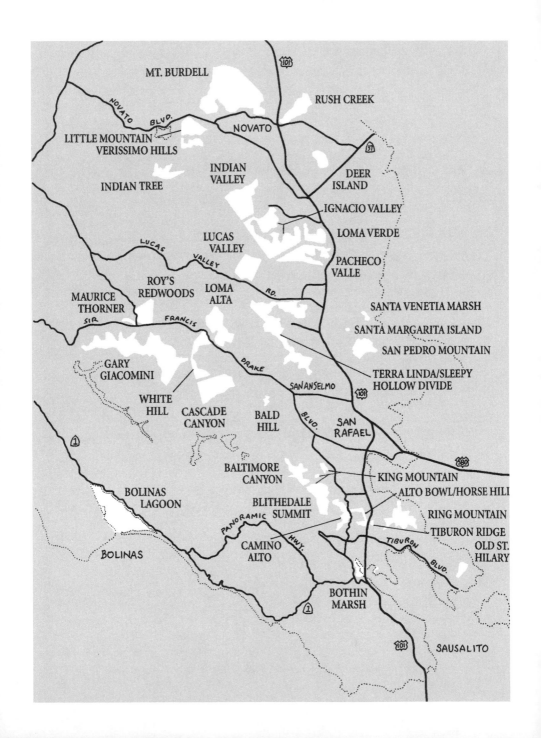

ALTO BOWL / HORSE HILL

Size: 97.3 acres   Elevation range: 40-360 feet

*Alto Bowl seems to me one of our most re-
markable preserves. Let's take a quick hike on
Bob Middagh Trail. About halfway along,
stop. Look around. We're standing in a beautiful, sloped grassy meadow. Now imagine this
area completely choked by non-native broom.
Believe it or not, this is what it looked like
before a handful of dedicated volunteers
cleared it. Talk about challenging work! These
folks help make the Open Space District what it is today. One of
the best parts of my job is working with neighbors like these who
feel as passionately about Open Space as I do.*
— *Canada Ross, Ranger*

THE ALTO BOWL-HORSE HILL AREA was part of 646 acres inherited by Maria Inez
Reed, daughter of original grantee John Thomas Reed. In 1864, Maria Inez married
Pennsylvania-born Thomas Deffebach, who had arrived in California in 1850 and
spent time in the gold fields.

The couple had 11 children; only four survived to adulthood. Maria Inez and
Thomas died within months of one another in 1883-84. The four children, three
under age eight, were put into the care of Maria's sister Hilarita and husband Benjamin Lyford on their Strawberry ranch. The Alto-area dairy lands were leased to
tenant ranchers.

The more northern ranch was called Tunnel Ranch, for the nearby Alto train
tunnel which opened in 1884. A dairy census of 1935-36 recorded 113 cows on the
ranch producing an average of 6,380 pounds of milk and 235 pounds of butterfat
yearly, most rushed fresh daily to San Francisco.

Just to the south was the Alto Dairy, owned and operated by Roque Moraes
from 1910. It was one of the first dairies in Marin to use milking machines and
pasteurization. The 1935-36 census listed 82 cows on the ranch, the heaviest at 448
pounds.

Moraes sold his dairy in 1940. The residential developments called Scott Valley and Alto Sutton Manor began after World War II over its old grazing lands.

Large-scale developments were planned in the 1960's over what is today's Preserve; some 900 homes on the Alto Bowl side, 1,200 apartments on Horse Hill.
These plans were turned back in the face of strong local opposition.

In 1974, what was still called the Marin County Regional Park District purchased two parcels totaling 18 acres for $100,000 in Alto Bowl. The District ac-
quired additional land in 1985 (19.3 acres) and 1990 (15.8 acres).

In 1982, developers submitted an application to build 61 homes on their 34.4-

acre Horse Hill parcel. The project was stalled by a building moratorium imposed by the City of Mill Valley. When the moratorium expired in 1988, a new proposal, for 13 homes, was made. But a group called the Save Horse Hill Committee collected donations from more than 5,000 individuals eager to keep the site pastoral . Horse Hill was purchased as open space, with full transfer to the District completed in 1995. The price of $2.4 million—contributed by the MCOSD, the City of Mill Valley, the Marin Community Foundation, and individuals—was then the District's most expensive acquisition (since topped in Tiburon). Today, Horse Hill is enjoyed visually by thousands of people who drive by daily.

The Horse Hill section of the Preserve is unique within the District as privately owned horses are grazed over 60 fenced acres (including adjacent land northwest of the Preserve belonging to the Mill Valley Meadows Homeowners Association). Today, the horses and limited equestrian facilities are overseen by the Alto Bowl Horseowners Association. A maximum of 14 horses are permitted. They graze new grasses in spring, then are fed hay during summer, winter, and fall at the corral area near Highway 101 (east end of Lomita Drive). The shelters at the corral area were erected in 1998.

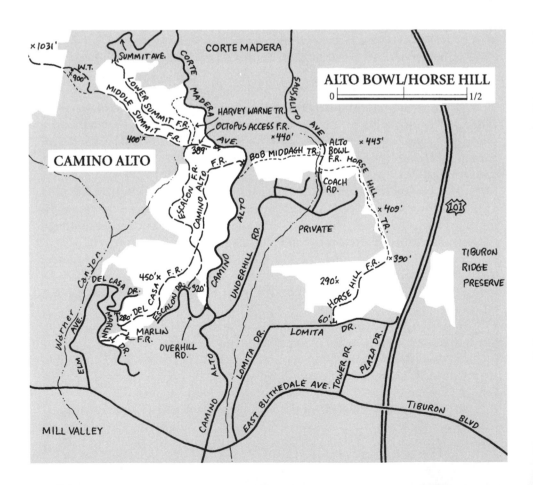

ALTO BOWL FIRE ROAD (.17 miles)
From Coach Road (Mill Valley) to Sausalito Street (Corte Madera)
Intersection: Bob Middagh Trail (.13m)

This short Fire Road connects residential areas of Mill Valley and Corte Madera. The lower end is at the MCOSD gate atop Coach Road, in the Scott Valley section of Mill Valley. On the right, off the base of Benson Circle, is the unsigned bottom of Horse Hill Trail.

Once choked with broom, Alto Bowl Fire Road is now being steadily cleared by a group of local residents, the Alto Bowl Open Space Volunteers. A creek runs to the left.

Near the Fire Road's north end, signed Bob Middagh Trail leaves left, over the creek. It runs a half-mile to Camino Alto, across which is an entry to the MCOSD's Camino Alto Preserve.

Alto Bowl Fire Road ends at an MCOSD gate at Corte Madera's Sausalito Street (hence the "Sausalito Pump Station" on the left).

BOB MIDDAGH TRAIL (.46 miles)
From Camino Alto (Mill Valley) to Alto Bowl Fire Road
Notes: A few parking spots in pullouts by Trailhead;
no parking west side of Camino Alto

Bob Middagh Trail links the Camino Alto and Alto Bowl Preserves. The Trailhead is on the east side of Camino Alto, near its crest (the Mill Valley/Corte Madera line). Fifty yards above the Trailhead and across the street is the gate onto Camino Alto Fire Road.

The Trail starts below, and parallel to, Camino Alto. The entry gate is on City of Mill Valley land. There are several coast live oaks, and, 200 feet in, the Trail passes under a particularly large one.

At 200 yards, Bob Middagh Trail bends right, away from the road. Splendid views of the San Francisco skyline open. Above is the fence line for a private estate once owned by the late rock impresario Bill Graham, who called it "Masada."

Bob Middagh Trail traverses the grassy south slope of Corte Madera Hill. The 2,194-foot long Alto Tunnel was blasted under this hill in 1884. It had a single track through which commute trains passed between Alto (Mill Valley) and Chapman (Corte Madera) stations. Beginning in 1903, the entire southern Marin commuter system was double-tracked with only the Alto Tunnel segment remaining single track. An elaborate signaling system at both ends controlled traffic.

Doomed by the opening of the Golden Gate Bridge in 1937, rail commuter service ended February 28, 1941. Some freight runs continued until the early 1960's. A slide on the Mill Valley end, plus concerns about the safety of children who ventured in, led to sealing the tunnel on both its ends.

Two short paths drop right through the grassland to signed entries on Upperhill Road in Scott Valley. The Trail rolls over the grassland before beginning a steady descent. The lower yards are lined by creekside vegetation such as blackberry and willow.

The Trail crosses over the creek and ends at its junction with Alto Bowl Fire Road. It is 70 yards up left to Sausalito Street in Corte Madera and one-eighth mile right down to Coach Road in Mill Valley.

Bob Middagh was in charge of real estate acquisitions for Marin County in the 1970's and '80's, playing a key role in purchases of many Preserves as well as County parks such as McInnis, Stafford Lake, and McNears Beach. After his retirement, the Trail was dedicated in his honor at a ceremony on March 7, 1992.

HORSE HILL FIRE ROAD (.34 miles)
From Lomita Drive (Mill Valley) to Horse Hill Trail
Note: No parking at Lomita Drive entry

This Fire Road is the most prominent route in the Preserve, clearly visible when traveling east on Mill Valley's Blithedale Avenue.

Horse Hill Fire Road begins behind an MCOSD gate opposite #43 Lomita Drive. At the start is an old stone foundation of unknown origin. A path takes off right along the fence line, going .2 miles toward the corral area. On the left a new (1999) fence encloses a long-time gully.

The Fire Road climbs through the disturbed grassland. Teasel (*Dipsacus*), a European import common in old pastures, lines the way. Poppies, lupines, buttercups, and mallow are some of the more common showy natives coloring the grassland in spring. Several paths criss-cross the hillside.

A quarter-mile up, the Fire Road meets a plateau with a dirt circle, subsoil from a nearby development project. It's a favorite spot for the resident horses. They are used to visitors but give them wide berth and do not feed them.

There are now stunning shots of the San Francisco skyline and Mt. Tamalpais. At one-third mile, unmarked Horse Hill Trail sets off left. The junction is considered the end of Horse Hill Fire Road, with the ridge top and Preserve boundary fence line 200 feet above. The District's Tiburon Ridge Preserve is just across Highway 101.

HORSE HILL TRAIL (.57 miles)
From Horse Hill Fire Road to Coach Road

Horse Hill Trail sets off west from the top of Horse Hill Fire Road. There are sweeping views. In 75 yards, the Trail enters an oak-studded crest enjoyed by horses (and others) for the shade, the breezes, and the quiet. Parallel paths have been worn.

There is then a short drop to another MCOSD gate, which encloses the grazing pasture. Be sure to close the gate.

The Trail skirts the fence separating the Preserve from private, gated Meadowcrest Drive (Corte Madera) on the true ridge line. Boundary posts mark where the Trail passes in and out of the private open space lands of the Mill Valley Meadows Homeowners Association. Oaks dot the hillside and the Trail passes through a dense grove.

At .42 miles, Horse Hill Trail meets a power line and bends left to follow the PG&E right-of-way down. (Straight, or north, to Corte Madera, crosses private property.) The descent is steep and slippery.

The route ends at an unsigned step-over barrier at the junction of Benson Circle (named for the dog of the Scott Valley developer) and Coach Road. To the right, Alto Bowl Fire Road rises to Sausalito Street, Corte Madera. To the left is the private Scott Valley Swimming and Tennis Club.

An early 1980's "Save Horse Hill" sign, part of the community effort that led to today's Preserve.

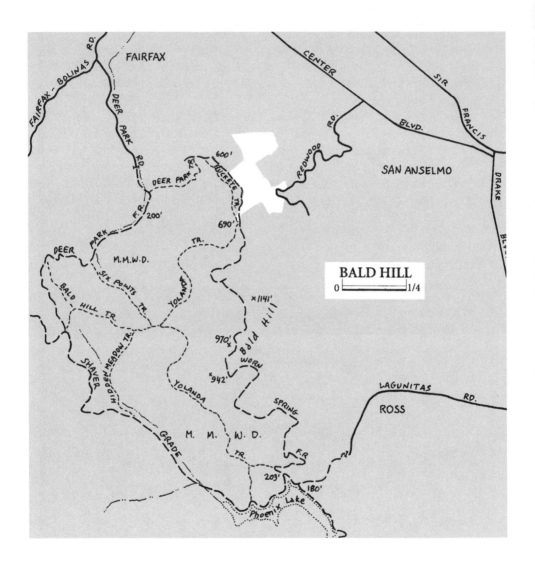

JONATHAN BRAUN is an example of a local hero. So are Mary Jo Rice, Pat and Jeanne MacLeamy, Nancy Knoble, Jerry Riessen, Bob Ritter, and David Moller. Local heroes are a special breed of volunteer. They are people who have led neighborhood and community efforts to raise funds needed to help the District purchase open space. Some are neighborhood activists. Others just seem to appear out of nowhere, get the job done, then disappear again. Without local heroes, many places that are now enjoyed as open space wouldn't be. And this book would be a lot smaller.

BALD HILL

Size: 31.7 acres   Elevation range: 225-697 feet

San Anselmo, the "hub" of Marin. Almost in the center of this "hub" is one of Marin Open Space's little known treasures, Bald Hill. Constantly fighting to keep it from being developed, the energetic San Anselmo Open Space Committee, along with neighboring towns, have saved beautiful hidden meadows, oak woodlands, and vistas that overlook Ross, San Anselmo, and Fairfax. I look at this mountain every day, and can't help to think how many dedicated, hard-working people have sacrificed their time to save what Marin cherishes the most. Simple, unchanged beauty. — Brian Sanford, Supervising Ranger

WHILE THE WEST SLOPE of Bald Hill (affectionately called "Baldy") has long been inside the MMWD, its other flanks, including the 1,141-foot summit itself, are privately owned. A joint San Anselmo-Ross effort in 1990 to issue bonds to buy the 60-acre summit parcel narrowly missed the required two-thirds vote. (Ironically, in the early 1970's, an earlier owner of the summit parcel had offered it for sale to the newly-created Open Space District. The County Board of Supervisors rejected the asking price of $7,500 per acre, not wanting to set a precedent at what then seemed a high figure.)

It was the threat of imminent development on a parcel above San Anselmo's Redwood Road—12 large homes were planned that would have been visible throughout upper Ross Valley—that led to creation of Bald Hill Preserve. The acquisition story is a complicated one, involving development deals and land swaps. The volunteers of the San Anselmo Open Space Committee, led by Jonathan Braun, played a large role. In 1994, $450,000 was paid—split equally by the District, the Town of San Anselmo, and the Marin Community Foundation's Beryl Buck Open Space Fund—for the Preserve's initial 18.56 acres. The same parties contributed an additional $450,000 the following year for 7.37 acres, then $105,000 for 5.05 acres.

Bald Hill Preserve may be reached over Marin Municipal Water District lands via either Worn Spring Fire Road (from Phoenix Lake or Fairfax), or Yolanda Trail (also from Phoenix Lake). There is also a limited access easement, signed "To Worn Springs Fire Road," across private property from the upper end of San Anselmo's Oak Avenue (but no parking). There are no maintained trails within the Preserve, but a boundless selection in the adjacent MMWD.

BALTIMORE CANYON

Size: 196.1 acres   Elevation range: 120-1,091 feet

An experience that everyone should seek is hiking up Baltimore Canyon during a rainstorm. As you meander underneath the giant redwoods and watch the swollen waters of the creek, you can't help but feel that you're in a world far removed from civilization. The reward for the hike is near the top—viewing the beauty of Dawn Falls. The extraordinary power of these falls is breathtaking! Baltimore Canyon is secluded, quiet and powerful. If you listen carefully, you might still hear the drumbeats of the old "Hippie" camp that was once here.   — John Aranson, Supervising Ranger

THERE WAS APPARENTLY logging in Baltimore Canyon during the Mexican era. In 1847, the newly-in-charge United States government erected a sawmill at the Magnolia Avenue/Doherty Drive intersection, which was then at the edge of San Francisco Bay, so convenient for transportation. But it was the discovery of gold in 1848, and the resulting insatiable demand for lumber to build (and to re-build after frequent fires) a burgeoning San Francisco, that doomed the canyon's impressive virgin stands.

The Baltimore & Frederick Trading and Mining Company, a Maryland-based partnership of 30 individuals each putting up $1,000, brought a mill around Cape Horn in '49. They placed it at the canyon mouth, on West Baltimore near Magnolia, accounting for the name Baltimore Canyon. The company soon disbanded, its members lured by the gold fields, and sold out to Benjamin Buckelew. (One partner who returned to Marin was Ai Barney. He and son Jerome founded *The Marin County Journal* newspaper, now the *Independent Journal*.)

Eyewitnesses say the canyon's redwoods were the tallest they had ever seen, some over 300 feet. They were all cut in less than a decade. Some of the redwood found its way to Hawaii (then called the Sandwich Islands). But, in a way, the giants live on. It is from their roots that today's circles of redwoods—genetic clones of their ancestors—sprouted.

By the late 1800's, the canyon had become a popular summer camping retreat for San Franciscans. Tiny 25x25 foot lots were sold for summer homes. Also, family tents, group tents, and guest cottages were available for rental. In 1906, tents in the canyon were filled with San Franciscans escaping the earthquake.

BARBARA SPRING TRAIL (.34 miles)
From Dawn Falls Trail to Southern Marin Line Fire Road

When entering Baltimore Canyon and Dawn Falls Trail via the bridge over Larkspur Creek at the end of Madrone Avenue, Barbara Spring Trail is 50 yards to the right (upstream). The MCOSD signpost at the start has been removed several times by vandals and visitors are creating a slightly different entry through a cluster of redwood trees.

Barbara Spring was never intended as a trail—a Larkspur fire chief cut it in the early 1970's as a training path for his firefighters—and it shows. The first yards are vague, slide-prone, and extremely steep, and the route doesn't get much better higher.

The Trail climbs in the woodland beside the canyon of Barbara Spring. In .1 miles, in a lovely area, two feeders merge at a small seasonal waterfall. There was a hippie encampment here around 1970. Barbara Spring Trail bends to follow the left fork higher.

Madrones have been the dominant tree following logging, but redwoods and Douglas-firs are rising above them and blocking the sunlight. Fallen madrones across the Trail are a regular obstacle, and side paths skirt them.

Barbara Spring Trail bends right (these bends give it an alternate name, "S Trail.") A final push up leads to Southern Marin Line F.R., the junction signed. The H-Line F.R. intersection is one-third mile to the right with Dawn Falls Trail, a loop option, another mile past.

DAWN FALLS TRAIL (1.84 miles)
From Baltimore Avenue (Larkspur) to Hoo-Koo-E-Koo Trail
Intersections: Barbara Spring Trail (.56m),
Contractors Trail (1.11m), Southern Marin Line F.R. (1.63m)
Notes: Entry to Dawn Falls Trail from West Baltimore Avenue
blocked by private property. Park only within delineated spaces.

Dawn Falls is a popular trail—long, deeply wooded, beside a roaring creek with a waterfall, yet near busy Magnolia Avenue.

There is no public entry to the eastern end of Dawn Falls Trail. Most users enter the Trail in its middle, by crossing the Larkspur Creek bridge at the west end of Madrone Avenue (technically Water Way). But the Trail will be described in full from east to west rather than split it into two sections.

Dawn Falls Trail sets off west from behind the last house (in which the late singer Janis Joplin once lived) on West Baltimore Avenue. The Trail follows Larkspur Creek's right bank. The creek was originally called Arroyo Holon when it formed the boundary between the Rancho Corte Madera del Presidio and Rancho Punta de Quentin land grants.

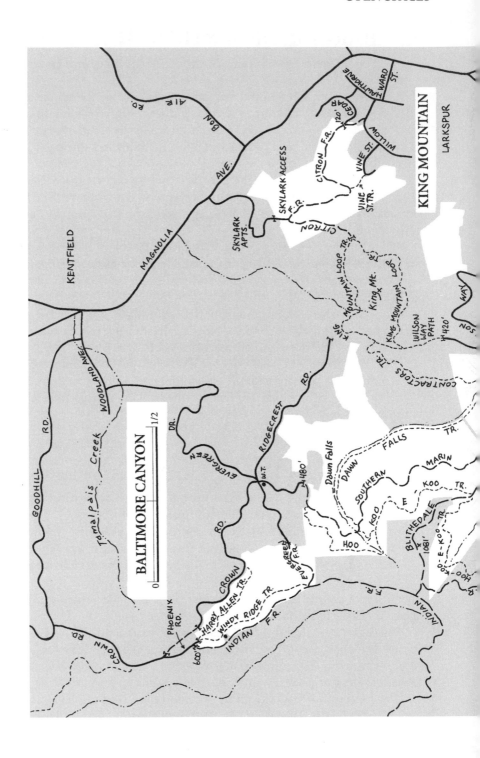

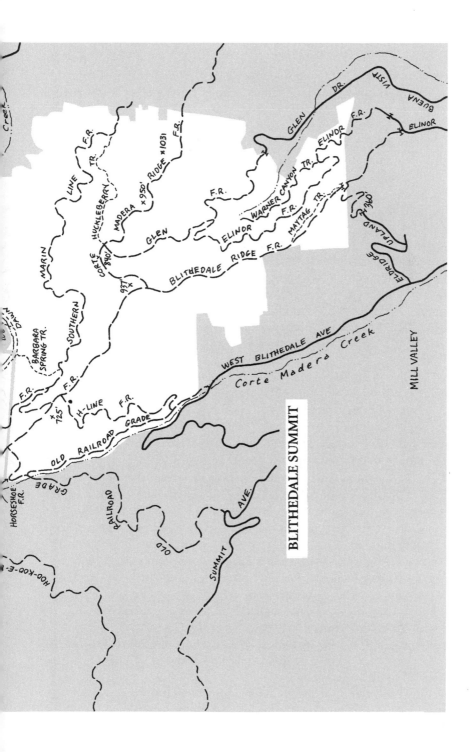

The easternmost .6 miles of Dawn Falls Trail have long been fire road-width, used as access for vehicles servicing the old dam upstream, but advancing vegetation is narrowing the way. The redwoods along the canyon floor are impressive, although nowhere near the 1,000-year-old giants that grew here prior to logging. A clearing on the left is known locally as "The Meadow." It was the scene of a major slide, and subsequent repair work, after the wet winter of 1982.

Trail plant (*Adenocaulon bicolor*) is abundant on the route's edge. The light-colored underside of the arrow-shaped leaves can be used to mark trails, hence the name. Homes are visible on the opposite bank of Larkspur Creek.

About a half-mile in is the westernmost bridge over Larkspur Creek. It was built by Boy Scout Troop 43. Across is Water Way, the western end of Madrone Avenue. Fifty yards beyond, very steep Barbara Spring Trail rises left to Southern Marin Line F.R.

Just ahead is an old fence. When it was erected in 1971, there were so many protests that an opening for hikers was finally provided, explaining the old City of Larkspur sign (now out-of-date) still dangling above. Earlier, long-time landowner Adolph Tiscornia and hired hands were known to warn trespassers off with rifles.

Dawn Falls Trail goes over a small hill. Look right to see remnants of the dam built around 1890 by the Larkspur Water Company. The Water Company was closed after a scandal in 1917; their pipes had been tapping into MMWD lines. The dam itself was dynamited in the 1920's after a drowning death.

Ahead on the left is the old quarry where blue basalt for the dam, the Blue Rock Inn, and other projects, was taken. The Trail follows the water's edge, and may be partially submerged in the very wettest conditions. (There's usually a way to scramble through.) Huge redwoods grow in the middle of the Trail.

Just over a mile in is a clearing on the right where ladybugs have been known to cover the foliage by the tens of thousands. Ladybird beetles (*Hippodomia convergens*), better known as ladybugs, ride thermals here from the Central Valley in fall, and return on them in spring. Recent disturbance of the site may have ended the cycle; hopefully not. Directly across the creek here, but nearly invisible, is the base of Contractors (sometimes called Ladybug) Trail, which climbs steeply to King Mountain Loop Trail.

The tree canopy lightens, then the Trail begins to noticeably rise. Climb and, suddenly, you are at Dawn Falls. Two forks of Larkspur Creek meet here, then plunge 25 feet. It's a torrent in winter, a trickle in summer, but always a delightful place to rest. The falls face due east, catching dawn's first light after the area had been logged, which may account for the name.

The climb beyond is eased by switchbacks added in the 1980's. Dawn Falls Trail meets Southern Marin Line Fire Road. It is .3 miles right to Crown Road and 2.5 level miles left to the Larkspur end.

Dawn Falls Trail continues directly across. A final tough climb through forest leads to Hoo-Koo-E-Koo Trail. Right returns to Southern Marin Line Fire Road and left leads up to Blithedale Ridge.

EVERGREEN FIRE ROAD (.23 miles)

From top of Evergreen Drive (Kent Woodlands) to Indian Fire Road
Note: Subject to winter closures

This very steep Fire Road rises from the top of Evergreen Drive high in Kent Woodlands. Downhill travelers need to exercise caution because of the slope, loose rocks, and deeply eroded ruts.

A light woodland lines much of the way. The route bends right beyond the last house. At 350 feet, at the one landmark, a water tank, the Fire Road bends left.

A bit higher, turn around to see Mt. Diablo. Then Mt. Tamalpais appears, and a glimpse of the San Francisco skyline.

The steep climbing ends and the second half of the Fire Road is almost level. Near the top, erosion exposes a water pipeline beneath the roadbed.

Evergreen Fire Road ends at its junction with Indian Fire Road and Windy Ridge Trail, at the boundary between MCOSD and MMWD lands. Indian goes up left to the top of Hoo-Koo-E-Koo Fire Road and then on to Eldridge Grade. Right, it drops to Phoenix Road in Kent Woodlands. Windy Ridge Trail (open to cyclists) is immediately right; it also descends to Phoenix Road.

The route was originally part of a longer Kent Fire Road. The surrounding land was graciously sold to the District by the Kent family for the extremely low price of some $400 per acre. No family is more associated with Mt. Tamalpais than the Kents. First to arrive were Albert Emmett Kent, who made a fortune as owner of Chicago's largest meat packing firm. His son William expanded the family holdings and at one time you could walk on Kent property from Kent Avenue, Kentfield, to the Pacific.

William Kent was elected Marin's representative in the United States Congress in 1910 and served three terms. He strived to create a national park on Tamalpais. He is also known for great generosity regarding his lands. His donations (with wife Elizabeth) include Muir Woods to the Federal government, other Tamalpais holdings, such as the Mountain Theater site, to the new Marin Municipal Water District (with a proviso they remain open to hikers), and Steep Ravine to the brand new Mt. Tamalpais State Park a day before his death, March 13, 1928. His five sons (Kent Lake is named for one, Thomas) and their families have continued the Kent tradition of community service. The old Kent family home (now owned by others) is on Woodland Road at the corner of Evergreen Drive.

HARRY ALLEN TRAIL (.44 miles)

From top of Phoenix Road to Crown Road (Kent Woodlands)

During a three-year period in the early 1920's, Harris (Harry) Stearns Allen built a trail connecting his home at 55 Olive Avenue off Larkspur's Madrone Canyon with Phoenix Lake. Allen, an avid hiker, had been president of the Tamalpais Conservation Club during World War I. He died in 1947. The development of Kent Wood-lands—lots on the initial 500 acres were first offered for sale by the Kent family in the late 1930's—covered some of the route. But parts remain, such as the one up from Phoenix Lake to Crown Road over MMWD land, and this section, within the MCOSD.

Three routes depart from the top of Phoenix Road, a short street above Crown Road's northern section. To the right is Indian Fire Road, on MMWD land. Behind the MCOSD-signed gate are Windy Ridge Trail (straight and up) and Harry Allen Trail, marked "Trail to Crown Road." (The unsigned top of the Phoenix Lake section of Harry Allen is a couple of hundred yards lower on Crown Road.)

Squeeze through two redwoods to start. Indeed, much of the Trail is narrow. Almost the whole route is through a forest of thin, tightly packed redwoods. They are returning to an area logged some 150 years ago and now crowd out madrones that first took advantage of the suddenly available sunlight. Huckleberry is an abundant shrub throughout.

The first quarter-mile of Harry Allen is level to slightly up. Then, by an MCOSD sign pointing the Trail left, the downhill begins. The path straight at the junction is overgrown and heads onto private property.

Just beyond the sign, the Trail goes over the roots of a madrone and redwood growing close together. A few yards ahead, there is a bit of clearing. Many tanbark oaks grow here, a common tree on Mt. Tamalpais. Some stand tall but quite a few are downed, victims of a fungus spread by beetles.

At a bend left over a small creek, there is a second "Trail" sign. It is then about 100 yards down to the Trail's end at Crown Road. Early-blooming fetid adder's tongue (*Scoliopus bigelovii*), in the lily family, is abundant by the Trail's base in February. The pedicels supporting the mottled, ill-scented, purple-brown flowers droop low to the ground. Right is Idlewood Road, then Evergreen Drive. Left, the street dead-ends, with a closed-to-cars section connecting up to the northern half of Crown Road.

HOO-KOO-E-KOO TRAIL (1.46 miles)

From Southern Marin Line F.R. to Hoo-Koo-E-Koo F.R.
Intersections: Dawn Falls Trail (.45m), Blithedale Ridge F.R. (.94m)

Hoo-Koo-E-Koo is one of the most colorfully named of Marin trails. The Trail's builders, the Tamalpais Conservation Club, apparently came across Indian middens during construction in 1915. So they chose a name (likely apocryphal) of a band of Coast Miwoks. Most users stress the first and third syllables, some the second and fourth.

The Trail rises off Southern Marin Line Fire Road about 100 yards from the gate at Crown Road. It originally started nearer the old rail line along Magnolia Avenue, but the lower section was covered by development of Kent Woodlands.

There is a steep start, but the rest of the uphill is more gradual. Less than 50 yards up is a seeming junction. Veer left; right is a remnant of the old route now blocked by homes.

There are glimpses down to Southern Marin Line F.R. through the trees. In a half-mile, amidst a redwood grove nurtured by Larkspur Creek's headwaters, is the signed top of Dawn Falls Trail. It descends to Southern Marin Line, then to the canyon floor.

Hoo-Koo-E-Koo leaves the woodland into chaparral. There are striking views to the east above the line of shrubs. Three of Marin's most aromatic plants grow abundantly here. Pitcher sage (*Lepechinia calycina*), in the mint family, has soft, hairy leaves that leave a pungent fragrance when rubbed. California sagebrush (*Artemesia californica*), in the sunflower family, has lacier leaves and a slightly milder fragrance. And, particularly near the Trail's crossing of Blithedale Ridge F.R., are masses of blue blossom, or California-lilac (*Ceanothus thyrsiflorus*). In March, ceanothus fragrance pervades the area.

The Trail reaches Blithedale Ridge F.R. and southern views suddenly open. Left on Blithedale Ridge F.R. leads to Mill Valley, right up to Indian Fire Road.

The next section of Hoo-Koo-E-Koo, called Echo Rock Trail on MMWD maps, is fairly level. There are views down across Blithedale Canyon, which the Trail circles.

Around one-quarter-mile past Blithedale Ridge, the Trail edges past Echo Rock. Face the rock and boom out a greeting; the echo is startling. Indeed, even whispered conversations may be heard across the canyon. The rock is an outcropping of greenstone basalt, formed in an ocean floor fissure. The mineral chlorite produces greenish tinges.

Beyond Echo Rock, the Trail leaves the Preserve into the Marin Municipal Water District. Soon, thin, tightly packed redwoods crowd the Trail; a mature grove will have greater spacing. The sound of Corte Madera Creek is audible in winter.

Hoo-Koo-E-Koo Trail approaches Hoo-Koo-E-Koo Fire Road, which is reached by climbing a few yards. To the left, Corte Madera Creek Trail follows the creek precipitously down, returning to MCOSD land by Horseshoe Fire Road. Hoo-Koo-E-Koo F.R. goes left to Wheeler Trail, then Old Railroad Grade. Right, it rises a quarter-mile to Blithedale Ridge Fire Road.

SOUTHERN MARIN LINE FIRE ROAD (2.78 miles)

From Crown Road (Kent Woodlands) to Sunrise Lane (Larkspur)
Intersections: Hoo-Koo-E-Koo Trail (.05m), Dawn Falls Trail (.28m), H-Line F.R. (1.24m), Barbara Spring Trail (1.56m)

Southern Marin Line Fire Road is well-used because it is one of the longest level roads in the County and near central Marin communities. Dog owners, and beginning bikers and runners, find it particularly appealing.

Most visitors enter the Fire Road from the Crown Road side high in Kent Woodlands, as there is no adjacent (and little nearby) parking on the Larkspur end. Indeed, the entire route is commonly referred to simply as "Crown Road." Park only on the left shoulder when driving in from Crown Road, do not block driveways, maintain required clearance from the road center, and refrain from any loud conversation until well clear of residences.

The unpaved portion of the Fire Road begins a few yards from the gate. There are fine views beyond Baltimore (also called Madrone, Redwood, and Larkspur) Canyon to Corte Madera Ridge ("Little Tamalpais") and well beyond. Private homes are above right until the Hoo-Koo-E-Koo Trail junction, less than 100 yards in. Hoo-Koo-E-Koo rises to Blithedale Ridge F.R., then goes another three miles, much of it as a fire road, to Matt Davis Trail on Tam's south side.

You may find the Fire Road lined with broom, or see little evidence of the hardy invader, depending on how recently the last major clearing occurred. Most other shrubs and trees—madrones, young redwoods and Douglas-firs, laurels—are Marin natives.

About a quarter-mile in, Dawn Falls Trail crosses. Right, it rises the short way to Hoo-Koo-E-Koo Trail. Left, it drops to Dawn Falls itself (about .2 miles down the switchbacks) and then continues through Baltimore Canyon.

Just beyond, the water pipeline to which the Fire Road owes its existence is visible over a gorge. The pipe's support structure has been dubbed "Little Golden Gate." All the rest of the way, the gently downsloping pipeline is hidden just under the roadbed. Through it, water flows from the Bon Tempe Treatment Plant to southern Marin storage tanks. Bon Tempe Dam (creating Bon Tempe Lake), the Treatment Plant, the pipeline, and the Fire Road all were built as part of the MMWD Southern Marin Line project just after World War II. Coded green posts placed by the MMWD in 1996 mark drainages. Valves and other signs of the pipeline are evident throughout.

There are fewer vista points as the increasingly wooded Fire Road travels south, although Tam views beckon when heading back. After a mile without an intersection the Fire Road widens at the H-Line F.R. junction. Several big pipes, each labeled with a letter, are enclosed in the pumping station area. From here, water is pumped up over Blithedale Ridge to Mill Valley. H-Line F.R. also goes over the ridge, then down to Old Railroad Grade in Mill Valley.

The redwood forest along the Fire Road is densest just after (and a bit before) the H-Line junction. A few bends lead to signed Barbara Spring Trail, which departs left and descends steeply to the canyon floor. There are then no more intersections along the Fire Road other than a couple of social paths.

Southern Marin Line winds around the eastern face of Tam, so many bends that some users find them wearing. One of the few landmarks are the two fences marking a major slide from the big January 1982 storm.

The Fire Road ends at another MCOSD gate. A few feet beyond, Huckleberry Trail rises right to Corte Madera Ridge. Beyond are residences in Larkspur. One, numbered 10, has given rise to the erroneous name "Fire Road 10" for the whole route. The paved road continues down as Sunrise Lane, which meets Marina Vista Avenue.

The water pipeline continues as well. It is again covered by a fire road, also through MCOSD lands, south from Corte Madera's Summit Drive into Mill Valley.

WINDY RIDGE TRAIL (.45 miles)

From top of Phoenix Road to Indian/Evergreen Fire Roads
Note: Open to bicyclists

A few years ago, this former fire road was so choked by broom that it was barely passable. The route has since been cleared and consequently reopened to bicycle users. Although the route is quite broad almost all the way, the very top and bottom remain narrow, so Windy Ridge is labeled as a trail.

Windy Ridge Trail sets off from the top of Phoenix Road, a short street rising off Crown Road's western section in Kent Woodlands. At the same spot, Harry Allen Trail begins a descent to Crown Road's eastern half. A few yards lower on Phoenix Road is the base of Indian Fire Road for which Windy Ridge Trail serves as a cooler, shaded, and less steep alternative.

At press-time, lower Windy Ridge Trail is again being crowded by broom but still comfortably open. A lone, non-native, acacia, 50 yards in, is covered with yellow blossoms in February, which then blanket the Trail in March. A dense stand of young redwoods lines just about all the rest of the route. Many bear fire scars.

At 250 yards, a brief clearing left opens views to the north. At .3 miles, a short connector rises right to Indian Fire Road.

Near its top, Windy Ridge Trail leaves the redwoods and again narrows. The Trail ends at a junction with both Indian and Evergreen Fire Roads at the MCOSD-MMWD boundary. The MMWD's Indian F.R., here in a saddle, rises left to Hoo-Koo-E-Koo Fire Road and Eldridge Grade. Right, it also rises, then drops back to Phoenix Road. Evergreen F.R. descends to Evergreen Drive over MCOSD land.

Giant trillium (Trillium chloropetalum), also called wake-robin, in the Lily family, found occasionally in the Preserves' redwood forests. Its sweet-scented, maroon/purple petals sit stalkless atop a whorl of three leaves. More common locally is western trillium (Trillium ovatum ssp. ovatum), with smaller leaves and whitish (aging to pink) petals atop a short stalk.

BLITHEDALE SUMMIT

Size: 560 acres   Elevation range: 80-1,031 feet

*This arm of Mt. Tamalpais juts out into Larkspur, Corte Madera,
and Mill Valley and divides the cities. But in a way it actually
unites their residents. I'm always surprised when patrolling the
ridge how many people I see coming up from the cities on the
various trails and fire roads. Most get up onto Blithedale Ridge
fire road and head up towards "The Sleeping Lady." As they head
back to their home town, they can experience redwood groves,
chaparral, oak/bay woodlands, and if they look hard enough,
beautiful creeks with immense ferns.*
                            — *Brian Sanford, Supervising Ranger*

BLITHEDALE RIDGE is the major spur of Mt. Tamalpais' southeast face. The uppermost part of the ridge is within the Marin Municipal Water District, the lower slopes
covered by homes on winding Mill Valley streets. The middle section forms the
heart of the Preserve.

John J. Cushing (1822-1879) brought the name "Blithedale" to Marin. He
was born in Rhode Island, came west during the Gold Rush, then practiced homeo-
pathic medicine in San Francisco. In 1873, he filed a homestead for 320 acres in the
future Mill Valley and opened a health resort there. He called it "Blithedale," from
his Bowdoin College classmate Nathaniel Hawthorne's novel, "The Blithedale Ro-
mance." The name became attached to the canyon and the road to it from the rail
line. After Cushing's death, the resort was expanded as a summer hotel by his son
Sidney. It closed after the 1910 season and the main hotel building was torn down
in 1912.

Blithedale Ridge is part of a broader area—which includes sections of Camino
Alto, Alto Bowl, and Baltimore Canyon Preserves—known as Northridge, for it
extends north from Mill Valley into the neighboring towns of Corte Madera and
Larkspur. Saving Northridge from development was a community priority in the
1970's, and local citizen's groups played a major effort in fundraising and publicity.
The largest single Northridge tract, 357 acres, was purchased in October 1976, for
$850,000. Of this, the OSD contributed one-half, the balance coming from the cit-
ies of Mill Valley and Larkspur, and the Friends of Northridge. Similar joint efforts
involving the District, the towns of Mill Valley, Larkspur, and Corte Madera, and
private donor groups were used in funding other Northridge acquisitions.

see map on pages 52-53

BLITHEDALE RIDGE FIRE ROAD (2.22 miles)

From Greenwood Fire Road to Indian Fire Road
Intersections: Maytag Trail (.05m, .17m), Corte Madera Ridge F.R. (.80m),
H-Line F.R. (1.30m), Horseshoe F.R. (1.51m), Hoo-Koo-E-Koo Trail
(1.77m), Hoo-Koo-E-Koo F.R. (2.16m)
Notes: Access roads are narrow and winding;
park only within white-outlined spaces

This long Fire Road along the spine of Mt. Tamalpais' Blithedale Ridge forms an open space link between Mill Valley and communities north. Be aware that the net elevation change between start and end points, 500 feet, vastly understates the amount of climbing, as numerous dips add to the uphill.

The southeast end of the Fire Road is over private property and there have been problems with access. The only all-public entry is via Greenwood Fire Road, atop Greenwood Way. The fire road rises one-eighth mile, over City of Mill Valley land, to Blithedale Ridge. Although the MCOSD boundary is 60 yards to the left, this junction is the starting point for the measurements cited. A problem with the Greenwood entry is that the drive to it is over extremely narrow and winding roads.

Blithedale Ridge is commonly called "roller coaster" but a better term for the opening section, to Corte Madera Ridge F.R., might be "staircase," as uphills are followed more by level or less steep sections than by corresponding downhills. But sensational views of Mt. Tamalpais begin immediately.

Just 100 feet beyond the MCOSD boundary sign is another MCOSD sign, "Trail," on the right. This is the public start of Maytag Trail, which runs parallel to the Fire Road a bit lower in the redwoods. Maytag rejoins the Fire Road, unsigned, 200 yards ahead.

Boundary signposts, one-quarter mile in, mark where the Fire Road briefly leaves the Preserve onto private property (through access is permitted). A fenced water tank sits on the crest. Not far beyond, an orange-red gate on the left bars the top of off-limits, private, Rider (or Cushing) Road. Dr. J. Alfred Rider sold 190 adjacent acres to the District in 1983. The Fire Road returns to MCOSD land at another pair of boundary posts 250 yards later.

There is a climb to another crest, then a steeper uphill to yet another. From the latter, northern views open, including Knob Hill at the end of Blithedale Ridge.

At .8 miles, in a wide clearing, Corte Madera Ridge F.R. comes in from the right. It tops the east wall, and Blithedale Ridge F.R. the west, of Warner Canyon. The crest just above the junction is at elevation 956 feet.

After a short rise, Blithedale Ridge F.R. begins its longest downhill. The descent opens with a straight-on shot of Mt. Tamalpais, then drops into a canyon lined with redwoods.

The plunge ends at an intersection, sometimes called Windy Gap, or The Notch, 1.3 miles in. Left, H-Line Fire Road drops to Old Railroad Grade. Straight, Blithedale Ridge F.R. starts up again. Right, H-Line drops to near the middle of Southern Marin Line F.R., which can be taken to Kent Woodlands or Larkspur.

The Fire Road climbs back up to the ridge. The roller coaster begins anew, again mostly up. The chaparral permits broad views. There are some trees, such as madrones, redwoods, and chinquapins, with their bur-covered fruits.

At the end of a downhill at 1.5 miles, Horseshoe Fire Road drops left, to Corte Madera Creek Trail and Old Railroad Grade. Ahead, in early spring, are masses of blue blossom, or wild lilac, providing pleasing fragrance and color.

A quarter-mile after Horseshoe, Hoo-Koo-E-Koo Trail crosses. Left leads to Echo Rock, then Hoo-Koo-E-Koo Fire Road at the top of Corte Madera Creek Trail. Right leads to the Kent Woodlands end of Southern Marin Line.

Blithedale Ridge F.R. circles the headwall of Blithedale Canyon. There is more uphill, much of it rocky, toward the prominent 1,091-foot summit of Knob Hill. Just before the signed junction with the top of Hoo-Koo-E-Koo F.R., Blithedale Ridge F.R. leaves the MCOSD onto MMWD land. Hoo-Koo-E-Koo F.R. drops to Hoo-Koo-E-Koo Trail, then continues around Mt. Tamalpais.

A final, steep, 100 yard climb leads to the end of Blithedale Ridge F.R. at its junction with Indian Fire Road. Left on Indian leads up to Eldridge Grade. Right drops to Kent Woodlands. The boundaries of three Mexican land grants met here; Punta de Quentin, Saucelito, and Tomales y Baulines.

CORTE MADERA RIDGE FIRE ROAD (.90 miles)

From top of Summit Drive (Corte Madera) to Blithedale Ridge Fire Road
Intersections: Huckleberry Trail and Glen Fire Road (.63m)
Notes: Access roads are extremely steep and narrow; very limited parking atop Summit Drive and no parking after sunset; do not block driveway of private home adjacent to Trailhead

This Fire Road is described from the Corte Madera end, where it is accessible by car. But the winding, narrow drive up is among the hairiest for any access point in this book. If the handful of parking places by the trailhead gate at the top of Summit Drive are taken, you'll need to retreat. Do not mistake the Fire Road with the private driveway to the left, nor with the broad path that goes up to the right immediately behind the gate.

Awesome views begin at once. Just 50 feet in you can look behind and see Richardson Bay. In ten more yards, the San Francisco skyline comes into view. By .1 mile, Oakland is added. Next are knockout views of Tam, first of the peak, then of its whole southern and eastern faces.

At .3 miles, the Fire Road bends left and encounters redwoods. The path that ran from the start atop the ridge enters, then departs again. Some 500 feet later, views to the north open, including of White Hill, Bald Hill, and Loma Alta.

There is then a downhill to a four-way junction at .63 miles. Right, with an MCOSD sign, is the top of Huckleberry Trail. It drops to the Larkspur end of Southern Marin Line. Left is Glen F.R., which descends a half-mile to Elinor F.R. and .4 additional miles to Glen Drive in Mill Valley.

The steep uphill ahead is rewarded with the best Tam vista so far and a nice perspective of King Mountain. Higher still is another view to San Francisco.

The Fire Road finishes atop a narrow ridge between Baltimore Canyon to the right (north) and the headwaters of Warner Creek to the left (south). Its end is the junction with Blithedale Ridge F.R. It is a mile left to Blithedale's end in Mill Valley. Right on Blithedale is a sharp drop (after a short initial rise) to H-Line Fire Road.

ELINOR FIRE ROAD (1.06 miles)

From Elinor Avenue (Mill Valley) to Glen Fire Road
Intersection: Warner Canyon Trail (.32m)
Notes: Elinor Avenue is narrow; park only within
designated white-outlined spaces

Near the upper end of winding Elinor Avenue, by the private drive leading up to addresses #300-302-310, Elinor Fire Road sets off right. One hundred feet in is a gate signed only "No Parking." The first 275 yards of the Fire Road are outside the Preserve.

Just inside the gate, a path drops right to Bay Tree Lane lower in Warner Canyon. A bit farther, an old roadbed is evident above on the left.

A second gate, signed "Blithedale Summit," marks entry into MCOSD lands, in which Elinor Fire Road then remains. There are views out to the Tiburon peninsula. Five hundred feet past the MCOSD gate, a path drops right 300 yards to Tartan Road.

Just over 100 yards later, in the middle of a big bend left, Warner Canyon Trail sets off right. It dead-ends, in .5 miles, at Warner Falls.

Elinor begins a half-mile section that involves steep climbing through a deep redwood forest. This is a wonderful stretch (although perhaps better enjoyed in the downhill direction!), far from any road. The redwoods are slender and densely packed, indicative of a young, second growth forest following logging. But some of the fire-scarred trees immediately bordering the Fire Road already are giants, nearly 150 feet tall, though without the girth of the virgin monarchs in Muir Woods.

At the next big bend, a path leaves left into the woods toward Blithedale Ridge. The small tree/tall shrub of hazel is abundant. Feel its soft leaves and look for the hard-to-find nuts.

The Fire Road gradually rises above the redwood belt and opens. Madrones and chaparral shrubs now line the way, and there are views down to the Mill Valley Municipal Golf Course at the base of Warner Canyon. The uphill is more gradual.

Warner Creek then flows directly over Elinor Fire Road (creeks are usually diverted under roads through culverts) at a wooded bend right. The seemingly promising path departing here left along the creek bank quickly deteriorates.

Elinor rises to more San Francisco views. The route ends at its junction with Glen Fire Road, which rises left a half-mile to Corte Madera Ridge F.R. and drops .4 miles to Glen Drive in Warner Canyon.

Elinor Burt (1899-1973) was the granddaughter of Jacob Gardner and daughter of John Burt, two of the pioneers of early Mill Valley. Jacob and John developed the Bolsa Tract, through which Elinor Avenue runs, just after World War I and named one of the streets for her. Elinor Burt became a teacher and served as a dietitian for the U.S. Air Corps during World War II. She wrote two cookbooks, *Olla Podrida* and *Far Eastern Cooking*. Her oral history is archived in the Mill Valley Public Library.

GLEN FIRE ROAD (.87 miles)
From Glen Drive (Mill Valley) to Corte Madera Ridge Fire Road
Intersection: Elinor F.R. (.44m)

Glen Fire Road begins behind an MCOSD-signed gate at the top of Glen Drive. Warner Creek, which carves Warner Canyon, is below left. The high ridges above are Blithedale to the left (west) and Corte Madera to the right.

The route is unrelentingly uphill, but the early going is steepest. Oaks dot the edge but offer little shade. Broom is abundant, crowding out native wildflowers.

About halfway up Glen, Elinor Fire Road comes in from the left. It traverses the west side of the canyon to Elinor Avenue in Mill Valley.

The final climb on Glen Fire Road is to the headwaters of Warner Creek. The Fire Road ends at a saddle in Corte Madera Ridge F.R. Left leads to Blithedale Ridge F.R., right to Summit Drive in Corte Madera. Directly across is the top of Huckleberry Trail, which drops to the Larkspur end of Southern Marin Line Fire Road.

The developer of Warner Canyon applied Scottish-sounding names to the new streets, Glen being one.

H-LINE FIRE ROAD (.89 miles)
From Southern Marin Line Fire Road to Old Railroad Grade
Intersection: Blithedale Ridge F.R. (.25m)

Few routes climb up one side of a ridge, then descend the other. H-Line F.R. was specifically built to do that, to provide access for vehicles servicing water pipelines crossing Blithedale Ridge into Mill Valley. Although the Mill Valley end of H-Line is closer to a trailhead, the route will be described in the direction the water is pumped.

H-Line Fire Road rises from Southern Marin Line F.R., 1.3 miles from the Crown Road end, 1.5 miles from the Larkspur end. The pump station and underground pipelines are visible here behind the fencing.

The Fire Road's uphill section is moderately steep, gaining 150 feet over a quarter-mile. A big switchback helps. Redwoods give way to madrones.

The Fire Road crests at elevation 660 feet and crosses Blithedale Ridge Fire Road at a key intersection called both The Notch and Windy Gap. Uphill to the right, Blithedale Ridge F.R. heads toward Hoo-Koo-E-Koo Trail and Indian Fire

Road. Left, it rises to Corte Madera Ridge F.R. and on to Mill Valley. H-Line continues, now descending.

Ahead is Mill Valley. Blithedale Canyon stretches below. At the base of the first big bend is a huge (500,000 gallon), new (1999), forest green, welded steel water tank. It replaced two older, smaller, redwood tanks on the route, one here and one lower, to improve water pressure for Mill Valley consumers. The MMWD calls it H-Line Tank. (Many visitors have long referred to this section of Fire Road between Blithedale Ridge and Old Railroad Grade as "Two Tanks." At press time, there are still two tanks; the new one and a temporary one beside it. Soon there will just be one.)

Acacias, non-native trees, line the way, although some have been cut. The lower tank stood at a bend right, where the route is briefly paved. H-Line descends a final .1 mile, out of the chaparral into the deep woodland of Blithedale Canyon.

H-Line ends at its junction with Old Railroad Grade. It is 200 yards left to the West Blithedale Avenue trailhead. Right is a seven mile rise to the East Peak parking lot.

The name arose because, when the Fire Road was first graded as part of the Southern Marin Line project of the early 1950's, its route fell on the "H" line of the MMWD's grid map.

HORSESHOE FIRE ROAD (.28 miles)
From Old Railroad Grade to Blithedale Ridge Fire Road
Intersection: Corte Madera Creek Trail (.10m)

Horseshoe is a very steep connector between Old Railroad Grade and Blithedale Ridge F.R., two key Mill Valley routes.

Horseshoe is the second intersecting fire road when climbing Old Railroad Grade from West Blithedale Avenue (H-Line is the first). Horseshoe Fire Road, .6 miles up from West Blithedale, rises from historic Horseshoe Curve. This bend over Corte Madera Creek was the sharpest of all 281 curves on the Mt. Tamalpais & Muir Woods Scenic Railway route. Today's downhill in the bend dates from 1982, when a storm-caused slide was filled; there were originally no such dips in the track. Horseshoe Curve also marks the boundary between the MCOSD and MMWD lands.

The Fire Road rises right beside the redwood-lined creek. At .1 miles, signed Corte Madera Creek Trail departs left at a MCOSD "Trail" sign. But it immediately leaves the Preserve onto MMWD land (so is not separately described), for an extremely steep climb to Hoo-Koo-E-Koo F. R.

Horseshoe F.R. veers away from the redwoods and into chaparral. The stiff, exposed grind up is rewarded with fine views out to the San Francisco skyline.

Horseshoe Fire Road ends at Blithedale Ridge F.R. There are loop options by going .3 miles left to Hoo-Koo-E-Koo Trail (followed by Corte Madera Creek Trail), or .2 miles right to H-Line Fire Road.

HUCKLEBERRY TRAIL (.61 miles)

From Southern Marin Line Fire Road to Corte Madera Ridge Fire Road

Huckleberry Trail is an important trail connector between two well-used fire roads. It is also one of the few sites in Marin County where rhododendrons grow naturally.

Huckleberry begins from an MCOSD signpost at the southern (Larkspur) end of Southern Marin Line Fire Road, just a few yards before the gate. The climbing is tough at once, with only a few respites the whole way up.

The Trail rises above the initial tree cover. There are fine views over Larkspur, Greenbrae, and Corte Madera, and well beyond to the north and east. The shrub huckleberry is abundant. Its tasty, but small, berries are edible when they blacken in summer. (District regulations regulate the amount of berries that can be picked, as berries are important in the diet of many wildlife species.) Chinquapin, in the oak family, is the common small tree. Its nuts are protected by sharp burs.

A quarter-mile in, when the Trail re-enters woodland through a few tanbark oaks, look left and right for several western rhododendrons, also called California rose-bay (*Rhododendron macrophyllum*). They are easy to miss, except when the showy, rose-colored, flowers (please do not pick) stand out in mid-spring. Of some 1,000 members of the rhododendron genus throughout the world, only two, this and the western azalea (*R. occidentale*), grow in California. Azalea is fairly abundant in Marin but rose-bay is native only here and at four or five other sites in the County. Master trail builder Ben Schmidt, who helped carve the route some 50 years ago, coined the original name of Rhododendron Trail.

The upper part of the Trail cuts through stands of young redwoods, including at the very top. Huckleberry ends at its junction with Corte Madera Ridge Fire Road. The Fire Road goes left to Summit Drive in Corte Madera and right, past a stunning view knoll a few yards up, to Blithedale Ridge F.R. Directly across Huckleberry at the junction is the top of Glen Fire Road, which descends Warner Canyon to Mill Valley.

MAYTAG TRAIL (.16 miles)

Between Blithedale Ridge Fire Road

When traveling Blithedale Ridge F.R. from the Mill Valley end (top of Greenwood Fire Road), quickly encountered are an MCOSD boundary signpost (left), then, 100 feet later, a "Trail" signpost (right) marking the public start of Maytag Trail.

Within 20 feet, Maytag is in redwood forest, where it remains. The Trail drops steeply for 100 feet, then bends left and levels. A path comes in right—it is actually part of the originally cut Maytag Trail—from private property.

Several members of the lily family associated with redwoods provide floral treats along the Trail in spring. A favorite is trillium, or wake-robin (*Trillium ovatum*).

Showy, white, three-petaled flowers, which age to pink, sit atop a triple-leaf base. Other lily family members include Solomon's seal (*Smilacina racemosa* and *S. stellata*), fetid adders tongue (*Scoliopus bigelovii*), fairy bells (*Disporum hookeri* and *D. smithii*), and Clintonia (*Clintonia andrewsiana*).

At a double-trunked bay laurel, a connector cuts back up to the ridge. A hundred yards later, a short steep pitch returns Maytag to its end at Blithedale Ridge Fire Road. This junction, 200 yards from the start, is unsigned.

The Trail was cleared by local boy scouts to provide a shaded alternative to Blithedale Ridge F.R. They came across a discarded Maytag appliance, thus the name.

OLD RAILROAD GRADE (.62 miles)
From West Blithedale Avenue to MMWD boundary/Horseshoe Fire Road Intersection: H-Line F.R. (.12m)

Old Railroad Grade and the Dipsea Trail are the two most famous routes in Marin County. Not coincidentally, they once both started from the same place, the railroad depot in downtown Mill Valley. For it was via the railroad (with ferry connection between San Francisco and Sausalito) that early visitors flocked to Mill Valley. These mostly summertime visitors then proceeded up Mt. Tamalpais either by foot (often on the Dipsea Trail) or by a separate rail line, dubbed "The World's Crookedest Railway," whose route is today's Old Railroad Grade.

The 8.3-mile, single-tracked, line up Tam was built in a remarkably short time, less than six months, in the pre-Environmental Impact Report days of 1896. Actually, there were strong local environmental objections—to the noise of the trains, to the cutting of redwoods, and more—but the railway's influential backers overturned an injunction in a hasty court proceeding, then rushed the project through before appeals could begin.

The grade never exceeded seven percent so engines could pull (actually they were soon switched to the rear to push) passenger cars up. Descent often was by gravity car, one of the great rides in the world. There were 281 curves, hence the line's nickname. There were originally 22 trestles over creek crossings; all were subsequently filled. A lavish tavern at the top of the line (today's East Peak parking lot) and a more modest one at the westernmost point of track (West Point) served day visitors and overnighters.

The Mt. Tamalpais & Muir Woods Railway was immensely popular and beloved. But the rise of the automobile, the paving of a road to the top, the terrible Mill Valley fire of 1929, and the Depression all served to doom it. There was a surprise winter closure after the runs of October 31, 1929, and service never resumed. The track was torn up in 1930. Sharp-eyed visitors may still find spikes after heavy rains. Luckily, plans to then pave the Railroad Grade as another auto road were beaten back.

The initial 1.2 miles of the line along Corte Madera Creek are now over private property. The public portion of the Grade begins at an MCOSD gate off West

Blithedale Avenue just beyond Lee Street. The few nearby parking spaces are invariably filled on weekends; come via carpool, foot or bicycle.

The Grade rises at its gradual, steady pace. Corte Madera Creek, which the old rail line had already crossed seven times from downtown to here, is to the left. Maples line the bank, creating perhaps the best fall color display in Marin. Across the creek are homes. MCOSD lands are to the right. In 200 yards, H-Line Fire Road rises right to Blithedale Ridge Fire Road.

At .6 miles from the gate, the Grade begins a broad turn left to make its eighth and last crossing of Corte Madera Creek. This is Horseshoe Curve, the sharpest on the entire route. On the near side of the curve, Horseshoe Fire Road begins its very steep rise. It passes the entry to Corte Madera Creek Trail and ends at Blithedale Ridge F.R. The MCOSD/MMWD boundary line is in the middle of the bend. The slight downhill there is the result of fill used to repair a washout during the El Niño winter of 1981-82.

The Grade continues its long, historic journey up. Try *The Crookedest Railroad in the World* by Ted Wurm and Al Graves or my *Tamalpais Trails* to guide the way.

WARNER CANYON TRAIL (.48 miles)
From Elinor Fire Road to Warner Falls
Note: Dead-end

Warner Canyon Trail begins, signed and named, off Elinor Fire Road, .3 miles from Elinor Avenue. The Trail leaves to the right in the middle of a big bend left.

The broad start indicates the route was once a road. A decade ago, French broom had narrowed it so much as to make the route virtually impassable. Now, broom clearings by OSD staff and volunteers keep it open.

The Trail rises almost imperceptibly. Redwood, maple, and madrone are the main trees. Hazel is the most abundant shrub, after broom.

Nearly a half-mile in, a final short uphill leads to Warner Falls and the Trail's end. The flow is lively in winter, barely a trickle in summer. This is a lovely, isolated spot. Trillium and other wildflowers add color in spring.

Dr. Alexander Warner was a Virginia-born dentist who came west at the suggestion of "Big Four" railroad builder Collis Huntington, one of his patients. Legend has it that, in the early 1880's, Warner gained title to the original 130 acres of the canyon to be named for him as settlement of a dental bill. The Warner family then spent summers in the canyon in tents and in a one-room house on today's Glen Drive. In 1917, the family added 35 acres of the upper canyon by paying $29.38 in delinquent property taxes. In 1919, the year Dr. Warner died, the Mill Valley Golf Course opened in the canyon's lower reaches. In 1930, the Warner house was torn down and its wood burned in a Tamalpais High School football rally bonfire.

Warner Canyon remained a pristine, semi-wilderness playground for Mill Valley youth until after World War II, when subdivision began.

Routes in the Northridge Preserves (Blithedale Summit, Camino Alto, Baltimore Canyon) offer unsurpassed views of Mt. Tamalpais.

A scene on the Mt. Tamalpais & Muir Woods Railway, now Old Railroad Grade. (Courtesy, Dewey Livingston)

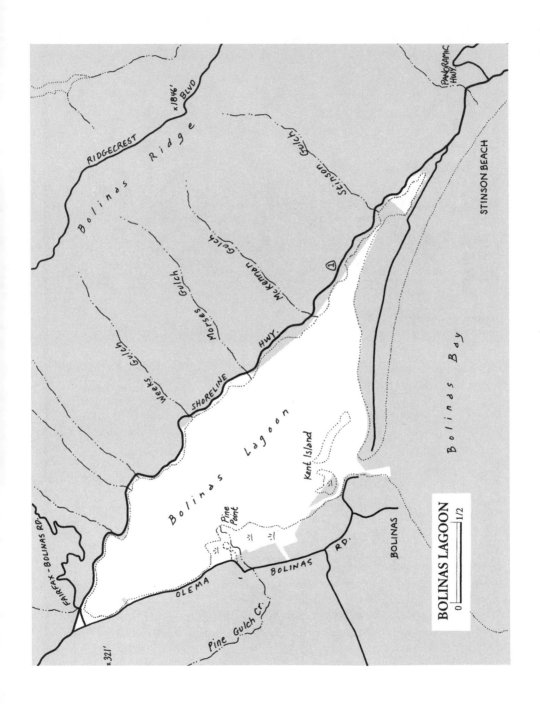

BOLINAS LAGOON

BOLINAS LAGOON

Size: 1,006.9 acres (mostly tidelands)   Elevation range: 0-15 feet

In addition to being beautiful, Bolinas Lagoon has a rich history. It is here that one can see the profound effects that modern civilization has had upon our natural environment. Imagine the surrounding hills covered with trees instead of deforested and over-grazed. The Pine Gulch Creek delta was once only a small spit of land which excessive erosion has now made large. It's hard to believe that we have had such a profound impact on this area in only 150 years.   — *Canada Ross, Ranger*

BOLINAS LAGOON lies directly atop the San Andreas Fault, the infamous, unstable, divide between the earth's North American and Pacific Plates. The Pacific Plate is drifting northward at the rate of some one-two inches per year, but occasionally moves more violently, nearly 25 feet during the 1906 Earthquake. The present Lagoon dates from some 8,000 years ago, when rising waters following the retreat of the most recent Ice Age began filling it.

In Gold Rush days, Bolinas was a busy shipping port for logged redwoods bound for San Francisco. Dairy products and other farm produce then became the main export, on schooners built right on the lagoon. For example, Hugh McKennan, for whom a trail within the GGNRA on the east shore of the Lagoon is named, raised ducks and shipped up to 1,000 eggs a day to San Francisco. The road to Sausalito, now Highway 1, opened in 1870. The first subdivision in Bolinas, called Grande Vista, dates from 1872.

The lagoon harbors one of the richer concentrations of bird life in the nation. Numerous and impossible to miss are the great blue herons and the all-white snowy and great egrets. All three species nest in the treetops inside adjacent Audubon Canyon Ranch (acquired to save the site) and feed in the nutrient-rich waters.

Kent Island in the lagoon is one of just nine year-round haul out sites for the harbor seal (*Phoca vitulina*) in the Bay Area. On land, the seals replenish oxygen exhausted after long dives for fish. Seal pups, born in early spring, are suckled there. And the seals haul out for up to 11 daylight hours each summer to accelerate their molt.

Harbor seals lack external ears and are unable to turn their hind limbs forward for locomotion on land. They are gray and about six feet in length. They may sleep under water, rising to the surface every quarter-hour or so to breathe, yet not waking.

The District has posted signs to reduce wildlife disturbance; keep yourself and dogs at least 300 feet away from any seals. Do not pick up solitary seal pups. Several are doomed each year by well-meaning visitors who "rescue" them while the mother is actually nearby, perhaps even looking on.

A grave threat to the Lagoon's wildlife and natural state emerged in 1957 when the State of California leased 1,200 acres of tidelands to the Bolinas Harbor District. Grandiose development schemes were proposed, such as a 1,400-slip marina, heliport, bridge, offices, and housing. Highway One was to be widened and straightened. The fascinating story of the counter-effort to keep the Lagoon as a nature preserve is told in *Saving the Marin-Sonoma Coast* by Dr. Martin Griffin, who played a major role.

One key element in thwarting development was the purchase in 1962 of the initial acreage of what came to be called Audubon Canyon Ranch by the Marin and Golden Gate Audubon society chapters. Another was the donation to the County (via the Nature Conservancy and Audubon Canyon Ranch) of Kent Island, at the mouth of the lagoon and essential to the marina plan, by the Kent family in the late 1960's. Pierre Joske, then General Manager of the County Parks system (and later of the new Open Space District), recalls that the County Board of Supervisors literally had only minutes to decide whether to accept the Kent gift or risk losing it to condemnation by the Harbor District.

In 1988, management of the Bolinas Lagoon Nature Preserve was turned over to the Open Space District, from the Marin County Parks Department. In 1998, Bolinas Lagoon was named a Wetlands of International Importance by the United States Fish and Wildlife Service through the International Convention on Wetlands.

Today, the greatest threat to the Lagoon comes from sedimentation. Previous land uses in the watershed, including logging and overgrazing, accelerated natural rates of sedimentation and caused a loss of tidal habitat. Mudflats are expanding and channels within the lagoon are slowly becoming shallower or disappearing altogether. At press time, the MCOSD and the United States Army Corps of Engineers are studying ways to address the problem.

With virtually no dry land, the Preserve has no real trails. Several paths lace marshy Pine Gulch peninsula where Pine Gulch Creek, which the District is helping to restore, empties into the west side of the Lagoon. There are two entries into the network, both signed and with roadside parking turnouts, off Olema-Bolinas Road just north of Horseshoe Hill Road. The outermost path is called Bob Stewart Trail, for the District's long-time naturalist who retired in 1997. Informal names are attached to other paths: Night Heron Trail (from the entry nearer Horseshoe Hill Road), Egret Trail, Kingfisher Trail. None of these paths through the willows and alders are separately described as they are all short and usually extremely muddy; wear boots. There is also a signed entry through a stile opposite #77 Olema-Bolinas Road.

There is controversy over the origin of the name "Bolinas." The original land grant covering the area was Rancho Las Baulines. Francisco de Bolanos served as pilot on the 1603 Vizcaino expedition that put ashore in west Marin. Hubert Bancroft, the great authority of early California history, is firm that the name comes from the Spanish word for whales, ballenas. Some say the name stems from the nautical "bowlines" knot. Others believe it is of Miwok origin. The town's post office has been "Bolinas" from 1863.

Bolinas Lagoon at low tide.

The Mill Valley-Sausalito Multi-Use Path, a railroad line for some 80 years, through Bothin Marsh Preserve. Coyote Creek enters on the left, crossed by a footbridge at the southern end of the Preserve. Mt. Tamalpais is reflected in the Marsh's waters.

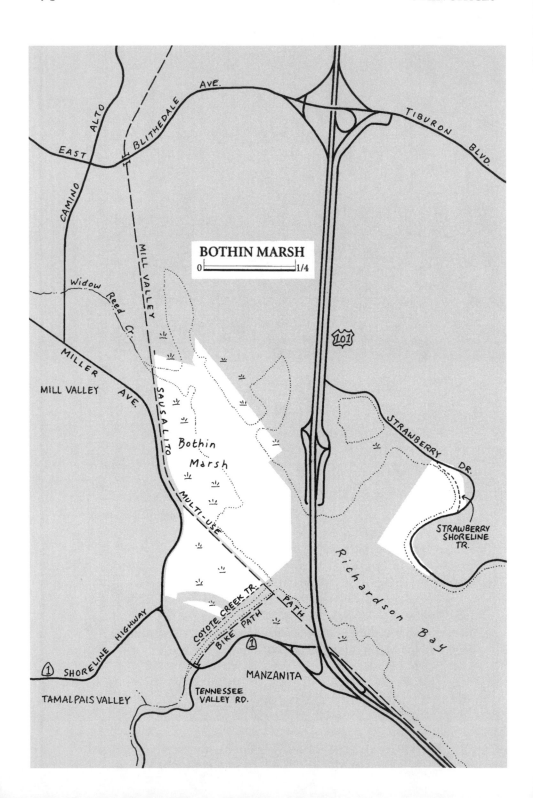

BOTHIN MARSH

Size: 94.5 acres   Elevation range: 0-15 feet

Each visit to this small Preserve reminds me that much of the wetlands in the Bay Area have been lost or altered—filled for houses, industrial complexes, roadways, and other uses. As I walk the levees from the bike path out to the channel, it is hard to imagine that originally there were 190,000 acres of historic tidal marsh in the Bay Area, with little more than 16,000 acres remaining today. It makes this Preserve more important, more precious. I hope that passing motorists, runners, bicyclists and dog walkers can see it too.
— *Chris Bramham, Chief Ranger*

MOST OF THIS PRESERVE is tidal marshland. The one route through is the raised old railroad bed, now the Multi-Use Path. When European settlers first arrived in Marin, upper Richardson Bay was deeper and larger. For example, in the 1860's and '70's, Samuel Throckmorton, owner of 19,000 acres of southern Marin, maintained a wharf where Tamalpais High School now sits. Lumber, tallow, hides, hay, and dairy products were loaded onto huge barges for transport to San Francisco. But silt from logging and development increasingly filled Richardson Bay.

The marsh and Preserve name comes from Henry Bothin (1853-1923). He was born in Ohio and came to San Francisco at age 21. Bothin invested in San Francisco real estate and made a fortune, although some 90 of his buildings were destroyed in the 1906 earthquake and fire. Bothin and his second wife, Ellen Chabot, lived in Ross in a mansion they built in 1908 at the west end of Lagunitas Road. He became one of Marin's, and the Bay Area's, most generous philanthropists (see Bothin Access F.R., White Hill Preserve chapter) and the Bothin Foundation is still making charitable donations in the Bay Area.

A developer, KSW Properties, acquired the Bothin marsh holdings in 1970 and began filling and building. The threat of a larger development—Tam Gateway—prompted the Trust for Public Land to secure a purchase option in 1975. A year later, the bulk of today's Preserve was acquired for $195,000. Of this, the MCOSD contributed $96,000, the City of Mill Valley $56,000, a local assessment district added $15,000, and the Marin Audubon Society donated $25,000.

An easement across the old railroad right of way (today's Path) was gained in 1977. The pathway was formally acquired in 1981, with assistance from the Federal "Rails to Trails" program. The California Department of Transportation (Caltrans) retains an easement over the route.

Note that the Preserve also includes some wetlands east of Highway 101, between Seminary Drive and upper Richardson Bay. There is a short path there called Strawberry Shoreline Trail.

MILL VALLEY-SAUSALITO PATH (.75 miles)

From Coyote Creek to Corte Madera del Presidio Creek
Note: Paved (dirt borders); maintained by Marin County
Parks Department (not MCOSD)

The three-mile, Multi-Use Path running from the north edge of Sausalito into Scott Valley in Mill Valley is among the most heavily used routes in Marin, and among the most historic. Three-quarters of a mile of it, between the mouths of Coyote and Corte Madera Creeks, is within the MCOSD's Bothin Marsh Preserve.

The southern entry to the MCOSD section is via a path that borders the right bank of Coyote Creek from Shoreline Highway. (There are plans to upgrade a connection from Tennessee Valley to here.) At the Multi-Use Path, turn left at the bridge and join the other walkers, bikers, runners, baby strollers, rollerbladers, etc. The traffic rule of etiquette is "Stay Right." Note the District's "Sensitive Wildlife Area" signs for Bothin Marsh on both sides of the Path; please keep dogs out of the marsh.

Handsome interpretive signs have been placed on the Path. The first encountered, by a bench, gives background on Richardson Bay Bridge, over which Highway 101 crosses Richardson Bay. It was originally a drawbridge constructed entirely of redwood, said to be the largest redwood structure ever built. Called Redwood Richardson Bay Bridge, it opened in 1931 to complete a gap in the newly opened Redwood Highway (a name still attached to Highway 101). The present concrete span dates from 1956.

In 250 yards, the Path crosses a small bridge. At low tide, look at the rocks beneath; they are covered with barnacles, limpets, and mussels. An interpretive sign just beyond introduces the ecology of Richardson Bay and some of its residents. (The route is sometimes called Richardson Bay Multi-Use Path.)

A quarter-mile in, a dead-end route called South Levee Trail goes right over marshland.

The Path enters Mill Valley City limits just before the first trees, all introduced. There is an entry at the Miller Avenue/Almonte Boulevard junction. In 1889, a spur off Marin's main railroad line was built from here to the future Mill Valley in preparation for opening the town to development. The track ran on today's Miller Avenue to downtown. The stop here was first called Bay Junction, then Mill Valley Junction, then Almonte, "to the mountain (Tamalpais)." The site is now served by a Golden Gate Transit bus stop. Note the San Francisco Bay Trail signs; the Path is part of a several hundred-mile public loop, not yet complete, of San Francisco Bay.

Tamalpais High School's athletic field, recently renamed for Bruce A. Grant, a long-time track coach, is to the left. After the school was built in 1908, its original football field frequently flooded.

The Multi-Use Path passes behind some townhouses. Another dead-end path (North Levee Trail) goes right. It once connected to the southern levee path before the dike was opened to help restore tidal circulation in the marsh.

The MCOSD section of the Path ends at the bridged crossing of the mouth of Corte Madera del Presidio Creek. This heavily channeled creek is called Widow

Reed on U.S. Geological Survey maps, for Hilaria Reed, widow of original Mexican land grantee John Thomas Reed.

The entire route is a former railroad bed, built by Chinese laborers in 1883. It replaced an earlier routing (See Tiburon Ridge Preserve) dating from 1873 that climbed over Corte Madera Hill. Key to the new route was the Alto Tunnel, which was blasted through the hill separating Mill Valley and Corte Madera.

In 1903, the southern and central Marin sections of the line were upgraded for an improved commuter service. The system was electrified with the addition of a third rail and the old coal-powered engines replaced by cleaner, more modern ones. The electricity came from the Sierra over a transmission line to the Alto Powerhouse, which stood just across the marsh by today's Roque Moraes Drive. Tracks were widened to convert from narrow to standard (3 feet, 6 inches) gauge. The entire line (save for the Alto Tunnel) was ultimately also double-tracked. New passenger cars were put into service, themselves replaced by even more modern, orange-painted, steel ones in 1929. In 1909, a new cutoff from Baltimore Park (Larkspur) through Greenbrae and the Puerto Suelo tunnel eliminated the need for San Rafael passengers to go through San Anselmo.

For decades after, fast, efficient commuter trains whizzed between Marin communities and Sausalito, where a fleet of up to seven ferries crossed the Bay to San Francisco. Travel times were usually shorter than today. For example, those boarding the 5:15 p.m. ferry from San Francisco pulled into downtown San Rafael (where the bus terminal is today) at 6:07. There were also special school trains from the Ross Valley to Tamalpais High.

But the rise of the automobile and the opening of the Golden Gate Bridge (1937) doomed the commuter service, replaced by Greyhound buses. The last passenger train on the Mill Valley spur ran September 30, 1940, and the last San Rafael-Sausalito commuter run was February 28, 1941. Ironically, America's entry into World War II a few months later made gasoline and tires rationed commodities, and the trains were immediately missed.

There continued to be passenger service to Eureka, but San Rafael was the southern terminus and the connection to San Francisco by bus. Some freight ran over the track until the early 1960's. This part (Coyote Creek north to Alto School) of the old rail route was paved in 1981. The section south, to Gate 6 in Sausalito, was acquired and constructed in 1986.

San Francisco Bay Trail

In 1989, the California State Legislature directed the Association of Bay Area Governments to develop a continuous recreational hiking and bicycle trail around the perimeter of San Francisco and San Pablo Bays. This San Francisco Bay Trail is neither a new route nor a separate jurisdiction, but a connection of 130 existing shoreline parks in a 400-mile loop that crosses seven bridges. The only section of the Bay Trail in an MCOSD Preserve is the Multi-Use Path through Bothin Marsh. Bay Trail signs are in place there. The project's telephone number is (510) 464-7935.

CAMINO ALTO

Size: 225.1 acres   Elevation range: 160-680 feet

Camino Alto, located along the Northridge, is one of the first Preserves I visited as the Open Space Resource Ecologist. The habitat consists of coast live oak, Doug fir forests, and chaparral. Due to many decades of fuel build-up, this Preserve is one of the primary locations within the Mt. Tamalpais Vegetation Management Plan. Part of my job is to implement this plan to reduce fire hazards, and enhance and maintain biological diversity.
— Mischon Martin, Resource Ecologist

CAMINO ALTO (the Spanish "high road") was for decades part of the main north-south highway in Marin County, and for a while even carried the designation "Highway 101." Its many turns were helpful in easing the grade when horses did the pulling. But those turns, and thus low speed limits, proved an annoyance to a rising tide of motorists. By the late-1920's, enough of the new 101, or Redwood Highway, was completed to bypass the Camino Alto hill. (The next section south of 101, over the new Richardson Bay bridge, opened in 1931. The remaining southern section was tied to the opening of the Golden Gate Bridge in 1937.)

Camino Alto Preserve is linked to Alto Bowl Preserve (by crossing Camino Alto road) and to Blithedale Summit Preserve (via Summit Drive in Corte Madera), opening longer travel routes. Camino Alto is laced with unmaintained, neighborhood "social" paths. They are tricky to follow and many cross into private property.

Initial acreage in the Camino Alto Preserve came through the Northridge acquisitions of the mid-1970's (see Blithedale Ridge Preserve).

CAMINO ALTO FIRE ROAD (.50 miles)

From Camino Alto to junction of Escalon Fire Road and Del Casa Fire Road
Notes: No parking on west side of Camino Alto, very few spots on east side

Camino Alto Fire Road rises directly from Camino Alto some 75 yards below the Mill Valley/Corte Madera boundary. The start is extremely steep, toughest of the journey, although there is more uphill ahead.

At the first bend left, just 250 feet up, is a spectacular view of San Francisco. Trees line much of the rest of the Fire Road. At a clearing, where the incline noticeably decreases, two unmaintained paths branch right, one before and one after the water tank fence.

Continue up. The east wall of Mt. Tamalpais comes briefly into view. At the point where Camino Alto Fire Road begins a steep, quarter-mile drop to its end, another path branches right. The downhill directly faces the downtown San Francisco skyline. Old fence posts remind that on MCOSD acquisitions, barbed wire barriers ultimately fall.

The Fire Road ends at a four-way junction (the Escalon Intersection). Veer left to Escalon Drive, proceed straight to Del Casa Drive, or go right to Octopus Junction.

DEL CASA FIRE ROAD (.48 miles)
From Del Casa Drive to junction of Escalon Fire Road and Camino Alto Fire Road

This Fire Road starts behind a MCOSD gate opposite 270 Del Casa Drive in Mill Valley. Marlin Fire Road, which descends to Marlin Avenue, is a few yards to the right (when facing the gate). Lower on Del Casa Drive, by #239, is another signed Preserve entry (but without a designated trail).

The opening 250 yards of Del Casa Fire Road are very steeply up, as inclined as any fire road in the district. There are views behind of Mt. Tamalpais. The prominent closer ridge is called Little Tamalpais. Broom incursions have altered the flora but lupine remains a colorful native.

The first house encountered right, where the Fire Road levels and begins a bend left, was formerly owned by singer Grace Slick. Broad views open, including of the San Francisco skyline.

Del Casa F.R. continues behind the homes, which are accessed via Escalon Drive. A path left into the broom enters the maze of social paths crisscrossing the Preserve.

The Fire Road drops. Near the base, two more paths go left into the redwood forest. Both have numerous unmarked intersections and are difficult to follow.

Del Casa F.R. ends at a four-way fire road junction. Left, Escalon Fire Road runs level to an even bigger intersection called "The Octopus." Right, it meets Escalon Drive. Straight ahead, Camino Alto F.R. rolls up to Camino Alto near the Mill Valley/Corte Madera border.

ESCALON FIRE ROAD (.67 miles)
From Escalon Drive to Octopus Junction
Intersections: Del Casa F.R. & Camino Alto F.R. (.12m)

As a rare, level fire road, and easily accessible, Escalon F.R. draws a steady stream of visitors. The MCOSD-signed entry gate is at the north end of Escalon Drive. There are a few parking places in the cul-de-sac.

Some 125 yards in, the Fire Road's oak tree border breaks, opening a view to Horse Hill and well beyond. At one-eighth mile is a four-way fire road junction, sometimes called the Escalon Intersection. Sharply left is Del Casa F.R., which rolls up, then drops, to Del Casa Drive. Right, and up, is Camino Alto F.R., connecting to near the summit of Camino Alto. Escalon F.R. continues across.

Another 50 yards ahead are blue MMWD markers labeled "A," "B," and "C," denoting three pipelines below the Fire Road surface. Escalon F.R. is the southern end of the Southern Marin Line Water Project (see Southern Marin Line F.R., Baltimore Canyon Preserve) and these are among several Water District markers along the way.

A bit further, the woodland border opens to reveal a stunning shot of Mt. Tamalpais behind Blithedale Ridge. An impressive live oak stands by the green MMWD post "SM 70" (the numbering of creek crossings and culverts along Southern Marin Line).

The Fire Road bends and another dramatic Tam vista appears, this time head-on. Fire-scarred redwoods join Escalon's wooded margin. Forget-me-nots, a non-native wildflower, line the right edge. A cluster of MMWD signs indicates the many pipelines below (A, B, C, D, E, F, G, H, J). Look left to see the green grass of the Mill Valley Municipal Golf Course. An old stone pillar is on the right.

Escalon Fire Road meets the junction known as the Octopus. Left, paved Sarah Drive drops to Mill Valley and a driveway rises to a private home. Clockwise, next is Middle Summit F.R., rising very steeply to Summit Drive, Corte Madera. Straight ahead, past the MMWD pump station, is Lower Summit F.R., another section of Southern Marin Line. It also goes to Summit Drive. Right is Octopus Access F.R., and just down it, Harvey Warne Trail. Immediately right is a path up to Camino Alto Fire Road.

HARVEY WARNE TRAIL (.18 miles)
From Corte Madera Avenue to Octopus Access Fire Road

Although signed and directly beside a main road, Harvey Warne Trail is little known. When coming up Corte Madera Avenue from Corte Madera, the trailhead is on the right, opposite house numbers 594-604-624. There are a few parking turnouts on both sides of the road. Be extra cautious when walking or cycling (or driving) on narrow, winding Corte Madera Avenue.

The opening few feet of Harvey Warne are a bit steep. Immediately bend left and the rest of the ascent is more gradual. The Trail passes through a redwood forest, a pleasant surprise so close to a busy road. Indeed, Corte Madera Avenue-Camino Alto, with all its curves, was once the County's main north-south highway.

see map page 52-53

Its status as Highway 101 ended with construction of today's routing in the late 1920's.

About 250 feet in, past a huge bay tree, the Trail begins veering away from Corte Madera Avenue. A pair of redwoods at the Trail's left edge are giants. Harvey Warne rises into a lighter woodland of toyon and hazel. The ridge line, Octopus Access Fire Road, and the MMWD pump building at Octopus Junction come into view.

Harvey Warne ends on Octopus Access F.R. a few yards below Octopus Junction (see Octopus Access or Escalon F.R. for the options here).

Harvey Warne was a long-time Corte Madera resident, naturalist, and Boy Scout leader. He died in 1986 in an automobile accident on his way to lead a hike in the Sierra. The MCOSD dedicated the Trail to him, the first in the District named for an individual, at a ceremony in May 1987.

LOWER SUMMIT FIRE ROAD (.58 miles)
From Summit Drive (Corte Madera) to Octopus Junction
Notes: Summit Drive is narrow and winding; park only in designated white-outlined spaces and not at all in the entry cul-de-sac

Lower Summit F.R. begins at an MCOSD-signed gate between the private residences of 151 and 159 Summit Drive, at a bend in the road. As parking is very scarce, foot travelers may wish to use the splendid nearby step system (called Hill Path), which begins at Corte Madera Avenue. The Lower Summit F.R. entry gate is between the bottom and top of the Spring Hill section of steps.

Lower Summit F.R. is basically level although there is a barely noticeable downward trend. This is to aid the flow of water in the pipes just below the surface; Lower Summit is part of the Southern Marin Line Project (see Southern Marin Line Fire Road). The first green MMWD marker, 100 feet in, is "SM 57," marking the culverts along the full Southern Marin Line.

The dense woodland left, and steep slope right, block most views but there are glimpses of San Francisco Bay. Laurels are the dominant tree. Before 300 yards, redwoods begin appearing both down and upslope. Paths drop left to Corte Madera Avenue and rise to Middle Summit Fire Road.

The Fire Road passes an MMWD pump building with a "Warning, High Voltage" sign, then ends at Octopus Junction (described in Escalon F.R. above). The continuation of the Southern Marin Line straight across is considered as a separate fire road, Escalon.

This is the lowest of three fire roads across MCOSD lands meeting Summit Drive, hence the name.

MARLIN FIRE ROAD (.19 miles)
From Marlin Avenue to Del Casa Fire Road at Del Casa Drive

This Fire Road rises from Marlin Avenue in Mill Valley, opposite #145. There is virtually no nearby parking. The non-MCOSD gate at the start is presently unsigned.

The Fire Road rises gradually. It runs along the edge of the Preserve, with private property left. Coast live oaks and broom border the way. A showy flower abundant in spring is Bermuda buttercup (*Oxalis pes-caprae*). It is a South African native that the *Jepson Manual* describes as a "pernicious urban weed." A seep makes for a muddy patch.

Marlin Fire Road exits opposite 270 Del Casa Drive. You must squeeze past a coast live oak to exit. This upper gate has an MCOSD "Camino Alto" sign. Immediately right, Del Casa Fire Road climbs to the Escalon Intersection.

MIDDLE SUMMIT FIRE ROAD (.54 miles)
From Octopus Junction to Summit Drive (Corte Madera)

Middle Summit is the uphill fire road option out of Octopus Junction. The early yards are very steep, and there's more of the same the rest of the way.

The opening section is treeless. The density of broom lining the way varies, depending on how recently the District has undertaken a fire hazard reduction clearing. The hardiness of broom—its ability to recover from cutting—has been evident here as shrubs are seemingly back in full force within months.

There is a single coast live oak 125 yards up. Higher, the Fire Road becomes lined with oaks and remains so to the top. The long driveway parallel left, leading to a private residence bordering the Fire Road, is a hint of earlier development plans for the area. It was only in 1996 that the District acquired 41.7 additional acres adjacent to the Fire Road, for $350,000, to stave off additional construction. One-third of the purchase funds came from the District, the balance from the City of Mill Valley, with financial support from neighborhood residents and the Tamalpais Conservation Club.

Beyond the house, the Fire Road drops very steeply, its only major downhill. There are fine views of Mt. Tamalpais. In the saddle before the next stiff rise, paths branch left and right. The grass left of the saddle is a mushroom garden after the first fall rains.

The uphill brings vistas to the north and east, including Mt. Diablo on clear days. The next two crests offer only short breathers before stiff climbing resumes. The second crest has also harbored a mushroom "forest."

The Fire Road bends right and broader views open of northern Marin and the North Bay. A path left, which bypassed paved Summit Drive for those continuing up to Corte Madera Ridge Fire Road, is now overgrown. The Fire Road ends at a gate with a small MCOSD sign above 337 Summit Drive. The old route behind the second gate left is also overgrown.

Corte Madera's narrow, twisting Summit Drive is making a bend (known as Jones Corner) on its way up Christmas Tree Hill to Corte Madera Ridge F.R., .2 miles higher. In the 1920's, PG&E replaced street lights on the hill with colored bulbs each Christmas season, giving the area (also called Little Tamalpais) a new name. The lighting custom was revived during World War II and continues to this day. The homes above the Fire Road form the point of the tree with its star. Ripley's "Believe It Or Not" once labeled the hill as the world's tallest Christmas display.

The name "Middle Summit" arises because two other MCOSD fire roads meet Summit Drive, one lower and one higher.

OCTOPUS ACCESS FIRE ROAD (.13 miles)
From Corte Madera Avenue to Octopus Junction
Intersection: Harvey Warne Trail (.12m)

This short Fire Road rises from an MCOSD gate west off Corte Madera Avenue, just below its crest at the Mill Valley/Corte Madera line. There are two small parking turnouts lower on Corte Madera Avenue, above the Harvey Warne trailhead.

Octopus Access Fire Road climbs steeply. The route was once paved, and much of the paving remains. Redwoods are among the forest trees. At .1 mile, a path branches left onto the hill known locally as Sugar Lump. Fifty feet below the Fire Road's top, signed Harvey Warne Trail, a short loop option, comes in on the right.

The Fire Road ends at the big Octopus Junction. Immediately left is another path onto Sugar Lump. Continuing clockwise are: Escalon F. R. to Escalon Drive (Mill Valley); the paved upper end of Sarah Drive (Mill Valley); a paved, private driveway uphill; Middle Summit F.R. uphill; and, to the right and level, Lower Summit F.R. to Summit Drive (Corte Madera).

Donations

Land is expensive in Marin. And land management expenses now claim a greater share of MCOSD's annual budget than ever before, meaning less money is available for land purchases. The Open Space and Parks Fund of the Marin Community Foundation has been established to accept contributions and distribute funds for the preservation and enhancement of open space and parks in Marin County. The Marin Community Foundation, established in 1986, administers this fund and encourages contributions (tax-deductible) of cash, securities, and most other forms of property.

For additional information, contact the Marin Community Foundation at 17 E. Sir Francis Drake Blvd., Suite 200, Larkspur, CA 94939-1727, or by telephone at 461-3333.

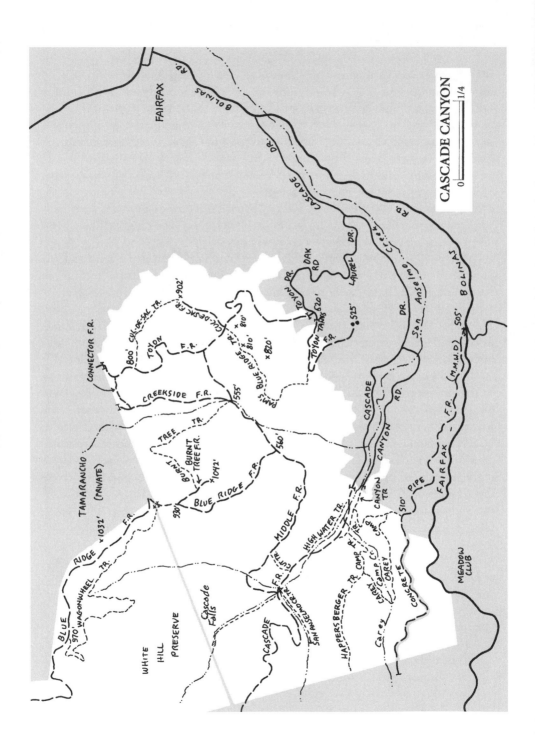

CASCADE CANYON

Size: 496.7 acres   Elevation range: 200-1,042 feet

*Water. Flowing water over rock, hiding in
    mossy cocoons.
Black oak and buckeye lean from grassy
    heights: like enraptured concert-goers
    with balcony seats, straining to get closer
    to the music.
Live water. Churning, rushing water. Tree
    frogs sing soprano.
Woodpeckers keep the beat.*

—*Jason Hoorn, Ranger*

THE BOTTINI RANCH covered Cascade Canyon around the turn of the century. The land remained pastoral with a great deal of weekend picnicking by San Franciscans arriving by railroad. In 1914, the Cascade Land Development Co. took control and began subdividing. See Pam's Blue Ridge Trail below for the story behind purchase of the Preserve's initial acreage.

The lower, canyon section of the Preserve had been acquired after World War II by Floyd Elliot, a Fairfax mayor, for the back taxes due. He used it as a private hunting preserve, patrolling the land on jeep. In the 1970's, after Elliot died, a 436-acre parcel passed to the City of Fairfax, then to the MCOSD. The sign, "Elliot Nature Preserve" still stands at the Cascade Road entry. Floyd Elliot's wife Roberta died in 1988, two days before her 100th birthday.

The Preserve encompasses three major creek canyons; Cascade, San Anselmo, and Carey Camp. These three creeks, plus their many feeders, all join on the floor of the Preserve, forming what is generally called San Anselmo Creek (and Corte Madera Creek downstream through lower Ross Valley).

Cascade Canyon, popular as a gateway to western Marin open space lands, has long been a focus of both access and biker-hiker conflicts. The District is currently developing a Management Plan for the Preserve, which hopefully will ameliorate many of these problems.

BLUE RIDGE FIRE ROAD/South (.63 miles)

From Middle Fire Road to Camp Tamarancho boundary
Intersections: Burnt Tree F.R. (.56m), Wagon Wheel Trail (.60m)
Note: The northern section of Blue Ridge F.R., separated by private
property of Camp Tamarancho, is described in White Hill Preserve

Long, lovely, and remote Blue Ridge Fire Road connects the Cascade Canyon, White Hill, and Giacomini preserves. As a portion of Blue Ridge Fire Road crosses private Camp Tamarancho, the route description is divided into southern and northern sections. The southern section is entirely within Cascade Canyon Preserve, the northern section in White Hill Preserve.

Blue Ridge Fire Road rises from Middle F.R. When traveling up Middle from Cascade Canyon F.R., the junction is in .6 miles, about 100 yards after a very steep, open, S-shaped bend.

The initial uphill, and much of the early going, are extremely steep. Caution is in order when descending. But more than compensating are splendid views of the headwaters canyons of the watershed.

After nearly .6 miles of steady climbing, the Fire Road reaches the spine of Blue Ridge itself. The fire road right, along the ridge line, is separately called Burnt Tree F.R., for it passes a burnt tree and Burnt Tree Trail before topping out at the 1,042 foot summit of Cascade Peak (well worth the detour).

Blue Ridge F.R. continues left. Within a few yards are old barriers marking the former Preserve boundary; the current boundary is now a few yards ahead. Just within the boundary, to the left, is the eastern end of 1.3-mile long Wagon Wheel Trail, the only public connection to the other half of Blue Ridge Fire Road. (Visitors are also wearing in an extremely steep connector a few yards ahead to the left. In 100 yards, this path meets the top of a short spur atop a knoll. Another 100 yards down leads to the section of Blue Ridge F.R. described in the White Hill Preserve chapter.) Just outside the boundary to the right is a hiker/biker trail over Boy Scout property. Straight, the Fire Road drops, beyond the gate, to the Central Camp area, which is closed to the public at all times.

The original 880 acres of Camp Tamarancho (now reduced by 390 acres after sales to the MCOSD) were once known as the Rivers property. Ken Bechtel, a president of both the Marin Council and then the national Boy Scouts of America, bought it in 1944. He then donated the parcel to the Marin Council. It was formally dedicated May 27, 1945, and has been a haven for local scouting ever since. The "Tamarancho" name was suggested by Bud Ruhland of Troop 11, Kentfield.

Access to selected routes on the Boy Scout property is offered to those purchasing a Friends of Tamarancho pass. The annual passes are sold through the Marin Council, Boy Scouts of America, 225 West End Avenue, San Rafael, CA 94901 (phone number 454-1081). The cost is presently $36 annually, $24 after June 30, and $50/$36 for family membership.

BURNT TREE FIRE ROAD (.17 miles)

From Blue Ridge Fire Road to Cascade Peak
Intersection: Burnt Tree Trail (.08m)

Burnt Tree F.R., although short and a dead-end, is a must for travelers anywhere near it. The breathtaking 360 degree panorama from the isolated, rocky, 1,042-foot summit of Cascade Peak is among the best in the County.

Burnt Tree F.R. starts at its junction with Blue Ridge F.R. When climbing Blue Ridge F.R. from Middle F.R., turn right at the summit ridge line.

In exactly 100 feet, on the right, is the burnt tree, a charred Douglas-fir, that gives the fire road its name. Some 100 yards later, on the left, is the signed top of Burnt Tree Trail, which drops very steeply to Middle Fire Road.

Continue up through the rocks to the highest point in the preserve, the summit of Cascade Peak. This is very much a place to linger. Landmark peaks such as Mt. Diablo, 40 miles east, along with Marin giants such as Tam, Big Rock, Loma Alta, White Hill, and Bald Hill, should be readily identifiable. You can even catch a glimpse of the top of the Transamerica Pyramid in downtown San Francisco.

There is no option out but to retrace your steps.

BURNT TREE TRAIL (.45 miles)

From Middle Fire Road to Burnt Tree Fire Road

Burnt Tree Trail is very steep, without a level or downhill pitch its entire length up. It begins at a potentially tricky four-way intersection off Middle Fire Road, .2 miles below Toyon Fire Road. It is the only trail option here, and is marked by a "Trail" signpost. The base of Creekside Fire Road is to the right. Ford the main creek, not always easy in winter, and begin the climb. The opening yards are extremely steep, toughest of the route.

About 400 feet in, the Trail passes under an impressive black oak. Note its large, bristle-tipped leaves, usually 6-lobed. They color and drop (although some hang on) in late fall. The shrub California hazel is abundant as is the vine, honeysuckle. The native bunchgrasses growing here in the deep shade often remain green all year. A log bench offers a resting spot.

At .3 miles, the Trail bends left. In the bend, a path departs right to private Boy Scout property. The tree cover is now lighter, the terrain drier. Monkeyflowers line the way. Douglas-firs rise above the oaks.

Higher still, the Trail briefly enters chaparral, with chamise the dominant shrub. Madrones accompany Burnt Tree's uppermost yards.

Burnt Tree Trail ends at its junction with Burnt Tree Fire Road. Be sure to take it left to its end, 150 yards away, at a stunning vista point. Right leads to the burnt Douglas-fir that gave the Trail its name, Blue Ridge F.R. (a loop option that is equally steep), then Wagon Wheel Trail.

CANYON TRAIL (.13 miles)

From Canyon Road to Cascade Fire Road
Intersection: Carey Camp Loop Trail (.11m)

Canyon Trail offers access to Carey Camp Loop and Happersberger trails when winter rains leave San Anselmo Creek unfordable. On the flip side, a strong-flowing creek can block the connection from Canyon Trail to the many routes off Cascade Fire Road.

The Trail begins at the end of half-mile long Canyon Road, the last intersecting street off upper Cascade Drive. (There is a fish ladder under the bridge at the start of Canyon Road, to aid the salmon struggling upstream.) An easement path, with a blue MCOSD sign, runs from between #195 and #200 Canyon Road to the Preserve boundary, where a green MCOSD sign marks the Trail's start.

The level Trail is entirely on the right bank of the main creek. Poison oak lines the way. It can be observed here in all its forms; low-growing plant, shrub, small tree, and vine. Its reddish leaves color the woodland in fall. In spring, members of the lily family—trillium, slim and fat Solomon, fetid adder's tongue, mission bells—are more pleasing floral treats.

At .11 miles, Canyon Trail meets easy-to-miss Carey Camp Loop Trail. The mile-long loop can be taken up to the left (clockwise) or straight ahead (counterclockwise).

Canyon Trail runs together with Carey Camp Loop for some ten yards before veering off right. Just 30 yards later, Canyon Trail ends when it meets Cascade Fire Road, which has just made the first of its un-bridged creek crossings (when traveling west from Cascade Drive). There is a "Trail" sign here.

CAREY CAMP LOOP TRAIL (.98m)

Loop off Canyon Trail
Intersection: Happersberger Trail (.75m)
Note: When San Anselmo Creek is high, the only dry access
to the Trail is via the Preserve's Canyon Road entry

Carey Camp Creek Trail offers a pleasant, loop walk from quite near a trailhead. But since it has been unmarked and somewhat difficult to follow, it is lightly traveled.

When entering the Preserve from Canyon Road, there are two faint entries to Carey Camp Loop Trail, a few yards apart, one-tenth of a mile into Canyon Trail. They offer a clockwise journey over the loop (as described here). If you miss the entries, cross the bridge just ahead and immediately go left. You'll then be following the Carey Camp loop in a counterclockwise direction. (When entering the Preserve from Cascade Drive, you need to cross the main creek once to reach Carey Camp Loop, which may not be possible in winter and early spring.)

Carey Camp Loop Trail rises gently into a woodland of bays (dominant), oaks, and madrones. Just 25 yards in, a path goes left; veer right and up.

One-sixth mile up, the Trail meets the lower of two nearby bridges. Some 50 feet above this first bridge, a path departs left, crossing private property as it rises steeply to Concrete Pipe (also called Pine Mountain Tunnel) Fire Road. The Preserve actually includes land just above Concrete Pipe F.R., but not the Fire Road itself.

Twenty-five yards later, the Trail crosses the upper of the two bridges. The Trail crests and becomes gently rolling. The lily Slim Solomon (*Smilacina stellata*) grows profusely here in spring. In fall, deciduous maples add yellow-orange-red tones to the oak and laurel woodland.

Carey Camp Creek is heard, then glimpsed. The Trail crosses a rivulet, then the creek itself in what can be a tricky fording after a rainstorm. Next is a short stretch up through open grassland. The Trail returns to woodland and 100 yards of steep descent that briefly eases in a tricky area with several junctions.

To the left, marked by an MCOSD "Trail" sign, Happersberger Trail rises onto the ridge separating the drainages of Carey Camp and San Anselmo creeks. An old jeep road, from the days when deer and quail hunters tracked through the area, also crosses. There is also a short path right to a knoll overlooking the creek.

At the base of another steep drop, the Trail joins the left bank of Carey Camp Creek. The District has undertaken streambank protection measures to reduce sediment entering the creek. A level stretch along the creek leads to a bridge, 100 yards west of where the Trail started. Just ahead is the confluence of Carey Camp Creek with San Anselmo Creek. Go right to complete the loop, left to Cascade F.R. and deeper into the Preserve.

Carey Camp was a one-time gun club/deer hunting camp in Carey Creek canyon. It was founded by Robert A. Carey, who played a major role in the original subdivision of the Cascades area of Fairfax. The creek was named for the camp.

CASCADE FIRE ROAD (2.50 miles)

From Cascade Drive to San Geronimo Ridge Fire Road
Intersections: High Water Trail (.04m, .13m, .26m), Canyon Trail (.07m), connector to Middle F.R. (.36m), Middle F.R. (.44m), Cascade Falls Trail (.46m), San Anselmo Creek Trail (.52m)

Although Cascade Fire Road is the chief artery through the Preserve, its lower section is impassable several months of the year. The Fire Road crosses San Anselmo Creek (also often called Cascade Creek) four times in the first quarter-mile, all without bridges. By late winter, even nimble rock hoppers will be challenged to complete a dry fording.

Cascade F.R., also known as Repack Road for the pioneering mountain bike races first held over it in the 1970's (see below), sets off immediately behind the gate at the end of Cascade Drive. There has long been a wintering ladybug colony just in, on the right.

The first of the four crossings comes within 200 feet. There is an Oregon ash (*Fraxinus latifolia*), a small tree in the olive family, on the right. When the creek is full, many pedestrians bypass all four crossings by taking narrow High Water Trail, which skirts the canyon wall right. Bikers must stay on the Fire Road.

This section of the creek still supports a run of steelhead salmon (*Oncorhynchys mykiss*), a species designated as threatened along the entire California coast in 1997. Adults that were born here, and who survive the journey downstream to the Pacific and life in the ocean, attempt to make their way back to spawn a new generation. Numbers are up somewhat from several years ago, but nowhere at levels of decades back, when fishing was a local pastime. Some of the salmon get trapped in the creek when it dries each summer and residents remove them for transport downstream.

Across the creek, a "Trail" sign marks the west end of Canyon Trail, with Carey Camp Loop Trail 30 yards ahead. There is much poison oak on the way to the second crossing, also the second junction with High Water Trail. You can see evidence of the District's creek restoration efforts. The third crossing follows 200 feet later.

The fourth of the unbridged crossings comes at one-quarter mile. On the far side, High Water Trail ends when it comes in from the right.

Cascade Fire Road begins rolling; later the uphill is steep and unrelenting. A trail post marks a short connector (no bikes) up to Middle F.R. In 400 feet is the base of Middle F.R. itself, which rises right (straight) as another access to the Preserve's uplands.

A few yards beyond, the Fire Road crosses Cascade Creek over a bridge. Just downstream is the confluence of San Anselmo and Cascade creeks. The boulder just past the bridge is a landmark, the finish line of the old Repack mountain bike races. Beyond it, Cascade Falls Trail sets off right, to the waterfall.

The Fire Road veers left and uphill. Some 100 yards past the bridge, on the far side of a boulder, San Anselmo Creek Trail leaves left at a signpost. In another 100 feet, a path has "No Bikes" and "Natural Area Restoration, Please Keep Off" signs; please heed them.

The very steep climbing begins in earnest and barely eases the remaining two miles to San Geronimo Ridge. The Fire Road runs on a ridge separating the deep canyons of San Anselmo Creek (left, south) and Cascade Creek (north). As the tree canopy thins, splendid vistas open; look back as well. There is a timeless feeling here above the pristine canyons, which shelter some of the wildest terrain remaining in the Bay Area.

Cascade F.R. leaves the Preserve at a joint MMWD/MCOSD signpost, 1.05 miles in from Cascade Drive. The climb continues another glorious, isolated, 1.45 miles to San Geronimo Ridge F.R. There are broad views over miles of open space, with great shots of White Hill and (behind) of Mt. Tamalpais above Bon Tempe Lake.

Cascade F.R. re-enters MCOSD land beyond an MMWD gate at the southern tip of Gary Giacomini Preserve, one-eighth mile below the ridge line. A pygmy forest of Sargent cypress trees lines the Fire Road's remaining yards.

The Fire Road gained lasting fame in the 1970's, when it was the site of some of the first mountain bike races anywhere. Many of the pioneers of mountain biking lived in the Ross Valley and fine-tuned their earliest test models on Mt. Tam and

Pine Mountain. In 1976, to settle the argument of just who was the fastest downhiller, a group of six decided to race, one at a time, down Cascade Fire Road, an elevation drop of 1,300 feet.

According to Charles Kelly, one of the six, that first race was timed by synchronizing an old navy chronometer and an alarm clock for the start and finish lines. Bob Burrowes (or Alan Bonds by another account) was the first champion.

The "one-time" only race soon became a regular affair. Digital watches were bought. They were synchronized by banging the start buttons together, then covering the reset buttons (to avoid accidental stoppages) with bottle caps. Start slots were pre-set at the bottom and racers had to make their way to the top in time.

The racers found that even one fast trip down the steep grade necessitated repacking the lubricating grease in the heavy early bikes' coaster brakes. Soon, the name "Repack" came to be attached to the races and to the Fire Road itself.

The last official Repack race was held in 1984. There were 94 participants and rangers treated 35 injuries. The races were then banned for safety and environmental reasons.

CASCADE FALLS TRAIL (.26 miles)
From Cascade Fire Road to Cascade Falls

This lovely Trail leads to the best known among many jewels within the Preserve, Cascade Falls.

Just under a half-mile into Cascade Fire Road from the Cascade Drive entry, Middle F.R. forks right and Cascade F.R. veers left over a bridge. On the far side of the bridge, Cascade Falls Trail departs to the right.

The broad Trail rises gently along the right bank of Cascade Creek. Across the creek, a grassy hill looms ever higher. Shaded woodland keeps the Trail comfortable even in summer. Abundant mosses attest to the cool and wetness. In fall, maples add color.

Halfway in, several shrubby hazels (*Corylus cornuta*) touch the Trail. The hairy leaves are soft to the touch. Finding the delicious, edible nuts is a challenge; squirrels and birds harvest them quickly. The plant's flexible stems were used in basket-making by many Native American tribes.

The Trail then gently drops. There is a final rise to Cascade Falls, which comes into view rather dramatically after climbing the first step or two. A white alder grows from the rocks just below the falls. The cascading torrent is, of course, strongest during and immediately after a heavy winter rain, but there is some flow most months of the year.

The very rough path above is lined with poison oak and steep slopes.

CONNECTOR FIRE ROAD (.16 miles)

From Toyon Fire Road to Creekside Fire Road

This short Fire Road connects Toyon and Creekside fire roads, opening additional loop opportunities between the upper and lower parts of Cascade Canyon Preserve. Both ends of Connector are relatively far (a mile or more) from any MCOSD trailhead. Joining from Toyon F.R. yields a steep downhill and from Creekside F.R. a corresponding stiff climb.

The unmarked entrance off Toyon F.R. is .1 mile from the Camp Tamarancho boundary fence and 100 yards downhill from Cul-de-sac Trail. Facing the entry, there is a madrone on the right and a toyon and laurel on the left.

Connector drops very steeply. A light tree canopy of oaks, madrones, and laurels provides shade and color year-round. Parts of the upper section are narrow.

The Fire Road nears the MCOSD/Tamarancho fence line. Connector ends at its junction with Creekside Fire Road, which drops left to Middle Fire Road. Right, a path leaves the Preserve into private Boy Scout land. Straight is a path that soon dead-ends.

CREEKSIDE FIRE ROAD (.35 miles)

From Middle Fire Road at Burnt Tree Trail to Preserve boundary

Creekside Fire Road rises off Middle F.R. in a deep woodland one-fifth mile below Toyon Fire Road. Also at the same junction, to the left (south), is the base of Burnt Tree Trail, which is signed.

Creekside F.R. immediately crosses a feeder to the main creek (the crossing to Burnt Tree Trail is broader), then rises very steeply. The creek is quickly left behind for drier grassland and light woodland, making the name "Creekside" somewhat misleading. But the creek's deep canyon borders the route up and, in winter, you can hear the sound of rushing water.

The steepness eases. The pristine, tree-covered, east wall of Blue Ridge rises appealingly to the left. One hundred yards up and on the left, you may notice a smaller tree amid the madrones, oaks, and laurels. It's silk tassel bush (*Garrya elliptica*), with drooping, early-blooming, inflorescences and wavy leaves with very hairy undersides. It's also called quinine bush, as pioneers used the bitter leaves as a substitute for quinine.

Creekside F.R. meets the MCOSD/Camp Tamarancho boundary fence. Left is a path that soon deteriorates. Straight ahead, a path enters private Boy Scout property. Right, within the Preserve, Connector F.R. rises very steeply to Toyon Fire Road.

CUL-DE-SAC FIRE ROAD (.19 miles) and
CUL-DE-SAC TRAIL (.34 miles)
Off Toyon Fire Road

This is an odd route, a semi-loop off Toyon Fire Road whose southern half is a fire road and northern half a trail.

The entry to the fire road section (open to bicycles) is at the crest of Toyon Fire Road, a half-mile when coming from Toyon Drive and opposite the signed top of Pam's Blue Ridge Trail. There are spectacular views at the start and all the way up. Note the honeysuckle (*Lonicera hispidula*). Like toyon, it has red berries. Honeysuckle is a twining shrub, wrapping itself around other plants. Unlike the widely cultivated Japanese honeysuckle, the Marin native is not fragrant.

The Fire Road tops out at what looks like a cul-de-sac, ringed by madrones. Inside the circle, beneath a coast live oak, is a small, Christmas-tree shaped bay laurel. Come in December for a surprise.

The route continues down as Cul-de-sac Trail. A sign at the top bars cyclists. This is a lovely stretch, winding and rolling amid a madrone and oak woodland. Halfway in, a path right is signed "Stop, End of Public Open Space." Please stay off.

Some 100 yards ahead, also on the right, is a stone monument bearing a plaque "For Emma, With Love From Your Friends and Family in Fairfax." The clearing is brightly colored in spring by green grass, red Indian paintbush, white yarrow, and blue dicks.

The Trail rejoins Toyon Fire Road .35 miles north of the Cul-de-sac F.R. entry.

HAPPERSBERGER TRAIL (.43 miles)
From Carey Camp Loop Trail to MMWD line

This Trail leads to Happersberger Point, among the lovelier areas in the County. However, the Trail is poor, there are extremely steep and slippery sections, and no through options.

Carey Camp Loop Trail can be followed in either direction to reach Happersberger's trailhead. It is closer to the Cascade Drive and Canyon Drive entries to take Carey Camp counterclockwise from its canyon floor bridge. Three hundred yards in on Carey Camp Loop Trail (be aware of intersecting paths), Happersberger Trail departs right from an MCOSD "Trail" signpost.

Happersberger Trail starts by rising steeply in the woodland. The climb eases (briefly) at a bend right in about 100 yards. Soon after, the Trail meets a grassy patch, then leaves the tree canopy completely, into grassland. Dramatic views immediately open, particularly of White Hill.

Happersberger Trail follows the spine of Happersberger Ridge, which separates the deep canyons of Carey Camp and San Anselmo Creeks. A small madrone grove is entered. Leaving it brings the steepest stretch on the Trail, which is even more of a problem—it's quite slippery—on the descent.

The Trail then rolls over a series of grassy crests. Each offers splendid views, including Mt. Diablo when facing back (east). South is Fairfax-Bolinas Road and the clubhouse of the Meadow Club. Cascade Fire Road is the near neighbor north.

There is an MCOSD trail signpost at the fourth crest (the third crest is a minor one). A pair of shrubby oaks and a rock outcropping also mark the end of Happersberger Trail. Beyond are lands of the Marin Municipal Water District. The continuing path is closed and overgrown, and has unavoidable poison oak

Happersberger Point is noted on USGS maps, but the reference appears over the whole ridge rather than a single spot. Frank Happersberger (1858-1932) was a noted sculptor and Fairfax-area landowner. His public works include the Pioneer Monument at San Francisco's Civic Center and the President Garfield statue in Golden Gate Park.

HIGH WATER TRAIL (.24 miles)
Between Cascade Fire Road

This narrow Trail, skirting the left bank of San Anselmo Creek, is, for several months each year, a pedestrian's only dry way into the Preserve from Cascade Drive. Cascade Fire Road, the usual access, has four creek crossings that can be too wide to jump and too deep to ford.

High Water Trail sets off right 200 feet in from the MCOSD gate at the end of Cascade Drive. There is a trail sign 100 feet later. The Trail is at its narrowest and rockiest a hundred yards in, when it barely clears the creek. Indeed, the Trail may one day have to be closed. A plank brings the Trail over a rivulet.

A pair of "Trail" signs mark the route near another creek/fire road junction. A rail-less bridge crosses a feeder stream.

High Water Trail ends as it rejoins Cascade Fire Road. Right leads to the trail to Cascade Falls.

MIDDLE FIRE ROAD (1.13 miles)
From Cascade Fire Road to Toyon Fire Road
Intersections: Blue Ridge F.R. (.59m), Burnt Tree Trail and Creekside F.R. (.93m)

As the key link between the upper and lower sections of the Preserve, this Fire Road is aptly named. Wooded and near water throughout, it is also quite lovely.

To reach the lower end of Middle F.R., follow Cascade F.R. (or High Water Trail when the creek is unfordable in winter) just under a half-mile in from the Cascade Drive entrance to the Preserve. Middle F.R. sets off right, uphill, just before

Cascade F.R. crosses a bridge by the confluence of San Anselmo and Cascade creeks.

Middle F.R. starts up steeply but most of the rest of the way, while still distinctly up, is gentler. The route is shaded, and remains so basically all the way, a relief on torrid summer days. Madrones, laurels, and oaks are the common trees.

In one-fifth mile is the signed top of a cutoff path whose base, on Cascade Fire Road, was passed on the journey in. At a half-mile, another path, signed "No Bicycles," drops steeply right onto private property at Cascade Drive. The canyon appears ever deeper as the Fire Road ascends.

There is a very steep section over a grassy area. The grind eases as the Fire Road returns to woodland. Madrones are still dominant but there are many Douglas-firs.

One hundred yards past the Cascade Drive cutoff is the base of Blue Ridge Fire Road. It rises to Blue Ridge, then continues to the summit of White Hill.

The Fire Road passes an old fence line. At .8 miles, seepage from a spring makes for a wet patch. A horse trough left, under a coffeeberry bush, collects some of the flow. You may see the first irises of spring here. Behind the trough is an impressive wall of rock. Just beyond, look into the creekbed to see an old dam and abandoned water pipeline. The Fire Road then crosses the creek, which can be a wet affair in winter.

Nearly a mile in is a four-way junction. Near left, across the creek, is signed Burnt Tree Trail, which rises extremely steeply to Burnt Tree F.R. just below Blue Ridge F.R. To Burnt Tree's right is the base of Creekside F.R., which goes up to Connector F.R. at the MCOSD/Camp Tamarancho boundary. Continue straight on Middle F.R. The next section is steeply uphill.

Near its top, Middle F.R. leaves the woodland into grassland/chaparral. The shrub baccharis (coyote brush), lines the way. It has separate male and female plants, readily distinguishable in winter when the females are topped by white "fuzzy-wuzzies" (technically, pappi) ready to carry the seeds away.

Middle F.R. ends at Toyon F.R. Left goes toward the Boy Scout's Camp Tamarancho. Right goes to Pam's Blue Ridge Trail and on to Toyon Drive in Fairfax.

PAM'S BLUE RIDGE TRAIL (.55 miles)

From Toyon Fire Road to Toyon Tanks Fire Road

Most users join Pam's Blue Ridge Trail at its upper end as the lower section is extremely steep and eroded. The upper trailhead, signed "Trail," is the four-way junction with Toyon Fire Road (in two directions) and Cul-de-sac Fire Road.

The views from the grassy ridgeline are immediately sweeping. Mt. Tamalpais, Pine Mountain, and White Hill are the tallest peaks. Blue Ridge, topped by Cascade Peak and higher than Pam's Blue Ridge, stands dramatically just to the west. A shortcut path from lower on Toyon F.R. joins on the left at the crest.

At another junction 70 yards later, the path left (straight) goes only the short distance to the top of the view knoll. Veer right. At the edge of the grassland right

The ceremony on March 23, 1975, marking the dedication of the Pamela Prentice Ettinger plaque on what is now officially designated as Pam's Blue Ridge. Flanking Pamela Ettinger's mother are two towering figures in Marin's conservation movement, Karin Urquhart and the late Peter Behr.

are stands of false-lupine (*Thermopsis macrophylla*). Its yellow flowers are in peak bloom in late spring.

The Trail slopes down into a serpentine rock outcrop. Serpentinite is the state mineral of California.

Five hundred yards in, opposite a grove of madrones, is another intersection. Pam's Blue Ridge Trail continues straight (right) but be sure to visit the left option. It winds, somewhat overgrown, 120 yards to a dead-end. There, on a serpentine boulder, is a plaque to the memory of Pamela Prentice Ettinger, the "Free Spirit" for whom the ridge is named.

Ettinger, one of 12 children of the family that founded the publishing house Prentice-Hall, was a member of the board of directors of the Educational Foundation of America. She had just moved to Fairfax and enjoyed running, hiking, and sketching in these hills. In 1974, returning from a visit to her twin sister Deborah in Woodside, Pam was killed in an automobile accident. She was 24.

The Ettinger family agreed to donate $80,000 to buy a 175-acre parcel in the new Preserve in her memory. A ceremony honoring the Ettinger's dedication of the ridge was held March 23, 1975. In November of that year, the United States Board of Geographic Names formally designated the previously unnamed mile-long ridge as "Pam's Blue Ridge." In 1994, after learning that neighborhood residents were attempting to add to the Preserve (the Toyon Tanks area), Deborah induced the Educational Foundation to contribute an additional $45,000.

The plaque area originally had a view; shrubs now obscure it. Shooting stars

(*Dodecatheon hendersonii*), with their distinctive, purple, reflexed corollas, brighten the circle in late winter and early spring.

Back on the lower remnant of Pam's Blue Ridge Trail, the whole Cascade Canyon drainage is visible. The Trail meets quartz-bearing "Crystal Rock." An MCOSD sign, however, warns that this is a sensitive area with no digging or collecting of minerals permitted. Bright red Indian paintbrush, poppies, yarrow, and sticky monkeyflowers grow out of the eerily shaped rocks.

The Trail enters light woodland. Indian warrior (*Pedicularis densiflora*) is abundant. They are in the same Figwort family as Indian paintbrush but a darker, deeper red-purple. Indian warrior is a partial root parasite, gaining nourishment from other plants.

The final 250 yards are very steep, with a gully down the center making travel even more tricky. At a junction, an "Erosion Control, Please Keep Off" sign blocks a former route down to private property. Veer left. The Trail passes an old gate. Just ahead is Toyon Tanks Fire Road between a pair of wood posts. Left leads to the end of Toyon Drive, right to a dead-end at a pair of water tanks.

SAN ANSELMO CREEK TRAIL (.21 miles)
From Cascade Fire Road along San Anselmo Creek

To reach the San Anselmo Creek trailhead, follow Cascade Fire Road a half-mile in from the Cascade Drive entry. One hundred yards above the first Cascade F.R. bridge (at the confluence of Cascade and San Anselmo creeks) and just beyond an eight-foot boulder, an MCOSD "Trail" sign on the left marks the start. Note that some 100 feet higher on Cascade F.R. is a path to the right marked only by a "No Bikes" sign.

San Anselmo Creek Trail, along the creek's left bank, is immediately striking. It is cool in summer. In fall, maples add a bit of New England color. In winter, San Anselmo Creek roars. In spring, the Trail is adorned with woodland flowers. One downside is abundant poison oak. Another is that the Trail dead-ends.

The Trail rolls gently its whole length. Laurels and oaks are predominant early, then buckeyes, then maples deeper.

At 400 feet, a slide briefly narrows the Trail. Nearly 300 yards in, the Trail crosses San Anselmo Creek. This will likely be a wet affair in winter, and possibly the end of the line for some immediately after a heavy rain.

In any case, the maintained part of the Trail ends soon after, at a wonderful small clearing in the forest. Maples line the creek bank. Quiet is assured.

The Trail continues as a path that rises steeply, with poison oak difficult to avoid.

TOYON FIRE ROAD (1.03 miles)

From Toyon Drive to Tamarancho line
Intersections: Pam's Blue Ridge Trail (.50m), Cul-de-sac F.R. (.50m),
Middle F.R. (.58m), Cul-de-sac Trail (.85m), Connector F.R. (.92m)
Notes: Access streets are narrow and winding; very little parking;
maintain six-foot clearance from center of roadway

Toyon Fire Road offers stunning Mt. Tam vistas and access to the Preserve's haunting Blue Ridge area.

The Fire Road begins behind an MCOSD gate opposite 88 Toyon Drive. (Note there is a second MCOSD gate just a few yards ahead at the end of Toyon Drive, from which the separate Toyon Tanks Fire Road departs.) Coast live oaks immediately provide shade, and are companions much of the rest of the way up. There is a private residence above left at the start.

The oak canopy lightens in about 100 yards. Note the several toyons (*Heteromeles arbutifolia*) on both sides of the Fire Road. These tall shrubs, usually 5-10 feet in height, are members of the Rose family. They have long elliptic to oblong evergreen leaves and, most distinctive, red berries in late fall and winter (hence its alternate name, Christmas berry). Tarweeds, in the Sunflower (Composite) family, make yellow carpets in the grassland in summer and early fall.

There are hints early of the great vistas to come. Above .2 miles in, clear shots of the entire north wall of Tam open.

At .45 miles, the uphill eases. One hundred yards beyond, at a crest, is a four-way junction. Left, signed, is Pam's Blue Ridge Trail, which leads toward the Pamela Ettinger plaque. Toyon F.R. continues straight. To the right is Cul-de-sac Fire Road, up the hill. Cul-de-sac F.R. returns to Toyon Fire Road .35 miles later (but note that the downhill side is a trail, not open to bicycles).

Some 100 yards down, Middle Fire Road comes in from the left, a connector to the lower part of the Preserve and several other route options.

Oaks rule here, as they once did over even more of California. Sedges grow out of a seep in the middle of the Fire Road. An old water trough sits to the right.

Toyon F.R. climbs to a junction with Cul-de-sac Trail, the far side of Cul-de-sac Fire Road. There are then a couple of hundred feet of descent to Connector Fire Road. Looking like a trail, it departs left, then begins a sharp drop to Creekside F.R.

The tree cover opens and there are views of White Hill and Loma Alta (right) ahead. Also visible lower left is the off-limits Tamarancho pond.

The MCOSD portion of the Fire Road ends at a chain and sign marking the boundary of the private Camp Tamarancho Boy Scout Reservation. Tamarancho is an active camp for scouts from throughout the Bay Area. See Blue Ridge F.R. above for access information.

TOYON TANKS FIRE ROAD (.32 miles)
From top of Toyon Drive to MMWD Water Tanks
Intersection: Pam's Blue Ridge Trail (.16m)

Toyon Tanks Fire Road crosses the most recent addition to Cascade Canyon Preserve. It departs from the upper end of Toyon Drive. Fifty yards behind, on the other side of 99 Toyon, is the base of Toyon Fire Road.

The route begins almost level, rising slightly. There are lovely Tam views. Broom grows profusely along the edges, beneath the oaks, madrones, and bays.

A short uphill leads to a pair of wood posts on the right. Between them, Pam's Blue Ridge Trail begins its climb to Toyon Fire Road. The second half of Toyon Tanks Fire Road is a dead-end.

The Fire Road drops to a saddle with a view over Cascade Canyon. A second, short, rise leads to a pair of MMWD tanks. They mark the end of the Fire Road, and give the route its name. A blue arrow painted on a madrone points to an off-limits path.

Before its acquisition as open space in 1994-95, the tanks area was slated for dozens of homes on small parcels, with the Fire Road to have been paved and extended to Laurel Drive. The Ettinger family (of Pam's Blue Ridge) contributed $45,000 of the $180,000 purchase price with the balance from neighbors, the District, and State Proposition 70 bond funds.

Cascade Fire Road crosses San Anselmo Creek four times within Cascade Canyon Preserve before the first bridge. Hikers use a bypass (High Water Trail) and equestrians proceed straight through; cyclists must take the "plunge."

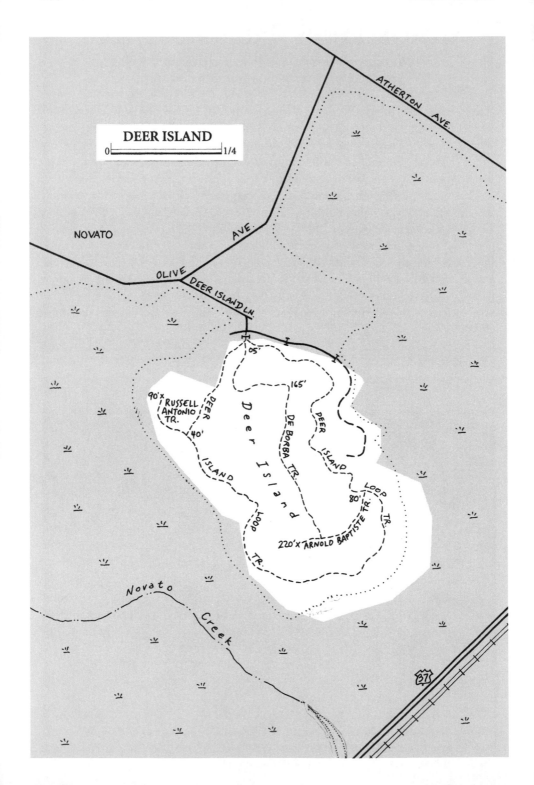

DEER ISLAND

Size: 134.8 acres   Elevation range: 0-200 feet

*Over the last several years, I've had the plea-
sure of living in the historic farmhouse on this
Preserve. Yes, the house with the barking dog
in the window. At least that's how most passing hikers tell it. I'm a history buff, and Deer
Island has so much! Beginning as a real island during the Miwok's days to a working
ranch and now an Open Space Preserve. Some
of its history can still be seen. Look for the rose
hedge, fig, and plum trees. See the old milk barn as Mother
Nature reclaims it. Come join the many different users such as
joggers, birders, dog walkers, horse riders and even the occasional
camper or two (who always have their permits), each finding
their own spaces for solitude.   — Karen Kilian, Ranger*

DEER ISLAND WAS INDEED an island, accessible only by boat, until late into the 19th
century, when much of Novato's marshland was diked and drained for pasture land.

In 1887, thousands of acres of the old Novato Rancho, including Deer Island,
passed to a group called the Home and Farm Company. Three years later, a dairy
centered on Deer Island was designated as the California Creamery Company. A
ranch house, still standing, was built in 1891. Manuel Branco was the first resident,
with wife Mariana and daughter Maria.

In 1893, Branco and partner Antone DeBorba (see DeBorba Trail below) took
over operation of the California Creamery and changed its name to Black Point
Creamery. High quality butter and cheese were shipped via barge to San Francisco.
Remnants of the Creamery's buildings are visible today. In 1903, DeBorba bought
outright the 395-acre Creamery, paying $11,347. A toll road, part of today's High-
way 37, was built across his property.

Manuel Branco died in 1908 and his widow and daughter moved out of the
Deer Island ranch house soon after. The next residents were Mary Agnes (1894-
1974), eldest daughter of Antone and Anna DeBorba, and her husband Manuel
Almada, who had worked at the Verissimo Ranch dairy. Five of their six children
were born on Deer Island before the family moved to Petaluma.

A DeBorba son, Frank (1892-1984), provides a glimpse into early days on
Deer Island in this reminiscence quoted in the book *Novato Township*: "Many years
before I left Novato to go to college in 1915, Johnny Mathias while hunting on Deer
Island on the back end of the ranch, saw something among the leaves and dirt....He
picked it up and it was a skull with all the upper teeth showing much wear." DeBorba
later used his professional training as a dentist to analyze the skull and concluded,
"I think the one we found at Deer Island was an Indian because many artifacts of

Indian origin were found on the ranch. In the area where the skull was found there was a cabin (one room) where Louis Rush, a Frenchman, lived for years. He was a wood chopper who cleared the area for my dad and we sold oak wood by the cord for $8 or $10 a cord."

In 1949, the Nunes family leased what was by then called Deer Island Ranch. From 1963 until 1981, the Antonio family lived in the Deer Island house. The Branco, DeBorba, Nunes, and Antonio families were all from the Azores Islands, as were most of Marin's early dairy ranchers.

The MCOSD acquired 125 acres of Deer Island in 1978 from the DeBorba family for $272,500. (The adjacent Flood Control District contributed $50,000.) Five years later, nine acres were added, for $121,000. Also in 1983, the Nunes' grazing lease ended and District rangers began residence in the Deer Island house.

Note that dogs must be on leash at all times within the Preserve.

ARNOLD BAPTISTE TRAIL (.11 miles)
From DeBorba Trail to dead-end atop Preserve

Arnold Baptiste Trail runs through the remotest part of the Preserve and is a dead-end, so is little visited. It begins, signed, off De Borba Trail, .6 miles when traveling from the main Preserve entry gate. (An alternate entry is a quarter-mile up DeBorba Trail from its other intersection with Loop Trail, on the southeast side of Deer Island.)

The short Trail runs along the 200-foot crest of Deer Island. The hilltop is studded with oaks and bays, adding to the pastoral charm but limiting views. Arnold Baptiste Trail ends at a meadow and signpost. Please do not continue down the hill.

Arnold Baptiste was a County Supervisor representing the Novato (District 5) area from the time the MCOSD was formed until 1979. He spearheaded the acquisition of Deer Island Preserve. Earlier, as president of the North Marin Federation, he led a successful fight against development of an 1,800-unit mobile home park not far from Deer Island.

DeBORBA TRAIL (.83 miles)
Between Deer Island Loop Trail
Intersection: Arnold Baptiste Trail (.58m)

DeBorba Trail is the one official route to the upper reaches of Deer Island. There are two entries to it off Deer Island Loop Trail; I'll describe the more-used one just twenty-five yards inside the main Preserve gate.

DeBorba climbs gently over oak-dotted savanna. There are fine views across the flood plain south and west to Big Rock Ridge. Bay laurels grow out of the rock outcroppings.

At .2 miles, DeBorba reaches the first of several crests, with much of the North Bay visible. The Trail rolls along over Deer Island's spine.

A half-mile in, the Trail rises out of a saddle into oak woodland. You may hear Highway 37. Otherwise the sylvan setting is likely much as it was in the late 1800's.

At .6 miles, signed Arnold Baptiste Trail departs right. It goes one-tenth of a mile, with no outlet, along the wooded summit ridge.

DeBorba climbs slightly for another hundred yards beyond the Baptiste junction. It then begins a moderately steep descent with a few slippery sections. (Some visitors may prefer to traverse DeBorba in the opposite direction, for a less steep downhill.) A huge multi-trunked bay laurel stands out in the lovely woodland.

DeBorba returns to Deer Island Loop Trail. It is .7 miles back to the start to the left, or 1.2 miles back to the right.

Antone V. DeBorba (1858-1923) was born in Portugal's Azores Islands, came to Marin County in around 1880 and to Novato five or six years later. He began acquiring Novato real estate (including Deer Island in 1903) and became a pillar of the community.

Antone and wife Anna Machado (d. 1911) had eight children. The eldest, Antonio Jr. (Tony, 1883-1942), opened DeBorba's Saloon on Novato's Grant Avenue in 1909. It is still in business today. During prohibition, when the saloon was closed, Tony founded DeBorba's Ice Cream Parlor on Novato's Redwood Road, then a section of Highway 101, and it too became a fixture.

The DeBorba's also donated 30 acres to the adjacent Flood Control District for a park.

DEER ISLAND LOOP TRAIL (1.90 miles)
Around Preserve
Intersections (clockwise from main entry gate): DeBorba Trail (.72m, 1.89m), Russell Antonio Trail (1.62m)

The nearly flat Deer Island Loop Trail circles the "island" and is the main route within the Preserve. A hillier, inner loop is possible in combination with De Borba Trail.

The Trail begins, signed, immediately inside the Preserve entry, a few yards from the parking area. DeBorba Trail is a few yards away on the right fork but the Loop will be described clockwise, so go left. The first quarter-mile of the Trail borders a light industrial strip that includes an auto graveyard. But to the right is a haunting forest of dense, tangled bay laurels.

As the Trail bends south it becomes more pastoral although Highway 37 is visible and audible. Grazing land and diked ponds now form the boundary left. Oaks rule, as they do over the rest of the loop. Many impressive ones date to Miwok days.

The Trail bends over a pair of rivulets. At .6 miles, a signpost reads "Deer Island Fire Lane," a short route to a Preserve gate onto private property.

In another .1 mile, signed DeBorba Trail rises to the right. It winds to the top of the island, then returns to Loop Trail back at the main entry gate.

Some 100 yards ahead is a fenced, spring-fed pond. Duckweed now covers the surface. Walk in to the opening to the right to see a deep shaft of unknown origin. Keep children safely clear. There is a second such shaft just ahead.

The Trail opens as it bends onto the west side of the Preserve. Ponds of the treatment plant below are a favorite of migrating and resident waterfowl, and the raptors who hunt them. Views extend out to Mt. Diablo and to all the Novato MCOSD Preserves. West of Deer Island is a County flood control plain, with winter overflow from Novato Creek channeled here rather than to formerly flood-prone developed areas. An MCOSD "double-poster" sign sits where some visitors have entered the Preserve over the adjacent dike system.

Loop Trail bends right onto the north side of the island. A sign points the way to Russell Antonio Trail, a short, dead-end route onto the knoll. One hundred feet ahead, an old ranch road cuts left. Next come the first of two small bridges.

The sizable ruins below left are from Deer Island's creamery era. The old building on the right edge of the Trail was once a ranch bunkhouse. The house left dates to 1891 (see above). Since 1983, it has been a residence for MCOSD rangers.

Loop Trail passes a signed entry to DeBorba Trail. Twenty-five yards later, the Loop returns back to its start.

RUSSELL ANTONIO TRAIL (.12 miles)
From Deer Island Loop Trail to dead-end atop knoll

Russell Antonio Trail is short and dead-ends beneath an electricity transmission tower, so is little taken. Indeed, the early yards become all but invisible when new grasses emerge each winter.

To reach the trailhead, follow Deer Island Loop Trail counter-clockwise (right) just over a quarter-mile from the Preserve parking area. A signpost marks the start.

Russell Antonio Trail gently rises northwest, past a rock sticking out of the treeless grassland. Gumweed is abundant along the route in the early yards. At 75 yards, the Trail passes through an old fence line and becomes easier to follow.

The marshland ahead is rich in bird life, particularly in winter. Bring binoculars to study the waterfowl, shorebirds, and soaring hawks.

The Trail ends at the crest directly beneath the transmission line. There are views over the oak savanna. Steps must be retraced to Loop Trail.

Russell Antonio was a son of the Antonio family that lived on Deer Island as caretakers from 1963 until 1981. He died at age 10 in a construction accident.

It has been more than 100 years since levees, plus silt, filled enough of San Pablo Bay to connect Deer Island to the mainland. But parts of the Preserve still retain an island feel. (David Hansen)

The "pygmy" Sargent cypress forest that lines the eastern half of San Geronimo Ridge Fire Road within Giacomini Preserve. Sargent cypresses (Cupressus sargentii) grow only in California. The Jepson Manual gives their height range as 10-20 meters. But here, although many are over 100 years old, they are 5-20 feet, stunted by the serpentine soils and wind.

GARY GIACOMINI

Size: 1,549.1 acres   Elevation range: 280-1,516 feet

*It's easy to feel as if you have found paradise on this Preserve.
Whether it is cool, redwood groves or sunny slopes you crave,
Gary Giacomini Preserve offers outstanding diversity. San
Geronimo Ridge Fire Road represents a great starting point for
spending hours (or days, or weeks) exploring. But don't forget to
keep track of your path, it can be easy to get lost up here.
The Preserve also stands out in my mind as a very special place
because of the community that surrounds it. Neighbors have a
sincere respect for the Preserve and take pride in its beauty and
diversity. It's easy to understand why after one has spent some
time exploring the vast system of roads and trails that exist here.
This Preserve is truly magnificent. — Canada Ross, Ranger*

THIS IS AMONG the District's newest Preserves. It covers 1,549 acres (just nine acres
shy of Mt. Burdell as the largest Preserve) on the south side of San Geronimo Ridge,
stretching from the floor of San Geronimo Valley to the ridge line more than 1,100
feet higher. It embraces some of the most remote and scenic parts of the County.
Adding to its appeal, the Preserve borders thousands of additional acres of MMWD
lands to the south and also connects with the MCOSD's White Hill Preserve.

Immediately prior to its acquisition by the County, the area was owned by
developers Sid Hendricks and Dennis Horne. They planned a gated community,
called Skye Ranch, to include homes high on the ridge. Substantial community
opposition stalled the development.

The first parcels acquired by the District were 88 acres in Bates Canyon and
196 acres in Forest Knolls in 1991. The heart of the Preserve was purchased from
Hendricks and Horne in 1995 for the substantially below-market price of $2.1 mil-
lion. Half the monies came from the District, the other half from the Marin Community Foundation. Hendricks and Horne retained some potentially developable
parcels near the valley floor.

Gary Giacomini served 24 years as Marin County Supervisor for District 4,
which includes San Geronimo Valley, and played a key role in the Preserve's acquisition. The new Preserve, originally called San Geronimo Ridge, was renamed for
him upon his retirement as Supervisor.

Visitors will come across more routes lacing this huge Preserve than are described here. Some cross private property, some are illegally carved, some are being
returned to nature. Others may be opened when a Preserve-wide plan is developed.
Be prepared when visiting Giacomini; its vast scale, adjacent wild lands, and numerous unmarked woodland routes make getting lost here likelier than anywhere
else within the District.

BATES CANYON TRAIL (.64 miles)

From Redwood Canyon Road to junction of Conifer Way and Carson Road
Notes: Only Giacomini Preserve entry with ample parking; seasonal
closure to horses; sections extremely muddy

The Bates Canyon Trailhead is on the San Geronimo Valley floor, thus avoiding the steep drives and parking problems associated with higher entries into the Preserve.

There are actually two nearby access gates by San Geronimo Valley Drive, one off Redwood Canyon Drive and one from Meadow Vista Lane (the former used here for measurement). These new streets serve a much smaller Skye Ranch subdivision than what was once planned over today's Preserve.

Enter the broad Trail behind the MCOSD gate to the right of lower Redwood Canyon Drive. There is immediately a feeling of having entered an enchanted area. A maple is the first tree across the grass. At 50 yards, a tall laurel stands beside a bench. There are even taller laurels in the redwood forest just ahead, such as one rising over 100 feet beside the bridge.

In spring, the forest floor is brightened yellow by masses of redwood violets (*Viola sempervirens*). Look also for trillium. At 150 yards, a sturdy bridge (this is a popular equestrian area) crosses Bates Canyon Creek. On the other side, it is 100 yards right to the Meadow Vista Lane entry gate. Just before the bridge, a very steep path climbs 40 yards to Redwood Canyon Drive at Chaparral Lane. (In winter, equestrians are directed onto Chaparral Lane Trail, which runs over a public easement from upper Chaparral Lane to Conifer Way, .1 mile below where Bates Canyon Trail exits.)

Continue straight (not crossing the bridge) and the Trail begins to rise. A path cuts up left to the top of Redwood Canyon Drive. A path comes in right, crossing the creek over a plank. A bit higher, a pair of wooden "banisters" have no steps between them. Maples and tanbark oaks join the redwoods and laurels.

Keep climbing. At .4 miles is the first (and worst) of two nasty mud patches in

Volunteers

Volunteers are a mainstay of MCOSD's efforts to manage and protect its lands. There are several ways to participate in the District's volunteer program.

~ Join the monthly workdays to plant trees, build trails, repair erosion damage, remove invading exotic plants, and clean up new properties. Tools, training, and snacks are provided.

~ Become a Trail Assistant or Ranger Assistant to work an eight-hour shift with staff rangers.

~ Adopt a Preserve or trail and work according to your own schedule through a plan approved by MCOSD. Training, materials, and advice are provided by rangers.

For more information about volunteer opportunities with the District, call (415) 499-3778.

winter. Be very careful trying to bypass them, as poison oak lines the Trail's edge. Above, as the Trail leaves Bates Canyon, the route is more open, edged with baccharis.

The Trail levels and returns to redwood forest. At .6 miles, a path rises right. It meanders through the forest, crossing private property, to high on Conifer Fire Road. Veer left for the final 50 yards to an unsigned gate. Just ahead is the junction of Carson Road and Conifer Way; take the latter up to meet Conifer Fire Road.

CONIFER FIRE ROAD (.74 miles)

From top of Conifer Way to San Geronimo Ridge Fire Road at Carson Meadow
Notes: Conifer Way is unmaintained, with no parking, above Carson Road; limited parking along Carson Road; maintain required six-foot clearance to center of road.

To reach Conifer Fire Road, follow unpaved Conifer Way above its junction with Carson Road. (The trailhead can also be reached off San Geronimo Valley Drive via either Bates Canyon Trail or the public easement over Chaparral Lane.) The uppermost section of Conifer Way is private property and passes a few homes; be respectful of neighbors. In .2 miles, an MCOSD gate marks entry into Giacomini Preserve and the start of the public (and measured) part of Conifer Fire Road.

The Fire Road climbs in the woods. Oaks, bays, and Douglas-firs are the most common trees. In just over 100 yards, the Fire Road bends right, by a wood water tank with solar panels on top.

Continue climbing through the forest. The canopy thins and vistas open. By .3 miles, the Fire Road enters grassland. From the saddle between two knolls on the right, a long, steep path sets off down to Bates Canyon. There are splendid views from the tops of the knolls.

At .66 miles, Conifer Fire Road forks. Both options meet San Geronimo Ridge Fire Road at Carson Meadow (also called the Woodacre Triangle), elevation 1,360 feet. The left option should be taken for travel east on San Geronimo Ridge F.R., toward Pine Mountain and Fairfax-Bolinas Road. The right fork passes a knoll crowned by laurel trees. Use it for travel northwest on the ridge, to Sylvestris F.R., Green Hill, and beyond.

HUNT CAMP FIRE ROAD (.43 miles)

From Sylvestris Fire Road to San Geronimo Ridge Fire Road

Hunt Camp F.R. is a trek from any access point. I'll describe it from the Sylvestris F.R. end, somewhat lower in elevation than the San Geronimo Ridge F.R. side.

To reach Hunt Camp F.R., climb Sylvestris F.R. .8 miles from the MCOSD gate atop East Sylvestris Drive. Hunt Camp, to the right, is the lone fire road intersection.

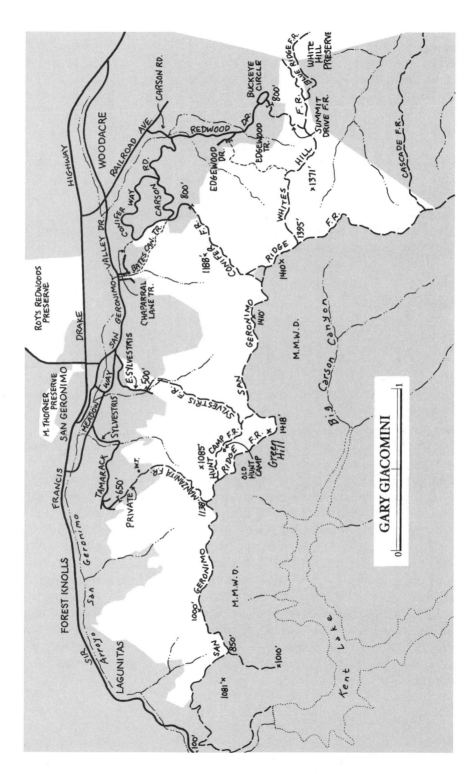

The Fire Road immediately enters a redwood forest. One hundred yards in, a path departs left. It runs 100 yards, cutting off a rutted, up-and-down section of the Fire Road, through a mass of huckleberry shrubs. The tasty but small berries ripen around August and are a favorite food for wildlife.

Then, in a redwood grove .4 miles in, is the delightful, little-known treasure of Hunt Camp. On a concrete slab are a sturdy table once used for carving the deer and other game taken, and tables and benches where meals were enjoyed. Just up left is the camp's water source. In the years just before the Preserve was acquired by the MCOSD, the camp was used by the Pine Ridge Gun Club, which had restored the historic site with running water and other amenities. Deer hunting was permitted during the fall rifle season on Saturdays, Sundays, and Wednesdays. Today's watering trough for horses was donated by the Marin Horse Council.

The Fire Road rises. A pair of giant, ancient redwoods rise above the others right. Douglas-firs and madrones are also abundant.

Hunt Camp F.R. ends at San Geronimo Ridge F.R., opposite an MMWD Watershed sign. The Ridge F.R. goes miles in either direction, left ultimately to Fairfax-Bolinas Road at Azalea Hill and right to Sir Francis Drake Blvd. at Shafter Bridge.

MANZANITA FIRE ROAD (.46 miles)

From San Geronimo Ridge Fire Road to northern boundary of Preserve
Note: There is no public access to Manzanita Fire Road from the north

Manzanita Fire Road drops from San Geronimo Ridge F.R. (at elevation 1,138 feet), one-sixth mile west of Hunt Camp Fire Road. There is then not another fire road down into San Geronimo Valley, when traveling west on the ridge, for two-and-a-half miles.

The descent is very steep, with few easier sections, through the forest. Most of the trees, such as the stands of thin, tightly packed redwoods, are young, but there are old, pre-logging era monarchs as well.

The Fire Road emerges into an open area, ablaze with ceanothus in spring. Some 50 yards before the MCOSD boundary post, a broad path departs left. A former fire road, it is now part of a network of paths skirting in and out of private property.

The MCOSD sign marks the Preserve boundary and the route's end; please respect private property owners rights. The remaining half-mile of the Fire Road (technically, Manzanita Avenue) is indeed lined with manzanita. It empties (passing one major fork to the right) onto the junction of Tamarack, Juniper, and Hemlock roads.

SAN GERONIMO RIDGE FIRE ROAD (4.80 miles)

From top of Cascade Fire Road to Preserve's west boundary
Intersections: White Hill F.R. (1.00m), Conifer F.R. (1.31m, 1.41m),
Sylvestris F.R. and Pine Mountain F.R. (2.36m), Hunt Camp F.R. (3.16m),
Manzanita F.R. (3.32m), Grassy Slope F.R. (4.51m)
Note: MMWD/MCOSD boundary runs through center of the Fire Road

San Geronimo Ridge Fire Road (also historically called Pine Mountain Truck Road) is one of the great routes of Marin, and longest in any of the 32 Preserves. It runs more than eight miles along the remote, unspoiled ridge, from Fairfax-Bolinas Road to near Sir Francis Drake Boulevard at Shafter Bridge. More than half of the Fire Road, between Cascade Fire Road and the western end of Gary Giacomini Preserve, touches MCOSD land. (The Fire Road marks the boundary of MMWD lands to the southwest.)

There are basically two ways to join the MCOSD section of San Geronimo Ridge F.R. at the southeastern tip of Giacomini Preserve. Both involve long journeys. One is to enter San Geronimo Ridge F.R. at Fairfax-Bolinas Road opposite the Azalea Hill parking area, above the Meadow Club. It is a two-mile trek in over MMWD land, passing the Oat Hill and Pine Mountain Fire Roads (both on the left), to the Giacomini Preserve boundary atop Cascade Fire Road. The second route is from Cascade Canyon Preserve and up Cascade (Repack) Fire Road to the summit, elevation 1,400 feet.

San Geronimo Ridge Fire Road, an up-and-down roller coaster, runs surprisingly level for its first half-mile past the Cascade F.R. junction. Bordering the route left and right are hundreds of stunted Sargent cypress (*Cupressus sargentii*) trees, called the "pygmy forest." Sargent cypress grows only in California. The world's two largest Sargent cypress trees, both over 80 feet tall, are in Marin County (on Mt. Tam's Mickey O'Brien Trail). Although many of the trees are over 100 years old, the serpentine-derived soils, plus the winds over the ridge, keep them low. There are other stunted cypresses in Marin, such as along Tam's Northside Trail, but nowhere is the forest so extensive. Note the rounded, woody, seed cones. The serpentine also produces some poorly drained sections and winter visitors should be prepared for muddy patches, even miniature "lakes."

About a half-mile in, a clearing on the right offers a stunning vista point out to both Tam and Mt. Diablo. Beyond, the Fire Road begins a steady descent.

To the right, separated by a small Sargent cypress cluster, are a pair of entries to White Hill F.R., which runs toward White Hill and then down to Sir Francis Drake Boulevard. There is a post, but no sign.

In another 1,000 feet is a splendid 360-degree vista point. Most of the tallest peaks in Marin County are visible, along with giants in neighboring counties. Find the lookout tower atop Barnabe Peak (elevation 1,466 feet). Then, clockwise, the highest visible Marin summits are: distinctively-shaped Black Mountain (1,280'), Shroyer Mountain (1,458'), Big Rock Ridge (1,887'), Loma Alta (1,592'), White Hill (1,430'), Mt. Tamalpais (2,571'), Pine Mountain (1,762'), and Green Hill

(1,418'), which is farther along San Geronimo Ridge Fire Road.

The Fire Road meets lovely Carson Meadow. On the right, Conifer Fire Road begins its descent to the Conifer Way/Carson Road junction in Woodacre. Veer left. A path heads left. The next fire road right is a fork of Conifer Fire Road, .1 mile from the first entry. One hundred yards later is an old gate and fence line.

There are more sensational view sites. Mt. St. Helena, 50 miles away on the Napa/Sonoma/Lake Counties border, is a distant landmark on clear days. Sargent cypresses densely line both sides of the Fire Road. The "pygmy forest" ends by the four way junction at 2.36 miles.

At this junction, marked only by an MMWD watershed sign, San Geronimo Ridge F.R. continues straight ahead. Right is Sylvestris F.R., which drops to Hunt Camp F.R., then Sylvestris Drive in San Geronimo. On the left is Pine Mountain F.R., which drops to near Kent Lake then continues back up to Pine Mountain for a long, tough loop.

The Fire Road climbs along the northwest face of Green Hill, which has been visible for miles. The Fire Road skirts just below Green Hill's true summit, but the views are impressive enough.

Kent Lake is suddenly, and dramatically, visible below and remains so for the next half-mile. Kent Lake, with deeply wooded forests rising above it, looks more like a mighty, pristine river of the Pacific Northwest than the reservoir it is. The deep canyon immediately left of the Fire Road is Big Carson, among the remoter lands in all Marin.

The wooded, rolling terrain beyond Green Hill is strikingly beautiful, with nary a sign of civilization. The prominent grassy clearing visible northwest across Kent Lake was used on an album cover by local musicians Sons of Champlin.

The Fire Road drops to a junction with the west end of Hunt Camp F.R., a loop possibility. Next is a rise to another crest, then a drop to the top of Manzanita F.R. on the right. Manzanita F.R. dead-ends as a public route at the Preserve boundary.

The Fire Road rises again, with redwoods bordering on the right. One crest is reached 150 yards beyond Manzanita F.R., then another some 100 yards later. The view dead ahead of the lookout tower atop Barnabe is framed by Douglas-firs. The very top of Black Mountain peeks out to Barnabe's right. Left of Barnabe is fire-scarred Mt. Vision. Eagle-eyed visitors might glimpse the Pacific Ocean right of Mt. Vision. Indeed, this may be the lone spot in all the Marin County Open Space District (save for Bolinas Lagoon and views of the Golden Gate from the Tiburon Preserves) where the ocean is visible.

San Geronimo Ridge F.R. continues rolling, although there is now more downhill. Trees, mostly stately Douglas-firs, line both sides of the route. A quarter-mile past Manzanita F.R., at a crest, a path goes left past a straggly madrone and through the serpentine chaparral to a Kent Lake overlook. Some of the County's densest stands of wild lilac fill the air with a pleasing fragrance in early spring.

Three-quarters of a mile past Manzanita, the F.R. enters a deep and dark grove of Douglas-firs. This is one of the quietest, most isolated parts of the County. A path goes left at a crest to a vista point. Huckleberry is abundant. Perhaps the most massive Douglas-fir yet encountered stands on the right on the ensuing downhill.

At .9 miles past Manzanita, a path drops right. It is part of a network of such paths, criss-crossing private property, above Lagunitas and Forest Knolls. The next clearing, just ahead, is dense with tree poppy (*Dendromecon rigida*) bushes on both sides of the Fire Road. Their large, yellow, four-petaled flowers, out in early summer, are among the County's showiest.

There is a tricky four-way junction at 1.2 miles beyond Manzanita Fire Road. Left, out of the Preserve, is an old Water District maintenance access route down to Kent Lake. It was abandoned (so not considered a fire road) after Peters Dam was raised. Straight and initially uphill is Grassy Slope Fire Road, also immediately leaving the Preserve. (Thomas Bros. maps identify this option as San Geronimo Ridge F.R.) Grassy Slope F.R. goes to Peters Dam, which forms Kent Lake, then again meets San Geronimo Ridge Fire Road.

Veer right and down to continue on San Geronimo Ridge Fire Road. The steady descent is through deeply shaded Douglas-fir woodland. There is a section bordered by MCOSD land on both sides. About two-thirds of a mile down, on the right, is an abandoned old road with an MCOSD sign, "No Trail Outlet," on the gate. The route behind it, to a water tank site, quickly leaves the Preserve and narrows.

Just below, at an unmarked boundary, San Geronimo Ridge F.R. leaves the Preserve and enters the Marin Municipal Water District. (Note that MMWD lands, unlike MCOSD lands, are closed to the public from sunset to sunrise.) There is an additional three-quarter mile drop to Grassy Slope F.R., below Peters Dam. It is then .2 level miles right to Sir Francis Drake Boulevard at Shafter Bridge by the confluence of Lagunitas and San Geronimo creeks.

The nearest parking for those wishing to join San Geronimo Ridge F.R. from this west end, or for those arranging a car shuttle, is .2 miles into Samuel P. Taylor State Park, on the north side of Drake Boulevard. During the winter salmon spawning season, the MMWD opens the small lot adjacent to Shafter Bridge on the opposite (left) bank of Lagunitas Creek from San Geronimo Ridge F.R. Parking there is limited to one hour.

SUMMIT DRIVE FIRE ROAD (.22 miles)

From above Buckeye Circle (Woodacre) to White Hill Fire Road
Note: No parking within six feet of any road center

To reach Summit Drive F.R., enter Buckeye Circle atop Redwood Drive (Woodacre) and veer right. Look for the Fire Road above #8 Buckeye; there is a blue MCOSD easement sign just uphill. The lower section is technically Summit Drive and private property, and new construction underway at press time will alter its appearance. Please respect the rights of neighbors and stay on the Fire Road.

There is a pleasant fragrance of bay laurels in the deep, cool woodland. The uphill is steep, and remains so. In 60 yards, a short fire road branches left to the water tank. Summit F.R. leaves the forest canopy. The actual Preserve boundary is marked by a sign, one-sixth mile up from Buckeye Circle.

Keep climbing. The Fire Road enters rocky serpentine; note the change in the shrubby flora lining the way. Long vistas open to the north. The Fire Road enters a forest of Douglas-firs.

Summit Fire Road ends at its unmarked junction with White Hill Fire Road. Left leads to the summit of White Hill, right to San Geronimo Ridge.

SYLVESTRIS FIRE ROAD (.95 miles)

From East Sylvestris Drive to San Geronimo Ridge Fire Road
Intersection: Hunt Camp F.R. (.79m)
Notes: Very limited parking opposite trailhead

To reach this Fire Road, climb narrow East Sylvestris Drive above Meadow Way in San Geronimo. Sylvestris F.R. begins on the left, behind an MCOSD-signed gate near the top, just before the pavement is blocked by a "private property" sign. (Note that there is a separate western section of Sylvestris Drive.)

The Fire Road sets off uphill and remains steep. Broom, both Scotch and French, is abundant low but the Fire Road soon enters forest. There are very muddy sections along with several erosion control sites.

Three hundred yards in, on both sides of the Fire Road, are clumps of the ancient and primitive common horsetail (*Equisetum arvense*). Horsetails preceded flowering plants and giant members of the family were browsed by dinosaurs.

The creek ahead usually flows all year, a rarity in Marin with its long, rainless summers. The bank is lined with big-leaf maples. Their leaves color brightly in October before dropping in fall winds. The small tree hazelnut is also abundant. Its hairy leaves are very soft to the touch. Higher on the Fire Road are many Douglas-firs, some branchless a long way up. The Fire Road again touches the creekbed.

Sylvestris meets Hunt Camp F.R., the only junction on the route. It goes right, into the redwoods, to the old deer camp (2,000 feet away) and then up to San Geronimo Ridge Fire Road.

Veer left for the final steep pitch on Sylvestris F.R. It ends at a four-way junction. Left, San Geronimo Ridge F.R. rolls all the way to Fairfax-Bolinas Road, with the next junction, Conifer F.R., a mile away. Right, San Geronimo Ridge F.R. heads toward Sir Francis Drake Boulevard, with the next intersection, Hunt Camp F.R., a nice loop option, .8 miles distant. Straight, by the MMWD Watershed sign, Pine Mountain F.R. drops toward Kent Lake, then climbs back up to San Geronimo Ridge.

WHITE HILL FIRE ROAD/West (1.57 miles)
From Preserve's northeast boundary to San Geronimo Ridge Fire Road
Intersections: Blue Ridge F.R. (.44m), Summit Drive F.R. (.63m),
Edgewood Trail (1.05m)

The southeast section of 3.3 mile-long White Hill Fire Road, from Bothin Access Road to the lower Flanders Ranch gate, is described in the White Hill Preserve chapter. The middle section, running roughly south from the upper Flanders Ranch gate to the Giacomini Preserve line, twice passes outside MCOSD lands (first onto Camp Tamarancho property, then through a private parcel to the west) so is not separately described. The western section, one-and-a-half miles from the Giacomini line to San Geronimo Ridge F.R., is presented below.

The Giacomini Preserve boundary line on White Hill F.R. has not yet been surveyed and is presently unmarked. Measurements cited are from the old gate above the entries into Camp Tamarancho.

The route is fairly level here. There is an old fence line to the left. Four hundred feet past the old gate is the first of two downed large wood posts. White Hill F.R. then enters an isolated, haunting, forest of bay laurels, far from any road. Lupine, purple larkspur and woodland star are among many wildflowers growing here in spring.

The Fire Road begins to rise, gaining West Marin views, then drops into another laurel grove. At .3 miles, the Fire Road passes a second downed old post. Another dip is followed by 150 yards of uphill to the junction with Blue Ridge Fire Road, one of the special places of Marin. Left, Blue Ridge F.R. (not White Hill F.R.) rises to the crest of White Hill, elevation 1,430 feet, and continues across White Hill Preserve to Cascade Canyon Preserve.

Veer right. The views are sweeping, spectacular. This crest that White Hill Fire Road tops is an important watershed divide. Rain falling to the right (west) will find its way to the Pacific via Tomales Bay. Raindrops on the left will enter the Pacific through San Francisco Bay and the Golden Gate. An illegally carved path left, closed to all, is signed "No Bikes."

White Hill Fire Road cuts over rocky terrain to meet Summit Drive Fire Road, which drops right a quarter-mile to the Preserve boundary, then down (over an easement across private property) to Buckeye Circle in Woodacre.

Here and above, young, fast-growing Douglas-firs are clearly winning the battle for space and sunlight with older oaks. Douglas-firs are vigorous colonizers of oak-studded grasslands that are no longer grazed. Indeed, some land managers consider them as invasives, to be removed. Man's suppression of the natural fire cycle also works against the oaks. So too does the rise of the deer population—they are now basically without predators—as oak acorn seeds are a favorite food. Some bemoan the oaks' fate; others enjoy the Douglas-firs and the succession.

Some 150 yards beyond Summit Drive F.R., a "No Bikes" signpost marks a second closed path. The Fire Road rolls through chaparral. A grassy meadow is passed on the left. After, the Fire Road drops steeply. It meets the broad top of what is called Edgewood Trail (a .6-mile route not separately described, as its lower section is heavily eroded). Climbing resumes.

There is a fairly sharp demarcation in the Fire Road between a band of rust-colored sandstone and the rocky, gray-blue, serpentine ahead. Serpentine dominates the crest of the San Geronimo Ridge. Sargent cypress, a tree which grows only in California and is associated with serpentine soils, replaces the oaks.

White Hill Fire Road ends at San Geronimo Ridge Fire Road at a small Sargent cypress grove forming a Y-intersection. Left leads to the fire road up Pine Mountain and to Fairfax-Bolinas Road. Right ultimately leads to Kent Lake's Peters Dam and then Sir Francis Drake Boulevard at Shafter Bridge. Across San Geronimo Ridge F.R. (the border is actually the center of the road) are lands of the Marin Municipal Water District.

White Hill, from the wild lands high on Giacomini Preserve. (Dewey Livingston)

IGNACIO VALLEY

Size: 449.8 acres   Elevation range: 200-1,444 feet

*Ignacio Valley, especially the upper reaches, remains one of the
most rugged Preserves. This trail-less area, surrounded by remote
fire roads, offers spectacular views for the hardy hiker. Ignacio
Valley remains a pristine area, not invaded by many of the
common exotic plants. The beautiful deep valleys and rugged
ridgelines are speckled with madrones, bays, and oaks. During
the winter the seasonal creeks come alive with torrents of water.
Ignacio Valley gives the visitor a glimpse of a true California
landscape. If one seeks solitude, Ignacio Valley might be the
Preserve for you.   — John Aranson, Supervising Ranger*

IGNACIO VALLEY IS CARVED by Arroyo San Jose. The Preserve covers the southern
headwaters of the creek. Most of the acreage was purchased in 1975 with neighborhood support through County Service Area (CSA) No. 20. Some was dedicated in
development of Marin Country Club Estates.

The Ignacio area has a rich history, long predating its incorporation into the
city of Novato. The locale was originally called Pacheco, for Mexican land grantee
Ignacio Pacheco. But when a post office opened in 1893, the Pacheco name had
already been assigned (in Contra Costa County), so Ignacio was substituted. A highly
visible landmark, just west of Highway 101 on Alameda del Prado, is the Pacheco/
Rowland family house (still lived in), dating from the 1870's. The Ignacio train
stop, on the Sonoma line, was in operation from 1888 to 1976. Hamilton Air Force
Base was constructed in the early 1930's on a parcel once known as "Marin Meadows." Completion of the Ignacio overpass in 1964 removed the last traffic light
between the Golden Gate Bridge and Novato.

There are hopes of one day expanding the Preserve to the northwest (off Fairway Drive), which would open to public access a now isolated section of District
ridge line running to the H Ranch boundary.

EAGLE TRAIL (.21 miles)
From top of Eagle Drive to Montura Fire Road

This poor, not officially designated Trail—one of many similar ones worn in from
MCOSD boundary gates—would ordinarily not be included here. But it serves as
access to lovely Montura Fire Road.

The Trail sets off behind the MCOSD barrier atop Eagle Drive. There is limited parking in the cul-de-sac; try lower on Eagle Drive to avoid overburdening
immediate neighbors.

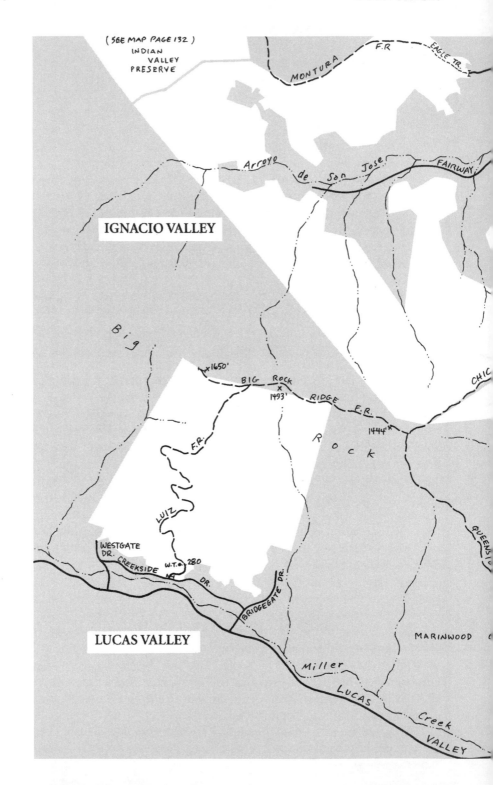

(SEE MAP PAGE 132)
INDIAN
VALLEY
PRESERVE

MONTURA   F.R   EAGLE TR.

Arroyo   de   San   Jose   FAIRWAY

IGNACIO VALLEY

Big

+1650'

BIG Rock
x
1493'   RIDGE F.R.

CHIC

F.R.   R o c k   1444' x

LUIZ

QUEENS

WESTGATE
DR.   CREEKSIDE   W.T. 280
DR.

BRIDGEGATE DR.

MARINWOOD

LUCAS VALLEY

Miller

LUCAS   Creek   VALLEY

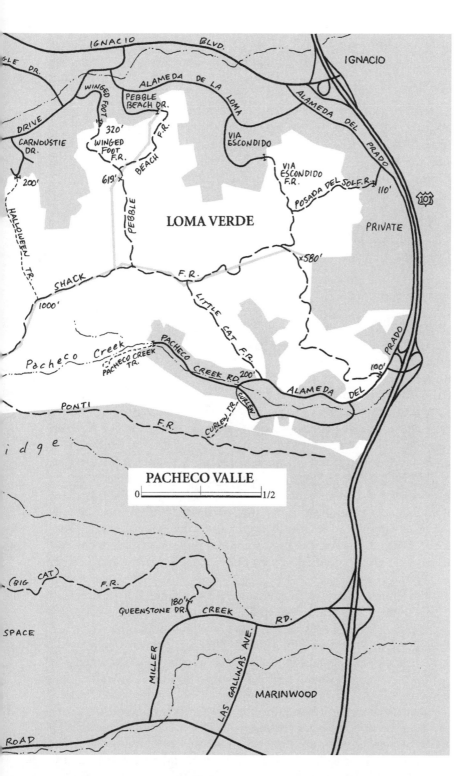

IGNACIO

IGNACIO BLVD.

GLE DR.

ALAMEDA DE LA LOMA

WINGED FOOT

PEBBLE
BEACH DR.

ALAMEDA DEL PRADO

DRIVE

CARNOUSTIE
DR.

320'
WINGED
FOOT
F.R.

F.R.

VIA
ESCONDIDO

VIA
ESCONDIDO
F.R.

200'

619'x

PEBBLE

BEACH

POSADA DEL SOL F.R.

110'

101

LOMA VERDE

PRIVATE

HALLOWEEN TR.

PEBBLE

F.R.

x580'

SHACK

LITTLE CAT F.R.

1000'

Pacheco Creek

PACHECO

PACHECO CREEK
TR.

PACHECO CREEK RD.

200'

PRADO

100'

PONTI

F.R.

CURLEY TR.

CURLEY

ALAMEDA DEL

idge

PACHECO VALLE

0   1/2

(BIG CAT)

F.R.

180'

QUEENSTONE DR.

CREEK

RD.

SPACE

MILLER

LAS GALLINAS AVE.

MARINWOOD

ROAD

The Trail rises over grassland and through light oak woodland. Irises are abundant in spring. An impressive stand of tall manzanitas, all bending south, is passed 400 feet in. There are fine views throughout of the headwaters of Arroyo San Jose. The Marin Country Club golf course, and its clubhouse, are prominent below. Paths branch off.

Eagle Trail ends at its one clear intersection. Right, Montura Fire Road drops, behind the chain barrier, over private property to the top of Montura Drive (no access or egress) off Ignacio Boulevard. Ahead, Montura F.R. tops the ridge toward Indian Valley College.

The "eagle" of the name refers to the coveted golf score.

HALLOWEEN TRAIL (.73 miles)

From Burning Tree Drive to Chicken Shack Fire Road

This is one of the steepest trails in the District, three-quarters of a mile of unrelenting climbing when taken uphill, or three-quarters of a mile of precipitous descent. But that steepness translates into a relatively short route from Ignacio Valley to Big Rock Ridge. Halloween Trail, particularly its upper half, is also quite peaceful and may have the highest concentration of irises of any route on MCOSD land.

Halloween Trail starts behind an MCOSD-signed barrier opposite 10 Burning Tree Drive. The Trail immediately bends right, then quickly left at the fence line of a private residence that sits high on Obertz Lane. The Trail then parallels, just on the other side of the fence, the home's winding driveway for the next 500 yards up.

On the climb, Halloween passes through a pleasant light woodland of madrones and of coast live, black, and valley oaks. But the proximity of the driveway and fence, with several "Private Property" warnings, somewhat diminishes the appeal.

Halloween finally leaves the private property border. It passes along the edge of a hillside laden with polypody ferns. If anything, the going is even steeper than before. Indeed, upper Halloween is so steep some may find it a bit scary to descend. Wear good footwear and proceed cautiously. The Trail is also narrow but, happily, almost free of poison oak.

Most of the hundreds of irises which line the entire route, and are usually at their peak here in April and May, are deep blue. But there are patches of creamy ones, and of countless other shades, as well.

At .38 miles, Halloween passes an MCOSD directional sign. Veer left, uphill. Soon after, the climb briefly eases at an attractive, level, grassy area. Another steep pitch ends with the lone downhill of the route by a second clearing, with a valley oak in the middle.

Yet another tough climb ends in a third, and last, meadow. Several black oaks, whose large leaves color in fall before dropping in winter, stand here. The deeply canyoned, tree-covered, north face of Big Rock Ridge can be glimpsed on the right. The Trail squeezes through a tall manzanita right and a coast live oak left, then meets Chicken Shack Fire Road. There is an MCOSD "Trail" sign at the junction, which is at a crest in the fire road. It is just under a half-mile left to Pebble Beach F.R.; its Winged Foot F.R. fork offering the nearest loop option. Chicken Shack also goes right to Ponti F.R., just under a half-mile away.

District field workers named the Trail "Halloween" because they completed its construction (in conjunction with the Marin Conservation Corps) on Halloween day.

MONTURA FIRE ROAD (1.11 miles)
From Eagle Trail to Preserve boundary

Montura Fire Road runs atop the ridge dividing two forks of Arroyo San Jose, which unite in the heart of Ignacio Valley. The Fire Road touches both Ignacio Valley and Indian Valley Preserves and sits on the boundary between MCOSD and College of Marin lands.

The east end of Montura Fire Road is reached via narrow Eagle Trail from the MCOSD boundary sign atop Eagle Drive. Eagle Trail rises .2 miles to meet Montura F.R. At the Eagle-Montura junction, a .1-mile stub of Montura drops right to Montura Way off Ignacio Boulevard, but it is over private property with no public access.

Montura Fire Road offers splendid views most all its length. To the left is formidable Big Rock Ridge, high above the main Ignacio Valley. To the right is the northern arm of Ignacio Valley, hemmed in by only slightly lower hills. Marin natives—oaks, madrones, bay, manzanita, monkeyflower, bunchgrasses—line the entire route, so the ridge likely looks as it has for centuries. The Fire Road itself only dates to 1976, when it was cleared as an access route for fire-fighting vehicles.

There are impressive stands of tall Parry's manzanita (*Arctostaphylos manzanita*) in the early going. The shrubs are particularly lovely in January, when their hanging, rose-white flowers stand out.

The uphill is steady, gradual to steep. Several crests passed along the way bring even better views. A few old fence posts dot the edges. Some .6 miles beyond the Montura Way intersection is the first of two very steep downhills, which can be quite slippery. They become correspondingly tough uphills on the return journey. You may see some people running along while carrying maps; the hills here are a favorite for Marin's orienteering community.

The Fire Road passes under a power line, which arcs across to the next ridge south. The Indian Valley ballfields come into view, then Pacheco Pond.

The Fire Road rises steeply to an intersection. Montura F.R. drops right, out of the Preserve (but open for travel), onto lands of the College of Marin, Indian Valley Campus. It continues very steeply down .4 miles to a paved road, just east of the College's swimming pool and parking lot #8. The broad route straight ahead runs less than .1 mile to a wide spot, then deteriorates badly. Just before the narrowing, High Meadow Trail (not separately described as it is in poor condition) descends right over the grassy slope to Pacheco Pond in Indian Valley Preserve.

WINGED FOOT FIRE ROAD (.32 miles)

From Winged Foot Drive at Carnoustie Heights to Pebble Beach Fire Road

Fire roads rise from the top of Winged Foot Drive and its nearby Country Club district neighbor, Pebble Beach Drive (see Loma Verde Preserve). The two routes merge at about the 600 foot level, then continue up to Chicken Shack F.R. The Winged Foot entry is one-eighth mile shorter.

The MCOSD entry gate is at the junction of Winged Foot Drive and Carnoustie Heights. The lowest section of Winged Foot F.R. is through a somewhat disturbed landscape. In spring, purplish-red vetches (*Vicia*), in the pea family, color the grass bordering the Fire Road's right edge.

A steep climb leads to views, looking back, of Mt. Burdell. At .22 miles, a broad road goes right the 60 or so yards to a water tank. Above, Pebble Beach is more pristine.

The Fire Road passes through a thick, double line of manzanita bushes. Oaks, madrones, and toyons become abundant higher. Several breaks offer views, including of Halloween Trail, a loop partner with Winged Foot.

Winged Foot F.R. ends at its unsigned junction with Pebble Beach F.R., which rises the remaining half-mile up to Chicken Shack Fire Road.

Erosion Control and Drainage Improvement

MCOSD must often assume the role of a "land doctor" after it acquires open space. Some of the first problems MCOSD corrects on newly acquired lands are related to erosion control and drainage. During an open space outing, you may notice one or more of the following as evidence of MCOSD's efforts to curb erosion or correct drainage problems.

~ *Trash racks* are lengths of pipe set in a V-shape in a stream channel just before a stream enters a drain inlet or culvert. These structures stop branches, rocks and other debris from entering and clogging drainpipes.

~ *Rock-lined stream channels* are created to repair steep, severely eroding stream banks. Before the rock is placed, the eroded banks are graded back to a gentler, less erosive slope.

~ *Low earthen dams* temporarily store storm water in locations where drain inlets might otherwise be overwhelmed by exceptionally heavy rainfall.

~ *Water bars* are logs or low ridges of earth installed at an angle across trails or fire protection roads to divert water and thus prevent the creation of gullies.

~ *Young, native vegetation protected by wire mesh cages* is often planted as part of stream bank protection work. The District raises much of its own stock for this purpose.

INDIAN TREE

Size: 242 acres   Elevation range: From 400-1,440 feet

Over the years Indian Tree has come up with some surprises. One day as the trail crew was taking a break, I was standing by a dead tree that was about ten feet tall. I pulled off a chunk of bark that looked like it was ready to fall off. Just as soon as the bark fell off a bat came flying out, within inches of my face. What a scare. — Carl Szawarzenski, Ranger

INDIAN TREE is one of two completely "land-locked" MCOSD Preserves (the other is Tiburon Ridge), with no part touching a road. There is public access, however, from the north, over land of the North Marin Water District.

The Indian Tree area was long part of F Ranch. Its last owners prior to public acquisition were Frank and Mary Rebelo. The parcel (242 acres, bought for $343,750) was part of a larger joint 1977 acquisition by the MCOSD and North Marin Water District. The current division of land between the two agencies was made in 1985, and Indian Tree designated a Preserve.

The Preserve name arises from a story surrounding the giant redwood atop the Preserve, reachable by Big Trees Trail. Apparently, a native American lived for some time in a hollowed portion (since re-grown) of the tree.

BIG TREES TRAIL (2.99 miles)
From Vineyard Road to the Big Trees Grove
Intersections: Deer Camp Trail (2.06m), Ship's Mast Trail (2.49m),
Indian Tree F.R., (2.90-2.92m)
Note: Part of Bay Area Ridge Trail (no bicycles)

Since a 1998 re-route added 1.1 miles, Big Trees is much the longest trail in the District. It is a meandering trail, several times crossing the now-closed shorter route, and may frustrate those in a hurry. But travelers who value the journey as much as the destination—and in this case, the destination is one of the treasures of Marin County—Big Trees Trail is a delight.

Access to Big Trees Trail is via the trailhead atop the unpaved section of Vineyard Road. The redwoods on the ridge, Big Trees Trail's destination, can be seen from the start. Big Trees Trail passes the last house on Vineyard Road over an easement through North Marin Water District land. Just before a gate, Upper Meadow Trail sets off to the right and Big Trees Trail veers left and up. (Current MCOSD signs label the section between Vineyard Road and the first intersection as Upper Meadow Trail.)

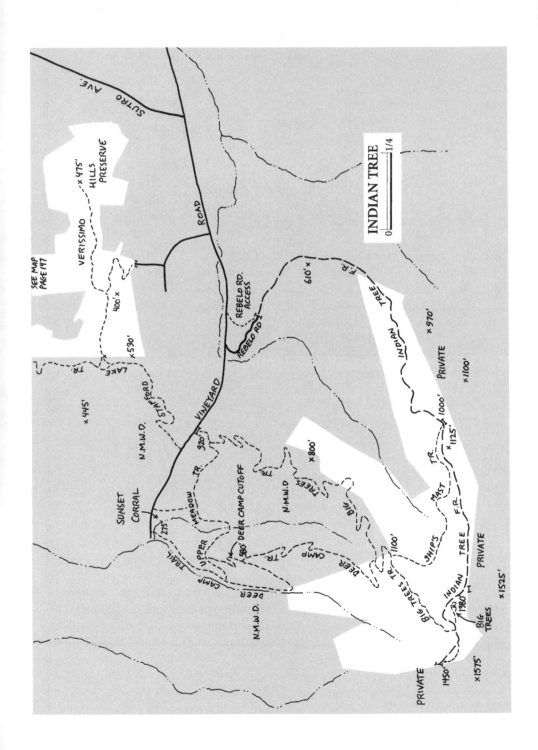

Fifty yards ahead, Big Trees enters woodland and remains shaded basically the rest of the way. Oaks and laurels are prevalent low on the route. Be alert to extensive poison oak at Trail edge.

The first switchback is to the left, with the former routing going straight. (Old routings of Big Trees Trail and of adjacent closed trails, Watershed and Horsemens, are deliberately blocked by cut foliage, and some have "Erosion Control" signs. Please stay off them.) These switchbacks, 11 within the first two miles, while lengthening the route, curb erosion and make the climb easy (5-10% maximum grade) for almost all visitors. There are also fairly long level stretches, even slight downhills.

It is above switchback #3 that the first views open, here of Stafford Lake Trail up to Verissimo Hills Preserve. The Trail crosses a patch of "sand cement" over a wet area beyond switchback #4. Views open to the peaks north of Stafford Lake, the tallest being Hicks Mountain and Mt. Burdell. By switchback #5 are the first looks northeast into Sonoma and Napa counties.

Just shy of a half-mile, three wood steps lead Big Trees Trail into its first grove of redwoods. The creek crossing here is no coincidence; redwoods require huge amounts of water. Just above is the first of several open areas. In spring, the grass is dotted with woodland stars (*Lithophragma affine*), in the Saxifrage family, with white petals three-lobed at their tips. Rising higher amid the grasses are tall-stemmed blue dicks. There are glimpses of Stafford Lake and Indian Valley Golf course.

After a section through a sea of twisted bay laurels at .8 miles, the forest lightens. Madrones become more numerous, and remain companions much of the remaining way. Ferns—sword, wood, deer, maidenhair, goldback, and more—carpet the hillside.

At 1.6 miles, the dam across Novato Creek that formed Stafford Lake in 1950 is first visible. On clear days, Mt. St. Helena, tallest peak in the Bay Area (4,343 feet on the border of Napa, Sonoma, and Lake counties), also is first seen here.

Less than 100 yards later is an OSD "Trail" post at a former routing; irises are abundant here. A few yards beyond, a vista opens east between the trees, to San Francisco Bay and Mt. Diablo. Just ahead is another signpost reading "Big Trees Trail to Big Tree."

The Trail returns to redwoods. Look for the many star-flowers (*Trientalis latifolia*). The pinkish flowers sit atop the most delicate of stems. The genus name "Trientalis" comes from the Latin, "one-third of a foot," for the plant's typical height.

At two miles is the first and only official trail intersection. Deer Camp Trail (marked only as "Trail" on the signpost), a loop option back down to Upper Meadow Trail, departs right at a fence line. (At press-time, there was another somewhat confusing Deer Camp Trail signpost .4 miles above.)

A bend right at 2.3 miles suddenly brings Big Trees into the dry chaparral of the hill's southeast slope. There is soon a return to madrone woodland. At 2.4 miles, new (1999) Ship's Mast Trail sets off left into the madrones. It runs, almost level, just under a mile to Indian Tree Fire Road.

At 2.6 miles, Douglas-firs, rivals to the redwoods in height and girth, make their debut. The shrub hazel grows in abundance in the deep woods. The Trail has its first somewhat steeper sections, all short.

After a last redwood grove, Big Trees Trail enters a high meadow, one of the special places in Marin. To the right, Indian Tree F.R. rises one-eighth mile to a fence, signed "No Trespassing," at the Preserve boundary with Ryan Ranch.

The Trail and Indian Tree Fire Road drop to a signed junction. A sign notes that this segment of Bay Area Ridge Trail is ending. Left, Indian Tree F.R. departs, first rising, then dropping the long way down to Rebelo Lane. It offers an appealing, six-mile loop option with Big Trees Trail (including stretches on Rebelo Lane and Vineyard Road, or the adjacent easement). A final short section of Big Trees Trail straight ahead leads to the highest grove of redwoods, the "Big Trees."

All the redwoods are impressive but three are particularly massive, One, known as "Big Tree," "Ship's Mast," and "Indian Tree," is king of them all. This tree has special significance as a longtime Novato landmark and holds a power over all who come to it. Not too long ago, the trunk was hollowed (it has since re-solidified) and legend has it that an Indian lived in it, hence one of the names. "Ship's Mast" arises because of the tree's appearance from distant points; it was even more prominent years ago before neighboring redwoods grew to match its height. There is a sweeping view over all Novato. Few visitors hurry to leave, for here is truly escape from the pace of the world below.

DEER CAMP TRAIL (1.58 miles)

From Big Trees Trail to Sunset Corral
Intersections: Deer Camp Cutoff Trail (.88m), Upper Meadow Trail (1.48m)

Deer Camp Trail is described downhill, as it makes an attractive, all-wooded loop partner with Big Trees Trail.

The top of Deer Camp Trail is two miles above the base of Big Trees Trail. There is a newer wooden fence at the junction and a "Trail" sign. Most all the trees here are madrones. Deer Camp Trail starts gently down, and remains an easy descent.

In 75 yards is the first of many glimpses of Stafford Lake and hills beyond. Adjacent to the upper Trail are a few redwoods, including one huge-girthed, ancient monarch to the left that somehow escaped loggers' axes. Note its spiraled bark and massive branches.

Deer Camp Trail passes through a lovely, quiet oak-madrone woodland. Miners-lettuce is abundant. Its green leaves were used in pioneer's salads, then the foliage reddens in late spring. You begin to hear, in winter and spring, the creek in the canyon left. You can spot the redwoods on the heavily-wooded far canyon wall by their upturned branches. Several old routings are passed, some with fences and "Erosion Control" signs.

The Trail meets a signed intersection with Deer Camp Cutoff Trail, heading downhill right. Take the Cutoff to Upper Meadow Trail, then go right to make a loop with Big Trees Trail.

Beyond the Cutoff, Deer Camp Trail continues to descend gradually. It drops into a lovely creek canyon amid a grove of redwoods. Many first-time visitors are delightfully surprised to come upon such a redwood forest low in northern Novato. The old deer hunting camp is on private property.

Right, Deer Camp Trail immediately leaves the Preserve. The remaining, broad nearly half-mile stretch through the canyon (a section sometimes called Jet Trail) is outside the Preserve but open to public passage. It passes the west end of Upper Meadow Trail, another loop option. The route then dead-ends at the private property of Sunset Corral.

DEER CAMP CUTOFF TRAIL (.29 miles)
From Upper Meadow Trail to Deer Camp Trail

Deer Camp Cutoff Trail plays a role in a few Preserve loop options. It sets off uphill from Upper Meadow Trail, .6 miles west from Big Trees Trail. A second, closer entry to the Cutoff is off Vineyard Road about one-third mile west from the end of the pavement. It is marked with both a blue easement sign and a green one reading "Upper Meadow to Indian Tree Open Space." Muddy and rutted, this entry runs one-eighth mile beside the fence of the Sunset Corral rental horse area.

The Cutoff rises gently, initially parallel to Upper Meadow Trail. An oak/bay woodland shelters the way. Some 150 yards in, by a hazel, a new (1999) reroute replaces a steep section with more gradual switchbacks. The old and new routes rejoin at .2 miles.

Deer Camp Cutoff ends at Deer Camp Trail. The intersection area has a dense concentration of shooting stars in late winter and early spring. Right is a short descent to the Preserve boundary in a redwood-lined canyon. Left is a climb to well up on Big Trees Trail. Both directions offer loop options.

INDIAN TREE FIRE ROAD (1.98 miles)
From Preserve's southwest boundary to Rebelo Lane
Intersections: Big Trees Trail (.13m-.15m), Ship's Mast Trail (.96m)

Indian Tree Fire Road skirts the southern edge of the Preserve. Since the Fire Road offers an ideal, long (six-mile) loop option with Big Trees Trail, it will be described downhill from its junction with Big Trees. This makes for a cool, shaded, gradual ascent and a steeper, more open trip back down, with splendid views.

The uppermost one-eighth mile of Indian Tree F.R. runs between the Preserve's southwest boundary, with the historic Ryan (earlier, Redmond) Ranch, and Big Trees Trail. (The only access is from below.) The original Ryan/Redmond Ranch buildings are now submerged under Stafford Lake, the owners having lost a legal battle to save them. The sign at the boundary fence warns "No Trespassing." Take it literally; the ranch still has legal deer hunting in fall.

Just off upper Indian Tree F.R. are extraordinarily appealing grand views over the pastoral geographic heart of Marin. All of central Marin, between Big Rock Ridge (on which you're standing) and Mt. Tamalpais, lies below. And just about all that is visible is green and pristine, dairy grazing land as it has been for some 150 years.

By the Big Trees Trail junction is a lovely grass meadow. This a peaceful area and a favorite of all who make the long journey to it. The Fire Road and Trail continue briefly down to a signed fork. Right, Big Trees Trail goes the short way up to the Big Trees themselves. A sign at the junction notes that there is a gap in the Bay Area Ridge Trail, the route south over private property still unsettled. Left, Indian Tree F.R. rises for 100 yards, then begins its long descent.

There are views out to Mt. Diablo. At .15 miles, a path comes in right. It connects the few yards back up to the Big Trees grove. At .2 miles, the Fire Road enters a woodland of oaks and bay laurels. There are several more such wooded stretches below, but most of the route is through grassland. The fence line right marks the boundary of the privately owned H (or Hill) Ranch.

Just before a half-mile, there is a view out to distant Mt. St. Helena, then of Mt. Diablo again. These are two of the monarchs of the Bay Area. But Mt. Tamalpais, Marin's giant, is blocked by Big Rock Ridge.

The Fire Road passes through its deepest stand of redwoods. Upon emerging to open grassland, new (1999) Ship's Mast Trail sets off left, going a level mile back to Big Trees Trail. Opposite is a gate into private H Ranch.

Immediately ahead is the first of several steep sections. They become very muddy and rutted in winter, and dusty and slippery in summer. Descend with caution. You can see the dam forming Stafford Lake.

Indian Tree F.R. crosses a creek. A short uphill brings another grand vista. Bay laurels grow from a rock outcropping left. Mules ears (genus *Wyethia*), with their large yellow sunflowers and big "mule-ear" leaves, dot the grassland.

In a meadow area, MCOSD boundary posts on the left mark where Indian Tree F.R. runs briefly outside the Preserve. Through passage is permitted. A gate right marks one end of Burnt Ridge Fire Road, on H Ranch property and not open to the public.

At 1.43 miles, Indian Tree F.R. leaves the Preserve for good through a barrier gate. The MCOSD sign on the other side reads "Big Rock Ridge to Indian Tree." There is a public easement over the remaining descent.

A water tank is passed 200 yards below the MCOSD gate. In another 200 yards, Wildhorse Valley Fire Road branches right over private property. Homes high in Wildhorse Valley are visible through the trees.

The Fire Road passes more signs of civilization, such as water and power lines, and there are views of the new, large homes below. A tennis court left marks the end, finally or all too soon depending on degree of fatigue, of the wilderness part of the long Big Trees Trail-Indian Fire Road loop

Indian Tree Fire Road comes out in a residential cul-de-sac above Rebelo Lane. (Frank and Mary Rebelo were owners of the Preserve land before its public acquisition.) A blue "Public Trail" sign just below 4 Rebelo marks an easement route to Vineyard Road. Note other off-road easements on the south side of Vineyard Road when you go left to complete the loop.

SHIP'S MAST TRAIL (.94 miles)
From Big Trees Trail to Indian Tree Fire Road

This is the District's newest trail, carved in the summer of 1999 and not slated to formally open until spring 2000. (It's so new I haven't had a chance to explore the spring-time flora.) Ship's Mast is a delightful Trail, deeply wooded and almost level. It offers a new loop option to those who make the long journey to the Preserve's upper reaches.

When descending Indian Tree Fire Road from Big Trees Trail, the Ship's Mast trailhead is just under a mile down, on the left. Opposite is a gate onto private H Ranch. Just ahead, Indian Tree F.R. leaves the tree canopy and begins its first very steep drop.

Ship's Mast enters the woodland of the north side of Big Rock Ridge and remains shaded and cool its whole length. In 100 yards, the Trail passes through the first of several redwood groves, here of tightly packed younger trees.

At one-third mile, past a grove of more mature redwoods, there is a clear view of Mt. Burdell. The Trail trends slightly up (and down a bit later), but the slope is barely perceptible as the route follows the hill's natural contour.

A bit over halfway in is the deepest redwood grove. Just beyond is a haunting forest of laurels, with ferns carpeting the understory. Next, Ship's Mast Trail enters a more open area of madrone trees.

Ship's Mast Trail ends at Big Trees Trail. It is .43 miles right to Deer Camp Trail. Left, it is exactly a half-mile up to Ship's Mast itself in the Big Trees Grove atop the Preserve.

UPPER MEADOW TRAIL (.74 miles)
From Big Trees Trail to Deer Camp Trail
Intersections: Rental Barn connector (.21m), Deer Camp Cutoff Trail (.60m)
Notes: Easement over land of the North Marin Water District; seasonal closure to horses

Although easement routes outside MCOSD Preserves are generally not described in this book, Upper Meadow Trail must be an exception as so many visitors to Indian Tree Preserve travel it.

Most people reach Upper Meadow Trail via Big Trees Trail, 500 feet from the trailhead at the end of the pavement on Vineyard Road. (The trailhead sign indicates the opening section is Upper Meadow Trail.) At the first junction, Big Trees Trail veers left to begin its three-mile climb to the Big Trees while Upper Meadow Trail goes straight through the self-closing cattle gate, designed so it can be opened by a mounted rider. Ahead, the Trail is posted as closed to horses in winter.

Upper Meadow Trail crosses a creek over a sizable bridge, six feet wide and railed to accommodate horses. The route enters a forest of bay laurels. Just ahead are remnants of the base of now-closed Watershed Trail. Heavy equestrian use has rutted sections of Upper Meadow Trail, its center depressed up to a full foot below the edges.

At one-fifth mile, an easement path veers right. It skirts Sunset Corral's rental horse area and meets Vineyard Road at an MCOSD signpost. Informally called "Rental Barn Trail," this easement is an alternate entry to Upper Meadow Trail.

The Trail crosses oak savanna; grassland with widely spread oaks. There is a second gate; again, be sure it closes behind. Upper Meadow reenters bay woodland.

A gentle up brings views over to Verissimo Hills Preserve and Mt. Burdell. The Trail borders Sunset Corral, formerly called Redwood Boarding Stables. The grassland is ablaze with yellow suncups and buttercups in spring. At .6 miles, Deer Camp Cutoff, signed, sets off left up to Deer Camp Trail.

The remaining section of Upper Meadow is deeply wooded and slightly downhill. The Trail ends at broad Deer Camp Trail in a delightful, cool, creek canyon on NMWD land. Right leads to private Sunset Corral. Left are loop options.

The uppermost reaches of Indian Tree Preserve, a long climb well worth the effort.

INDIAN VALLEY

Size: 653.7 acres   Elevation range: 40-1,080 feet

I was hired in 1992 by the Open Space District to help plant and maintain native plants in areas in need of restoration. Though I grew fond of all the District's restoration sites and even some individual plants, the most memorable site is Arroyo Avichi in Indian Valley Preserve. Of course I remember the challenge of digging holes in the extremely dry and compacted soil of the Indian Valley Fire Road, but more importantly, I remember the high volume of visitors. Some folks would stop a while and chat with me, others would nod as they passed. But most people, no matter what the user type, were pleasant toward each other and me and that's great.   *— Ari Golan, Ranger*

TODAY'S INDIAN VALLEY Preserve was part of an approximately 1,000-acre dairy that the Pacheco family, the original Mexican land grantees, called "the Back Ranch." The family sold a 333-acre parcel of the Back Ranch in 1964 for $860,000 to create a second College of Marin campus. Called Indian Valley Colleges, it offered its first classes in 1971 and formally opened in 1975. Also in 1975, the balance of the Back Ranch, less some 100 acres that were developed, was sold to the MCOSD for just under $1 million, the core of Indian Valley Preserve. A neighborhood assessment district—the bonds now paid off in full—helped finance the acquisition.

There has been local debate about the Indian Valley name. Some say the college is really in Ignacio Valley and that traditionally designated Indian Valley is to the northwest, the drainage of Arroyo Avichi. Indian Valley Road was formerly called Arroyo Avichi Road.

AD & GLORIA SCHWINDT TRAIL (.81 miles)

Between Indian Valley Fire Road

This mostly wooded Trail opens a pleasant loop option on the north side of Indian Valley. The entries to both ends of Ad & Gloria Schwindt are off Indian Valley Fire Road. The Trail will be described from the Indian Valley College side.

Schwindt Trail rises to the right 25 yards inside the Preserve gate behind the College fields. (From the westernmost parking lot, walk past the ballfield bathrooms, where there is a water fountain.) Schwindt climbs through the grassland. At 100 yards, a shortcut path from Indian Valley F.R. comes in left.

The Trail briefly leaves the Preserve onto Indian Valley College land (open to the public) as it passes through a fence line. A path right goes across college land. A pushup station from the old college fitness parcourse provides an unexpected chance to exercise arm muscles as well.

The Trail re-enters the Preserve at the next signed entry gate. The route is wide, then returns to Trail width.

A second crest is reached in exactly one quarter-mile. Schwindt Trail begins a

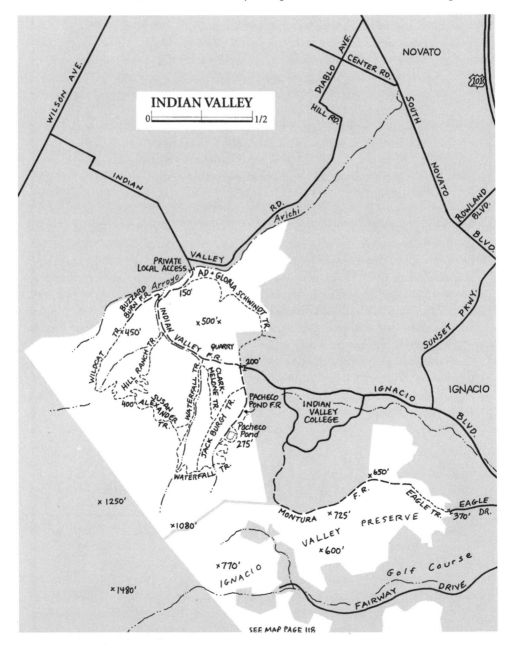

SEE MAP PAGE 118

gentle descent into a cool, lovely woodland. A few oaks and madrones dot the forest, but bay laurels rule, pervading the air with their pleasing scent.

The Trail meets the canyon floor, then follows the left bank of Arroyo Avichi. The name appears on an 1859 map of Rancho de Novato, the meaning unknown. The 1880 *History of Marin County* calls it "Arroyo Achiva." Usually dry, the Arroyo comes to life during winter storms. But its salmon run, fondly recalled by old-timers, is gone.

At a half-mile, there is a Schwindt signpost at a short connector used only by residents of private, adjacent Pencil Belly Ranch. Schwindt Trail then begins rising gently through the forest. Ferns are abundant.

Schwindt Trail then descends to its end. The Indian Valley Road entry to the Preserve is 150 yards to the right. It is three-quarters of a mile left on Indian Valley F.R. back to the start.

Ad and Gloria Schwindt were Indian Valley open space activists.

BUZZARD BURN FIRE ROAD (.34 miles)
From Indian Valley Fire Road to Wildcat Trail
Note: Dead-end for bicyclists

Buzzard Burn F.R. rises south off the floor of Indian Valley, one-fifth mile in from the Indian Valley Road entrance. The uphill is very steep to begin with, and steepens even more above. Use caution when descending.

The Fire Road cuts through a hardwood forest. At a crest there is a break in the tree cover and views stretch from the valley floor out to Mt. Diablo.

An MCOSD post on the oak-studded knoll here marks the end of the designated Fire Road section, the part maintained for vehicular access. The next section up, while as broad as below, is officially designated as Wildcat Trail. Bicycles are not permitted beyond. Wildcat Trail rises to an area signed as closed for restoration, then veers left to meet Hill Ranch Trail.

Just 70 yards ahead, the route (as Wildcat Trail) passes beneath a power line. In the 1980's, a turkey vulture, a bird sometimes mistakenly called a buzzard, landed on one of the wires, killing the bird and setting off a fire that gave the route its name.

CLARK-MELONE TRAIL (.33 miles)
From Waterfall Trail to Jack Burgi Trail

Clark-Melone Trail has a common start with Waterfall Trail, off Indian Valley Fire Road. Clark-Melone branches left while Waterfall goes straight.

The Trail is at once steeply uphill. By .1 mile, the incline eases as the Trail enters a lovely woodland of madrone and manzanita. There's even a bit of downhill as the tree canopy shifts to bay, oak, and toyon.

The climbing resumes. Clark-Melone cuts through a forest of twisted manza-

Dedication of Clark-Melone Trail (Indian Valley Preserve), 1994. From left, MCOSD General Manager Frances Brigmann, Woody Melone, Bob Clark, Susan Alexander.

nita. Higher, there are stately oaks.

A steep final pitch leads to open terrain and a junction with broad Jack Burgi Trail. There are views of Mt. Burdell and, to its west, Hicks Mountain. Jack Burgi rises steeply right to Waterfall Trail, a nice loop option. Left, it drops, also steeply, to Pacheco Pond Fire Road, another loop possibility.

Bob Clark and Woody Melone are two Indian Valley residents who were heavily involved in securing the Preserve as open space.

HILL RANCH TRAIL (1.02 miles)

From Indian Valley Fire Road to Preserve boundary
Intersections: Susan Alexander Trail (.50m), Wildcat Trail (.76m)

Hill Ranch Trail sets off south from the mid-point of Indian Valley F.R., between the Waterfall Trail and Buzzard Burn F.R. trailheads. The junction is signed.

Hill Ranch Trail goes under a blue elderberry tree, then crosses Arroyo Avichi over a bridge. Left of the bridge are numerous flowering currant (*Ribes glutinosum*) bushes. The Trail enters a deep, quiet forest, where it remains all the way up. The creek is just to the right, with multi-trunked bays growing at its edge.

At 150 yards, two forks of Arroyo Avichi merge at the nose of a hill. The Trail follows the left fork's canyon.

The uphill grade steepens but switchbacks help. At exactly the half-mile mark, amid a deep stand of buckeyes and tall bays, a signpost points the way left onto (Susan) Alexander Trail. It runs .6 miles to Waterfall Trail and can be taken as part of a well-wooded loop.

Another 250 yards of climbing brings Hill Ranch Trail to the clearing known as Log Cabin Meadow, for a structure now gone. Masses of blue brodiaeas color the grassland in spring. The first broad views on the journey open. At the fence, signed "Erosion Control, Please Keep Off," is a fork. The slightly more prominent route up to the right is considered as Wildcat Trail. It connects to the top of Buzzard Burn F.R., a loop partner. Hill Ranch Trail continues up and left, past a great old valley oak.

The upper quarter-mile of Hill Ranch is a dead-end (except for equestrians holding permits for travel onto private Hill Ranch above) but still worth traveling. It snakes through a quiet hardwood forest of bays, oaks, madrones, buckeyes, and toyons. Hill Ranch Trail ends at an unsigned gate through the barbed wire fence marking the Preserve boundary with Hill (or H) Ranch.

In the 1890's, the dairy operations of the old Novato land grant were divided into seven ranches, labeled A through H (there was no G, as it looked too similar to C as a cattle brand), plus the Home Ranch around the DeLong house. The H Ranch, at 2,450 acres, was much the largest. Each ranch was leased to tenants, some of whom became owners when the Novato Land Company began selling the ranches in 1908. The H Ranch has long been owned by the Hill family, and is now called both H Ranch and Hill Ranch..

INDIAN VALLEY FIRE ROAD (.85 miles)

From Indian Valley Road to Preserve boundary with Indian Valley College
Intersections: Pencil Belly access (.03m), Ad & Gloria Schwindt Trail
(.08m, .83m), Buzzard Burn F.R. (.22m), Hill Ranch Trail (.42m), Waterfall
Trail (.62m), Clark-Melone Trail (.62m), Pacheco Pond F.R. (.84m)

Flat, shaded, easily accessed, and meeting so many of the Preserve's trails, this Fire Road is understandably the most traveled route in Indian Valley. Almost any time of any day, you'll find many hikers, dog walkers, and horse and bike riders sharing its wide course. The Fire Road will be described from the Indian Valley Road (north) end, but can just as easily be joined from the Indian Valley College side. Those parking must leave a minimum of six feet clearance from the center of Indian Valley Road. Entry is via a public easement across a private, gravel lane (dogs must remain on leash, and please be quiet) near Old Ranch Road. An MCOSD gate marks the Preserve boundary.

A forest of bay trees lines the Fire Road on both sides. The corral immediately left, on private property, has been signed "John's Mule Farm." Also at the gate, a well-trod but unofficial path veers right, to rejoin the Fire Road in .1 mile.

Fifty yards in, a sign points the way left to a path called Pencil Belly Trail. It runs .08 miles to a dead-end at private Pencil Belly Ranch. Beware the leafy poison oak vine climbing the bay tree by the sign. In another 250 feet, a sign left marks one end of Ad & Gloria Schwindt Trail; it loops back to the far end of Indian Valley Fire Road.

The alternate entry path re-enters on the right. The Fire Road crosses over Arroyo Avichi, usually dry but roaring during big winter rainstorms. The MCOSD has financed an extensive creek restoration project along the Fire Road.

At .2 miles, a shortcut path to Buzzard Burn F.R. rises right. The signed, official entry to Buzzard Burn is just ahead. It offers a loop option with Wildcat and Hill Ranch Trails. The bay forest lightens a bit, and there are more oaks and open areas.

At .4 miles, Hill Ranch Trail sets off right, across a bridge over Arroyo Avichi, to Wildcat Trail and then the Preserve boundary with Hill Ranch. Blackberries and sedges line the watercourse. In late summer, the mint pennyroyal adds fragrance and color in damp patches of an otherwise dry channel.

At .6 miles, a path goes left into the old rock quarry, soon to rejoin the Fire Road. Indian Valley F.R. now runs through grassland. A one-eighth mile connector path to Pacheco Pond F.R. cuts right.

Two signs reading "Sensitive Wildlife Area, No Dogs Allowed Beyond This Point" stand 100 feet apart, flanking a small, former farm pond. It is home to many frogs. Between the signs, a path goes left to Schwindt Trail.

A few yards before the Fire Road's end, Schwindt Trail itself returns on the left and Pacheco Pond F.R. rises right. The latter passes Jack Burgi Trail, then goes on to Waterfall Trail and Pacheco Pond.

The Fire Road gate marks the Preserve boundary with Indian Valley College. The path around the two new lighted ball fields can be taken left or right to the nearest parking lot ($1 fee on weekdays).

JACK BURGI TRAIL (.56 miles)

From Pacheco Pond Fire Road to Waterfall Trail
Intersection: Clark-Melone Trail (.23m)

Jack Burgi Trail (signed as "O'Burgi") offers the best views of the several routes that climb south off Indian Valley. It alone runs atop a ridge, the others in deeply wooded canyons. But very steep sections make Burgi a challenge to some.

Jack Burgi Trail starts at the crest of the section of Pacheco Pond F.R. between the two main Indian Valley campus Preserve entry gates. The Trail is broad its entire length up the ridge.

The initial climb, although perhaps the route's steepest, is indicative of what's ahead. Pause, turn, and enjoy the views. They are particularly striking at a crest reached at one-sixth mile. Madrones, manzanita, and oaks are the prominent Trailside flora.

After one-quarter mile of climbing, the Trail drops to a saddle and its lone intersection. Signed Clark-Melone Trail descends right to a common junction with Waterfall Trail at Indian Valley Fire Road. A particularly impressive Parry's manzanita (*Arctostaphylos manzanita*) stands here. Once measured at 25 feet high with a circumference of 4 feet, 3 inches, and crown spread of 24 feet, it was nominated for inclusion into the American Forestry Association's Big Trees Registry.

Jack Burgi Trail continues very steeply up. Behind are views over San Pablo Bay to Sonoma and Napa counties. A second crest is reached. The next section, gently rolling up, is particularly lovely and leaves visitors wishing for more of the same.

A third crest amid an open area is reached 200 feet before the Trail's end. Jack Burgi meets Waterfall Trail at a crossing of ridges. It is the highest point on Waterfall, which goes left and right. Directly across is a path, one of several very poor, unmaintained, social routes lacing what some call Billy Goat Hill.

Jack O. Burgi was active in Novato civic affairs, including the saving and restoration of Pioneer Cemetery. A grove of trees is dedicated to him in Miwok Park.

PACHECO POND FIRE ROAD (.39 miles)
From Indian Valley Fire Road to Pacheco Pond
Intersections: Jack Burgi Trail (.11m), Waterfall Trail (.29m)

Pacheco Pond is a popular attraction, so this route to it is well-traveled.

Pacheco Pond F.R. sets off 15 yards inside the Preserve entry gate on the far (scoreboard) side of the lighted Indian Valley ball fields. A sign "Pacheco Pond Trail to Jack O'Burgi Trail" points the way left off Indian Valley Fire Road.

Pacheco Pond F.R. immediately climbs a short hill that tends to be muddy and slippery in winter. The first climb crests at 200 yards. Jack Burgi Trail begins here, rising to Waterfall Trail. The Fire Road drops another 200 yards to a gate and sign, "Pacheco Pond Fire Road to High Meadow Trail." Many users enter the Fire Road here, as it is a bit closer to the nearest parking.

Pacheco Pond F.R. now rises gently. Some 150 yards up is a fork. A sign points the way left for the start of Waterfall Trail, which makes a 1.6-mile semi-loop back to Indian Valley Fire Road.

The Fire Road enters an oak-bay woodland. The first tree encountered, on the left, actually appears to be a combined coast live oak and bay. You'll have to look carefully at the trunks to separate them.

A path goes right on the last uphill. The Fire Road ends at the dam that creates Pacheco Pond. On the left side of the dam is Waterfall Trail. (And also the start of High Meadow Trail, a route presently in too poor condition to describe separately.) The right side of the pond loop also meets Waterfall Trail, for a journey up into the heart of the Preserve.

Pacheco Dam, creating the pond, was built in November 1947, to provide a reliable water source for the 200 cows grazing what the Pacheco family called their 1,000-acre "Back Ranch." It was soon after stocked with bass and blue gill, emptied into the pond from milk cans. The earth fill dam is 25 feet high and 135 feet thick across the top. The pond has a surface area of about one acre, and can hold five million gallons of water. The dam was formally called "Tom Pacheco Dam," for one of the owners of the ranch. "Farm Pond" is another name.

A contemporary newspaper account described the pond's "clear water reflecting the heavy verdure of the hills." Now the pond and its denizens are being overrun by Brazilian waterweed (*Egeria densa*), a native of South America cultivated for aquarium tanks. (Someone apparently once emptied their aquarium here.) Volunteers have been working on Egeria's removal.

SUSAN ALEXANDER TRAIL (.59 miles)

From Waterfall Trail (two entries) to Hill Ranch Trail
Note: No horses

Well-wooded, up-and-down, Susan Alexander Trail adds to the loop options within the Preserve.

The route—called "The Alexander Trail" on signposts at either end—begins at the waterfall on Waterfall Trail. When arriving on Waterfall Trail from Indian Valley F.R., the creek must be crossed at the waterfall. (There is a second entry just higher on Waterfall Trail.)

The Trail starts steeply up through an oak/bay/madrone woodland. Most striking along the way are numerous large manzanitas (*Arctostaphylos manzanita*). Some lie prostrate, others rise eerily in twisted shapes. Their delicate blossoms begin to appear in December and are carpeting the Trail here by February.

The uphill eases a bit, setting a pattern of steep and gentle sections. The alternate entry branches back to Waterfall Trail. Native grasses hold their green all year. In winter, water flows in the canyon to the right.

The Trail reaches its highest point a quarter-mile in. There are limited views northeast over and through the madrones, which dominate here. Susan Alexander rolls along near its highest elevation. Views open to the northwest as well.

The Trail descends sharply over its final one-sixth mile. It ends when it meets Hill Ranch Trail at a switchback. Left, Hill Ranch Trail rises to Wildcat Trail, then the Preserve boundary with Hill Ranch. Right is a half-mile down to Indian Valley Fire Road, a loop option.

In 1996, the route was named for Susan Alexander, a local open space advocate.

WATERFALL TRAIL (1.63 miles)

From Indian Valley Fire Road to Pacheco Pond Fire Road
Intersections: Clark-Melone Trail (.01m), Susan Alexander Trail (.26m),
Jack Burgi Trail (.82m)

This is a long, deeply wooded, lovely Trail, well-used by Preserve regulars but little known by others. Most of the grade is gentle, making Waterfall Trail a good choice for a family hike.

Waterfall Trail runs as a semi-loop from the floor of the Preserve and both its ends are easily accessible. It will be described from the Indian Valley Fire Road junction, as it is much nearer the waterfall itself and has a less steep downhill.

The signed Trailhead is off Indian Valley F.R., .2 miles from the Indian Valley College side and .6 miles from the Indian Valley Road gate. The start is shared with Clark-Melone Trail, which rises left to Jack Burgi Trail.

Waterfall Trail enters woodland, and remains shaded and cool its entire length. In less than 25 yards, the Trail goes over a bridge. While this creek will be crossed seven times above, this is the only bridge. But the watercourse is near dry most of the year and, even in winter, only the next two fords might call for rock hopping. The Trail follows the creek's left bank for 200 yards, to the next crossing.

An alternate path runs to the right, closer to the creek. Other deer paths branch off as well. At one-quarter mile, Waterfall Trail encounters the appealing falls that gives it its name. The creek drops some 25 feet but flow is strong only during and after a good winter or spring rain. The rocks here can be slippery and wet, use caution.

Just above the waterfall, Susan Alexander Trail departs right and climbs to Hill Ranch Trail. A shortcut path to Alexander Trail, for those traveling on Waterfall Trail in the opposite direction, is passed 400 feet later.

This next stretch of Waterfall Trail is one of the more tranquil in the District, through bay and oak woods and far from any urban sights or sounds. The creek is

The orchard, one of the largest in the world, on the old Rancho de Novato land grant, c. 1900. (Courtesy, Dewey Livingston)

crossed and crisscrossed. A few sections are steep, but switchbacks help. Delicate wood rose (*Rosa gymnocarpa*) grows along the creek bank. In fall and winter you may see its reddish fruit, rose hips. A stand of gnarled manzanita is passed, whose pink-white, urn-shaped, flowers blossom here as early as mid-December.

At .8 miles, halfway through, Waterfall Trail reaches a crest at a junction. Left, Jack Burgi Trail drops to Pacheco Pond Fire Road. The seeming route right is unmaintained and very rough. There are views through the trees.

Waterfall Trail now descends easily over ten consecutive switchbacks. The woodland is a bit lighter. At a creek crossing, the smaller ferns goldback, polypody, and maidenhair grow in profusion. Goldback delights youngsters as pressing its underside against dark clothing leaves a clear imprint.

Waterfall then meets Pacheco Pond, another treat. Veer right to continue on Waterfall Trail. (Straight leads to the top of Pacheco Pond Fire Road). Cattails line the pond. Willows have been planted. At the far end is the dam that formed the pond in 1947. An overgrown path (High Meadow Trail) rises over the grassland to Montura Fire Road.

Waterfall Trail descends below the dam. The Trail ends .1 mile lower when it meets Pacheco Pond F.R. Continue on Pacheco Pond F.R., past the Indian Valley College ball fields, to Indian Valley F.R. to complete the Waterfall loop.

WILDCAT TRAIL (.45 miles)
From Buzzard Burn Fire Road to Hill Ranch Trail

Although the steep route south off the Indian Valley floor called Buzzard Burn Fire Road remains broad its full length, District field staff divides it into two sections. The lower one-third mile is maintained for vehicular access and is so designated a fire road. The section above the "No bikes" signpost is not cleared for vehicles and called Wildcat Trail.

Seventy yards above this signpost, Wildcat Trail passes under a PG&E power line (see Buzzard Burn F.R. above for an anecdote). The climbing is very steep.

Bordering the upper Trail are tall, twisted manzanitas (*Arctostaphylos manzanita*). "Medusa-like" is an apt description by one observer of a particularly convoluted shrub. Their bark peels, similar to the related madrones.

Wildcat Trail meets a junction and its highest point. The route straight ahead and up is posted as closed by the District for restoration. Wildcat Trail bends left. (The MCOSD signpost says "Hill Ranch Trail;" the word "To" should be added.)

Wildcat Trail continues in a madrone woodland. The tree canopy thickens ahead and there are a couple of easy creek crossings.

Wildcat Trail ends at Hill Ranch Trail at a wood fence, signed "Erosion Control, Please Keep Off," atop a grassy meadow. Left, Hill Ranch Trail drops three-quarters of a mile to the floor of Indian Valley. Right, it rises to a dead-end at the Preserve boundary with private Hill (H) Ranch.

KING MOUNTAIN

Size: 103.8 acres (in three parcels)   Elevation range: 120-640 feet

*It took three seasons to build the King Mountain loop trail. It was
truly a labor of love. I don't think there is a better place in Marin
to view the "Crown Jewel" of the County, Mt. Tamalpais, other
than from King Mountain. On many occasions, as I walked to
work in the morning, I marveled at the beauty of Mt. Tam
shrouded in fog like a white blanket. On other mornings, the
Mountain would be so crystal clear that you could seemingly
reach out and touch her. King Mountain remains close to my
heart. I grew up in this area. The loop trail hike is one of my
favorite walks in the District.*
— *John Aranson, Supervising Ranger*

IN 1869, Patrick King and William Murray bought 1,233 acres, including 780-foot-tall King Mountain, from the family of the late James Ross. The price was $4,500 in gold coins. The partners agreed to split the parcel with King getting the southern half, the future heart of downtown Larkspur.

King built a farmhouse by today's 105 King Street and ran a cattle and dairy ranch. In 1887, San Francisco land developer Charles Wright bought King's 600-plus acre ranch for about $21,000 and began subdividing. (The story is told is that Wright's English-born wife mistook lupine flowers for larkspur, so "mis-named" the town.)

In the 1930's, most of King Mountain passed into the hands of Adolph Tiscornia, a lawyer and astute land investor. He kept King Mountain strictly off limits while his goats grazed freely. Tiscornia died in 1967, age 82. The property passed to his granddaughter, Mary Tiscornia; his only child, Marine Capt. Edward Tiscornia, died at Okinawa in 1945.

In 1990, after years of negotiations, Mary agreed to sell 116 acres of the lower slopes to the County as a Preserve for $3,065,000, and to establish an open space easement over an additional 129 acres. (The first 15 acres of the future Preserve, the Lauterwasser parcel, had been acquired separately in 1988.) Tiscornia was given permission to erect four homes high on King Mountain. Funds for the purchase came one-third from the District, one-third from Larkspur's King Mountain Assessment District, and one-third from a challenge grant offered through the Beryl Buck Open Space Fund administered by the Marin Community Foundation.

In 1997, one family bought the entire private parcel atop King Mountain.

see map pages 52-53

CITRON FIRE ROAD (.59 miles)
From Cedar Avenue to King Mountain Loop Trail
Intersection: Vine Street Trail (.27m)

There are several "paper" streets on the southwest slope of King Mountain, part of a never-built subdivision. Citron Street is one; an unpaved road with no street signs or houses. Most all of it is now within King Mountain Preserve.

Citron technically starts off Willow Avenue. The opening 500 feet are unpaved, with a sidewalk, but outside the Preserve. Citron then meets Cedar Avenue (#1 Cedar is just to the right) in a circular, dirt area. There is some parking here but do not block the Fire Road gate or the turnaround for emergency vehicles. A fence with an MCOSD "King Mountain " sign marks the Preserve entry.

Begin a steady, moderately steep uphill. There is an impressive valley oak beside the Fire Road in 50 yards. Otherwise most all the trees, shrubs, and grasses are non-natives. Many of these aliens are being removed by local volunteers, the "Green Gorillas," as part of an ongoing fire-break program. The two largest eucalyptus trees were felled in 1998 but more remain upslope. Acacias, also an Australian import, add yellow color in February and March but also bring allergy woes to many. Broom is abundant, although less so after years of broom pulls. (But to the dismay of those pulling, non-native thistles, even harder to remove, are sprouting in broom's place.) There are also many plum trees, which still bear colorful blossoms and some fruit.

You may notice a sidewalk in the canyon below left. It is part of another "paper" street, Spring Lane. A hippie commune camped in the canyon during the 1960's and remnants of their stay can still be found. Across the canyon, at the end of Sycamore Avenue, stood the impressive 80-room Larkspur Inn (distinct from the Hotel Larkspur downtown). It was built in 1891 by Charles Wright, the man behind Larkspur's first subdivisions. The hotel burned to the ground in 1896. The Wrights then built their family home, called "Elfwood," on the hotel site. It too was destroyed by fire, in 1929.

At 250 yards, the Fire Road crosses a wet seep, one of several on the hillside. The Fire Road runs up alongside another spring to a bend left.

Around the bend, views open across San Francisco Bay, to Mt. Diablo. At the base of the next bend, Vine Street Trail cuts down left. It drops just under .1 mile (so not separately described) to Vine Street, where there is an MCOSD sign. Around the bend, the steep climbing eases. Views suddenly open to the north. A final wet patch—very muddy in winter—brings Citron Fire Road to a junction in the saddle between King Mountain (left) and Little King Mountain (right).

To the right, a broad road leads, in less than 200 feet, to an old basalt (blue rock) quarry. The rocks were crushed by a heavy metal ball dropped from a crane. Piles of rocks remain. The continuing path is choked by broom. There was also an unprofitable gold mine near here; old-timers can still locate the tunnel shaft.

Some 400 feet higher, the Fire Road bends left opposite a fence. (The continuation up is sometimes called King Mountain F.R., but is considered part of Citron F.R. here.) On the other side of the fence, a paved road drops left to the water tank and right 50 yards down to an MCOSD boundary fence above the Skylark Apartments and Skylark Drive.

Veer left and again steeply up. Citron ends some 250 yards higher, where King Mountain Loop Trail crosses. Blue MCOSD easement signposts mark the junction. The short stub of a fire road higher dead-ends at a private property fence.

There is some debate over the route's proper name, with Citron and Cedar Fire Roads both commonly used.

CONTRACTORS TRAIL (.46 miles)
From King Mountain Loop Trail to Larkspur Creek

Contractors Trail, signed "To Dawn Falls Trail," drops off King Mountain Loop Trail 200 yards, clockwise, from the Wilson Way connector and .4 miles, counter-clockwise, from the Ridgecrest Road access.

Just into the descent is a vista point, clear of trees, that offers one of the most breathtaking views of Mt. Tamalpais anywhere. Contractors continues down steeply through the hardwood forest.

In a quarter-mile is a clearing amid the madrone trees and coffeeberry shrubs. This was the site of a hippie encampment in the 1960's and many remnants are still evident. The blue blossoms of hounds tongue are now reclaiming the site.

The remaining descent is very steep, beneath usual MCOSD trail standards. Proceed with caution.

Contractors Trail meets Larkspur Creek. If it is flowing strongly, there is no option but to retrace steps. But most of the year the fording is an easy hop. Across is the clearing beside Dawn Falls Trail that once housed a sizable ladybird beetle, or ladybug (*Hippodomia convergens*), colony each winter. (Hence the Trail's alternate name, Ladybug.) They rode thermals here from the Central Valley in fall, overwintered on the foliage, then wafted back on wind currents in spring. But the site was disturbed a few years ago and the ladybugs have yet to return. Hopefully they will.

Fences and Barriers

Good fences make good neighbors. Sadly, this old adage bears considerable truth. Without fences and other barriers defining their boundaries, MCOSD lands would face a constant invasion from off-road motorized vehicles. Where MCOSD lands adjoin subdivisions, fences can often prevent encroachments (both purposeful and accidental) of landscaping or other residential improvements. On lands where horses or cows are pastured (as at Horse Hill and Mt. Burdell), fences also protect springs and riparian vegetation from trampling hooves. So while fences and boundaries may run counter to the concept of open space, they are necessary measures to protect the wildland resources under MCOSD's charge.

This route has long been called Contractors Trail by District field staff, as some contractors cut it on their way to a project.

KING MOUNTAIN LOOP TRAIL (1.95 miles)
Around King Mountain
Intersections: Connector to Wilson Way (.85m), Contractors Trail (.96m), connector to Ridgecrest Road (1.36m)

Although MCOSD-owned easements across privately owned land are not generally described in this book, exceptions are made here for King Mountain Loop Trail and for connecting Contractors Trail. The lovely Loop Trail is well-used as a destination route. Its construction helped ease concerns about possible development on the pristine top of King Mountain. And there is a chance that the land surrounding the Loop may someday pass into the District.

The nearest auto access points to King Mountain Loop Trail are 100 yards distant each, at the tops of Wilson Way in Larkspur and Ridgecrest Road in Kent Woodlands. Wilson Way is a narrow, winding street with limited parking. The Ridgecrest Road entry may change if the summit parcel is developed. So the Loop will be described, clockwise, from its crossing of Citron Fire Road (described above).

A pair of blue trail easement signposts stand at the Citron F.R./Loop Trail intersection. Go left, past the massive old oak. In 50 yards a clearing makes for a splendid vista point, including a perspective of most all of Larkspur.

This part of the Loop Trail trends slightly up. Oaks, madrones, and other broad-leaf trees line the way, but not densely enough to block views. Striking is the tree-covered north wall of Corte Madera Ridge across Baltimore Canyon.

A bit of down leads to a blue-signed (easement) junction. Left is the connection to Wilson Way. Right is an old summit route, over private property and closed.

There is a second, signed junction 200 yards later. The steep half-mile route left and down, signed "To Dawn Falls Trail," is Contractors (or Ladybug) Trail. When Larkspur Creek is high and unfordable, it is a dead-end.

The Loop Trail now begins its most noticeable uphill grade. A final rise leads to the connection left to Ridgecrest Road. Cross to continue on the Loop Trail.

Steps and railings drop the route through the wetter, more densely wooded, north side of King Mountain. Redwoods line the way. A few are massive, having somehow escaped the logging that claimed all the rest of the stand here some 150 years ago. Also in the forest are California nutmeg trees (*Torreya californica*), in the Yew family. They have sharp needles and a seed that bears a resemblance to nutmeg, hence the name. It is hard to believe this quiet woodland is but a mile, as the crow flies, from Magnolia Avenue. All too soon, the idyll, and the Loop, are over with a return to Citron Fire Road.

King Mountain Loop Trail was designed and built by MCOSD Senior Ranger and "Trailsman" John Aranson in 1994-95, soon after the easement was acquired. It follows old routes with some sections, particularly on the north side, completely new.

LITTLE MOUNTAIN

Size: 220.7 acres   Elevation range: 80-806 feet

Nature's wild citizens still weave their way over the rolling hills. Rather than roads, there are trails. Rather than cars, trucks and buses, there are deer, foxes, and hawks. Rather than clustered houses, obstructing fences and more pavement, there are open meadows, flowing streams and shady oak trees. I see, hear and feel all of this from our backyard, day and night. It never fails to move me and always reminds that the view, the land, and most importantly, our community, would be different.
— *Tina Torresan, Open Space Intern and Open Space Neighbor*

LITTLE MOUNTAIN, 806 feet tall, was long part of historic E Ranch. It remained pastoral grazing land for some 100 years. Efforts to acquire the south slope as public open space began when plans surfaced for a development, called Doe Hill, on the slide-prone hillside. Bob Ritter was one of several local "citizen heroes" in the fundraising effort. In 1995, the property was bought for $895,000 from the Sanchez family, donors of Verissimo Hills Preserve just to the south. Funds came equally from the District's Proposition 70 bond fund, the Marin Community Foundation, and the 471-parcel Little Mountain Open Space Assessment District. An additional $450,000 was raised for slide repairs.

Landslides, mudflows, and other forms of earth movement are not uncommon occurrences in Marin County, and examples can be found throughout MCOSD lands. Look for "rippled" (as opposed to smooth) slopes, crescent-shaped scarp, bulging "toes," and tilting fence posts or trees. In certain locations (the south side of Little Mountain is a good example) the MCOSD has taken steps to protect nearby homes from natural but potentially catastrophic earth movement. You may, for example, notice white pipes protruding at an angle out of a grassy slope. The pipes are evidence of a landslide repair and were installed for the purpose of inspecting and cleaning out a drainage system that functions to "dewater" a slide-prone area. Elsewhere, you may notice a gabion wall built across a canyon. These walls, constructed of rock-filled, wire mesh baskets, are meant to stop debris flows originating higher up the slope. Because landslides are natural phenomena, the MCOSD does not repair them in remote areas far from homes.

DOE HILL FIRE ROAD (.80 miles)

From Kathleen Drive to end of Center Road
Intersection: Little Mountain Trail (.05m)

Doe Hill Fire Road runs some 20 yards from a line of residential backyards, but is important nonetheless. For one, it is the main route through the Preserve. For another, it was designated in 1998 as part of the Bay Area Ridge Trail, planned to one day completely circle the Bay Area. For now, it is a link in an eight-mile, public route from Olompali State Park to the top of Indian Tree Preserve.

The eastern end of the Fire Road is off Kathleen Drive, a small street reached via Trish Drive and Center Road. At the entrance, and at other parts of the route, you will see evidence of the District's slope stabilization and drainage improvement work. Note that one of these gabion walls is slightly leaning, having done its job of holding back a sizable debris flow from the upper canyon.

In 100 yards, Doe Hill Fire Road meets the new Little Mountain Trail. It is the extension north of Bay Area Ridge Trail for hikers.

Doe Hill Fire Road veers left. It then very gently rolls the rest of its length alongside the homes of Trish Drive, Taurus Drive, and Daryl Avenue. Paths left between the houses are signed, alternate entries (in east-west order, between 98-100 Trish, 112-120 Trish, 35-25 Taurus, 50-60 Daryl, then 90-100 Daryl).

The view right is dramatic; the grass-covered, southern slope of Little Mountain. Its highest point is at elevation 806 feet, more than 600 feet above. Adjacent right are cone-shaped metal structures, drop inlets for runoff, behind small earthen debris dams. Residents recall mud flows from the hill crossing neighboring streets in the wet winter of 1982 and at other times.

Doe Hill Fire Road bends left to exit at the end of Center Road. Ahead is the fence demarcating lands of the North Marin Water District. To continue on the Bay Area Ridge Trail, veer left to the Stafford Lake Trail entry gate across Center Road. It passes just below Verissimo Hills Preserve, then drops to cross Vineyard Road, where the Bay Area Ridge Trail continues in Indian Tree Preserve.

LITTLE MOUNTAIN TRAIL (.30 miles)

From Doe Hill Fire Road to O'Hair City Park/Reuben Kaehler Memorial Trail
Intersection: Connector to Michele Court (.12m)
Note: Entire length part of Bay Area Ridge Trail (no bicycles)

This is one of the District's newest trails, opened in 1998. It is part of a new public link, and section of the Bay Area Ridge Trail, between Mt. Burdell and Big Rock Ridge.

When entering Doe Hill Fire Road from Kathleen Drive, Little Mountain Trail branches off right, signed, in 100 yards. At press time, the area is undergoing re-seeding and other restoration work; the hillside is prone to sliding.

Little Mountain Trail climbs very gently past lovely old valley oaks. At 250 feet is another MCOSD sign. The Trail crosses a creek bed over two new bridges. At each, gabion slide protection dams block debris flows from upstream.

At the first big switchback left, a 100-foot path right connects to Michele Court, an alternate entry. A huge coast live oak has branches "resting" on the ground, a not unusual characteristic of the species. More climbing brings a view of Mt. Burdell.

The Trail leaves Little Mountain Preserve into City of Novato's O'Hair Park at an MCOSD signpost at .3 miles. The continuing route, an additional .3 miles, enters a forest of mostly bay laurels. There is a gradual descent, aided by switchbacks, through the deep and cool woodland.

Little Mountain Trail ends at broad Reuben Kaehler Memorial Trail in the heart of O'Hair City Park. Straight ahead, Novato Creek flows through the canyon. To the right is the park's Sutro Avenue entry. To the left is Novato Boulevard and, across it, San Marin High School. A trail easement, part of the Bay Area Ridge Trail, will cross school grounds and connect with Dwarf Oak Trail in Mt. Burdell Preserve.

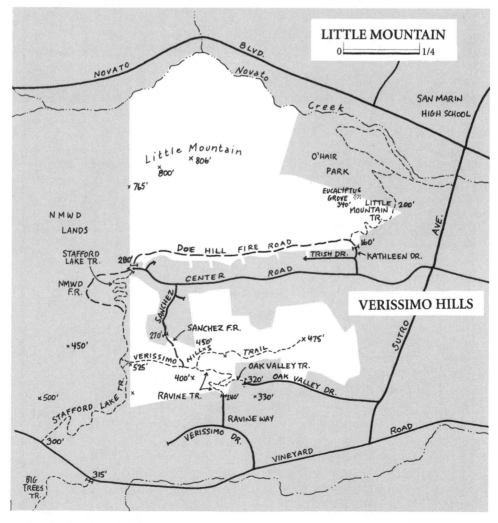

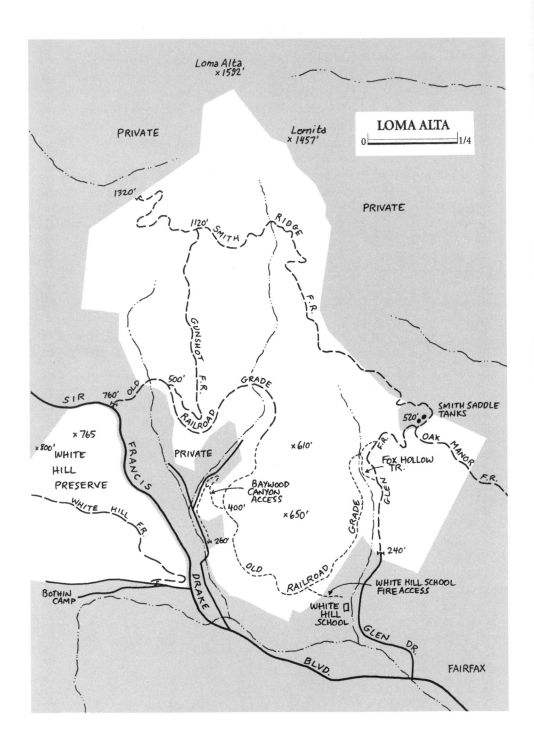

LOMA ALTA

Size: 484.7 acres   Elevation range: 240-1,560 feet

*Every October, the wind-swept mountain puts me up to the
challenge. I accept, and run the footrace known as "Run to the
Heavens." From San Domenico School in Sleepy Hollow, all the
way up to the peak of Loma Alta. A mere four miles uphill! I get
delirious, hot and short winded, but upon reaching the summit, I
know why I challenged myself to run the race again. The unprec-
edented views of Marin and beyond!*
— Brian Sanford, Supervising Ranger

AT 1,592 FEET, Loma Alta ("tall hill" in Spanish) is the fourth highest peak in Marin,
after Mt. Tamalpais (2,571'), Big Rock Ridge (1,887'), and Pine Mountain (1,762').
No paved roads cross it, necessitating a 25-mile drive to fully circle it.

Loma Alta has been dairy and beef cattle grazing land since Mexican days,
when it was divided among three huge *ranchos*. It remains, save for portions of its
lowest edges, undeveloped, pastoral grassland.

The MCOSD Preserve, the first and only public section of Loma Alta, covers
much of the southern slope. Most of the Preserve was previously part of the Smith
Brothers' Ranch, and earlier the Chambers Dairy. (Today's Smith Ranch Road in
northeast San Rafael was on a separate Smith brothers holding.) The lowest part of
the Preserve includes the original route of the historic North Pacific Railroad. Note
that the Preserve extends up to within yards of the Loma Alta summit, but the
highest point itself is on private property.

The initial 34.7-acre parcel within Loma Alta Preserve, the Trestle Glen tract,
was gained in 1988 as part of a subdivision dedication. The adjacent 252.4-acre
Blosser-Tarrant parcel was purchased a year later for $970,000. In 1990, the 117.6-
acre Fox Hollow area was purchased from developer James Helfrich for $1,116,000.
Equal one-third contributions came from the District, the Marin Community Foundation, and from Proposition 70 bond proceeds. Such joint financing was also used
for some other smaller Preserve additions.

FOX HOLLOW TRAIL (.13 miles)

From Glen Fire Road to Old Whites Hill Grade
Note: Open to bicyclists

When traveling Glen Fire Road from the Glen Drive trailhead, Fox Hollow Trail
sets off left in .2 miles, after a short downhill. Do not confuse Fox Hollow Trail with
the path that runs below and parallel to Glen Fire Road from the entry gate to here.

A dense canopy of bay trees keeps Fox Hollow Trail cool and fragrant throughout the year. Some 100 yards in is a concrete foundation. Even old-timers debate its origin— remnant from an old deer hunters camp, foundation of a chicken coop, and other guesses. Ten yards later, Fox Hollow drops to the first of two easy creek crossings.

At 150 yards, the Trail edges by a magnificent bay. Although many of its several trunks are fallen, the tree is very much alive. Indeed, some of the downed trunks send up perfectly vertical fifty-foot branches.

Fox Hollow Trail passes an old barbed wire fence, then ends when it meets a newer fence at a narrow section of Old Whites Hill Grade. It is 150 yards right back to Glen F.R. and two miles left on Old Whites Hill Grade to Gunshot Fire Road.

The gray fox (*Urocyon cinereoargenteus*) is native to Marin and can still be seen in many of the District's preserves.

GLEN FIRE ROAD (.55 miles)

From Glen Drive to Oak Manor F.R. and Smith Ridge F.R.
Intersections: Fox Hollow Trail (.18m), Old Whites Hill Grade (.33m)
Note: Glen Drive passes White Hill Middle School, drive with caution

Glen Fire Road is the most-traveled route within the Loma Alta Preserve. It sets off from an MCOSD gate at the north end of Glen Drive, off Sir Francis Drake Boulevard. Adequate trailhead parking is part of Glen F.R.'s appeal, as is its easy terrain.

The first two trees left are impressive valley oaks, followed by a bay laurel, then a buckeye. Buckeyes and valley oaks are leafless in winter.

Glen Drive and this opening section of Glen Fire Road were part of the original North Pacific Coast Railroad route, opened in 1873. There was a stop on today's Glen called Roy's, for the nearby house on John Roy's 773-acre ranch.

Glen F.R. enters a forest of mostly bay laurels, which keeps it pleasantly cool even on torrid summer days. A path runs parallel to the Fire Road left along the canyon floor, and there are entries to it.

It was at .2 miles, where the Fire Road bends left and makes a short drop to Fox Hollow Trail, that the old railroad track veered right (or straight)—the bed still evident—to enter a tunnel. This tunnel looped under the slope that Glen F.R. climbs ahead, meeting what is now called Old Whites Hill Grade to the left (west).

The downhill brings a view of the Loma Alta summit at the far end of the Preserve. At the base, Fox Hollow Trail leaves left, a shortcut to Old Whites Hill Grade.

Glen Fire Road rises. Where it leaves the tree canopy into grassland, the Fire Road passes over the western end of the old tunnel. Old Whites Hill Grade, here trail-width, sets off left, going two miles to Sir Francis Drake Boulevard.

Glen F.R. makes a big bend left and keeps climbing. Two huge water tanks, sometimes called the Saddle Tanks for their placement in the dip, come into view. Water from Nicasio Reservoir, via the San Geronimo Treatment Plant, is stored here. You may hear water flowing beneath wood coverings right.

The Fire Road ends at its junction with Oak Manor Fire Road, which goes right to Oak Manor Drive in Fairfax, and with Smith Ridge Fire Road, which circles the water tanks on a long climb up Loma Alta.

GUNSHOT FIRE ROAD (.75 miles)
From Old Whites Hill Grade to Smith Ridge Fire Road
Note: Part of Bay Area Ridge Trail

Gunshot Fire Road is very steep. But that steepness makes it a quick route to high on Loma Alta. It is also part of a long loop option, with Smith Ranch F.R., Glen F.R., and Old Whites Hill Grade, over the entire Preserve. In 1999, Gunshot was dedicated a segment of the Bay Area Ridge Trail.

Join Gunshot by traveling one-sixth of a mile on Old Whites Hill Grade from Sir Francis Drake Boulevard. (Some maps, such as Thomas Bros., label the connection with Drake as part of Gunshot as well.) An MCOSD-signed gate marks the base of the ascent. The climb starts steep, and remains unrelentingly so.

Views are the highlights of Gunshot Fire Road. Save for a grove of laurels just over halfway up, the Fire Road is basically treeless, permitting broad, ever-widening vistas over the grass and coyote brush. You may see cows grazing the privately owned upper slopes.

At one-third of a mile, between a bend left and then one right, a path known as Shortcut Trail cuts right, into the grassland. At .6 miles, the Fire Road passes an area of slumping—the steep slope is unstable—and there is significant erosion.

Gunshot ends at its junction with Smith Ridge F.R. at elevation 1,130 feet. Signs on a post indicate that the Bay Area Ridge Trail continues up left on Smith Ridge F.R., which dead-ends a half-mile above at the Preserve boundary. Right, Smith Ridge F.R. drops to the water tanks atop Glen Fire Road.

OAK MANOR FIRE ROAD (.37 miles)
From Glen Fire Road to Preserve's east boundary

Oak Manor Fire Road sets off east from the top of Glen F.R., at the two Saddle Water Tanks. This intersection is also the base of Smith Ridge F.R., which sets off circling the big tanks.

The opening uphill is stiff but offers broad views over the grassland. Baccharis shrubs line the way, with a few oaks. In late spring, thousands of clovers border the route. In late summer and early fall, red penstemon flourish on the large outcropping of graywacke (mudstone) midway along the route.

The Fire Road's crest is at .3 miles. A path crosses a cleared plateau to the right. The panorama is outstanding, particularly given the modest elevation of 700 feet.

Oak Manor F.R. begins to descend. A broad path branches right. It is some-

time called 7-Eleven Fire Road because it rolls (entirely on private property) all the
way to the 7-Eleven convenience store on Sir Francis Drake at Oak Manor Drive.

Another 25 yards later is the MCOSD boundary gate, with a Loma Alta sign.
The remaining 250 yards of the Fire Road, to the junction of Oak Manor Drive and
Manor View Road, are on private property although the District is in the process of
acquiring a public trail easement over it.

OLD WHITES HILL GRADE (2.02 miles)
From Sir Francis Drake Boulevard to Glen Fire Road
Intersections: Gunshot F.R. (.17m), Baywood Canyon Access F.R.
(1.03m), White Hill School F.R. (1.42m), Fox Hollow Trail (1.94m)
Note: Full route open to bicyclists

This is one of the more historic routes in all Marin County, and one of the oldest in
the District that can be accurately dated. It follows the track traveled by the North
Pacific Coast Railroad from 1874 to 1904 from a stop called Roy's to the White Hill
Tunnel. (The eastern section remained in use until 1933.) Today, the route has a
few decidedly un-railroad-like, narrow, up-and-down, sections over creeks—these
were former trestle sites. Also gone are the two tunnels, a short one by the east end
of the route and the main 1,300-foot one under White Hill at the west end.

The Sacramento Union of September 5, 1874, had an account of the building
of this section of the rail line (quoted in Bray Dickinson's book, *Narrow Gauge to
the Redwoods*):

"The track of the narrow-gauge was laid in the little tunnel on Monday. This
is about two miles from the big tunnel under White's Hill. There are three trestles
yet to build to span the approaches to the tunnel. The work for a long distance up
the hill is of a very difficult and expensive character, and the spectator is filled with
astonishment that the enterprise has ever been prosecuted over such difficulties....As
soon as it is finished, a train will be run from Saucelito to that point....[The work
was done by] an army of Chinese coolies, wearing basket-like hats and hair in long
pigtails, who hacked at hillsides with pick and shovel. Charges of giant powder sent
rocks flying while wheelbarrow and horse-drawn dump carts carried dirt and rubble
to make fills."

Dickinson also describes how the trains then negotiated the tough east-west
(Fairfax-San Geronimo) grade:

"Little engines—with huge funnel-shaped stacks—puffed and snorted, stut-
tered, and spun driving wheels as they dragged loads up long grades and in and out
of ravines. The trains would climb as much as three-fourths of a mile to gain 100
yards in elevation. They would roll over creaking trestles, through smoke-filled tunnels, and around hairpin curves where passengers saw their locomotive headed in
an opposite direction from themselves. Such was White's Hill, heaviest grade on the
road, with a rise of 121 feet to the mile.

"A 1,300 foot tunnel at the top [actually, at elevation 528 feet in the saddle

The tallest and longest of several railroad trestles, erected in 1874, along today's Old Whites Hill Grade. The trestles spanned canyons that today's travelers must negotiate. (Courtesy Fairfax Historical Society)

between Loma Alta] of White's Hill was constructed on a steep grade which made it difficult for a laboring engine completing the climb. To make matters worse, the water dripping from springs made the track wet and slippery. Many long trains became stalled inside the tunnel while a sweating fireman furiously stoked his fire to get up more steam. The passengers nearly suffocated from the smoke."

Old Whites Hill Grade today begins (it is described west-east because the west end is auto-accessible) at a green, non-MCOSD gate on the north side of Sir Francis Drake Boulevard, across from milepost 9.61. Drake's crest is .1 mile above. The opening hundred yards of steep downhill, graded after the railroad era as part of a water pipeline project, are along a public trail easement.

The actual old railroad portion begins by the hill's base. Nearby was the east portal of the first White Hill Tunnel. (A few years ago, a railway buff found the long-sealed and overgrown entrance.) Trains from Fairfax entered the tunnel here while trains from the stop west, called Lilliard's, exited. The 1,300-foot tunnel went under today's Sir Francis Drake Boulevard.

The Fire Road bends over the creek, the head of Baywood Canyon. Just ahead, Gunshot F.R. sets off left behind the MCOSD gate. Gunshot climbs very steeply to Smith Ridge F.R. The Grade runs by the boundary line between MCOSD land north and the private Baywood Canyon development below.

Not far ahead is the first view of Tam's summit. The stables of Baywood Canyon is below. There are several signs of the water pipeline buried below the Fire Road.

A half mile in, at another creek crossing, a fire road drops right, out of the Preserve, and dead-ends at a new home atop Hunter Creek Road in Baywood Canyon. (A new trail connection may one day be built.) The Grade now drops as well; the track here, and at other dips at creek crossings ahead, was carried over trestles long removed. Look over the edge of the Grade throughout to see old benched-out areas that were footings for trestle supports.

At the base of the downhill is Fairfax Falls, the destination of many visitors. A bench is conveniently placed for viewing the falls. In winter, Fairfax Creek drops some 25 feet before going under the roadbed. During times of heavy rains and high water, the falls may split into three sections. Buckeyes are the deciduous trees between the bench and falls, with many bay laurels to the side and above. Wildflowers, such as Indian warrior and Indian paintbrush, grow in profusion beside the falls in spring, as does poison oak. Bobcats have been seen drinking here.

There is another up-and-down formerly bridged by trestle. Coyote brush narrows the way. The downhill steepens as the Trail enters a bay laurel forest. At the low point, a stream crossing, a 25-yard connector from Baywood Canyon comes in right.

A steep up leads to a return to level terrain and the old track bed. The Grade leaves the tree canopy. Non-draining, clay soils keep this area waterlogged and puddled well into spring.

Just past a road cut about a mile in, the Grade meets a three-way junction. There are several MCOSD boundary signposts; the junction itself is just outside the Preserve. To the right is a 250-yard fire road down to Baywood Canyon. Pipeline Fire Road bends left. There are several MMWD structures. The Fire Road immediately re-enters the Preserve.

Next comes a .4-mile level section. A path drops right. The next junction is with White Hill School Fire Road, which enters on the right. It drops 400 feet to a Preserve entry behind White Hill Middle School. To the right of the junction, a path dead-ends at the top of the knoll. Bend left.

The next half mile of the route meanders through a lovely laurel woodland. It is wider than most trails, narrower than standard fire roads. Several rivulets are crossed. On the far side of a wood fence right is one end of Fox Hollow Trail. It goes along the canyon floor back to Glen Drive.

Just ahead, the route passes the western portal of an old railroad tunnel, long blocked and now also covered with poison oak (see Glen Fire Road). The final steep uphill was not part of the old grade. The route climbs, narrow and rutted, to upper Glen F.R., which goes left up to the water tanks, right to the Glen Drive entry gate.

In 1904, the railroad completed a bypass of much of the old route. It ran over the valley floor, via a long trestle, toward the new Bothin Tunnel, lower in elevation (and therefore substantially longer) than the older White Hill Tunnel. The Bothin Tunnel exited White Hill in Woodacre, at the head of today's Railroad Avenue. Some of the trestle foundations for this newer route are still in place, such as opposite 6 Deer Creek Court in Baywood Canyon. The new routing cut 2.1 miles of slow westbound climbing off the original track, which was then abandoned. Portions of the old grade were later incorporated into an MMWD pipeline project.

SMITH RIDGE FIRE ROAD (1.77 miles)
From intersection of Glen and Oak Manor Fire Roads at Saddle Water
Tanks to Preserve's northwest boundary
Intersection: Gunshot F.R. (1.30m)
Note: Section above Gunshot F.R. part of Bay Area Ridge Trail

Smith Ridge Fire Road offers sensational views. Although unrelentingly uphill, its grade is reasonable by most users' standards.

Smith Ridge Fire Road begins at a three-way junction beside the two giant Saddle Water Tanks. Here, Glen F.R. drops to Glen Drive in Fairfax, Oak Manor F.R. climbs west to the Preserve boundary, and Smith Ridge F.R. rises beside the tanks, almost circling them. Some 200 yards up, the Fire Road passes an MCOSD gate signed "Loma Alta." This gate once marked the District boundary before adjacent land was acquired and added to the Preserve.

The views are already impressive and do nothing but broaden over the long journey up. Mt. Tamalpais joins the vista just above the gate and remains in constant sight. A few yards higher, views open out to San Pablo Bay.

The Fire Road meets a fence line; the private land beyond is the Triple C Ranch, accessed through Sleepy Hollow. At .3 miles, an extremely steep path rises right.

Invasive star-thistles line the Fire Road edge and cover the grassland. Tarweed, also yellow, is one of the native floral holdouts. Baccharis, a native shrub which often returns to local grasslands after grazing ceases, is clearly multiplying. Oaks dot the hillside. Before a half-mile of climbing, the San Francisco skyline joins the ever-widening panorama.

The Fire Road crosses feeders of Fairfax Creek, which nurture groves of bay laurels and oaks but also produce mud in winter. The Richmond-San Rafael Bridge becomes visible about 1.1 miles up. The last stream crossing before Gunshot Fire Road is of Fairfax Creek itself.

At 1.3 miles, Smith Ridge F.R. meets the top of Gunshot F.R. Gunshot drops steeply three-quarters of a mile to Old Whites Hill Grade and can be part of a loop with Smith Ridge. Although Smith Ridge F.R. ahead presently has no public outlet, it is worth taking for the even more expansive views. The upper section was dedicated and signed as a segment of the Bay Area Ridge Trail on May 17, 1999. The fragrant mint pennyroyal lines the route in summer.

Seven hundred yards above Gunshot, in the middle of a final big bend left, a path departs right toward the 1,457-foot top of Lomita, a subsidiary peak of Loma Alta. In another 150 yards, views suddenly open west and northwest, out to Point Reyes. A few yards higher, Smith Ridge F.R. reaches the Preserve boundary.

Signs note this as the end of public land and of the Ridge Trail segment. Across the barbed wire fence are privately owned, off-limits, dairy ranches. This fence marks one of Marin's oldest boundaries, between three Mexican land grants.

The Smith brothers were previous owners of the ranch the Fire Road traverses. A sensational 1945 headline in the *San Rafael Independent* read "3,500 lives lost in Fairfax fire," but was referring to a blaze in the Smith brothers' henhouse.

LOMA VERDE

Size: 379 acres   Elevation range: 80-640 feet

*Just west of Highway 101, Loma Verde allows for a quick trek
into the wilderness. This section of the Big Rock Ridge area offers
uncommon beauty, solitude, neat views, and ample hiking.
Whether you walk the oak-lined fire roads or explore the deep
canyons, you'll agree Loma Verde is special. — Ari Golan, Ranger*

LOMA VERDE ("green hill" in Spanish) covers the northeasternmost slope of Big
Rock Ridge, running down to the residential development near the Highway 101
corridor. It is grouped, with several other Preserves, in the District's Big Rock Ridge
management unit.

Much of the Loma Verde area was the dairy ranch of Tony Bettencourt. In
1945, the Army planned on evacuating the area's few residents as soon as it finished
construction of a new ammunition depot on what is today's Marin Country Club
golf course. Work on the depot began in May 1945, and was 25 percent complete in
early August, when the war ended. Residential development of Loma Verde began
in 1956, with construction of 500 homes priced in the $25-$40,000 range.

PEBBLE BEACH FIRE ROAD (.92 miles)

From Pebble Beach Drive to Chicken Shack Fire Road
Intersection: Winged Foot F.R. (.46m)

The Fire Road atop Pebble Beach Drive connects the Country Club residential district with Big Rock Ridge, which is visible from the opening gate. Pebble Beach F.R.
straddles the Loma Verde-Ignacio Preserve boundary and its lone intersecting route
and nearest loop partner, Winged Foot F.R., is described in the Ignacio chapter.

Climb through the light oak and bay woodland, idyllic from within yards of
the start. At 100 yards, there is a bend right and fine views open to the southeast.
You may hear the sounds of children playing at nearby Loma Verde Elementary
School.

Views are added north, to Mt. Burdell and beyond, as the Fire Road steadily
gains elevation. An old barbed wire fence, remnant of ranching days here, is passed.
Local boy scouts have removed many other such fences.

The moderately steep climb eases briefly at .3 miles. Black and valley oaks are
prominent here, with coast live oaks more prevalent elsewhere along the way.

A steeper pitch leads to a junction (at elevation 600 feet) with Winged Foot

see map on pages 118-119

F.R., which drops one-third mile to the top of Winged Foot Drive, west of Pebble Beach Drive. This is exactly the halfway mark of Pebble Beach Fire Road.

Similar-looking young madrones and tree-like Parry's manzanita shrubs stand at the intersection, so it is a good place to compare them. Both are early bloomers, with their delicate flowers sometimes out in December. Both also have peeling bark. But although Parry's has among the largest leaves of any manzanita species in California, they are still only one-half to one-third the size of typical madrone leaves.

The upper half of Pebble Beach F.R. is rolling and generally less steep. Indeed, the first downhill of the route comes 100 yards above the Winged Foot junction. In the saddle ahead, there is a view right to the prominent house whose driveway is skirted by Halloween Trail. Very steep Halloween offers another loop option with Pebble Beach F.R. (with Chicken Shack F.R. the connector on top and residential streets as the loop's base).

An easy up and down leads to another saddle sheltering several black oaks. The uphill steepens. The Fire Road passes rounded wood posts left and right and ends 50 feet later at its junction with Chicken Shack Fire Road. A rusted, four-foot metal post stands at the otherwise unmarked intersection.

Streets bordering Marin Country Club have names related to golf; Pebble Beach and Winged Foot are two of America's most famous courses.

POSADA DEL SOL FIRE ROAD (.34 miles)

From Posada Del Sol to Via Escondida Fire Road
Notes: No parking by base of Fire Road;
adequate parking lower on Posada del Sol

This Fire Road sets off behind the uppermost apartments in the Posada West development atop Posada Del Sol. An MCOSD gate marks the start. The first 200 feet are paved, and very steep. Turn back for a perspective of the newly developed Hamilton Air Force Base site.

The first tree left beyond the pavement is a coast live oak. The second is a valley oak which for several years now has harbored a European honeybee colony in its trunk, some five feet up. Pass quickly.

Ahead is a sylvan landscape of mostly oaks. A brief easing of the uphill gives way to another very steep section. A couple of bends brings a nice framing of Mt. Burdell. At .3 miles, the Fire Road passes under a power line (the same one encountered along several other District routes in the Novato area), and over a gas line.

Fifty yards later, after a downhill, Posada Del Sol F.R. ends at its junction with Via Escondida F.R. Uphill leads to Chicken Shack Fire Road. Down leads to Via Escondida in the Ignacio section of Novato.

"Posada del sol" means "home of the sun" in Spanish.

VIA ESCONDIDA FIRE ROAD (.54 miles)
From Via Escondida to Chicken Shack Fire Road
Intersection: Posada Del Sol F.R. (.29m)

This Fire Road sets off from an MCOSD gate atop Ignacio's residential Via Escondida (Escondido on some maps). There is a junction in 100 yards, by a yellow fire hydrant. The left option enters a meadow, where paths drop to additional signed Preserve entries from Calle de la Selva and Arboleda. Continue right and up.

In another hundred yards, Via Escondida F.R. half-circles an older, fenced, green water tank bordered by eucalyptus trees. The climb continues with nice views over the oak-dotted grassland. The towers atop Big Rock Ridge can be sighted.

At .3 miles, Via Escondida F.R. meets Posada del Sol F.R., which rose from the top of the Ignacio street of that name. Again, veer right. A power transmission line is just below left.

After a bend, the uphill steepens. That just means more chances to pause and turn for the views over the oak savanna. Peaks in Sonoma and Napa counties are often visible.

Just 100 feet from its end, Via Escondida F.R. meets the top of a path known as Los Robles Trail (descends to private property). The final yards to Chicken Shack F.R. are downhill. A mile left is the base of Chicken Shack at Alameda del Prado and Clay Court. Right, Chicken Shack goes more than two miles to Big Rock Ridge Fire Road. The nearest loop option off Chicken Shack, which involves some street travel, is with Pebble Beach F.R., .8 miles right.

Escondida means "hidden" in Spanish.

LUCAS VALLEY

Size: 737.3 acres   Elevation range: 200-1,600 feet

*As our field office is next to this Preserve, sometimes I get my
after work exercise by hiking the slopes of Lucas Valley. Some days
the wild turkeys gobble at me on my way. Other times the wild
flowers and native grasses spread their generous beauty to
encourage my motivation. Scampering lizards, singing birds, and
even bobcats have been my partners during these excursions. The
best reward for making it to the ridge is the expansive view from
Mount Burdell to the Golden Gate. It is here you unexpectedly
discover just how much wild land exists, and feel like you really
earned this glorious view by making it to the top.*
— *Chris Bramham, Chief Ranger*

THIS PRESERVE covers the grassy slope of central Big Rock Ridge, which rises so
steeply and dramatically above Lucas Valley. The Preserve's initial 285 acres were
acquired from the Nunes family in 1975, financed by a 25-year neighborhood bond
issue approved by 95.8 percent of local homeowners. Additional acreage came in
1986, '89, '90, and '96, all part of development approvals along the floor of Lucas
Valley.

Most all the rest of Big Rock Ridge's upper southern wall between the Preserve and the Highway 101 corridor is also open to the public. Immediately east of
the Preserve are County lands managed by the Lucas Valley Homeowners Association. Further east are lands of the Marinwood Community Services District, then
the MCOSD's Pacheco Valle Preserve.

The properties west of Lucas Valley Preserve are private ranches, several owned
by movie mogul George Lucas (including the former Bulltail Ranch, now Skywalker
Ranch). But the name Lucas Valley dates to around 1860, when John Lucas lived
here on his 7,600-acre ranch.

BIG ROCK RIDGE FIRE ROAD (1.00 mile)

From Chicken Shack Fire Road & Queenstone (Big Cat) Fire Road
to MCOSD boundary
Intersection: Luiz Fire Road (.75m)

Big Rock Ridge Fire Road runs exactly one mile from its eastern end to a private
property gate. There may not be a mile of fire road with more sweeping views anywhere else in Marin County off Mt. Tamalpais.

Big Rock Ridge Fire Road begins west from the junction of Big Cat
(Queenstone) and Chicken Shack Fire Roads, at the southernmost edge of Pacheco

Valle Preserve. (Some maps show Big Rock Ridge F.R. beginning to the east, at the Ponti Fire Road intersection; the distinction is somewhat arbitrary.) Only Big Cat is signed here. A long climb is required to reach this intersection from anywhere accessible by car, so serenity is assured from the start. Visitors will have already enjoyed sensational views on the way up; these vistas will now expand with even more uphill.

The start is by the junction of three Mexican land grants; Rancho San Pedro Santa Margarita y Las Gallinas to the south, Rancho San Jose to the north, and Rancho Nicasio to the northwest. The Fire Road skirts the boundaries between Preserve lands, open-to-the-public lands of the Marinwood Community Services District and of the County-owned Lucas Valley Homeowners Association on the south, and private lands west-northwest. The Fire Road is actually only wholly within the MCOSD for the quarter-mile west of Luiz Fire Road.

A hundred yards in, a path rises left to the top of a view knoll (at 1,444 feet elevation), then rejoins the Fire Road. The snow-capped Sierra can sometimes be seen from here in winter. Highway 37 into Napa County is clearly visible left. Mt. St. Helena, 4,434 feet, looms highest on the northern horizon, just to the right of 1,558-foot Mt. Burdell.

Oaks and madrones adjoin the route on a brief downhill. Then, at one-third mile, a rutted, narrowed fire road drops to the left. It deteriorates lower on its way toward Rubicon Drive in Lucas Valley.

Keep climbing. The views above the grassland and through the oaks are stunning and, save for a short section in a road cut, continuous.

Big Rock Ridge meets Luiz Fire Road at one of the most spectacular spots anywhere within the District. The elevation is 1,493 feet and, particularly on a sparkling winter day, the views are all-encompassing. Luiz F.R. drops 1.6 miles, without an intersection, to the floor of Lucas Valley.

Next is a quarter-mile uphill section of Big Rock Ridge F.R. There are no through options but it is certainly worth the journey as even grander vistas are gained. All of Novato's high ridges, many protected as MCOSD Preserves, stretch below.

The public portion of Big Rock Ridge Fire Road ends at a gate at the boundary between Lucas Valley Preserve and private ranches ahead. The elevation here (1,600 feet) is the highest within the Marin County Open Space District. The highest point on the entire ridge (1,887 feet) is on private property, topped by a pair of communication towers.

LUIZ FIRE ROAD (1.59 miles)

From Creekside Drive to Big Rock Ridge Fire Road

Luiz Fire Road is highly visible from the south; the cut of its grade—long and unrelentingly steep up towering Big Rock Ridge—stands out clearly against the grassland. This sight intimidates many visitors while beckoning others. In summer, the unshaded Fire Road absorbs the full heat of a southern-facing slope. But on a cold, clear, winter day, you'll be treated to one of the best experiences within the District.

Luiz Fire Road departs behind an MCOSD gate in the middle of Creekside Drive, across from the tennis facility. There are two other nearby, signed, Preserve entries (both without trails), off Red Cedar Court and further east off Creekside.

The first 200 yards, up to the water tower, are paved. Coast live oaks dot the hillside and the Fire Road passes beneath a large one a quarter-mile in. A bit ahead, the grade briefly eases and you can see a lone oak that will passed higher on the route.

Thousands of poppies dot the grasslands. The striking, four-petaled, purplish-red flowers of farewell-to-spring (*Clarkia amoena*) become abundant, appropriately, late in May.

The views will hold any visitor rapt. The Bank of America building in San Francisco is first visible a half-mile up. At .7 miles, the Fire Road bends right, leaves the tree line (for a while), and views of Mt. Tam begin. The lookout atop Mt. Barnabe appears above .87 miles. At a bend right one mile from the start are the first sightings of the very top of Big Rock Ridge, with its communication disks. The first sweeping San Francisco Bay view comes at 1.14 miles and the first glimpse of Mt. Diablo just after.

Oaks begin reappearing alongside the Fire Road at around 1.4 miles. The campanile on the campus of the University of California in Berkeley will be visible on clear days. Basically all of Marin between Tam and Big Rock Ridge spreads below. At 1.5 miles, Carquinez Strait is visible. On the clearest of days, you may spot the snow-capped Sierra summit ridge, some 160 miles east, through this gap in the Coastal Range. A bit higher, a sweeping North Bay vista is gained. Far below is the huge boulder, also called Big Rock, adjacent to Lucas Valley Road.

Luiz Fire Road ends when it meets Big Rock Ridge F.R. at a stunning vista point, one of the best in Marin, at elevation 1,493 feet. Suddenly, Novato and the rest of Marin north of Big Rock come into view. Mt. St. Helena stands directly behind much nearer Mt. Burdell. The wild-looking northern slope of Big Rock Ridge drops sharply below.

Big Rock Ridge F.R. goes left a quarter-mile to a gate marking private property and there is no public through-passage to the ridge's highest point (elevation 1,887 feet). Right, Big Rock Ridge F.R. descends along the ridge line and meets Big Cat (Queenstone) F.R. in three-quarters of a mile. A loop can be made with Big Cat, but the stretch from the base of Queenstone back to Creekside Drive is a long one on residential streets.

The Luiz family held ranches on both sides of Lucas Valley Road for generations. An old sign advertising the fresh milk of the Lucas Valley Dairy is still painted onto the wall of the Lagunitas Deli in the town of Lagunitas.

see map on pages 118-119

MAURICE THORNER MEMORIAL
Size: 32.83 acres   Elevation range: 320-523 feet

*It's a real joy for me when I'm working on the trail in this
preserve and see a school group enjoying themselves taking a
hike.*   — *Carl Szawarzenski, Ranger*

THIS SMALL Preserve forever protects a ridge in the heart of the San Geronimo
Valley. It was acquired by the District in 1981 from Daniel & Cecelia A. Thorner
and Robert & Nancy Jean Thompson as part of a development dedication. It was
named in honor of Daniel's father, Maurice, who had died the year before at age 84.
Maurice Thorner practiced law for some 60 years and was best known for battling,
unsuccessfully, against the internment of Japanese-American citizens during World
War II.

More than 100 years ago, the Mailliard family operated a low-yielding, money-
losing, gold mine on the slope just south of the Preserve line.

THORNER RIDGE TRAIL (.67 miles)
From Lagunitas School Road to ridge crest
Note: Please do not park in school lots during school hours

The Trailhead is on the north side of Lagunitas School Road, at the near edge of the
school parking lot and just beyond a private driveway.

Thorner Ridge Trail rises over the grassy hillside. There may be muddy stretches
in winter. Several switchbacks keep the grade easy. In spring, blue-eyed grass, a common flower in grassland throughout Marin, grows in particular profusion here. So
too does checkerbloom (*Sidalcea malvaeflora*), with its striking, many-petaled, pink
flowers. In June, the striking yellow mariposa lily (*Calachortus luteus*) is the star.

At .2 miles, the Trail enters an unexpected and delightful woodland. Oaks,
madrones, and bays are the main trees, hazel the common shrub, and ferns abundant. Unfortunately, so too is poison oak. The old madrones are huge, but several
have recently fallen.

Above the woodland, Thorner Ridge Trail rolls gently through grassland.
Coyote brush, and boulders, dot the hillside. To the northeast is Dickson Ridge, the
upper part of Roy's Redwoods Preserve. Behind, the lookout tower atop Mt. Barnabe
is a landmark. San Geronimo Golf Course stretches below.

At .55 miles, the start of a new trail (there was a work party on National Trails
Day, June 12, 1999) sets off left. It is planned to slope down to the privately owned
golfer's bridge over Nicasio Valley Road and connect to Roy's Redwoods Loop Trail,
but work is stopped at press-time.

Thorner Ridge Trail then climbs to its high point, elevation 523 feet. The

Marin County Fire Department, headquartered in nearby Woodacre, calls the area "John's Hill," for John Costa, who was burned here in a late 1970's fire. Atop the crest is a 10-foot pole, which may or may not be in the shape of a cross. The original cross, placed by the late Pastor Fredericksen (a close friend of the Thorners) of the San Geronimo Valley Presbyterian Church just below, was damaged first by a storm, then by vandals. The summit also holds a "Miwok prayer bench," an extrusion of igneous rock.

This crest marks the end of Thorner Ridge Trail and steps must be retraced.

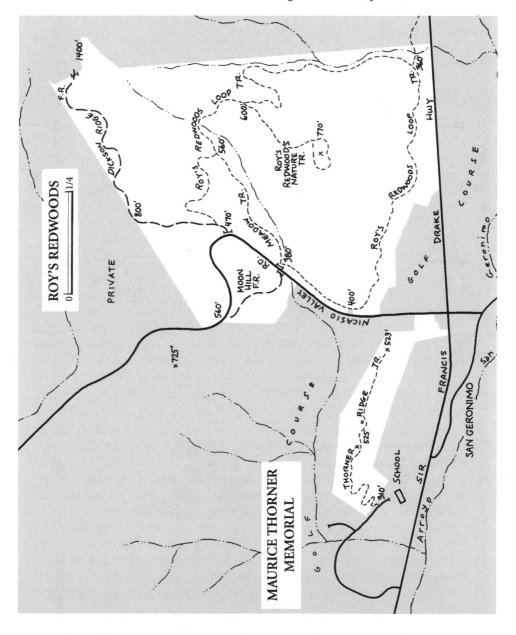

MT. BURDELL

Size: 1,558 acres   Elevation Range: 40-1,520 feet

*Walk through the coast live oaks with their bright green leaves
and cumbersome limbs until you reach the forest of black oak
and buckeye. The air is fragrant with new spring blossoms, which
bees are eagerly working. Walk until you reach the open sea of
grasses bobbing in the wind and hiding the creatures of the night.
Feel the warmth of the sun on your skin. Walk until you reach the
water's edge of the pond up on the mountain. Be still. It is here
you can feel the life of living things.*
        — *Mischon Martin, Resource Ecologist*

MT. BURDELL, 1,558 feet in elevation (oddly, the Preserve is also 1,558 acres in size),
is the fifth highest peak in Marin County. The MCOSD Preserve covers the southern face of Burdell, above the homes that rise to about the 300-foot level. Immediately east is the new Buck Center for Aging Research. Olompali State Historic Park
covers the northeast slope of Burdell, adjoining the Preserve along the summit ridge.
The northwest and west slopes of Burdell are privately owned dairy ranches.

    Galen Burdell (1828-1906), for whom the mountain and Preserve are named,
was born in New York. He began practicing dentistry at age 19. In 1849, Burdell was
visiting an uncle in Brazil when word of the discovery of gold in California arrived.
He promptly joined, as dentist, the San Francisco-bound ship *Duxbury* (it later
went aground off Bolinas on what is now called Duxbury Reef). Burdell set up an
office in the City, invented a tooth powder, and became wealthy.

    In 1863, Burdell married Mary Augustina Black (1845-1900), half his age. She
was the daughter of James Black (1810-1870), a resident of Marin since 1834, the
County's first tax assessor, judge, and coroner. By then, Black was Marin's second
largest landowner, behind only the Shafter brothers at Point Reyes.

    As a wedding gift, Black gave Mary the Olompali Rancho and 800 head of cattle.
(Olompali was the name of a major Miwok village, inhabited continuously, or nearly
so, for 8,000 years. The Miwoks called the mountain Olompais. Mt. Olompali was
another early name.) Black had bought the rancho in 1852 for $5,200 from Jose Camilo
Ynitia, the last Miwok *haipu* (headman) and only native American to have received a
land grant in Marin. (Ynitia was also the only native American in northern California to win legal title before the Land Commission). Ynitia's adobe, the oldest surviving building in Marin, still stands, in poor condition, at Olompali.

    But disaster struck four months after the marriage. Black's wife Maria died
under anesthesia in Burdell's dental chair. James Black never forgave Galen. In 1866,
Black remarried, to the widow (also named Maria) of Ignacio Pacheco, one of Marin's
original land grantees. Weeks later, Black secretly changed his will, disinheriting
Mary, his only surviving child, and leaving most of his sizable fortune to his new
wife and her children.

The Burdells had two children, James and Mabel. Galen used much of his own money in improving the Rancho and turning it into a showplace. Mary rewarded him with a 950-acre parcel at the head of Tomales Bay, upon which he founded the town of Point Reyes Station. Burdell also reclaimed extensive marshland east of today's Highway 101.

James Black, broken by his wife's death and having taken to drinking, died in a fall from his horse in 1870. After Mary was read the will, she tore off her father's signature with her teeth and swallowed it. The signature was never found and Mary was arrested. But there were copies.

Mary sued to break the will, saying her father had been deranged by alcohol and under undue influence of his new wife when it was changed. The case was among the most celebrated of the era. The first three trials in San Rafael all ended in hung juries. Running low of potential jurors in sparsely populated Marin, the trial was moved to San Francisco. In 1874, the jury basically found for Mary, breaking the will. Black's lands were divided between her and Mrs. Pacheco Black, each receiving more than 5,000 acres, and raising Mary's holdings to some 20,000 acres.

The Burdells held on to thousands of Marin acres (such as private Black Mountain) as grazing land for decades. Both Mt. Burdell Preserve and adjacent Olompali State Park, which was acquired with MCOSD assistance, are legacies. In 1969, when Olompali was leased to a hippie commune, a fire destroyed the Burdell mansion (which had included Ynitia's adobe). Ruins are still visible in the State Park, along with the Burdell family gardens and other plantings.

In 1962, the Sunset International Petroleum Company bought the 2,165-acre Freitas C Ranch, much of which is today's Preserve, for $3 million. They planned a new city of 4,000 homes called Greenborough. Only 254 acres were to be left as greenbelt. The somewhat scaled down development, renamed San Marin, began a year later. The upper section of the property was ultimately absorbed by Exxon. (Note that it was Gulf Oil's plan to place thousands of homes in the Marin Headlands' Gerbode Valley that helped trigger formation of the GGNRA.)

In 1977, the District bought 1,439 acres on Mt. Burdell, mostly from Exxon, but also parcels from the Nunes family and others. The OSD contributed just over $1 million and San Marin's Community Service Area No. 25 an additional $700,000.

ANDREAS COURT FIRE ROAD (.33 miles)
From Andreas Court to San Marin Fire Road

This Fire Road rises from between #11 and #17 Andreas Court, a street off San Andreas Drive. Pass through quietly. There is an MCOSD-signed gate at the start. The first 100 feet are paved.

At 50 yards, beyond the last house on the left, is a fork. The route straight up dead-ends 100 yards higher at an off-limits, fenced, telephone facility. Andreas Court F.R. veers left.

The Fire Road rises steadily over the Preserve border area, which is kept clear

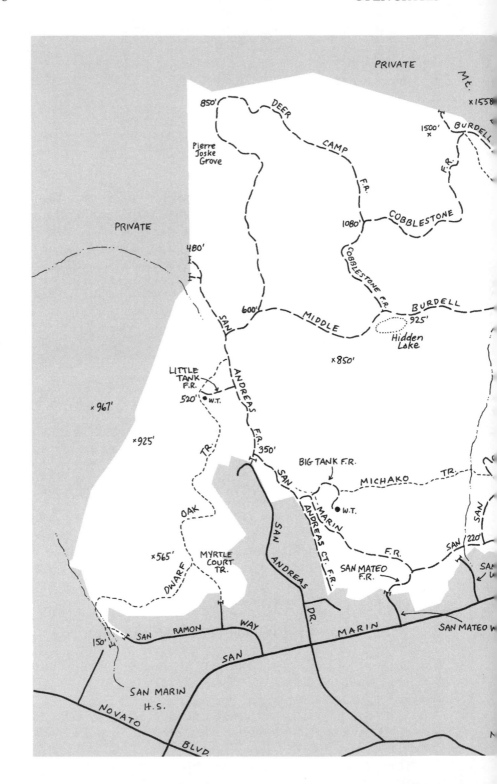

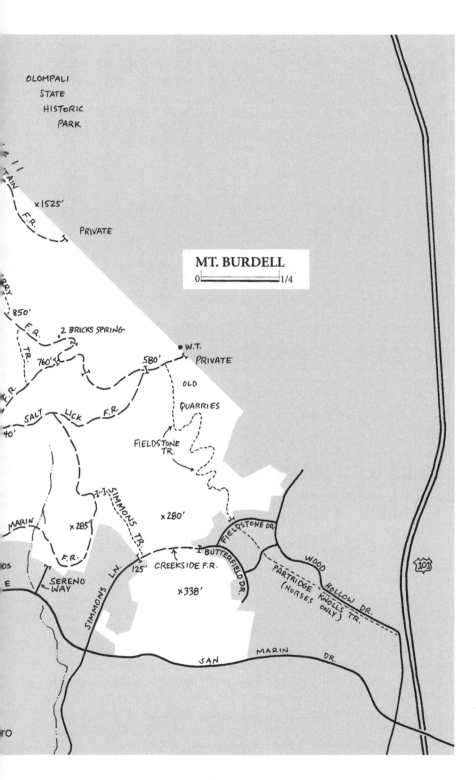

OLOMPALI
STATE
HISTORIC
PARK

x1525'

PRIVATE

F.R.

MT. BURDELL
0 ‖━━━━━━━━━━‖ 1/4

850'

F.R.

2 BRICKS SPRING

760'   580'   ● W.T.
                PRIVATE

OLD

QUARRIES

SALT LICK F.R.

FIELDSTONE
TR.

40'

SIMMONS TR.

MARIN   x285'   x280'

FIELDSTONE DR.

F.R.

125' CREEKSIDE F.R.   BUTTERFIELD DR.   WOOD HOLLOW DR.

SIMMONS LN.

PARTRIDGE KNOLLS TR.
(HORSES ONLY)

SERENO
WAY

x338'

101

SAN   MARIN   DR.

for fire protection. There are no trees or shrubs, only invasive thistles above the grassland. Left are the backyards of homes on San Domingo Way. Right is a drainage culvert for some of the several springs—10 by one count—off Burdell's southern slope. About 100 yards up, look beyond the fence to spot an old, green-topped, stone structure which also catches spring flow.

Andreas Court F.R. ends at its junction with San Marin Fire Road. Left leads to the Preserve entry atop San Andreas Drive. The next junction right is with Big Tank Fire Road.

BIG TANK FIRE ROAD (.15 miles)
From San Marin F.R. to Big Tank fence

Big Tank F.R. is a short, dead-end route. It sets off from San Marin F.R., about a quarter-mile from the San Andreas Drive entry. Since there is also a prominent "social" path here, which cuts directly across the grassland east to Michako Trail, the junction can be somewhat confusing.

Big Tank F.R. makes a wide arc right through the grassland. Valley oaks dot the hillside above. A spring-fed stream runs under, through a culvert.

Big Tank F.R. meets Michako Trail, which heads to San Carlos Fire Road. Big Tank F.R. drops 70 yards to end at the fence surrounding a North Marin Water District tank. It is called Big Tank in comparison to the second NMWD "Little Tank" within the Preserve, due west.

BURDELL MOUNTAIN RIDGE ROAD (.56 miles)
From Cobblestone F.R. and Old Quarry Trail to northeast boundary
Notes: Paved; part of Bay Area Ridge Trail (all users)

A trip across Burdell Mountain Ridge Road is reward for the climb up the mountain. Ridge Road itself is fairly level, and the views spectacular.

There are just two routes to Burdell's summit ridge from within the Preserve; Cobblestone Fire Road (part of the Bay Area Ridge Trail) and very steep Old Quarry Trail. Both meet Burdell Mountain Ridge Road at the same point, its western end, elevation 1,480 feet. From this junction, a paved option goes 150 yards west to the fence surrounding a telecommunication facility owned by AT&T. Also, a path rises north to the rock wall on the summit ridge. The 1,558-foot summit of Burdell is just outside the Preserve boundary to the northwest, topped by another antenna.

Burdell Mountain Ridge Road heads east, just below the true ridge top. The summit area is capped by andesite rocks from ancient volcanic flows. In the 1870's, Chinese laborers used these rocks to build the four-foot high wall along the summit ridge. All the rocks were hand-placed, fitted without mortar. The ridge line was the historic boundary between the Olompali and Novato ranchos.

The views are breathtaking. All of Novato, which covers the valleys between Burdell and Big Rock Ridge, stretches below. Mt. Tamalpais and Bolinas Ridge rise behind Big Rock. San Francisco, the Bay, Oakland, and Mt. Diablo are all visible. Turn to see Stafford Lake, Black (Elephant) Mountain, and the dairy lands of northwest Marin, into Sonoma.

Halfway in, a route branches left to a fence and gap in the rock wall. On the other side of the fence and ridge is 700-acre Olompali State Historic Park. (The MCOSD contributed half of the $700,000 used to purchase Olompali in 1977.) In 1999, the poor connecting fire access into Olompali was improved to become the northern extension of the Bay Area Ridge Trail (for hikers and equestrians). Olompali is rich in history, from its days as a major Miwok village, to a battle during the Bear Flag Revolt producing that conflict's only fatality, to its rock musician and hippie commune days in the 1960's. The main entrance to the park is off Highway 101 (southbound direction only) two miles north of the Atherton/San Marin exit.

The southeast face of Burdell drops precipitously below. The steep slope was caused by a massive landslide within the last few thousand years.

Ahead, broken rocks on both sides of the Road are remnants of a quarry (the main pit is still discernible). In *Novato Township*, Mae Ungemach writes of quarrying on the west slope of Burdell in 1888: "Patrick Gallagher's crews were up on Mt. Burdell earning $4 to $5 a day cutting out blocks for cobblestones to be used in the streets of San Francisco. The blocks of stone were cut out, hauled by wagons from the top of Mt. Burdell to Black Point, then shipped by schooner and barge to San Francisco."

Beyond is a sensational vista point. The Road descends into light woodland. The public portion of Burdell Mountain Ridge Road ends at a private property fence ominously signed, "Keep Out, Bull Pasture." There is a lovely view over the Petaluma River out to the Napa ridges.

COBBLESTONE FIRE ROAD (.99 miles)

From Middle Burdell F.R. to Burdell Mountain Ridge Road/Old Quarry Trail Intersection: Deer Camp F.R. (.35m)

Cobblestone is the lone Fire Road to Burdell's summit from within the Preserve. The only other route up is extremely steep Old Quarry Trail.

Cobblestone rises from Middle Burdell F.R. at a signpost by the west end of seasonal Hidden Lake. Large coast live oaks border the Fire Road, with an open grassy area on the right. The uphill steepens. The route is very rocky.

The views, already impressive, expand further at the first bend right. By 500 yards, the grade eases slightly. Look behind Big Rock Ridge to see the tip of Tam peeking over.

The Fire Road enters a grove of oaks and bays. It meets the top of Deer Camp F.R. (part of the Bay Area Ridge Trail), which drops left back down to Middle Burdell Fire Road for a lovely loop option. Cobblestone brings the Ridge Trail (all users) higher.

All three of Tam's peaks are now visible. So too are the mountains of Sonoma County. At one-third mile above Deer Camp F.R., the vistas rapidly expand to San Francisco Bay, then over all Novato. There is also a dramatic view of Burdell's steep southeast face plunging down to the Fireman's Fund complex by Highway 101.

A shortcut path veers off right. It will rejoin 200 yards higher. Between, another shortcut path goes left; it too returns, in 250 yards. A half-mile up from Deer Camp F.R., the telecommunications tower atop Burdell comes into view.

Cobblestone F.R. ends on the summit plateau area at a vista point and four-way junction. Left, a paved road goes to the AT&T tower. Right, Old Quarry Trail drops precipitously to Middle Burdell F.R. for a loop option. Between them, paved Burdell Mountain Ridge Road heads east to a dead-end. Burdell quarries provided cobblestones to pave San Francisco's streets.

CREEKSIDE FIRE ROAD (.19 miles)
From Simmons Lane to Butterfield Drive

The extreme southeast tip of Mt. Burdell Preserve extends to San Marin Drive, providing a permanent open space break. Creekside Fire Road crosses that tip of the Preserve and connects two residential areas.

From the MCOSD gate at the north end of Simmons Lane, veer right on to flat Creekside Fire Road. Simmons Trail also sets off here, uphill behind the cattle gate.

Creekside F.R. is never far from homes. But the oak-studded hillside above, and the creek right, make for pleasant passage nonetheless. The creek is bordered with rushes, snowberry shrubs, and willow, buckeye, and oak trees.

The Fire Road passes a gate and exits onto Butterfield Drive in the new Partridge Knolls subdivision. (This one-fifth mile connection between residential districts for walkers is some two miles for those driving.) The next street is Fieldstone Drive. Take it 100 yards left to Fieldstone Trail, which rises to Middle Burdell F.R.

DEER CAMP FIRE ROAD (1.45 miles)
From Middle Burdell Fire Road to Cobblestone Fire Road
Notes: Entire length is part of Bay Area Ridge Trail (all users)

A trip up or down Deer Camp Fire Road on a cool, clear day is one of the choicer treats in all the District. The entire route is gently graded, through a classic California oak setting, with sweeping views. Several special places along the way all but demand long rest stops.

Deer Camp F.R. rises from Middle Burdell F.R., one-fifth mile in from San Andreas F.R. Deer Camp takes the Bay Area Ridge Trail from Middle Burdell up to Cobblestone Fire Road.

Deer Camp climbs gradually over a lovely, mature, oak savanna. Valley oaks,

Hidden Lake, off Middle Burdell Fire Road. (David Hansen)

bare in winter, and rounded coast live oaks (a monarch presides to the left some 50 yards in) dot the grassland. Mt. Burdell is specifically cited as a place to view oak woodland in the book *Oaks of California*, and it's easy to see why. Also present are huge, old bay trees and a particularly massive one, 400 yards in, is of record-caliber size. There are broad views over pastoral hills south and west.

At .4 miles, a fence left encloses Pierre Joske Grove from cattle that graze here in winter. The signed entrance is a hundred yards ahead. Just inside this entry was the site of an old deer hunting camp, where the day's catch would be prepared. Remnants of the camp, begun by Samuel Freitas on this portion of the old C Ranch, are still evident.

The Grove is a most inviting place to sit or lie in the shade of an oak or bay. The grass carpet is a rich green here in late winter. There is a portable toilet (summer only) and hitching posts and troughs for horses. Pierre Joske was General Manager of the Marin County Open Space District from 1973 until his retirement in 1983. Sixteen of today's Preserves were acquired all or in part during his tenure. By a 1994 resolution of the MCOSD Board of Directors, the old deer camp site was renamed in his honor.

Beyond the Grove's fence, the Fire Road bends right and begins to run below Burdell's imposing summit ridge. There are impressive rock outcroppings above. At .8 miles come the first glimpse of Mt. Tamalpais; the tip of East Peak pokes up as a pyramid on the southern horizon. Not far ahead, by a huge bay tree on a knoll to the right, there is another Tam view. This too is an appealing spot to linger. Higher still, all of Novato is visible. Bolinas Ridge is first glimpsed beyond a saddle of Big Rock Ridge.

Almost 1.2 miles into the climb is the first downhill, a short one. The prominent telecommunications complex high on Burdell suddenly seems close. The Fire Road runs level through lovely grassland.

Deer Camp F.R. ends at its junction with Cobblestone F.R., which is signed "To Summit." Cobblestone carries hikers, bikers, and equestrians on the Bay Area Ridge Trail to near the top of Burdell.

DWARF OAK TRAIL (1.49 miles)

From San Andreas F.R. to San Ramon Way (planned to Novato Boulevard)
Intersection: Myrtle Place Trail (.95m)
Notes: Entire length part of Bay Area Ridge Trail (hikers, equestrians);
through Sensitive Wildlife Area (no dogs)

This is a long and lovely Trail over classic California oak savanna. Dwarf Oak is also a segment of the Bay Area Ridge Trail, part of a new public connection between Mt. Burdell and the District's Little Mountain and Indian Tree preserves to the south.

Dwarf Oak Trail begins .4 miles up San Andreas F.R. from the San Andreas Drive gate in an area called the "Bowl." Go left. Bay Area Ridge Trail hikers and equestrians coming from the opposite direction (upper Burdell and Olompali) may follow Dwarf Oak, while bikers continue on San Andreas F.R.

One hundred feet in, the Trail passes through a gate to enter a Sensitive Wildlife Area. Dogs are not permitted within any of the District's such areas, which harbor particularly sensitive habitats.

This early section of Dwarf Oak Trail is often very muddy in winter. Oaks, planted by volunteers as part of a restoration program, grow within protective casings on the hillside beside the Trail. A short rise leads to a view over Novato, to Highway 101, and beyond to San Pablo Bay. The rest of the long route is gently rolling, mostly downhill.

At 200 yards, the Trail descends into a stream canyon watering the deepest woods of the route. Just beyond some boards over wet areas, a connector path goes left. It runs 40 yards to Little Tank F.R., and some visitors use Little Tank as an alternate entry. Due to the exposure of volcanic rock and shallow, stony soils, the coast live oaks above and below here are shrub-like "dwarfs," smaller than mature oaks elsewhere in the Preserve.

The woodland lightens. Views open to the top of Mt. Burdell. The pattern is set for the next mile; rolling in and out of light woodland and over grassy oak savanna, with long views. On the ridge west are the redwoods of Ship's Mast atop Indian Tree Preserve, and the towers on the high point of Big Rock Ridge.

At .8 miles, Dwarf Oak passes through another gate and into a delightful grove.

The first tree left is a valley oak, the second a buckeye; both lose their leaves in winter. The Trail drops over a stream crossing. One hundred yards after Dwarf Oak Trail re-enters grassland, Myrtle Place Trail branches left. It drops to the edge of the Preserve, then over an easement to Myrtle Place at San Ramon Way.

The grassland ahead is rich in wildflowers. Blue-eyed grass, brodiaeas, mallows, buttercups, linanthus, and mules-ears are just some of the more colorful ones. Well above, San Marin High School students chalk the current graduating class year in huge numbers. The Trail approaches the line of houses along the Preserve's southwest boundary but arcs away, extending the pleasant journey.

The final section of Dwarf Oak meets the construction area for a new (1999) development called Novato Chase. (Local residents rejected an opportunity to assess themselves to buy the parcel, then called Brookside Meadows, as open space.) Veer left of the tree-lined creek to the signed exit/entry at the end of San Ramon Way. Dwarf Oak Trail (and with it, the Bay Area Ridge Trail) will ultimately run longer, through San Marin High School grounds to Novato Boulevard. Across is O'Hair Park and connection to Little Mountain Preserve.

FIELDSTONE TRAIL (1.16 miles)
From Fieldstone Drive to Middle Burdell Fire Road

Fieldstone Trail starts between 473 and 477 Fieldstone Drive. The trailhead sign notes "To Two Bricks Spring;" although it is Middle Burdell Fire Road, which Fieldstone meets, that actually passes the spring. Opposite Fieldstone Drive at the entry gate is a blue MCOSD easement sign for Partridge Knolls Trail (equestrians only in lower section).

Less than 50 yards in is a cattle gate; be sure to close it as there is seasonal grazing here. The initial climb is steep; higher, switchbacks ease the grade.

The Trail crosses a bridge. Impressive old oaks dot the adjacent hillside. There are views west to the District's Indian Tree and Little Mountain Preserves. East, the vista extends across Highway 101 (which, unfortunately, can be heard as well) to Rush Creek Preserve, the Petaluma River, San Pablo Bay, and beyond.

At .8 miles, Fieldstone Trail meets jumbled masses of broken rock. A path leads to a former quarry, apparently in business in the 1950's. The andesite rock found here was used in widening Highway 101 through Novato and for other projects. Andesite is an extrusive rock, originally molten within volcanoes or fissures. It has more silica than the closely related, abundant lava rock, basalt. (There is another quarry site higher, on Burdell Mountain Ridge Road. The Novato Historical Society also refers to an earlier quarry on the west side of Burdell, from which San Francisco's paving stones were cut.)

Above the quarry, Fieldstone Trail passes through a pleasant woodland. A meadow nurtures some planted fruit trees, survivors of an earlier era. A path veers right; continue left/straight. There is another delightful meadow, this time on the right.

Fieldstone Trail ends at its signed junction with Middle Burdell Fire Road. It is 100 yards left to Salt Lick F.R., one-third mile to San Carlos F.R., and a half-mile to Two Bricks Spring. Right, it is 100 yards to the Preserve boundary fence. This was also the boundary between the Olompali and Novato land grants.

LITTLE TANK FIRE ROAD (.14 miles)
From San Andreas Fire Road to the Little Tank
Intersection: Dwarf Oak Trail (.12m)

This is a short route, used to service the water tank at its end. It has a limited role as a shortcut to Dwarf Oak Trail from the Preserve's San Andreas Drive entry.

When climbing San Andreas F.R. from San Andreas Drive, Little Tank F.R. sets off left in .2 miles. It immediately passes through a gate. Inside is a Sensitive Wildlife Area, so off limits to dogs.

The route rises moderately steeply through a charming oak/bay woodland. Near the North Marin Water District tank itself, at a signpost, a 40-yard connector goes right to Dwarf Oak Trail. Right on Dwarf Oak leads back to San Andreas F.R. Left is a winding journey to Mt. Burdell Preserve's southwest tip.

MICHAKO TRAIL (.50 miles)
From Big Tank Fire Road to San Carlos Fire Road

Michako Trail plays a part in several loop options. It sets off east from Big Tank F.R, .08 miles from Big Tank's junction with San Marin Fire Road. (A slightly shorter social path to Michako has been worn in from the Big Tank-San Marin Fire Road intersection.)

An easy down leads to a crossing of a seep. An old stone structure here collected spring water coming out of the hillside. On the other side is a magnificent valley oak.

Another muddy seep is crossed. At near a half-mile, Michako goes over a more sizable creek. A pair of great horned owls have recently nested in the trees here. The Trail goes through a cattle gate and hikers' stile.

Michako ends at San Carlos Fire Road, which goes up left to Salt Lick F.R. and Middle Burdell F.R., and right down to San Marin F.R. Note the scores of acorns that have been firmly embedded in the valley oak at the junction. Many acorn woodpeckers contribute nuts to this "granary tree," which may then be removed by all members of the local acorn woodpecker population.

Michako is the Coast Miwok word for deer. A Miwok midden, indicating a long-used camp, was found near the Trail. Miwok petroglyphs have also been identified on Mt. Burdell.

MIDDLE BURDELL FIRE ROAD (2.00 miles)

From San Andreas Fire Road to Preserve's northeast boundary
Intersections: Deer Camp F.R. (.20m); Cobblestone F.R. (.71m);
Old Quarry Trail (1.20m and 1.26m); San Carlos F.R. (1.58m);
Salt Lick F.R. (1.89m); Fieldstone Trail (1.94m)
Note: Section between San Andreas F.R. and Deer Camp F.R.
is part of Bay Area Ridge Trail

This long Fire Road crosses the west-east width of the Preserve. It's a favorite of visitors, running just high enough to offer broad views and also passes appealing woodlands.

Because San Andreas Drive is a popular entry into the Preserve, most users join Middle Burdell F.R. on its western end, .6 miles up off San Andreas F.R. (A well-used but environmentally dubious shortcut to the Middle Burdell-Deer Camp F.R. junction departs San Andreas 200 yards earlier.) This end is also lower in elevation than the eastern side. Go right and begin a steady uphill. This opening section is an all-user segment of the Bay Area Ridge Trail.

The first intersection, in one-fifth mile, is with Deer Camp F.R., which carries the Bay Area Ridge Trail left, higher on the mountain. Look behind for a vista of pastoral northwest Marin, including 1,532-foot Hicks Mountain and the irrigated fields of Grossi Ranch on Burdell's northwest slope. In winter, you may see Holsteins grazing beside the Fire Road. To the right, a fence encloses a Sensitive Wildlife Area from cows.

At .71 miles, Cobblestone F.R., signed "To Summit," rises left. To the right is Hidden Lake, a two-acre, landslide-related, sag pond. (Some say it was created by the 1906 Earthquake, others say the quake reduced it in size.) Certainly, the pond was once deeper, even used as a water source for a school at Burdell's base and by

---

Bay Area Ridge Trail

The Bay Area Ridge Trail is a planned 400-plus mile, multi-use (hikers, bicyclists, equestrians) route around San Francisco Bay. It too uses existing routes, and all parts of the trail remain under the jurisdiction of local public land managers or private landowners. At press-time, 217 miles of the route had been dedicated. The Bay Area Ridge Trail presently crosses four MCOSD Preserves; Mt. Burdell, Little Mountain, Indian Tree, and Loma Alta.

The Bay Area Ridge Trail Council (established in 1987) office is at 311 California Street, Suite 510, San Francisco, CA 94104; (415) 391-0697 (or 391-9300 for hike information); www.ridgetrail.com.

ranchers. Old-timers recall swimming in the pond. Now usually dry or boggy due to silting, it becomes a sizable, although shallow, lake only in wet winters, as in 1998 and '99. The lake is a Sensitive Wildlife Area (no dogs allowed), enclosed by a fence which can be entered through stiles here and elsewhere. A path circles the water's perimeter, a favorite walk with children as the lake teems with tadpoles in spring. Visitors have reported frogs (mostly Pacific treefrogs) so abundant that care was needed not to step on them!

Middle Burdell rolls on. There are glorious views of the near-treeless wall rising to Burdell's summit ridge. The former quarry along the summit ridge is evident. In a wooded area, the Fire Road crosses a stream which is usually unnoticed but roars and requires rock-hopping to ford after winter storms.

The Fire Road enters another open area. It rises to its highest point, elevation 850 feet, at the first of two intersections with Old Quarry Trail. Here, Old Quarry goes left up to the summit. One hundred yards later, at the second junction, Old Quarry drops right to San Carlos F.R. Between the two segments is an extremely steep scar straight up the hillside. Please help it heal by keeping off.

Beyond the second Old Quarry junction, Middle Fire Road returns to oak/bay woodland, among the densest in the Preserve. The route remains wooded the rest of the way. At 1.4 miles from its start, the Fire Road passes the source of Two Bricks Spring. Two, old brick enclosures, one still with a cover, caught the spring's water, where it was then piped for livestock troughs and other uses downslope. Directly opposite the enclosures, on the right edge of the Fire Road, is a huge, multi-trunked laurel. Below are clumps of giant chain ferns (*Woodwardia fimbriata*), which only grow near streams or springs. They are the largest of Marin's fern species, to nine feet in height.

Middle Burdell F.R. passes a trough and another fence and gate. The route drops to an open area. Milk and Italian thistles, two invasive species, grow in abundance in the clearing left, along with several buckeye trees. Here, San Carlos Fire Road drops to Salt Lick F.R., then San Marin Fire Road.

Middle Burdell descends gradually in a wide arc. The next intersection is with Salt Lick F.R., which drops right to San Marin F.R. and San Carlos F.R.

A final cattle gate is crossed and there is another water trough. Fieldstone Trail comes in on the right. It switchbacks down to Fieldstone Drive.

The final hundred yards are a dead-end. Middle Burdell F.R. ends at the fence line which once separated the Rancho Olompali and Rancho de Novato land grants. (A species of Navarretia, a small flower in the phlox family, found nearby was not listed in John Thomas Howell's definitive *Marin Flora* because, when attempting research here in the 1940's, he was chased away at gunpoint!) A water tank for the new (opened 1999) Buck Center for Research in Aging complex is on the off-limits, privately-owned, east side of the fence.

MYRTLE PLACE TRAIL (.13 miles)
From Myrtle Place and San Ramon Way to Dwarf Oak Trail

There is a blue MCOSD easement route sign at the corner of Myrtle Place and San Ramon Way. Quietly follow the path up between the houses for .1 mile to the Preserve boundary. Myrtle Place Trail then rises through the grassland.

There is a striking serpentine rock outcrop just 100 feet up, a good place to sit and enjoy the vista. A few yards higher, there is a glimpse over to Rolling Hills Club, directly below. Paths cross.

Myrtle Place Trail ends at its junction with Dwarf Oak Trail. Left leads to the far end of San Ramon Way and a planned connection across Novato Boulevard into O'Hair Park and Little Mountain Preserve. Right, it is one mile to San Andreas F.R.

OLD QUARRY TRAIL (.98 miles)
From San Carlos F.R. to Burdell Mountain Ridge/Cobblestone Fire Roads
Intersection: Middle Burdell F.R. (.23m-.28m)
Note: Upper half is very steep and rocky; not recommended for horses

This is the steepest signed Trail within the District, grueling going up and hairy when descending. Old Quarry is not for everyone, particularly as there are attractive alternate routes, Cobblestone and Deer Camp Fire Roads.

Old Quarry Trail rises from San Carlos F.R. at a marked junction amid an area of lovely old oaks. An old, closed route is adjacent, and remains nearby throughout. This opening section is not steep. In 250 feet, the Trail passes through a gate which separates pastures for rotational grazing during the winter and spring cattle season. Paths branch left and right.

In a quarter-mile, Old Quarry Trail meets Middle Burdell F.R. Go left. The Trail and Fire Road run together uphill for 100 yards. Just past the forbidding looking "scar" straight up Burdell's south face, Old Quarry Trail departs to the right, also signed.

The serious climbing now begins. But there are rewards. When the Trail is not deep in woodland, the views behind are sweeping. For example, the tip of Tam's East Peak begins poking out just 100 yards in. The wooded sections, beside Jacinto Creek, are appealing as well. They offer shade in winter and are alive with birds— nest holes are abundant—and other wildlife the year around. There is a particularly impressive ancient laurel on the right 250 yards above Middle Burdell F.R.

The Trail emerges to spend its uppermost 500 feet in the open oak savanna of Burdell's summit ridge. The views are glorious.

Old Quarry ends at a four-way intersection. Left is Cobblestone F.R., part of the Bay Area Ridge Trail. Cobblestone drops to Middle Burdell F.R. for a loop option. Left is the access road to the telecommunications tower. Right is paved Burdell Mountain Ridge Road, which runs to an old quarry and the Preserve's east boundary.

SALT LICK FIRE ROAD (.59 miles)

From San Carlos Fire Road to Middle Burdell Fire Road
Intersection: San Marin F.R. (.21m)

This is a pleasant route; reasonably level, through grassland and oaks, and just high enough to offer broad views. The start is at a signed intersection with San Carlos Fire Road a half-mile up from San Marin F.R, a quarter-mile up from Michako Trail. Veer right. San Carlos Fire Road continues up to Middle Burdell F.R.

You'll likely encounter some of the common, colorful birds of Burdell's grasslands here; goldfinches, western bluebirds, and western meadowlarks. Goldfinches—lesser or American—are tiny, some five inches. Their undulating flight reveals flashes of yellow (adult males are brightest), along with black and white. They hang onto thistles, plucking seeds. Bluebirds fly about catching grassland insects. Here too it is the male that has the classic color. Meadowlarks flush out of the grass, where they forage for insects and seeds. Both sexes have a yellow breast and white outer tail feathers.

At one-fifth mile, Salt Lick F.R. crosses the eastern end of San Marin F.R., which drops right to Simmons Trail. Ranchers traditionally place salt licks (blocks of salt) near here for the cows, accounting for the Fire Road's name.

Salt Lick rises slightly, then levels. Valley oaks dot the hillside above and below. A seep makes for a muddy section in winter.

There is a dense line of oaks, bays, and buckeyes to the right. Salt Lick then begins rising. It ends at Middle Burdell F.R. by a water trough. Left, Middle Burdell is signed "To Two Bricks Spring." Right, Middle Burdell meets the top of Fieldstone Trail.

SAN ANDREAS FIRE ROAD (.73 miles)

From San Andreas Drive to Preserve boundary
Intersections: San Marin F.R. (.03m), Little Tank F.R. (.21m),
Dwarf Oak Trail (.39m), Middle Burdell F.R. (.58m)
Note: Part of Bay Area Ridge Trail, San Andreas Drive to Middle Burdell F.R.

This well-traveled Fire Road begins at the gate atop San Andreas Drive (half-mile north from San Marin Drive), at elevation 350 feet. There is ample parking on the east side of San Andreas Drive, but no parking on the west side.

From the stile, a shortcut path goes right to San Marin F.R. while San Andreas F.R. rises. To the left is a tree-lined creek. A fence separates the western section of Mt. Burdell Preserve, which is designated a Sensitive Wildlife Area (no dogs). Fifty yards in, San Marin F.R. departs right to Michako Trail and beyond. At .1 mile, San Andreas F.R. crosses the creek. There is a seasonal pond on the other side of the stile here.

At .2 miles, Little Tank Fire Road goes left, through a gate. It runs 700 feet to a water tank and an entry to Dwarf Oak Trail. Just above is a gate closed during the winter/spring cattle grazing season. A few yards higher, a 200-foot retaining wall borders the Fire Road. It was placed in preparation for a planned, but never built, residential development.

Immediately beyond the wall, views open across the meadow known as the "Bowl" to upper Burdell. Sharp-eyed viewers may see the rock wall along the summit ridge. There is a closer section of wall on the near ridge, ahead to the left. These walls were built by Chinese laborers in the 1870's. The near one marked the Rancho de Novato border with Rancho Nicasio, the summit one with Rancho Olompali.

At .4 miles, Dwarf Oak Trail sets off left. Dwarf Oak provides a connection for Bay Area Ridge Trail hikers and equestrians to O'Hair Park and Little Mountain Preserve. This is also the highest point on the Fire Road.

San Andreas descends gently through the oak savanna. To the left, many more oaks have been planted and are protected in casings. The District has been actively restoring historic oak habitats. Posts mark an underground phone cable. At an old wood post, a shortcut path goes up right to Deer Camp F.R. and Middle Burdell F.R.; the District discourages its use.

San Andreas F.R. meets Middle Burdell F.R., which takes Ridge Trail travelers up the mountain. San Andreas F.R. veers left; its remaining section a dead-end.

The final 800 feet of San Andreas passes an area that sees heavy cattle use in winter, so can be muddy. The route ends at a gate with a "No Trespassing" sign along the Preserve's western boundary. Beyond is a private ranch.

SAN CARLOS FIRE ROAD (.80 miles)
From San Marin F.R. to Middle Burdell F.R.
Intersections: Michako Trail (.24m), Salt Lick F.R. (.50m),
Old Quarry Trail (.61m)

San Carlos F.R. rises from San Marin F.R. at the end of Verdad Way, a short street off San Carlos Way. There is an entry from the end of San Carlos Way as well.

Lower San Carlos F.R. passes through grassland colored with a broad belt of wildflowers each spring. The Fire Road veers toward a seasonal stream, and climbs its right bank. Bend left at a trough.

About a quarter-mile up from Verdad Way, San Carlos F.R. meets the east end of Michako Trail. It goes left to Big Tank Fire Road. The valley oak at the junction is filled with holes, many with acorns fitted tightly inside.

San Carlos rises through a delightful, light oak woodland, a favorite of all who travel through. A quarter-mile above Michako, Salt Lick F.R. sets off right to San Marin F.R. and Middle Burdell F.R.

In another .1 mile, on the left, is the base of Old Quarry Trail, signed "To Summit." It crosses Middle Burdell F.R. and continues very steeply to the summit ridge. (A few yards away is the base of a now-closed, even steeper route straight up.)

San Carlos winds its way up. It passes a cattle gate, then ends a few yards later at its junction with Middle Burdell Fire Road. Left leads to Two Bricks Spring, Hidden Lake, and the base of Cobblestone F.R., right to the tops of Salt Lick F.R and then Fieldstone Trail.

SAN MARIN FIRE ROAD (1.99 miles)
From San Andreas Fire Road to Salt Lick Fire Road
Intersections: Andreas Court F.R. (.20m), Big Tank F.R. (.25m), San Mateo Fire Access (.68m), San Carlos F.R. (.91m), Simmons Trail (1.67m)

San Marin F.R. usually serves more as an access route than a destination. As the lowest in elevation of the Preserve's fire roads, its views pale in comparison to those higher. The entire route is within close sight of, often bordering, residential back-yards. And, in winter, when grazing cattle pass through after a rain, the Fire Road becomes a quagmire, even capable of sucking off loose shoes. Still, because it is the first route reached from most Burdell accesses, it is well traveled and plays a role in many loop options.

While San Marin F.R. touches many streets, its two ends are inland. It will be described west-east. A shortcut path to San Marin Fire Road sets off directly from the stile at the Preserve entry atop San Andreas Drive. The true start is to the right less than 50 yards up San Andreas Fire Road. The shortcut path comes in at 120 yards. A culvert carries a seasonal stream under the Fire Road. At 700 feet, San Marin F.R. reaches a crest and views open to the east.

In one-fifth mile, Andreas Court F.R. enters, having risen from Andreas Court, a short street off San Andreas Drive. In another 100 yards, Big Tank F.R. departs to the left, passing Michako Trail then ending at the water tank. A lower, more direct path to Michako Trail has been worn in from here as well.

San Marin F.R. reaches another crest, elevation 400 feet, and there are long views, out to Mt. Diablo on clear days. The Fire Road drops below the fence housing the "Big" water tank. The fragrant mint Western pennyroyal (*Monardella villosa*) grows abundantly each summer in a seep soon crossed. There is a line of coast live oaks.

At .68 miles, a signpost marks the short route, called San Mateo Fire Access, down to San Mateo Drive. Over the next mile, San Marin F.R. rolls up and down past several connectors to adjacent streets just above San Marin Drive. Grazing can leave stretches extremely muddy. It is along this section that narrow-leaf milkweed (*Asclepias fascicularis*) grows. Found in only one other locale in Marin, this milk-weed is eaten by monarch caterpillars, providing the butterflies with a toxin that makes them unpalatable to predators.

After heavy rains, the creek ahead announces itself with a roar. The rest of the year, it's barely a trickle. A fire road gate, stile, and cattle gate are at the entry to the end of San Carlos Way. But the signpost marking the start of San Carlos F.R. is 60 yards ahead, off Verdad Way. San Carlos F.R. climbs past Michako Trail and Salt Lick F.R. to Middle Burdell F.R. There is an entry to Sotelo Way. A seasonal creek is crossed.

In late winter, the grassland here is blanketed with zigadene, or star lily (*Zigadenus fremontii*), usually the earliest blooming of Burdell's showy flowers. The

Fire Road comes to the edge of houses, and there is a stile at Jacinto Way.

Veer left around the fence protecting the oak restoration along Jacinto Creek. Another seasonal stream is met. In winter, you may need to hop across the conveniently placed rocks to ford. That seems a world away on the hot dry days of summer. A signpost stands at an access from Sereno Way (1.36 miles).

The Fire Road begins to trend uphill. There is a lovely view of valley oaks dotting the knoll above left; the Fire Road soon loops even closer to them. San Marin leaves the residential border.

The next signed intersection is with the top of Simmons Trail, which goes right across a bridge and down to Simmons Lane. Veer left and begin the steepest climbing of the route. Where there is a brief leveling, the Fire Road passes just left of a broad coast live oak, with several massive limbs resting on the ground.

A final stiff climb brings San Marin F.R. to its end at Salt Lick F.R., which goes left to San Carlos F.R. and right to Middle Burdell F.R.

It is odd that despite exhaustive research, the origins of the County's two most significant names, Marin and Tamalpais, remain shrouded in mystery. The popular story attributes the County name to Chief Marin. He was a Coast Miwok in mission days whose prowess over local waterways—he lived for a while off the San Rafael shore on what came to be called the Marin Islands (now the Marin Islands National Wildlife Refuge and State Ecological Reserve, owned by the U.S. Fish and Wildlife Service and acquired with funding from the MCOSD and others)—helped him resist capture by Mexican authorities. He was finally taken, then died in 1834.

But the local Miwoks did not have chiefs and the "r" sound is not found in their language. So while Marin was a real personage, the name was probably given to him by the Mexicans, apparently due to his skill as a "marinero," or mariner.

Although administered last rites, Marin was not sainted. Still, "San Marin" was attached to the northern Novato residential district, its main street, and high school (opened in 1968). But there is precedent in that "San" was also long ago appended to his fellow Miwok fugitive Quintin (or Quentin).

The more prosaic story dates the Marin name to a 1775 map drawn by Juan Ayala, first European to sail into San Francisco Bay. He notes a "Bahia de Nuestra del Rosario, la Marinera." A more complete account of the naming controversy is found in Louise Teather's *Place Names of Marin*.

Grazing is a land management tool employed by MCOSD only at Mt. Burdell, where it is used to reduce fuel loads and to increase the diversity of native plant species in the grasslands. Per a grazing management plan and a lease with a local rancher (the Silveira Ranch on Burdell's northeast slope), Holstein dairy cows are resident during a grazing season that typically extends from mid-January to mid-June, depending on weather and forage conditions. The herd is periodically moved between four separate fenced pastures during round-ups led by members of MCOSD's Volunteer Mounted Patrol. Pasture A, covering the northern half of the Preserve, is the largest. Gates need to be re-closed during the grazing season, or use adjacent stiles.

SIMMONS TRAIL (.25 miles)

From Simmons Lane to San Marin Fire Road

Two routes depart from the MCOSD gate at the north end of Simmons Lane. Creekside Fire Road goes to the right, to Butterfield Drive. Simmons Trail rises to its left, behind the cattle gate. Be sure to close this and other gates above as there is seasonal grazing.

The Trail rises moderately steeply over the grassland. Mud makes for slippery conditions in winter. In January, certainly by February, the grassland is dotted with the lovely white flowers of zigadene (*Ziganedus fremontii*), in the lily family. Look closely and you may also notice a different white flower, with a nodding head. It is fragrant fritillary (*Fragaria liliacea*), also a lily. This fritillary is rare, on the State's threatened list. Blue-flowered brodiaeas are abundant here later in spring.

An underlying serpentine mass makes even oaks sparse on this hottest and driest of Burdell's slopes, the southeast. A lone valley oak, at 150 yards, stands out.

A second cattle gate is crossed, a bridge, then a third gate. Simmons Trail ends when it meets San Marin F.R. Left leads back down to residential San Marin streets, right up to Salt Lick F.R. with options for climbing still higher.

The historic, four-foot high, rock wall along the summit ridge of Mt. Burdell, the divide between the Rancho de Novato and Rancho Olompali land grants. The wall was built in the 1870's by Chinese laborers from volcanic andesite rock strewn atop Burdell. All rocks were hand-placed and fitted without mortar.

OLD ST. HILARY'S

Size: 117 acres   Elevation range: 100-600 feet

*This Preserve has become a special place for me. It's not just
because there are rare flowers, ones that are found nowhere else
in the world. It's not the endless vistas of Angel Island and the
entire Bay, nor is it the babbling creek that runs through the
middle of its lush grass lands. It is the feeling I have knowing how
intensely many people worked to save these acres from being
turned over to the "Condo Commandos."*
— Brian Sanford, Supervising Ranger

Sᴛ. Hɪʟᴀʀʏ's Roman Catholic Mission Church was built in 1888 to meet the spiri-
tual needs of families of Irish and Italian railroad workers, Portuguese dairy farm-
ers, and Reed descendants. The building's architectural style is Carpenter's Gothic.
Construction was financed by railroad mogul Peter Donahue, with labor believed
to have been provided by carpenters from the Tiburon railroad yard. The church
and original half-acre site were dedicated by San Francisco's Archbishop Riordan in
1888. The first marriage there was performed October 24 of that year.

In 1954, the church was deconsecrated and services moved to St. Hilary's Par-
ish Church (765 Hilary Drive). The old building stood "empty and forlorn" (*Pictorial History of Tiburon*). In 1959, local residents responded by forming the Belved-
ere-Tiburon Landmarks Society and bought the property from the Diocese. The
site was designated Old St. Hilary's Historic Preserve. The beloved landmark is open
to the public on Sundays and Wednesdays, April through October, from 1-4 p.m.

Two adjacent acres also were acquired to protect rare wildflowers. The lower
slope is named the John Thomas Howell Botanical Garden for the author of *Marin
Flora* and charter member of the Landmarks Society. Howell called the site, "One of
the most interesting and beautiful wildflower gardens in California, and thus in all
the world." Two plants first discovered there—Tiburon jewelflower (*Streptanthus
niger*) and Tiburon Indian paintbrush (since reclassified as a subspecies *Castilleja
affinis*, ssp. *neglecta*)—are unique to the site and endangered. Howell and Phyllis
Ellman co-authored a floral guide, *Saint Hilary's Garden*, published by the Landmarks Society. The upper slope encompasses the Caroline Livermore Vista Point,
so designated to honor Marin's preeminent conservationist.

Meanwhile, the grasslands above Old St. Hilary's—the 101-acre former
Harroman property above and the 15.8-acre former Jay property down to the
Tiburon Peninsula Club—were increasing in value for subdivision as some of the
choicest residential sites in the nation. The story of their acquisition as public open
space is a tangled one involving lawsuits, foreclosures, the nationwide savings and
loan debacle, the overthrow of the Marcos regime in the Philippines (the Harroman
interests had investments there), the Internal Revenue Service, last-minute dead-
lines, and more. Ultimately, the citizens of Tiburon and Belvedere overwhelmingly

approved two separate bond measures, in 1993 and '97, to acquire the parcels. The Harroman property was purchased for $6.8 million and the Jay property for $1.1 million. Together, they were, and remain, the most expensive open space purchases ever involving the District.

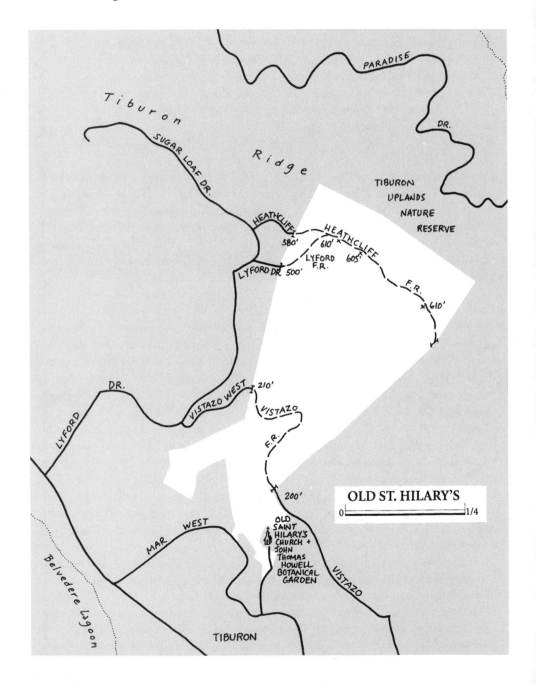

HEATHCLIFF FIRE ROAD (.45 miles)

From Heathcliff Drive to Preserve boundary
Intersection: Lyford F.R. (.12m)

Heathcliff offers spectacular views, certainly among the best in Marin from any fire road both below 1,000 feet in elevation and directly accessible by car. Of course, summer fog often obscures these views. Try coming on a clear day in winter, when Tiburon registers some of the County's warmest temperatures.

The Fire Road begins from an MCOSD gate at the upper end of Heathcliff Drive. It starts, and remains, atop the summit spine of the Tiburon Peninsula. The highest point on the ridge, called both Mount Tiburon and Sugar Loaf, at 748 feet, is just behind (west-northwest) and covered with multi-million dollar homes. Homes were also planned for Heathcliff Fire Road before its acquisition as public open space.

Heathcliff Fire Road starts uphill. In 150 yards, a path drops left, quickly leaving the Preserve toward the Tiburon Uplands Nature Reserve. The Reserve was once part of the Tiburon Naval Net Depot. At the start of World War II, a 6,000-ton metal net was built there and strung seven miles from Sausalito to San Francisco to keep out enemy submarines. The 24-acre Reserve parcel passed from Federal to County ownership in 1958, when the naval station closed, and is now administered by the Marin County Parks Department. The main entry, to the Reserve's one route (Uplands Loop Trail), is off Paradise Drive.

Heathcliff Fire Road reaches the first of three 600-foot crests at a junction with Lyford Fire Road, an alternate entry from Lyford Drive, coming in from the right. Virtually all of San Francisco is visible.

A downhill is followed by a rise to crest #2. Water views dominate; San Pablo Bay to the north, San Francisco Bay west, the Golden Gate south, and Richardson Bay to the east. A test is to spot the campanile on the University of California campus in Berkeley. The yellow violet known as johnny-jump-up or yellow pansy (*Viola pedunculata*) is one among many colorful spring wildflowers here.

The entire Tiburon ridge was dairy grazing land from the 1830's until after World War II. It was only in the 1950's that homes first began creeping up an extended Lyford Drive. Now bracken fern, a post-grazing forerunner to coyote brush, then to trees, is also advancing up the grassy slopes.

The third crest, one-third mile in, adds, among other landmarks, the Bay Bridge and Raccoon Strait, which separates the Tiburon Peninsula from Angel Island. There is an unusual view down to privately owned Keil Cove at water's edge by Bluff Point; note Keil Lagoon and the impressive residence, which dates from 1902.

The steep drop beyond the level crest area has a dead-on view of Angel Island above Ayala Cove. At .45 miles, Heathcliff Fire Road meets a fence line. Old-timers call this area "The Bull Pasture," for its former denizens. Although the Fire Road continues another 500 yards to Ridge Road, an MCOSD sign notes the fence as the end of public land. At press-time, there is a proposal to build 34 luxury homes on the 110-acre parcel beyond the fence.

Two paths depart to the right from the end of Heathcliff at the fence line. The one closer to the fence drops to the middle of Vistazo Fire Road at the lower end of the Preserve. The other roughly parallels Heathcliff Fire Road, back to Lyford F.R.

Kurt Heath was a post-World War II immigrant from Belgium who developed the area by the Fire Road's start.

LYFORD FIRE ROAD (.14 miles)
From Lyford Drive to Heathcliff Fire Road

This short Fire Road is an alternate access to Heathcliff Fire Road. A chain barrier marks the start at the upper end of Lyford Drive. Pampas grass crowds the left side of the entry. One hundred feet up, a path, which parallels Heathcliff Fire Road, leaves right.

Stunning views of San Francisco, the Golden Gate, and the headlands above Sausalito open. A bit higher, the vista extends to the north, then to the east as well.

The Fire Road ends when it meets Heathcliff F.R. at a spectacular view site. It is 200 yards left to Heathcliff Drive and 600 yards right to the Preserve boundary.

Dr. Benjamin Franklin Lyford (1841-1906) came to San Francisco after he was discharged from the Union Army—he served as an embalmer—at the end of the Civil War. In 1872, he married Hilarita Reed, heiress to more than 1,000 acres of lower Tiburon peninsula. Childless themselves, the Lyfords raised the orphaned children of Hilarita's sister, Maria Inez.

The Lyford house, part of the couple's Eagle Dairy, was built on Strawberry Point in around 1878. It was saved from demolition and barged across Richardson Bay on a very high tide, December 4, 1957, to become the landmark of the Audubon wildlife sanctuary at Greenwood Beach.

VISTAZO FIRE ROAD (.34 miles)
Between two sections of Vistazo West

This Fire Road crosses the lower end of Old St. Hilary's Preserve, connecting two sections of Vistazo Street. Although the level Fire Road is at a modest 200 feet in elevation, the views are superb. Starting from the west side (chosen here) showcases San Francisco; from the east side highlights Mt. Tamalpais.

A creek runs below the pavement by the gate at Vistazo West. The striking yellow color here in March just outside the Preserve is from masses of acacia trees.

Immediately, the vista (except when the area is engulfed in fog, as is common mornings and late afternoons in summer) sweeps from the San Francisco skyline, across Belvedere Island and the bay, to both towers of the Golden Gate Bridge and on to the Headlands. You can also glimpse the twin crosses atop historic (erected 1888) Old St. Hilary's Church by the Fire Road's eastern end.

Colorful wildflowers abound in spring. The Landmarks Society brochure for

Hilarita Reed (1839-1908), daughter of John Thomas Reed, the first land grantee in Marin County, and wife Hilaria Sanchez. Hilarita inherited 1,020 acres of lower Tiburon peninsula, all of Strawberry peninsula, and, ultimately, Belvedere. In 1872, she married Dr. Benjamin Lyford, a Canadian-born embalmer during the Civil War and in San Francisco. He ran dairies on his wife's lands, using the most hygienic practices of the time.

Hilarita donated land for a church to the Archdiocese of San Francisco. Opened in 1888, the church was named for her patron saint, and that of her mother, St. Hilary. (Courtesy Marin County Historical Society)

the adjacent St. Hilary's Botanic Preserve reads, "Nowhere else in California can so many kinds of wildflowers be found in so small a space as on the few acres surrounding the old church."

Two hundred and fifty yards in, Vistazo Fire Road bends right as it crosses a creek. Horsetails, a primitive and ancient plant browsed by dinosaurs, grow here. A path rises very steeply beside the creek bank, which harbors much invasive pampas grass. Willows line the bank downslope.

Easy to miss, particularly if you're enjoying the views, is an entry to Old St. Hilary's Botanic Preserve Trail on the right. It drops a few yards, then runs parallel to the Fire Road. It leaves the Preserve to the church, with stone benches along the way to enjoy the views. Baby-blue-eyes (*Nemophila menziesii*) dot the Fire Road edge.

A wall of serpentine lines the left edge of the Fire Road cut. It is the harsh soil formed from serpentine rock that contributes to the many unusual flowers here. The flat land below, down to the Tiburon Peninsula Club, is the former Jay property, a choice building site that will now remain pristine.

The Fire Road ends at the MCOSD Preserve boundary gate, where Vistazo West resumes. Just ahead are two paths on the right, both marked by "Welcome to Old St. Hilary's Botanical Preserve" plates. The first (in about 50 yards) goes to Caroline S. Livermore Vista Point, then to Old St. Hilary's. The second is Dakin Lane, also down to the church.

PACHECO VALLE

Size: 786.2 acres   Elevation range: 120-1,310 feet

It's not unusual to get calls from Open Space neighbors wondering about animals that they've encountered in Open Space. One afternoon a few years ago I got a call from a woman trying to describe something she had seen earlier in the day, while jogging. She breezily rattled off the description of the animal and I repeated her description aloud as I wrote down the details. To my co-workers, it must have sounded like a Bob Newhart telephone routine. "So it was large and black with beady little eyes and it grunted at you...okay." When she said that she thought it was a panda bear, it was all that I could do to keep from laughing, and my co-workers rolled on the floor. I finished the report to the best of my ability and later went up to Pacheco Valle to find the bear in question. I didn't see anything but that's not to say that it wasn't happily munching on some backyard bamboo. I'm still waiting for the call about the koala bears on San Rafael Ridge!
— *Scott Rasmussen, Supervising Ranger*

PACHECO VALLE (the Spanish spelling of "valley" is traditionally used) covers the upper areas surrounding Pacheco Creek. The area was completely undeveloped when the owner offered the District a chance to buy it in the early 1970's. "It was a series of lovely meadows," then MCOSD General Manager Pierre Joske recalls. But the County Board of Supervisors turned the proposal down, instead using the available funds to purchase what is today McInnis Park. The bulk of the Preserve was acquired in 1975 through a County Service Area.

In the early 1990's, after homes had been built in Pacheco Valle, residents became upset when a "no trespassing" sign was placed over an old route at the head of the canyon (Pacheco Creek Trail). Pat and Jeanne MacLeamy led a community effort to save the pristine upper canyon. In 1995, an additional 179 acres were acquired for $740,000. One-third of the monies came from the District, one-third from the Marin Community Foundation, and one-third from a local assessment district.

see map on pages 118-119

CHICKEN SHACK FIRE ROAD (3.21 miles)

From Alameda del Prado at Clay Court to Big Rock Ridge Fire Road
& Big Cat (Queenstone) Fire Road
Intersections: Via Escondida F.R. (1.02m), Little Cat F.R. (1.56m), Pebble
Beach F.R. (1.81m), Halloween Trail (2.27m), Ponti F.R. (2.73m)
Notes: Adjacent parking difficult on weekdays;
Caltrans parking lot is for commuters only

At 3.21 miles, Chicken Shack is the second longest fire road in the MCOSD, behind only San Geronimo Ridge. It journeys through some of Marin's more pristine lands, offering great views all along the way. Although its start is just yards from a Highway 101 exit (Alameda del Prado), Chicken Shack remains lightly traveled because of its steepness.

Note that Chicken Shack F.R. touches three Preserves—Pacheco Valle, Loma Verde, and Ignacio Valley—but is included here because its lower end is within Pacheco Valle.

The Fire Road rises behind a metal MCOSD gate signed Big Rock Ridge and Pacheco Valle. The first, steep quarter-mile is newly paved. It is open to vehicular use (infrequent) by Pacheco Valle residents, with keys, using four private tennis courts perched on the hillside. The courts sit above tanks used to boost water pressure. The chicken coops that gave the route its name once stood here. There is a water fountain on the lower, near side of the courts. Taking a drink is all but mandatory in summer, when the area can record the highest temperatures in Marin.

The pavement ends at the tennis court parking lot and a second MCOSD gate marks the start of dirt fire road. The uphill continues steep, with only brief respites.

Chicken Shack traverses a classic oak woodland that likely looks little different than it did in Miwok days. The generous spacing between trees typical of such woodland keeps views open. Mt. Tam looms south and Mt. Burdell north. Behind (east) are views out to San Pablo Bay and beyond. Ahead is the steep, oak-covered head of Pacheco Valle. The barbed wire fence on the right, which runs the length of the Fire Road, marks old property lines. The land beyond it is now largely within Loma Verde Preserve.

At .86 miles, at the end of a relatively level stretch, an old, overgrown ranch road branches right. It dead-ends 150 yards below at a gate marking the private property of Pacheco Ranch.

The steepness eases for a while as the Fire Road begins rolling, although still clearly trending up. Highway 101 noise finally disappears.

At just under one mile, a path goes off right and up to a crest where a United States Coastal & Geodetic Survey Marker, placed in 1955, is embedded. There is a dead-on view of Mt. Diablo; the Mt. Diablo Base Line and Meridian is the standard for measuring property lines in central California.

One hundred yards later is the first true intersection as Via Escondida F.R. departs right. Lower, Via Escondida F.R. forks and continues down to the Ignacio streets of Via Escondida (left fork) and Posada del Sol (right).

The terrain opens over Chicken Shack's first substantial downhill. About a mile-and-a-half in is a junction. Most of the old "stencil" signs and arrows are gone, but "Big Rock" remains. Left is Little Cat Fire Road, down to Hummingbird Way at Alameda del Prado in Pacheco Valle.

A quarter-mile later, after a tough uphill, is another fire road junction, marked only by a lone, old metal post. Pebble Beach F.R. drops right toward the Marin Country Club golf courses (which can be glimpsed). A half-mile down it, Pebble Beach F.R. branches to meet the tops of Winged Foot (left) and Pebble Beach (right) Drives.

A few yards above the junction, another seeming fire road rises right. It's part of a path that runs above Chicken Shack whenever the Fire Road is on the south side of the true ridge crest. This path re-joins and re-departs Chicken Shack ahead.

As Chicken Shack continues, and climbs relentlessly, the vegetation shifts to drier chaparral. Chamise (greasewood), the dominant shrub of Marin's chaparral, becomes increasingly abundant. There are views right that take in virtually all of Novato.

At a short crest 2.27 miles in is the signed top of Halloween Trail, departing right, through a break in the old barbed-wire fence line. Halloween Trail descends steeply for three-quarters of a mile to Burning Tree Drive.

There is then a brief respite in the uphill. A striking view of the east wall of Big Rock Ridge is framed on the right. The stiff climb resumes. Several vantage points offer views over seven or more counties. In crystal clear weather, the vista extends to the Sierra through Carquinez Strait.

At a crest, Ponti Fire Road comes in from the left; an old "stencil" sign remains. Ponti drops 1.4 miles to Curlew Way and Alameda del Prado in Pacheco Valle. (Some maps consider this as the end of Chicken Shack F.R. and the continuation as Big Rock Ridge F.R.) A brief level stretch gives way to a downhill, but climbing again resumes. The views, if possible, are even more sensational.

Chicken Shack ends at an unmarked three-way fire road junction. Left, Queenstone (also called Big Cat) Fire Road begins a long descent over Marinwood Community Services District land to Queenstone Drive off Miller Creek Road in Marinwood. The option right is Big Rock Ridge F.R., heading toward the MCOSD's Lucas Valley Preserve and even more stunning vistas.

LITTLE CAT FIRE ROAD (.54 miles)

From Alameda del Prado (Pacheco Valle) to Chicken Shack Fire Road

Little Cat Fire Road passes through a picture-perfect California oak woodland as it climbs atop a ridge.

The Fire Road starts up from behind an MCOSD gate on Alameda del Prado just east of Hummingbird Way. There is a second, narrower entry, also with an MCOSD sign, some 75 yards up Alameda del Prado, past Hummingbird Way.

Little Cat Fire Road passes two houses. The going is very steep, and, basically, unrelenting. The alternate entry comes in left some 400 feet up. At .2 miles, the Fire

Road passes a sizable water tank serving Pacheco Valle.

The Fire Road keeps climbing the ridge between the two forks of Pacheco Creek. Oaks dominate, creating a timeless, pastoral feel.

Little Cat ends at its junction with Chicken Shack Fire Road. The stenciled sign "Little Cat" is now half gone. There is a nice view from the junction, through a gap in the trees, toward the southeast. Chicken Shack's two ends are about equidistant, a mile-and-a-half away, up left to Big Rock Ridge F.R., or down right to Alameda del Prado by Highway 101.

Marin harbors two wild members of the cat family; bobcat, which may be considered the "little cat," and mountain lion, the "big cat."

PACHECO CREEK TRAIL (.26 miles)
From Pacheco Creek Drive to waterfall
Note: Dead-end

This Trail sets off from the westernmost edge of the Pacheco Valle residential area, the end of Pacheco Creek Drive.

A few yards in are two stately oaks. The first is a coast live, the second a valley oak. The differences in their leaves are obvious—oval and convex on the coast live oak, larger and lobed on the valley oak. In winter, only the valley oak loses its leaves. Also note the differences in their bark, the valley oak's is more deeply fissured and checkered.

Some 400 feet in, the Trail fords a rivulet joining Pacheco Creek. There are then four crossings of Pacheco Creek in rather rapid succession. The last brings the Trail back to the left bank (the creek to the left).

Beyond, Pacheco Creek Trail begins deteriorating as it rises and narrows. But it is worth walking, particularly after heavy rain, the extra .1 mile to a lovely waterfall. The Trail is considered to end at the falls, with the continuing path extremely poor.

PONTI FIRE ROAD (1.40 miles)
From Curlew Way at Alameda del Prado to Chicken Shack Fire Road
Intersection: Heatherstone F.R. (.27m)

This is a lovely Fire Road through a light oak-madrone woodland that provides shade but still offers nice views.

Ponti F.R. sets off from an MCOSD gate on the west side of Curlew Way, a small street off Alameda del Prado. The lowest yards are steep and rocky. The initial climb is through a deep woodland dominated by madrones.

At a quarter-mile, the Fire Road bends right. In the middle of the bend, Heatherstone Fire Road departs left. A Marinwood Community Services District (C.S.D.) sign is at the junction. Heatherstone F.R. goes two-thirds of a mile (entirely outside the Preserve on private property) to Heatherstone Drive in Marinwood. There are two fire roads off Heatherstone F.R. back into Pacheco Valle—to Sage Grouse Road and to Red Hawk Road—both of which briefly cross MCOSD land.

Ponti continues up, now out of sight of Pacheco Valle homes, through a most appealing woodland. One-quarter mile above the Heatherstone junction, an old blue Ford pickup truck rests at the left edge of the road. Nature is turning the cargo area into a planting box.

Steep sections vary with reasonably level ones. About three-quarters of a mile up, views start to open. Sticky monkeyflower, with orange-yellow flowers, is abundant. Higher, manzanita becomes the most common shrub.

Ponti F.R. ends at its junction with Chicken Shack F.R. on Big Rock Ridge. It is one-half mile of glorious views left to Big Cat (Queenstone) F.R. and Big Rock Ridge F.R. The next junction to the right is also one-half mile, with Halloween Trail.

The Fire Road's name is a shortened version of a previous owner of the Pacheco Valle, Ponticopoulos.

Marin's tallest manzanita species (Arctostaphylos manzanita), abundant on the slopes of Big Rock Ridge, as here in Pacheco Valle Preserve

RING MOUNTAIN

Size: 405.6 acres   Elevation range: 10-602 feet

One evening I was standing on top of Ring Mountain as the sun sank in the west horizon, and at the same time a full moon rose in the east. What an incredible experience. Hiking up to the top I stopped to look at the ancient petroglyphs. On the way down I made sure to stay on the trail so I wouldn't step on the Tiburon Mariposa Lily in the dark. It was a tough day at work.

— *Leonard Page, Ranger*

RING MOUNTAIN may be the best known and most studied of the District's Preserves. The battle in the 1970's to save what had been pristine grazing land from massive development was well publicized. So too was the story of the discovery of the Tiburon mariposa lily, which grows only on this ridge and nowhere else in the world. A visit to Ring Mountain has become a staple for local schoolchildren. Others, including many families, come to walk the informative and lovely nature loop.

The earliest Miwok village site on Ring Mountain has been dated at 370 BC. (There is a midden just off lower Phyllis Ellman Trail.) Ring Mountain was part of the 8,000-acre rancho granted to John Thomas Reed in 1834. His heirs grazed cows and horses on the fenced-off site—part of Reed Ranch—for 130 years, until 1965.

The mountain itself had no formal name. George E. Ring (1841-1911) came to Marin from New Hampshire as a young man. He amassed a fortune in local real estate, with sizable holdings in Novato, Nicasio, Greenbrae, and on the Tiburon shore at the foot of the mountain (Ring Point, now called Paradise Cay). Ring acquired the latter holding—the site of Benjamin Buckelew's grandiose but failed California City plan of the 1850's—in 1879. He lived there the rest of his life, with wife Ella and son William. Ring was a well-known figure in Marin and a popular County supervisor and his name became attached to the mountain.

In the Cold War days of the 1950's, the Army installed four 90mm anti-aircraft guns and support structures on Ring Mountain's summit. The facility was deactivated as obsolete in the '60's.

Also in the 1960's, Thomas Deffebach, descendant of Thomas Boileau Deffebach, who had married John Thomas Reed's daughter Maria Inez, sold 435 acres of Ring Mountain to a development company, Ring Mountain Ltd. The mountain's grazing days were over. The company's development plans triggered a lengthy preservation fight. Phyllis Ellman was one of the key opposition organizers.

In 1972, Dr. Robert West discovered a new plant high on the mountain and submitted it to the University of California's Jepson Herbarium. A year later, Albert J. Hill published its description as *Calochortus tiburonensis*, Tiburon mariposa lily. Other rare and endangered endemic plant species, notably the Tiburon indian paintbrush (*Castilleja neglecta*) and the Tiburon jewel flower (*Streptanthus niger*), were also identified. So too was the Tiburon blind harvestman (*Sitalcina tiberona*), a tiny arachnid living under rocks only on Ring Mountain. Also, Miwok petroglyphs were discovered. They have since been identified on some 30 of the mountain's rock outcroppings.

The mountain was already famous for its geology. It was here in the 1890's that a new mineral, lawsonite, named for University of California geology professor Andrew Lawson, was first identified. Prominent local geologist Salem Rice wrote, "Most of the rare and unusual rock types at Ring Mountain have been found at....other localities. However, it appears that the diverse assortment of such rocks at Ring Mountain is unique and not known to occur elsewhere."

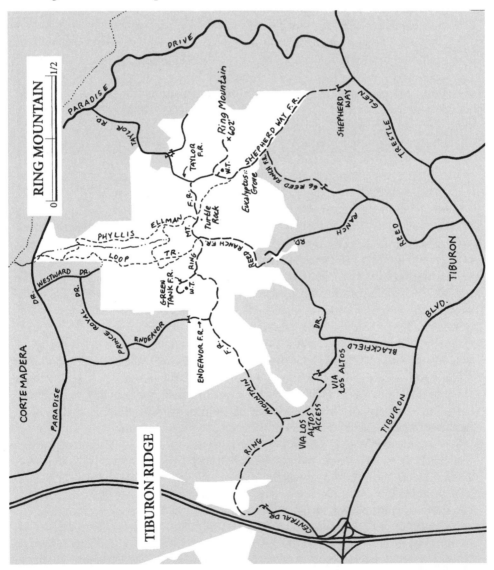

In 1981, the San Francisco-based Nature Conservancy purchased the most environmentally sensitive, uppermost 72 acres of Ring Mountain. Two years later, Ring Mountain Ltd. deeded the Conservancy another 45 acres and gave them joint management control of 260 additional acres. Ring Mountain Preserve was dedicated April 23, 1983.

The Nature Conservancy managed Ring Mountain Preserve until November 1995, when they turned it over to the Marin County Open Space District.

Note that dogs must be leashed at all times within this Preserve

ENDEAVOR FIRE ROAD (.10 miles)
From top of Endeavor Drive (Corte Madera) to Ring Mountain Fire Road

This short Fire Road atop Endeavor Drive is the highest Preserve entry from the Corte Madera side of Ring Mountain. There is an MCOSD-signed gate at the start.

Endeavor Fire Road rises steeply to meet Ring Mountain Fire Road. Left leads to Phyllis Ellman Trail and Turtle Rock and right to the Preserve's southwest edge.

GREEN TANK FIRE ROAD (.15 miles)
From Ring Mountain Fire Road to water tank
Note: Dead-end

Green Tank Fire Road departs 200 feet east of the crest of Ring Mountain Fire Road and the path to the John Thomas Howell bench. It is to the right when heading uphill, left when descending.

Green Tank F.R. descends gently over the grassland. There are sweeping views north. A path leaves across the grass at a left bend. The Fire Road dead-ends when it meets the green, wooden, water tank so the route must be retraced out.

PHYLLIS ELLMAN LOOP TRAIL (1.76 miles)
Keyhole from Paradise Drive (Corte Madera)
Intersections: Ring Mountain F.R. (.87m-.99m), Reed Ranch F.R. (.99m), Post 14 Spur (1.09m)

Phyllis Ellman Loop (or Nature) Trail is one of the most popular of all District trails. It starts directly behind the Ring Mountain entry gate on Paradise Drive and makes a long and lovely loop up through the heart of the Preserve. The Nature Conservancy, which saved Ring Mountain from development, placed 16 numbered nature trail signposts (all except #1 standing at press time) along Phyllis Ellman Nature Trail. Seasonal interpretive brochures, keyed to the signposts, are available through the MCOSD. They were written by Larry Serpa, former Nature Conservancy manager of the Ring Mountain Preserve.

In 50 yards, a bridge, dedicated to the memory of George John Mouton, crosses the slope's main creek. Just beyond, a sign honors donors (including Phyllis Ellman) to the Nature Conservancy's acquisition fund for Ring Mountain, and dedicates the effort to Patricia Bucko-Stormer. It reads, in part, "Pat's commitment to conservation and enthusiasm for the natural world were an inspiration to all who knew her." An information signboard announces events and reminds visitors of the importance of keeping dogs leashed within the Preserve. A few feet beyond, opposite a toyon (and Post #1), is a "Phyllis Ellman Trail" sign.

Views over the grassland open quickly and remain a feature of the route. There is a nice perspective of San Quentin, a State prison since 1852. You may hear gunshots from the prison target practice range. More pleasing sounds come from children playing outside Marin Country Day School just below. The Richmond Bridge, opened August 31, 1956, is prominent. It replaced ferry service between San Rafael and Richmond.

At 1,000 feet, a sign ("Nature Loop Trail") points left. This is the start of the loop portion of the keyhole-shaped route, which will be followed left (clockwise), the direction of the numbered posts. The first post encountered is #2, in less than 30 yards. Posts then come reasonably regularly, an average of 100 yards apart. There are many paths across the hillside, several confusing. If you miss a numbered post, keep uphill and you'll likely rejoin Phyllis Ellman Trail. A summary of the post descriptions follows.

#2—Discusses the seasonal creek and the vegetation it supports. Wildflowers here include pink onion, blue Ithuriels spear, then, in summer, yellow tarweed.

#3—The largest boulders in the Preserve are complicated schists, composed of 12-15 different types of minerals, including shiny specks of mica. Colorful lichens, a union of fungi and algae, grow on many of these rocks.

#4—Shooting stars and buttercups are common wildflowers here.

#5—Describes the adjacent coast live oak, and how water percolates as springs from the serpentine higher in the Preserve.

#6—Yellow false lupine is abundant here in spring, followed by the clover butter-and-eggs. Black field crickets live in holes in the soil. Some attribute special significance to the rock outcrop above, with a boulder seemingly balanced atop.

#7—Molehills have been observed near here. Moles are carnivores who dig through the soil for crickets, spiders, and earthworms. Wax myrtles and chain ferns line the water course.

#8—Talks of the threats this huge coast live oak has faced in recent decades, and of resident grey tree squirrels and nocturnal deer mice.

#9—Discusses ecology within this "tree island." Note the grand laurel. Some 15 trunks rise out of the rock. Exposure to wind keeps them all relatively short. A view of Mt. Tamalpais opens beyond the grove.

#10—Relates how San Francisco Bay is relatively young. It was only some 10,000 years ago that a rising Pacific Ocean first re-penetrated what had been a valley during the most recent Ice Age.

#11—Notes some of the more than 30 species of grasses found within the Preserve. Most are introduced but there are natives such as purple needle grass, California oat, and serpentine reedgrass.

One hundred feet above Post #11, Phyllis Ellman Trail meets Ring Mountain Fire Road at a signless post. Left leads to Taylor Ridge Road and the summit of Ring Mountain. Across is a path to Turtle Rock. To continue on the loop, go 200 yards right on the fire road to the Phyllis Ellman Trail sign. There is a breathtaking view of San Francisco Bay and the City skyline. Post #12 discusses nearby Turtle and Petroglyph rocks. Go right onto the broad Trail.

Post #13 refers to some of the plants here, such as the early-blooming milk-maids, California buttercups, meadow barley (nicknamed caterpillar grass), and the serpentine rock succulent called sea lettuce. One hundred feet later, the route splits at a signpost in a somewhat confusing area. A handwritten arrow points the way left to Post #14.

The "Post 14 Spur" runs .28 miles, or 500 feet longer than the right-hand fork that rejoins below. The Spur has very steep downhill sections but leads to prime habitat for the Preserve's most famous wildflower, and what Post #14 is all about.

The Tiburon mariposa lily is a bulbous perennial. Its shiny, linear leaves emerge in February but flowers do not appear until late May. Early June is usually peak bloom. The flowers, generally 2-3 per plant but up to eight, are light yellow-green, flecked purplish brown. This mottled appearance blends in with dried grasses and makes the plant hard to find. But identify one and you'll likely then see many more. The plant can be up to two feet high, but is usually shorter.

The Tiburon mariposa lily is abundant in the serpentine here but its extremely restricted range—on this ridge and nowhere else—contributes to its official classification as Threatened. Albert Hill, who described it for science, observed, "Had this species not been noticed soon, it might well have become extinct without ever having been recorded." One wonders how often that has already happened, and is happening, elsewhere. Needless to say, do not pick or trample this or any wildflower, in any Preserve or public open space.

The two route options merge at a post with a similar handwritten arrow as above, in another tricky area. Directional arrows guide the way but new paths have been worn. Signpost #15 directs attention to a knoll between the freshwater marsh and Marin Country Day School. The knoll dates from a prehistoric landslide; there have been more recent slides.

Post #16 is last of the series. The interpretive brochure for spring talks of the Douglas iris, narrow-leafed mules ears, morning glory, and other wildflowers here. There are muddy patches near the water course.

Among many striking spring wildflowers in the lower grassland is the hairy, white Oakland star-tulip (*Calachortus umbellatus*). It is not to be confused with its close relative, the elusive Tiburon mariposa lily (*C. tiburonensis*) found higher.

Phyllis Ellman Nature Trail crosses a brook and the loop portion ends. If the .18 miles back to the gate is added, the total length of the route is raised to 1.94 miles.

Phyllis Ellman was a leader in the effort to organize community support against the plan for housing atop Ring Mountain. She accompanied John Thomas Howell on some of his early botany explorations on Ring Mountain, which helped her realize what a unique flora was present, and endangered.

REED RANCH FIRE ROAD (.32 miles)
From Reed Ranch Road to Ring Mountain Fire Road and Phyllis Ellman Nature Trail

Reed Ranch Fire Road starts at the top of Tiburon's Reed Ranch Road, nestled between two homes and behind a gate with an MCOSD "Ring Mountain" sign. In 1964, in preparation for construction of homes on upper Reed Ranch Road, a prominent outcrop of metamorphic rock was blasted and bulldozed. It was in that outcrop, in the 1890's, that lawsonite, now recognized as an important indicator mineral in metamorphic rocks throughout the Coast Ranges, was first identified.

The spine of the Tiburon Peninsula has "million dollar" views—homes here are among the most expensive in the County—and Reed Ranch Fire Road doesn't disappoint. Even from the start, the views, particularly behind, are sensational.

The initial climb is moderately steep. A grove of eucalyptus, the only tall trees in the heart of the Preserve, and Turtle Rock are landmarks. To the right, invasive pampas grass sends up long stalks. After a brief easing in the uphill, a path goes right to Turtle Rock and one drops left to Petroglyph Rock, both favorites of Ring Mountain visitors.

Petroglyph Rock, a blue metamorphic schist, contains oval-shaped forms pecked (not carved) by early Native Americans. (The technical name is Pecked Curvilinear Nucleaforms, or PCN's.) Some guess they are fertility symbols. Petroglyphs have been identified on some 30 of Ring Mountain's rock outcroppings. Unfortunately, the rock also contains graffiti. The new sign and rail at the rock are attempts by the MCOSD and others to stop such vandalism.

Less than 100 yards later, Reed Ranch F.R. crests and ends at a key intersection. Directly ahead is signed Phyllis Ellman Trail. It drops to Paradise Drive, Corte Madera. Right, Ring Mountain F.R. climbs to Taylor Ridge Road and the summit of Ring Mountain. Left, Ring Mountain F.R. rises to the John Thomas Howell bench.

John Joseph (Juan Jose) Reed (1837-1899) was the oldest child of John Thomas Reed, Marin's first land grantee, and Hilaria Sanchez. He was also among the first (possibly first) non-natives born in Marin. Upon his son's birth, John Thomas went to the top of Mt. Tamalpais to plant a huge cross.

John Joseph inherited more than 2,000 acres of the upper Tiburon peninsula and built his ranch home at what is now 21 Barn Road. He continued ranching on the land (Reed Ranch) and kept alive many of the *Californio* traditions from the Mexican era, including gracious hospitality, rodeos, and other fiestas. He married a Mexican (Carlota Suarez) and Spanish was the household tongue. John Joseph, Carlota, and their only son, John Paul Reed (1865-1919), are buried in Mt. Tamalpais Cemetery.

RING MOUNTAIN FIRE ROAD (.93 miles)

From Taylor Ridge Road to Preserve's southwest boundary
Intersections: Phyllis Ellman Loop Trail (.14m-.26m), Reed Ranch F.R.
(.26m), Green Tank F.R. (.41m), Endeavor F.R. (.66m)

Ring Mountain Fire Road is an unofficial name for the main route across the Preserve. It offers stunning views its entire length.

Ring Mountain F.R. departs west from Taylor Ridge Road. On the descent, look above left at the huge boulder of metamorphic schist, Turtle Rock. It could not have been more aptly named; almost everyone recognizes a turtle shape riding on top. Rock climbers have long honed their techniques here; observe MCOSD rules.

The respected local geologist Salem Rice helped explain the presence of such rocks in an article in *California Geology* (May 1991).

"The Ring Mountain area is made up of detached rock slices or wedges emplaced by a dynamic thrust fault system that juxtaposed older rock units over younger ones. Younger sedimentary rocks occur in the lower strata of the mountain while much older metamorphosed rocks are on top.

"....Much of the crest of Ring Mountain is capped by large sheets of serpentine rock. Serpentine is formed by igneous processes and is thought to originate in the Earth's mantle that lies deep beneath the crust. It most certainly formed far deeper than did the sedimentary units that now lie beneath it. Although these serpentine sheets have not been dated, they are perhaps the oldest rocks on the Tiburon Peninsula, probably more than 150 million years old.

"The serpentine sheets that cap the two hill crests in the Ring Mountain area are separated from the underlying sandstone by a thick zone composed principally of intensely sheared Franciscan complex melange. The melange represents an ancient fault zone....In places the melange is only a few tens of feet thick. However, under the main saddle between the two crests [the Turtle Rock area], the melange is much thicker and is perhaps several hundred feet in thickness.

"Many prominent dark colored blocky masses occur as outcrops principally downslope of the serpentine sheets. These unusual weather-resistant metamorphic rock bodies are instrumental in making Ring Mountain a celebrated geologic locality. In general, each of these monolithic masses has a different assemblage of minerals than the nearest adjoining rock mass. Most of these bodies are coarse-grained, massive to schistose rock types....Some have such unusual mineral compositions that none of the standard rock names apply."

A path rises right to the bay laurel grove in the rocky outcropping above. It leads to a stone bench commanding a great view. A plaque reads:

THE PAUL L. AND PHYLLIS WATTIS FOUNDATION
IN GRATEFUL APPRECIATION FOR ITS SUPPORT OF THE
RING MOUNTAIN PRESERVE   APRIL 23RD, 1983

Fifty yards lower, a post on the right identifies the top of the section of Phyllis Ellman Loop Trail covering posts #2 through #11.

At a quarter-mile, at a great San Francisco skyline vista point, is an important intersection. Right, signed is Phyllis Ellman Loop Trail (posts #12 through #16). To its left is Reed Ranch F.R., which descends to Reed Ranch Road in Tiburon. A path also drops to Petroglyph Rock (see Reed Ranch F.R.).

Ring Mountain F.R. now begins an uphill on the ridge's north slope. There is a chance of seeing the rare Tiburon mariposa lilies here in June. Forty yards before Reed Ranch reaches the crest, Green Tank F.R. drops right to dead-end at a water tank. Mt. Tamalpais rises directly behind the subsidiary peak (partly within the MCOSD's Blithedale Summit Preserve) known as Little Tamalpais.

The Fire Road crests a ridge which, at 588 feet, is just short of the highest point (602 feet) in the Preserve. A path goes left the few yards to the John Thomas Howell bench, dedicated to him on his 80th birthday. The late Howell, along with Alice Eastwood, who preceded him as Head Botany Curator for the California Academy of Sciences, were the two towering figures of modern botany in Marin. He described many plant species new to science, and several are named for him. His *Marin Flora* has remained the definitive work since it was published in 1949. (Howell completed supplements published in 1970 and '80 and the Marin chapter of the California Native Plant Society is now preparing a posthumous, updated re-issue.) The plaque on the stone bench reads, "For John Thomas Howell, Friend and Teacher of California Botany and Botanists, In Honor of His 80th Birthday." The 360-degree views are magnificent.

The Fire Road rolls, mostly down, along the ridge. A few deer paths and short-cuts cut across the open terrain. Five hundred yards beyond the Howell plaque, a fire road right drops the short way to Endeavor Drive in Corte Madera.

A dense line of oaks and bays edge the Fire Road west. The MCOSD's Tiburon Ridge Preserve is part of the remaining undeveloped land bordering the near side of Highway 101. The MCOSD's Alto Bowl/Horse Hill Preserve is just across the highway.

Ring Mountain F.R. exits the Preserve onto Town of Tiburon Open Space at a gate. In 1884, a railroad tunnel was blasted under the hill here (see Tiburon Ridge Preserve chapter).

The Fire Road's remaining .3 miles to the water tank atop Via Los Altos (Tiburon) are open to public travel. (A stairwell built in 1999 connects the Fire Road to upper Via Los Altos.) It passes two entries on the right to an unnamed fire road that runs down into and through the Tiburon Ridge Preserve, but there is no public exit. The new luxury homes atop Via Los Altos emphasize the significance of the Ring Mountain preservation effort as the highest slopes would likely have been similarly developed.

SHEPHERD WAY FIRE ROAD (.26 miles)
From Taylor Ridge Road to Preserve boundary

A paved road departs Taylor Ridge Road to the new water tank. One hundred feet in, the water tank entry bends left and Shepherd Way F.R. sets off straight ahead.

Ring Mountain has fantastic views just about everywhere and Shepherd Way F.R.

is certainly no exception. The panorama over the open grassland includes San Pablo Bay, the Berkeley Hills, Oakland, Angel and Alcatraz islands, San Francisco, Belvedere, the Golden Gate, the Marin Headlands, and Mt. Tamalpais. The highest point on the Trail comes within fifty yards, but views remain impressive on the descent.

At 100 yards, a path goes right down to Petroglyph Rock. Shepherd Way F.R. leaves the upper serpentine belt and becomes less rocky. It passes the lone eucalyptus grove on the upper mountain. The biggest tree there is huge, a hearty survivor in the winds for at least a century.

The Trail ends at the Preserve's boundary with Town of Tiburon Open Space land. There is an old fence line and MCOSD signpost. Two routes continue down. The one right drops to the driveway of 64-66 Reed Ranch Road, with an option to Indian Rock Court. The one left drops—steep, rutted, and muddy—to Shepherd Way at the private parking lot of Shepherd of the Hills Lutheran Church. Cross Trestle Glen Drive and go up to the end of Hacienda Drive to continue on the officially designated cross-Tiburon path.

TAYLOR RIDGE ROAD (.36 miles)

From Preserve boundary above Taylor Road to Ring Mountain summit
Intersection: Ring Mountain F.R. (.10m), Shepherd Way F.R. (.19m)
Note: Paved

Paving of upper Taylor Road to accommodate the new luxury homes built there has yielded a high trailhead into the Ring Mountain Preserve. Actually, three gated routes, all paved, rise from the circle atop Taylor Road. Only the road right (north), marked by a blue "Public Trail" easement sign, is a Preserve entry. The sidewalk (which quickly ends) and blue-gated road to the left access private residences.

Inside, signs remind visitors that private property is being crossed. The MCOSD gate and Preserve boundary fence are .1 mile away.

The views are immediately stunning. Tam and Diablo stand as sentinels, 40 miles apart. San Francisco Bay stretches below. Thirty yards in, a broad path drops steeply to the Preserve boundary. Its connection on to Robin Drive, used as an access by local residents, crosses private property.

At .1 mile in from the Preserve gate, Ring Mountain F.R. departs right. It goes to the junction of Reed Ranch F.R. and Phyllis Ellman Trail and beyond. The uphill eases. There are paths through the grassland.

The next big fork is with the paved entry to the new water tank. To the right is access to the water tank and Shepherd Way Fire Road, 100 feet in. Continue straight.

The old paving is giving way, returning upper Taylor to a dirt road. The grassy humps are mounds, now covered with vegetation, from when the summit was graded for the military base. The towers of the Golden Gate Bridge come into view.

Taylor Ridge Road meets the broad Ring Mountain summit area. The vistas are stunning. In 1954, four anit-aircraft guns were placed here to defend the Bay Area from Russian attack.

The pavement, and Taylor Ridge Road, end. A path continues down. Fifty yards below is an overturned old brick and stone fireplace chimney, one of many remnants here of the military presence. Other paths branch off.

A sea of tidy-tips, cream cups, and other wildflowers on Ring Mountain.
(Steve McCormack)

ROY'S REDWOODS

Size: 377 acres   Elevation range: 320-1,200 feet

I don't need to follow a white rabbit in the enchanted forest called Roy's Redwoods when I give night hikes to the public. It's easy enough to find magical places on my own to share. With Indians, Napoleon Bonaparte, Paul Revere, and stories of the "hippie occupation" there is plenty to talk about besides the plants and animals. It's easy to put your imagination to work in this preserve. George Lucas imagined Ewoks here.

— Leonard Page, Ranger

THE ROY BROTHERS, James (b. 1834) and Thomas (b. 1840) were both born in Caledonia County, Vermont. They arrived in California in 1861 and both were Marin residents by the following year. James never married. Thomas wed Mary Somers (1852-1940), from the same Vermont county, in 1871. They had one child, Ralph (1890-1954).

In 1877, the Roy brothers received 420 acres from Adolph Mailliard to settle a $20,000 loan they had made to him. (In 1883, a first cousin, John Roy, bought 773 acres on the Fairfax side of White Hill for $23,000, now the heart of Loma Alta Preserve.)

The Roy brothers family home stood by the duck pond of today's golf course. In 1981, it was purchased by a film company, moved to Nicasio, and featured in the movie *Shoot the Moon*. James died in 1893, his remains returned to Vermont, where the Roy family still maintains a farm. Thomas died in 1932.

In the 1950's, a golf course was opened on former Roy grazing land. Parts of other former Roy lands were acquired by developers anticipating that a planned freeway into west Marin would trigger growth. The freeway plan was beaten back and the lands leased for grazing. In 1978, the MCOSD bought the Preserve's initial 306 acres for $420,000. At the time, some 50 members of a hippie commune were living in the redwood groves.

Note that there is a section of the Preserve on the west side of Nicasio Valley Road. It may be entered by the MCOSD gate opposite the main Preserve entry. (Another gate just lower is marked "No Trespassing.") There are presently no official routes within this western section, sometimes called Moon Hill, longer than .1 mile. This may change as there are plans for transfer of 463 adjacent acres from the new French Ranch development (opened August 1999) to the District.

Also note that this Preserve is for day use only, and is closed nightly from 8 p.m. to 4 a.m.

see map on page 163

DICKSON RIDGE FIRE ROAD (.88 miles)

From Nicasio Valley Road to Preserve's northeastern boundary
Intersections: Roy's Redwoods Loop Trail (.00m and .04m)

Dickson Ridge Fire Road (mislabeled as Dixon on some maps) runs four miles, from Nicasio Valley Road to the edge of Loma Alta Preserve high on Loma Alta. Only the lower, westernmost mile, within Roy's Redwoods Preserve, is on public land. The climb is very steep and some visitors might find it overly strenuous.

The Fire Road starts behind an MCOSD gate on the east side of Nicasio Valley Road, a half-mile from Sir Francis Drake Boulevard and .1 mile above the main Preserve entry gate. Just 15 feet in, Roy's Redwoods Loop Trail enters from the right at a signpost, having risen from the main entry. The two routes run together for 50 yards, when the Loop Trail departs right at another signpost.

The steepness begins immediately. If you don't like it, turn back, as there's barely any relief the entire way. Great views, however, are a reward.

A private house, accessed via Nicasio Valley Road, sits prominently on the hill above left. The Fire Road runs along the property line's fence. To the right, coyote brush is the common shrub in the grassland, with rows of sage (Artemesia) as well.

At just under a quarter-mile comes the first look at Mt. Tamalpais and Tam views remain a constant of the journey. The Fire Road passes under some trees, then meets a fire road gate to the left. Dickson Ridge F.R. is on the edge of the Preserve boundary, so all the heavily wooded land left (west) and ahead (north) is private. Enjoy a brief leveling.

The steep climbing resumes. A notable landmark to the west is Black Mountain, which rises abruptly, without the long ridges typical of most Marin peaks, from its surrounding lowlands. Another is Barnabe Mountain, with the fire lookout.

A half-mile up, the Fire Road bends left and views out to the Richmond Bridge open. The San Geronimo Treatment Plant is prominent on the valley floor. Loma Alta, the still-distant end of Dickson Ridge Fire Road, comes into sight.

The Fire Road passes a now open fence line. Less than 150 yards above, the Fire Road meets a locked gate with an MCOSD sign, "Stop, End of Public Open Space." Spirit Rock Meditation Center owns the land ahead but permits low-impact travelers. The elevation is 1,200 feet and the views are sweeping, close, but not quite, to the Pacific Ocean.

The Dickson brothers—David, William, and John—were from the same county, Caledonia in Vermont, as fellow San Geronimo landowners, the Roy brothers. They came to California in the mid-1850's, and all three were dairying and stock raising in the San Geronimo Valley before 1860. Munro-Fraser, in his 1880 *History of Marin*, wrote the Valley then "was sparsely settled; traveling was done mostly on horseback, fences were almost unknown, bear were plentiful, often killing stock in the night."

In 1869, when Adolph Mailliard sold off part of his San Geronimo ranch, John Dickson bought 630 acres east of San Geronimo and William an additional 500 acres. The family still retains Valley holdings.

MEADOW TRAIL (.23 miles)

Between Roy's Redwoods Loop Trail

Meadow Trail starts near the main entry gate to the Preserve; just go left on the Loop Trail for 175 feet. An MCOSD sign directs equestrians left, away from the meadow, while Meadow Trail sets off across it.

The 200-plus yard walk through this beautiful, haunting meadow—a special place to so many—is as far as some Preserve visitors get. (For information about holding an event, such as a wedding, in the Meadow area, call 499-6405). On the right are towering redwoods. Just in front of them are bays, willows, and buckeyes. To the left are bays, madrones, oaks, and elderberry.

The Trail leaves the meadow into some impressive redwoods. To the right is a huge ring of redwoods, locally called the "Fairy Ring" or "Council Tree." They sprouted from roots of the redwood that once stood in the center. The size of the ring shows that the mother tree must have been massive, and the "offspring" sprouts are now giants in their own right. One, at 243 feet, is just shorter than the tallest redwood in all Marin County, a 254-footer in Muir Woods' Bohemian Grove. Enter the circle, as many do, to better appreciate the majesty. A laurel is an interloper on the outer edge.

Left is a redwood with a circumference of 38 feet, one of the biggest of any tree in Marin. It appears to be several redwoods fused at the base. Ahead is a forest of laurels. George Lucas filmed portions of his *Star Wars* movies here in 1984 and '85.

Meadow Trail continues, the floor brightened by yellow-colored redwood violets in spring. A creek is crossed. A huge eight-trunked bay is just beyond. Several laurels downed in a 1980's storm lie where they fell.

Meadow Trail rises to its end at Roy's Redwoods Loop Trail, having served as a quarter-mile shortcut. There is an MCOSD "Trail" signpost at the junction.

ROY'S REDWOODS LOOP TRAIL (2.48 miles)

Loop around Preserve
Intersections (clockwise): Meadow Trail (.03m, .45m), Dickson Ridge F.R. (.14m-.17m), Nature Trail (.66m), connector to Spirit Rock (1.49m)
Notes: Very muddy sections; seasonal closure to equestrians

A long loop trail circles the heart of Roy's Redwoods Preserve. Most visitors rate the west and north sections among the loveliest in the District. But the southern half—bordering busy Sir Francis Drake Boulevard, through disturbed grassland, and often muddy—has fewer admirers.

Most all users join the Trail at the MCOSD gate on the east side of Nicasio Valley Road, .4 miles from Sir Francis Drake Boulevard. There is adjacent road shoulder parking, and, uncommon on OSD lands, portable toilets. The loop will be described clockwise.

Go left, immediately beside huge redwoods. At 175 feet, a sign directs horse riders left, off the fragile meadow. Straight is Meadow Trail, which rejoins the Loop Trail above as a shortcut. The Trail rises along the fence line, passing a horse trough. There is a good perspective across the meadow of the tops of the big trees.

At 250 yards, the Trail joins Dickson Ridge F.R., which begins a few feet away at a gate off Nicasio Valley Road. The Trail and Dickson Ridge F.R. run together for 50 yards, then Roy's Redwoods Loop Trail splits right. A seasonal horse closure sign is placed here when winter rains begin. Dickson Ridge F.R. climbs along the northern edge of the Preserve, then leaves Roy's Redwoods at the Spirit Rock Meditation Center boundary.

The Trail goes in and out of the grassland and light woodland of lower Nicasio Hill. In spring, the grassland above is carpeted with blue brodiaeas, lupine, and buttercups. At .42 miles, a bridge fords a creek. Bordering the bridge on the left is a tall California coffeeberry (*Rhamnus californica*) shrub. In the Buckthorn family, it has no relation to coffee (genus *Coffea*) other than dark berries in fall.

Sixty yards later, Meadow Trail rejoins from the right, at a "Trail" sign. The Loop continues gently up, passing a dead-end path right posted "No Horses."

Just under .1 mile later are a pair of junctions. First, right, an MCOSD sign marks the start of Roy's Redwoods Nature Trail, a keyhole-shaped route with no outlet. A few yards beyond, a short path with an MCOSD "No Horses" sign goes left.

Roy's Redwoods Loop then enters a deep, quiet, haunting forest and begins a steady descent. This section of Trail was only built in 1990. Most of the densely packed trees are bay laurels, with a sprinkling of oaks, madrones, and massive Douglas-firs. Ferns carpet the forest floor. This is hiking heaven for woodland lovers.

Deep into the canyon, the Trail crosses a second bridge (.9 miles). Switchbacks bring the Trail down into grassland and lighter oak cover. An MCOSD sign at 1.2 miles marks the other end of the Trail's winter closure to horses. Continuing down, the Trail crosses a creek. Restoration work has been done here, including planting willow trees and placing rocks to shore the banks. The creek flows south into San Geronimo Creek, which harbors a salmon run.

The route now follows an overgrown road. The low-lying land can be a veritable bog in winter, testing visitors' footwear. The San Geronimo Treatment Plant, one of the MMWD's two filter plants through which all central and southern Marin's drinking water passes, is visible directly ahead.

At 1.5 miles, the Loop Trail veers right to parallel adjacent Sir Francis Drake Boulevard. At the bend, Spirit Rock Trail departs left. It goes 150 yards to the gate marking the boundary between the Preserve and private land of the Spirit Rock Meditation Center, then continues over a public easement to Dickson Ranch Stables.

Roy's Redwoods Trail now runs through grassland between a blackberry-lined channel bordering Drake and the hillside. The route, not as well-maintained as the first half, rolls up over short hills and down across muddy seeps. There are a couple of jogs right, adding to the distance.

The Trail then runs near the paved road into the golf course clubhouse. The restaurant is open to the public but the course itself is off-limits except to golfers. Above the clubhouse, the Trail bends right. A bridge, used by golfers going from the

The beloved meadow of Roy's Redwoods Preserve, just yards from the main entrance off Nicasio Valley Road. Some of the tallest and most massive redwoods in Marin rise at the far end.

18th hole to the clubhouse, crosses Nicasio Road. The District hopes to complete a connection over the bridge to Thorner Ridge Trail in Thorner Memorial Preserve.

The next section, through a light woodland parallel to Nicasio Valley Road, is broader. About 100 yards before the Loop's end, a sign directs horse riders left over a bridge. Straight leads to deep redwoods. Go left past the outhouses back to the start.

ROY'S REDWOODS NATURE TRAIL (.68 miles)
Keyhole from Roy's Redwoods Loop Trail
Note: No horses

This is a very lovely woodland Trail that, because it has no outlet, is relatively little traveled. Also deterring visitors is extensive poison oak at Trail's edge, perhaps more than on any other route in this book. Nature Trail is keyhole-shaped; an out-and-back section (.23 miles), followed by a loop (.21 miles). The distance cited above reflects counting the initial out-and-back section twice.

Nature Trail rises to the right when circling Roy's Redwoods Loop Trail clockwise. An MCOSD signpost marks the start, just before Loop Trail enters woodland. In spring through fall, the poison oak makes its presence known immediately, and caution is demanded throughout.

Most of the trees are laurels, but there are Douglas-firs, oaks, and madrones as well. Many contain woodpecker and other bird nests. At least six species of ferns form a dense forest understory. Pink star-flowers are abundant in late spring.

The Trail meets its first redwoods, large and fire-scarred, 500 feet in. Go left at the sharp bend ahead. There is another seeming junction 25 yards later; veer right.

At .21 miles, there are options left and right as Nature Trail begins its loop section. Take either fork. The Trail rises to the high point of the hill, the 780-foot summit of Nicasio Hill. Madrones, being crowded out by redwoods on the surrounding slopes, reign here at the relatively sunny summit.

A downhill brings Nature Trail back to the start of the keyhole loop section. There are no other options but to retrace steps and return to the Trail's start.

Rush Creek Preserve has become a popular lunch-break escape for office workers along the nearby Highway 101 corridor.

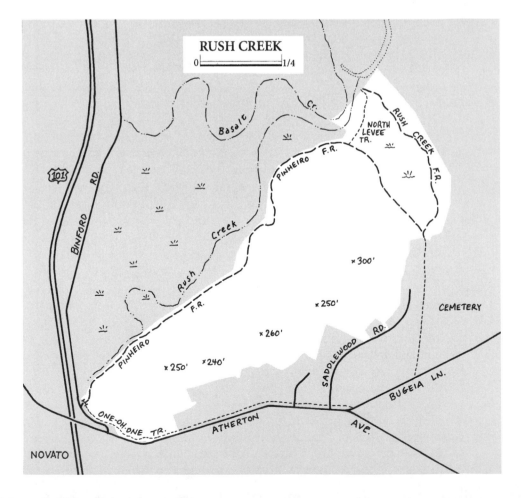

RUSH CREEK

Size: 314.4 acres   Elevation: 0-280 feet

*Looking for solitude and beauty all wrapped up in a great little
package? Take a hike along the fire road that borders the marsh.
Whether you're a birder, a biker, or just a nature enthusiast, this
preserve has much to offer. Personally, one of my favorite things
to do is bring binoculars and bird book and just wander along the
fire road. It's easy to see something new every visit.*
                                             — Canada Ross, Ranger

CARL PETER RUSH (originally Rusch, then anglicized) was born in Denmark in
1827, went to sea at age 15, came to the gold fields as a '49'er, and apparently made
a sizable amount of money. Around 1860, he bought 406 acres of Rancho Novato
by the creek that came to bear his name. Rush Creek was then considerably deeper
and wider, and he was able to barge supplies in and farm produce out. Rush brought
his future bride, Anna, from Europe and the two were married in 1864.

In 1877, Rush was murdered, one of the more sensational homicides of the
era. The Governor of California, on behalf on an outraged citizenry, offered a reward. Below is Munro-Fraser's account of the crime in his 1880 *History of Marin*:

"On June 1, (Rush) went out to his field to work, taking his luncheon. He left
at the house his wife and an Indian boy. A man employed by Rush on the place
started for Petaluma that morning, leaving the house first. The man returned about
five o'clock. Rush was expected in early to do the chores, and as he did not come,
the boy was sent out for him, but could not find him. The man finished up his
chores, and then, taking a lantern he and the boy went out to look for Rush. About
half an hour after they had left, as Mrs. Rush was sitting at the window reading, a
gun was discharged through it, large shot perforating her book, the flying glass
scratching her neck, and the shot lodging in a bed, was setting fire to it....The next
morning word was sent to Sweetser & De Long's, and a force of fifteen or twenty
men....commenced an active search for the missing man. All that day was spent in
the hunt....The search was resumed on the 3rd, and in the afternoon, the murdered
body of Peter Rush was found, in the field adjoining where he had been at work. He
had been shot in the back....The body had been dragged by hand to a fence....and
there covered up with grass and brush....His estate was estimated at from twenty to
thirty thousand dollars."

Such an estate was a veritable fortune then and Anna was considered a sus-
pect. She was arrested and indicted, but later cleared by a grand jury. A former
Marin County sheriff pursued the case for 16 years. In 1893, he identified the al-
leged murderer, a man already hanged for another crime.

Anna died in 1901 at age 78 and was buried beside her husband in a small
pioneer cemetery within today's Preserve. (The Rush bodies were later exhumed
and reburied in Colma.) The property passed to a nephew, Johannes Braun, who

had a chicken ranch there. Next it went to Johannes' widow, Carrie, then their son, Heinrich Braun. In 1940, Frank Pinheiro bought the ranch for $40,000.

In 1995, construction of 89 homes—800 had originally been planned—began on the southeast side of the property. Only a few of the some 16,000 trees on the site were cut. The MCOSD received 261.8 acres, the heart of today's Preserve, from the developer. Thirty-five acres of wetland (Rush Creek Marsh) went to the California Department of Fish and Game, and 19 acres were reserved for a community park.

NORTH LEVEE TRAIL (.22 miles)

From Pinheiro Fire Road to Rush Creek Fire Road

This short trail provides a link in hiking around the full perimeter of the Preserve.

When traveling Pinheiro F.R. from the Binford Road entry, North Levee Trail departs left, unmarked, 1.24 miles in, amidst the Fire Road's deepest tree cover. The Trail drops to the levee that forms the northwestern boundary of the Preserve's brackish Cemetery Marsh.

A few small eucalyptus trees manage to survive on the right margin; many other eucalyptus were removed by the District to restore native vegetation. More typical of marshes are the pickleweed underfoot and tules at the water's edge right.

North Levee Trail passes between a pair of overflow ponds, where snowy egrets and night herons often gather by the pipes to snare a meal. The Trail then ends at another levee, at the Preserve boundary.

This is a somewhat confusing area. This second levee, to the left, dead-ends. To the right is one end of Rush Creek Fire Road. It bends right to follow the pond margin to Pinheiro Fire Road. There is also a broad route quickly forking left off Rush Creek F.R. It leaves the Preserve and winds, as a trail over private property, along the marsh to the Bahia district of Novato.

ONE OH ONE TRAIL (.28 miles)

From Binford Road Gate to Preserve boundary by Atherton Avenue

One Oh One Trail (a name adopted by OSD field staff) starts at the Binford Road Gate, to the right of Pinheiro Fire Road. It rises into oak woodland, seemingly to offer a peaceful loop with Pinheiro Fire Road. But a quarter-mile in, just when the sounds of Highway 101 are fading, the Trail drops out of the Preserve and alongside busy Atherton Avenue.

A pedestrian and an equestrian path then run east past the new homes. In about a half-mile, just before the Valley Memorial Park Cemetery boundary, a path goes left. It follows the line of eucalyptus trees back into the Preserve by the far end of Pinheiro Fire Road, which fulfills the promise of a loop.

PINHEIRO FIRE ROAD (1.67 miles)
From Binford Road Gate to Preserve boundary at Rush Creek Fire Road
Intersection: North Levee Trail (1.24m)
Note: Sections can be extremely muddy in winter

Pinheiro Fire Road is the main route within the Preserve. When traveled from Binford Road, the landscape—pristine oak-studded hillside and marshland—appears little changed from 19th century Marin. Sounds of nearby Highway 101 and the occasional plane heading into Gnoss Field just to the north remind one of changes. Bring binoculars as the birdwatching is outstanding.

The trailhead is off Binford Road, named for Woody Binford, who ran a flying school at Gnoss Field after World War II. Just inside the MCOSD gate are two options; One Oh One Trail up right and Pinheiro Fire Road left. The Fire Road hugs the marsh.

The first yards are paved and downhill; the rest of the route is dirt and all but flat. The marsh teems with birdlife, particularly in winter, when migrants from the north visit or stay. In late fall, I've seen more than 500 great and snowy egrets feeding at once. Great blue herons, avocets, and black-necked stilts are among the other common long-legged birds. Smaller waders are yellowlegs, dowitchers, killdeers, plovers, and sandpipers. White pelicans, once considered endangered, are often found a bit farther in, scooping up their meals. In winter, ten or more species of ducks—ruddy, canvasback, pintail, widgeon, mallard, gadwall, ring-necked, scaup, goldeneye, bufflehead—plus geese, are routinely resident. Hawks and other raptors fly overhead.

Tall cattails (genus *Typha*) and tules line the marsh. They are a favorite haunt of red-winged blackbirds. Just under 200 yards in, a valley oak carries many huge galls, looking like golden apples, on its limbs. Galls, which vary greatly in appearance, are a host tree's response to chemicals secreted by wasp larvae (of more than 200 species). The galls, which apparently do not harm the oak, provide protection, not always fail-safe, for the developing wasps. Just beyond, look left in fall for clusters of white snowberries. The main channel of Rush Creek becomes clearer.

The Fire Road and fence line mark the old boundary of the Rancho Novato land grant to the south from the Rancho Olompali grant north. Rush Creek Marsh itself is under the jurisdiction of the California Department of Fish and Game. Shooting stars and buttercups (and poison oak!) line the Fire Road. In spring, the grassland to the right has broad patches of meadow foam (*Limnanthes douglasii*), whose creamy white flowers are streaked with purple veins. The Rush house stood on the prominent knoll to the left at least into the 1920's.

At the one-mile mark, the F.R. enters a line of bay trees. Next is a slight rise into a deeper woodland. Inside this tree canopy, North Levee Trail sets off left. It offers, with Rush Creek Fire Road, a loop of Cemetery Marsh or of the entire Preserve.

The Fire Road continues along the edge of the Pinheiro Ridge hillside, which rises to 300 feet. Cemetery Marsh is on the left. Somewhat jarring is the single, new (1999) home atop a knoll directly ahead.

Pinheiro's reverie is broken as the Fire Road approaches the edge of more homes in the new Rush Creek Estates development, and ends. The District is planting oak trees to "hide" the development, and there will be new entries here when construction is complete. A route continues to the right of the eucalyptus trees to Bugeia Lane and Atherton Avenue. Left across the channel—a tricky fording finally bridged in 1999—is Rush Creek F.R. It follows the opposite shore of Cemetery Marsh to North Levee Trail.

RUSH CREEK FIRE ROAD (.58 miles)

From Pinheiro Fire Road at Preserve's southeastern boundary to North Levee Trail

Rush Creek Fire Road is actually the Preserve half of a road that also goes through private property of Valley Memorial Park Cemetery.

One public access is along a path that begins near Bugeia Lane and runs a half-mile along the west side of the row of eucalyptus trees and a ditch. There will soon be closer entries off streets by the new homes under construction at press-time. From the southeastern end of Pinheiro Fire Road, ford the ditch over the new (Fall, 1999) bridge. There is an MCOSD "Rush Creek" sign just in.

Some 200 yards along, a pair of trees, an ancient valley oak left and a buckeye right, flank Rush Creek Fire Road. The oak is now protected by fencing and a "Keep Off" sign. Please stay away. This oak has been part of the life cycle of countless creatures over the centuries; hopefully it will endure. There are only two other, well-spaced trees on the left side of the Fire Road, an equally impressive second valley oak and then a coast live oak. But the hillside above right is covered with oaks.

There are fine views out to Mt. Burdell. You'll more likely be looking at the rich variety of birdlife in Cemetery Marsh. (There is actually a path closer to the marsh but visitors should stay on the Fire Road.)

A single metal gate post is passed and the oak beside it carries old "No Hunting, No Trespassing" signs. About 75 yards past, a path rises right. It leaves the Preserve into a privately owned oak woodland. A few yards ahead, a fire road to the right also leaves the Preserve at a signed gate less than 100 yards up. It continues, as a trail over private property, along the marsh edge.

Masses of the fragrant shrub California sage (Artemesia) then border the Fire Road on the right, with shrubby eucalyptuses to the left.

The Fire Road bends left to meet North Levee Trail. A route also goes right, to join the fire road encountered just earlier. North Levee goes left between two outlet ponds and connects with Pinheiro Fire Road for a loop. The levee path straight ahead dead-ends. You may see evidence here of the project, completed in 1999, to improve tidal circulation through the marsh.

SANTA MARGARITA ISLAND

Size: 9.1 acres   Elevation: 0-50 feet

*I grew up in Santa Venetia, so it's no wonder that Santa
Margarita Island is one of my favorite Open Space Preserves.
When I was a kid, I wasn't aware of the clapper rail or the salt
marsh harvest mouse or that the Island was anything more than
a beautiful place for me to play. I spent many a day swinging on
a rope swing over the canal and jumping off the bridge rails.
Though these activities were a whole lot of fun, I must say I'm
now more interested and concerned with the Island's colorful
history and its rich wetland habitat. I'm overjoyed that the
community and the Open Space District appreciate and protect
Santa Margarita Island's unique attributes and natural
resources.*   *— Ari Golan, Ranger*

AT JUST NINE ACRES, Santa Margarita is the smallest of the Preserves. It is also the
only true island Preserve, completely surrounded by the South Fork of Gallinas Creek.
The island itself is only 4.61 acres, some of which—the flat north end—is landfill.

There have been several attempts to develop Santa Margarita Island. The most
ambitious was early in the 20th century by the colorful Mabry McMahan. In November 1914, more than 3,000 people attended a grand opening celebration to view
McMahan's plans for a new Venice centered around the island. He had already spent
$160,000 on landfill and in building canals. Eighty-foot wide boulevards were to
line the canals and homes built in the Venetian style. Santa Margarita Island was to
house a 500-room hotel with "a mighty waterfall" on top, visible from the railroad.

Nothing came of the scheme and McMahan, near poverty, died after being hit
by a car. The foundations of his Santa Venetia estate off today's Oxford Drive are
now weed-covered, but the palm trees he imported to line the driveway still thrive.
Other evidence of McMahan's vision—cement canal walls, at least one of the old
light posts, a palm tree—remain on Santa Margarita Island. There is also a Mabry
Street, and an Adrian Way named for his son, in today's Santa Venetia district.

In 1963, the Billings and Hutchinson Gravel Company bought Santa Margarita
with the intent of filling in the approach canal, building a road across it, and developing the island. Community pressure turned back the plan.

The island was sold to the Rubini and Farina families, who put forward Santa
Margarita Islands ultimately last development effort. It called for 124 condominium
units, a swimming pool, and a restaurant. Today's bridge was built in anticipation
of the project. After community and conservation groups voiced formidable objections, the plan was vetoed by the County's Board of Supervisors.

Community reaction to development threats helped lead to the District's purchase of Santa Margarita Island in 1978 for $350,000. Of this, $20,000 was contributed through a neighborhood fund and $20,000 donated by Mrs. Clara-Belle

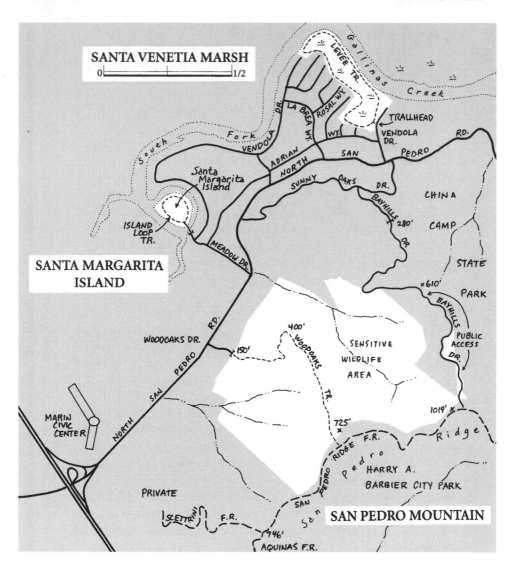

Hamilton (who also contributed $50,000 toward Northridge-area purchases in Blithedale Summit and Baltimore Canyon Preserves).

Note that dogs must be leashed at all times while on the Island, and kept out of marsh areas.

SANTA MARGARITA LOOP TRAIL (.30 miles)

Loop around Preserve

The Loop Trail circles Santa Margarita Island at water's edge. It is joined by crossing the bridge, built in 1970 over the South Fork of Gallinas Creek, at the end of Meadow Drive. The lights atop the four corner pedestals are gone. The District once attempted to cover the bridge with plantings. Swallows nest underneath in spring.

Just across the bridge, look left to see McMahan's old cement wall, with a light pillar. Directly ahead, left of the boulders, is a path to the Island's 50-foot high, wooded summit. Left and right are young valley oaks, unusual within District lands. Most of the valley oaks within Preserves such as Mt. Burdell, Rush Creek, and Deer Island are old-timers, many dating back hundreds of years. A sign reminds visitors that dogs must be leashed while on the Island because of its sensitive wetland habitat.

The marsh edging the Island is a home to the endangered California clapper rail (*Rallus longirostris levipes*), a secretive bird more often heard—its calls sound like clapping—than seen. Still, marshes around Santa Margarita Island are one of the best potential viewing areas in Marin. The pickleweed is also prime habitat for the endangered salt marsh harvest mouse (*Reithrodontomys raviventris*). White-tailed kites (*Elanus leucurus*), a threatened raptor, nested here before the bridge was built and have tried again since, unsuccessful due to disturbance by people and pets.

The loop will be described counterclockwise. Despite the homes lining the opposite bank of South Fork of Las Gallinas Creek, and the non-native grasses and weeds, the Island has a timeless quality. Before landfill, the island rose more abruptly from the water, with a minimum of perimeter grassland.

Some two-thirds around the circuit, the summit path from the start re-enters. Note the yellow, summer-flowering grindelia plants, with their milky sap. There was a major fire here in 1974. It was extinguished using saltwater from the channel.

On the east side, a marshy area is filled with reeds. Look left for a palm tree, one of many planted by McMahan. The loop returns to the start.

Santa Margarita Island and the as-yet untouched Santa Venetia and Civic Center areas, looking east across the Northwestern Pacific railroad track. The picture may have been taken around 1910, just before Mabry McMahan began dredging for his grandiose, but failed, scheme to develop Santa Margarita Island. (Marin County Historical Society)

SANTA VENETIA MARSH

Size: 32.67 acres   Elevation: 0-10 feet

*In the summer of 1988 we completed the loop
trail around the marsh by installing two large
foot bridges where the levees had been
breached. I spent a lot of hours in the mud
and hot sun with the Marin Conservation
Corps crew, digging and setting up the
footings, pumping in the concrete, and
installing the wooden structures of the bridges.*
  *The neighbors immediately showed appre-
ciation for the new access as evidenced by the dusty footprints on
the bare stringers of the bridges even before we had a chance to get
the deck and handrails installed!*   — Rich Gibson, Ranger

TODAY's Santa Venetia Marsh was part of San Pablo Bay prior to diking. The site
was used for soil disposal during development of Santa Venetia after World War II.
There was also extensive dumping of dredging spoils here in 1969, then again in
1987 after the Mosquito Abatement District dug drainage channels for better flow.

The non-profit Trust for Public Land acquired the marsh from the Santa
Venetia Land Corp. in 1973. Three months later, the Trust re-sold the 32.67-acre
parcel to the County for $72,200.

The original 1914 development plans for the adjacent area (see Santa Margarita
Island Preserve) were drawn with a more famous canal city—Venice, Italy—in mind.
Indeed, there were to have been gondolas (hence the adjoining street name, Ven-
dola) plying the channels of the new community, to be called Santa Venetia.

The marsh is a sensitive wildlife habitat. Dogs must be leashed at all times
within the Preserve, and kept on the levee, out of the marsh.

SANTA VENETIA LEVEE TRAIL (1.19 miles)

Loop around Preserve
Note: No bicycles allowed

A levee system circles Santa Venetia Marsh and the perimeter of the Preserve. The
western section of levee, bordering the homes, is part of the low-lying area's flood
control system. The surrounding community has suffered from floods, the most
recent major ones in 1982 and '83. The separate bayside levee is no longer used for
flood control as two breaks, now crossed by bridges, have been opened to permit
tidal action within the marsh.

The loop may be joined from nine signed trailheads at street-ends just north of San Pedro Road. All are in residential neighborhoods; please be courteous. Footbridges, many improved in 1998, cross the ditch. I'll start at the easternmost entry, closest to China Camp State Park, on Vendola Drive opposite the former McPhail School site. There is parking near the MCOSD gate. (Note that there is also a Preserve entry off west Vendola Drive.)

Enter past fenced-in pump station #4. The pump stations, drains, and levee bordering the residential area are maintained by the Las Gallinas Sanitary District and Marin County Flood Control. The loop will be described counter-clockwise so go right and cross the first of two bridges, 20 yards away. A sign reminds visitors that the Preserve is a home to the endangered California clapper rail.

Santa Venetia is a remnant of the once far more extensive salt marshes that ringed San Francisco and San Pablo Bays. More than ninety percent have been lost since settlement began in earnest in 1850. On the outer edges, closer to open water, cordgrass (*Spartina foliosa*) is the most common plant. A bit higher, within the inner marsh, pickleweed (*Salicornia virginica*) is dominant. Also on slightly higher ground is gumweed (*Grindelia humilis*), a yellow-flowered shrub. Several invasives grow on the levee itself, notably a sea of non-native grasses, anise- or licorice-scented sweet fennel (*Foeniculum vulgare*), and patches of iceplant.

The Levee bends left. Ahead is the South Fork of Gallinas Creek, which flows from Civic Center Lagoon into San Pablo Bay, just to the east. Terns hunt with swift, precision dives. Redwinged blackbirds cling to tall tules.

In just under a half-mile, the Road bends left again, heading due west toward Mt. Tamalpais. The North and South Forks of Gallinas Creek meet here. The golf course and driving range in John F. McInnis County Park are across the channel. Even closer is the San Rafael Airport (formerly named Smith Ranch Airport), still used by light planes.

The Road bends left here, passing Pump Station #5 (at .6 miles) by the other (west) end of Vendola Drive. The inner Levee Road, here lined with fennel, runs behind the backyards of homes. It passes seven more access points within the next half-mile. The street ends are, in order (all "Ways"): Rincon, Hacienda, Descanso, Rosal, Estancia, Palmera, and La Playa. The loop ends back at Pump Station #4.

A peaceful walk, babe in arms, over the levee.

SAN PEDRO MOUNTAIN

Size: 357 acres   Elevation: 40-950 feet

*Tony Bennett may have left his heart in San Francisco, but I left a
yard of my hide on San Pedro Ridge. I was investigating an
illegally built trail that had recently cropped up on the ridge
when I heard voices in the distance. I switched into a stealth
mode hoping to catch the trail building culprits red-handed. I
crept along, took a misstep, and rolled head over heels downhill
for about 70 feet. A friendly redwood tree broke my fall. I must
have laid there for 20 minutes assessing the damage. I knew that
I had broken some ribs and that the only way out was to crawl
back to my truck. I eventually made it back to our corporation
yard to dutifully let my chief ranger know that I'd had an
accident and was soon on my way to the emergency room in the
back of an ambulance.*

— *Scott Rasmussen, Supervising Ranger*

SAN PEDRO MOUNTAIN (also called San Pedro Ridge), forms the spine of the peninsula of the same name. In 1844, it was included in the Mexican land grant—the three ranches of Las Gallinas, Santa Margarita, and Punta de San Pedro combined as one and totaling 21,680 acres—awarded to Timothy Murphy.

Around 1868, brothers John and George McNear acquired 2,500 acres of the southern half of the peninsula. They quarried basalt and established a brick making operation (still in business) on San Pedro Point, and grazed livestock on the hills. Part of their holdings are now in China Camp State Park, part developed as Peacock Gap. The 24 acres known as McNears Beach were purchased by the County in 1970 for a park. The San Pedro shore also supported a thriving Chinese shrimping village, with a peak of some 500 residents in the 1880's.

In 1887, Edward Stetson (brother-in-law of Sidney Cushing, who built the Mt. Tamalpais Railway) acquired the land that would become the bulk of today's Preserve. The Stetson farm house was on the site of the former YMCA Building (now the Northview subdivision) on North San Pedro Road. The land remained in Stetson family hands for more than 80 years.

During World War II, anti-aircraft artillery was installed atop San Pedro Ridge to defend Hamilton Air Force Base just a few miles to the north. In 1954, during the Cold War, the Ridge became home to one of 11 Nike missile sites ringing San Francisco Bay. The facility was closed in 1974, when new technology had rendered Nikes obsolete.

By the late 1960's, development pressures on San Pedro Ridge intensified to the point where community leaders and others recognized the need to act quickly if it was to be preserved. A huge housing project, with individual units accessed by "hill-evators," was proposed for the slope above North San Pedro Road. In 1969, the City of San Rafael purchased a 539-acre tract from entertainer Frank Sinatra on the south side of the ridge. It is now Harry A. Barbier Memorial Park, the largest city-owned open space in Marin. In 1977, the State of California, with financial assistance from the MCOSD, acquired more than 1,000 acres on the east slope owned by a developer. It now forms the heart of 1,512-acre China Camp State Park.

In 1971, the Stetson family sold their 257-acre parcel to Jack and Gertrude Fierman. Three years later, just prior to a planned subdivision, the County paid $461,000 for the acreage. There were three small additions, and one of 40 acres (for $70,000), during the following three years. In 1999, a 53-acre parcel was purchased from Daniel and Rose Koo for $200,000 to bring the Preserve to its present size of 357 acres.

Several routes have been illegally cut through the wooded heart of San Pedro Mountain Preserve; please stay off them.

SAN PEDRO RIDGE FIRE ROAD (1.12 miles)
From junction of Scettrini and Aquinas Fire Roads to Bayhills Drive
Intersection: Woodoaks Trail (.43m)

San Pedro Ridge Fire Road forms the Preserve boundary with the City of San Rafael's Harry A. Barbier Memorial Park open space immediately south. To reach any part of the Fire Road requires a long, uphill trek.

The west end of San Pedro Ridge Fire Road (start of measurement) is at the union of Scettrini and Aquinas fire roads, elevation 750 feet. Scettrini F.R. rises one mile from Newcastle Court in the Meadow Oaks development; there is no public parking and the Fire Road crosses private property. Some visitors use a path to Scettrini from San Pablo Avenue opposite the Marin County Law Library. In 1956, Marin County bought the 140-acre Scettrini Ranch for $193,000 in a condemnation proceeding. Upon it was built the Frank Lloyd Wright-designed Civic Center, the first wing of which opened in 1962.

Aquinas Fire Road starts considerably higher than Scettrini and is steeper, so offers a shorter (half-mile) route to San Pedro Ridge Fire Road. The trailhead is the top of Aquinas Drive, off Dominican Drive on San Pedro's southwest slope.

From the unmarked Scettrini/Aquinas junction, San Pedro Ridge F.R. actually opens with a downhill. There will be other dips later, adding to an already tough climb. An MCOSD sign marks where San Pedro Ridge F.R. enters the Preserve.

San Pedro Ridge F.R. reaches a flat, treeless, crest (dubbed "The Bald Spot") offering splendid views. The panorama is almost complete, save to the north-north-east. It is also a great spot to look for raptors such as red-tailed and red-shouldered

see map page 214

hawks, bald and golden eagles, black-shouldered kites, northern harriers, great horned owls, and kestrels and other falcons. Several nest within the Preserve.

The canyon north, the 53-acre former Koo parcel, was only acquired in 1999. A path drops left, part of an illegally built route that has no public exit.

After 60 yards of downhill, San Pedro Ridge F.R. bottoms in a saddle where two trails branch off left over MCOSD land. First is another entry to the path just encountered. Some 10 yards beyond, Woodoaks Trail, marked by an MCOSD sign, begins by rising on the true ridge crest. It drops to Woodoaks Drive, above North San Pedro Road. Opposite, on the right, is a path that winds a mile-and-a-half along the hillside to Gold Hill Fire Road.

Some 100 yards later, the Fire Road passes a trio of utility poles, with two more sets to be passed later. Electricity is being carried up over the deep canyon to the summit ridge via this literally circuitous route.

The Fire Road's longest downhill follows. When reaching the saddle, look left to spot a redwood grove a few yards in. The difference in fog cover, temperature, and rainfall is so marked between the north and south facing slopes that redwoods can thrive so close to chaparral.

San Pedro Ridge Fire Road ends at a gate atop Bayhills Drive. The elevation is only some 100 feet below the ridge's highest point, 1,058 feet, to the southeast. Left and down, the MCOSD owns an easement (hence the blue MCOSD sign, for a right of public passage across private property) over Bayhills Drive. The paved street runs one-and-a-quarter miles to an electronic gate. There is a trail off it right, .3 miles down, to China Camp's Bayview Trail. Bayhills Drive below the gate is an alternate access to San Pedro Ridge F.R., although there is virtually no parking along it.

To the right, the paved road enters Harry A. Barbier Memorial Park. The former Nike missile site is just yards away, at a splendid vista point. The road continues along the ridge, winding between Barbier (right and south) and China Camp State Park (left and north), to the communication towers that were visible during much of the ascent of San Pedro Ridge Fire Road. There are several options down, all making for long loops.

WOODOAKS TRAIL (.98 miles)

From Woodoaks Drive to San Pedro Ridge Fire Road

Woodoaks Trail begins at the top of Woodoaks Drive, a dead-end street off North San Pedro Road. The Trail starts from the right side of the fence, by the MCOSD San Pedro Mountain sign, then veers left.

Barely 100 feet in, madrone and Marin's tallest manzanita species (*Arctostaphylos manzanita*) grow side by side. One of the manzanitas here rises to the supposed height limit of the species, 25 feet.

The Trail crosses a small stream. It then remains on the east side of the ever-deepening creek canyon. The grade is steep most of the way and several sharp bends in the Trail's lower section are precipitous.

At .3 miles is an island of pampas grass, a hard-to-remove invader from South America. Soon after, the woodland temporarily gives way to an open area affording broad views north over the bayside marshlands. Gallinas Creek, which passes two MCOSD preserves, Santa Margarita Island and Santa Venetia Marsh, is clearly visible snaking its way to San Pablo Bay. The perspective of Santa Margarita Island here is perhaps the best anywhere.

A bit above are some pits, dug for brush disposal after a fire here in the 1980's but never filled. When back in light shade, note that many of the native bunchgrasses are green, even in fall.

By .6 miles, look left to see a stand of redwoods that rises with the Trail for a couple of hundred yards. Northern slopes are cooler and wetter than their southern counterparts and thus able to meet the high, year-round water requirements of redwoods.

Just before its high point, the Trail forks around an island of oaks and bays. The two forks meet at the far side of the circle, then the Trail continues right over what was once a fire road.

Views from the true ridge line are glorious. Breaks provide vistas both south, including the San Francisco skyline, and north, including the peaks of White Hill, Loma Alta, Big Rock Ridge, and Mt. Burdell, all MCOSD Preserves. The Trail follows the ridge down for 200 yards, between lines of manzanita.

Woodoaks Trail ends at its junction with San Pedro Ridge Fire Road, in a saddle. Right on San Pedro Ridge F.R. leads to the Preserve boundary, then the junction where Scettrini and Aquinas Fire Roads split off. Bayhills Drive is .7 miles left.

Marin County Parks

Marin County Parks share the same elected governing Board, appointed Commissioners, and General Manager with the Open Space District. But County Parks are managed under different standards—geared to public recreation—from Open Space Preserves.

There are presently 12 County Parks: McNears Beach (55 acres), Paradise Beach (19 acres), Stafford Lake (139 acres), John F. McInnis (441 acres), Deer Park (54 acres), Civic Center Lagoon (20 acres), Agate Beach (6.6 acres), Tiburon Uplands Nature Reserve (24 acres), Black Point Boat Launch (1 acre), Miller Park Boat Launch (6 acres), Bolinas Park (2 acres), and White House Pool (24 acres). Day use fees are required at McNears Beach, Paradise Beach, Stafford Lake and at the two boat launch sites.

TERRA LINDA/SLEEPY HOLLOW DIVIDE

Size: 1,168.8 acres   Elevation range: 80-880 feet

I think the Terra Linda/Sleepy Hollow Divide is a great example of what the District is all about and displays the unique issues we face as a land management agency.

Our staff is challenged by the multiple access points, and the Preserve is almost completely surrounded by urban interface concerns. The terrain and vegetation are somewhat varied and fragile.

The Preserve's highly visible location separates most of Central Marin's developed areas with wildlands. This provides habitat and a corridor for wildlife, and a nearby escape for our neighbors to step out on a trail, or to ride a fire road with great views of the bay and surrounding lands. — Rich Gibson, Ranger

HORSESHOE-SHAPED Terra Linda/Sleepy Hollow Divide Preserve covers the ridges above Santa Margarita Valley. It is, in many ways, the most "complicated" of the Preserves. There are some 75 signed entries, by far the most of any Preserve, and none are particularly more used than the others. Numerous parcel acquisitions were involved. The Preserve is split into two, unconnected halves, called Southern and Northern. Even the Preserve's name differs on signs, with San Rafael Ridge, Terra Linda-Sleepy Hollow Divide, and San Rafael-Sleepy Hollow Divide all in use.

The first public part of the future Preserve was acquired even a few months before the MCOSD was created. Property owners in the Mont Marin area agreed to form an assessment district to buy 184 acres of the old Pimentel Ranch from developers for $317,000. One of the first land purchases made wholly by the MCOSD was also in this Preserve, a 9.57 acre-site above Mission Pass bought July 25, 1973, for $60,000.

The core of the northern section was acquired in early 1977, some 700 acres ringing Santa Margarita Valley. The Freitas family owned most of the south ridge, the Nunes family the north ridge. The $2 million cost came from the District, a City of San Rafael open space bond, and a local open space bond (County Service Area No. 23, approved with a 76 percent "yes" vote in November, 1975).

Manuel T. Freitas (1853-1923), a native of the Azores Islands, bought the 1,200-acre Home Ranch of Santa Margarita Rancho from John Lucas in 1896. His large ranch house stood at the end of a eucalyptus-lined driveway from the highway (a site now occupied by St. Isabella's Church and the Maria B. Freitas Senior Community). Freitas had eight children and bought an additional ranch each time he had a new son. Of the six ranches he owned, three were in the Terra Linda area—Home Ranch, Butcher Ranch, and Upper Ranch—and sections of each are now part of the District. (The Butcher Ranch was later owned by Manuel Pimentel, the Upper Ranch by Tom Nunes.) The Terra Linda subdivision of Freitas' property began in 1953,

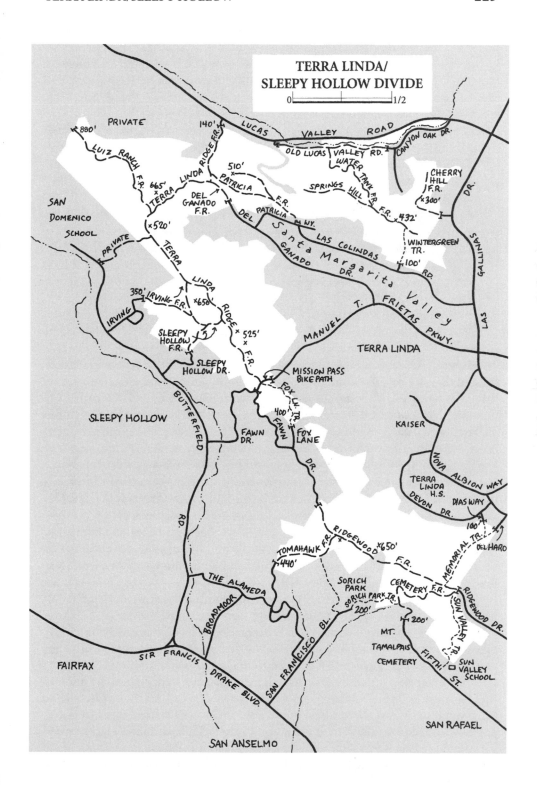

TERRA LINDA/ SLEEPY HOLLOW DIVIDE

0   1/2

and its main street is named for him. All of Terra Linda was annexed into San Rafael by 1972.

Fifty-two acres forming the nucleus of the Preserve's southern section were purchased in 1978 for $168,000. There is a colorful story behind the adjacent 43-acre Hozz parcel (see Ridgewood Fire Road below). In 1988-89, the 69-acre Lang property above Sleepy Hollow was added.

From 1981 through 1987, some 1,000 adult sheep, plus even more lambs, roamed the Preserve, munching vegetation to lower the fire danger. On-site shepherds moved the flocks around. The overgrazing resulted in loss of wildflowers and aided the invasion of non-native plants such as star thistle.

SOUTHERN SECTION (San Rafael Ridge)

CEMETERY FIRE ROAD (.71 miles)
From Preserve boundary at Mt. Tamalpais Cemetery to Ridgewood F.R.
Intersections: Sorich Trail (.00m), Sun Valley Trail (.48m)

The only public access to lower Cemetery F.R. is via Sorich Trail from Sorich Park at the end of San Francisco Boulevard (San Anselmo). Sorich Trail, described below, meets Cemetery F.R. a few feet above the Preserve boundary gate with Mt. Tamalpais Cemetery. (Note that the lower 250 yards of Cemetery Fire Road, not part of the distance cited above, are on cemetery property. The Cemetery has long permitted quiet, respectful, through travel; the 5th Avenue gate in the Sun Valley district of San Rafael is open 8 a.m. to 5 p.m. Dogs must be leashed on cemetery grounds.)

The uphill is steady. Eucalyptus trees are abundant, although the forest has been thinned to reduce fire danger and to help restore native vegetation. Some old, dead eucalyptus were deliberately left standing for the bird nesting sites they provide.

A bend right passes an old quarry site. Views open, and continue to expand. Poison oak borders the route, and all shortcut paths are covered with the dreaded shrub. In mid-spring, hundreds of harvest brodiaea (*Brodiaea elegans*), with clusters of blue flowers atop tall stems, rise out of the grasses.

As the Fire Road nears the ridge crest, several junctions, all to the right, are passed. First, Sun Valley Trail, marked with a signpost, drops to Sun Valley School and 5th Avenue in San Rafael. Take 5th Avenue back to the cemetery for a loop. Next is a path to Los Altos and Crestwood Drives. Then a connector runs the few yards to Ridgewood Fire Road, just in from Ridgewood Drive.

Cemetery Fire Road bends left along the line of eucalyptus to parallel Ridgewood F.R. This .2-mile section offers better views of Mt. Tamalpais, while Ridgewood has views north. Great horned owls roost in the eucalyptus trees and are heard, and sometimes seen, at sunrise and sunset. They are Marin's largest owls.

Just yards from its end, Cemetery F.R. passes a fireplace from a long-gone religious retreat. Note the tin cans in the stones. A short bend right, over a narrow section, brings Cemetery Fire Road onto Ridgewood Fire Road.

Mt. Tamalpais Cemetery was incorporated May 21, 1880. Its original 112 acres were donated by Henry Dubois in return for half the proceeds of cemetery plot sales. Pioneering Marin physician Dr. Alfred Taliaferro laid out the grounds. (Another account says a citizens committee led by Taliaferro purchased the land.) Members of many prominent Marin families, such as Barney, Boyd, Cushing, Dollar, Eldridge, Mailliard, Reed, and more, rest there. New burials are still accepted.

MEMORIAL TRAIL (.45 miles)

From Del Haro Way (Terra Linda) to Ridgewood Fire Road

This very steep, eroded, slippery route would not ordinarily be included, but it has particular local significance and plays a role as access to San Rafael Ridge from the north.

The Trail is a memorial to Bob Hoffman and Mark Platzek, Terra Linda High School cross country runners who trained on the hill in the mid-1970's. They died in an auto accident in 1977, and team members dedicated the route to them.

The Trail starts from an MCOSD-signed entrance atop the short cul-de-sac of Del Haro Way. There has been an unofficial "Memorial Trail" sign on the alternate entry (the one used by the runners) off Dias Way to the west; it is down at press time.

Climb steeply up the grassland. There are many valley oaks in the lower half of the route. Paths left and right lace the hillside but the Trail, ever up, is reasonably clear. Within 100 yards you can look back to a glimpse of San Pablo Bay.

At .14 miles, a fork presents two options up; the one right is marginally less steep. Where these two forks rejoin is a view over the Terra Linda High School campus, including the track where Hoffman and Platzek ran.

The Trail veers left to a view knoll (more easily reachable off Ridgewood F.R.) that is popular with local visitors. Immediately above the knoll, two forks branch. Take the one left if going to Ridgewood Drive, Sun Valley Trail, or Cemetery Fire Road. Follow the one right for travel west on Ridgewood Fire Road.

RIDGEWOOD FIRE ROAD (.86 miles)

From Ridgewood Drive (San Rafael) to Fawn Drive (Sleepy Hollow)
Intersections: Memorial Trail (.04m), Cemetery F.R. (.04m, .23m), Tomahawk F.R. (.71m)

Ridgewood Fire Road begins behind a gate at the upper, west end of San Rafael's Ridgewood Drive. There are immediately fine views north to the Civic Center, San Pablo Bay, and well beyond.

The story behind the acquisition of the 43-acre opening section, called the Hozz property, is a bizarre one. In 1983, a man saying he was the property owner telephoned an offer through a realtor to sell for $150,000.

The Trust for Public Land in San Francisco promptly stepped in with the funds, as a loan, until the City of San Rafael and the County, as equal partners, could complete the purchase. No one, including at the title company, ever saw the man. He had the $135,000 (the price less ten percent realtor's fee) wired to his account, quickly converted the money into gold coins, and disappeared. No problem was suspected until 1988, when the parcel's true owner, Morris Hozz, called to say he was ready to sell.

Even the F.B.I. was brought into the ensuing investigation but the con man was never caught. Years of legal hassles followed, with several of the parties suing one other. Ultimately, the title company reimbursed the Trust for Public Land and, in turn, accepted a smaller out-of-court settlement from the City of San Rafael and the County. Hozz "re-sold" the property for $400,000, the transaction finally completed in 1993.

Within a few yards, to the left just beyond the fenced-in water tank and communications tower, is a key short connector to three other routes. Cemetery Fire Road goes down to Mt. Tamalpais Cemetery. A social path runs parallel to and below Ridgewood Drive, to Los Altos and Crestwood Drives. And Sun Valley Trail, marked by a signpost, drops to 5th Avenue in San Rafael. To the right is Memorial Trail, which drops very steeply to Del Haro Way in Terra Linda.

The eucalyptus trees lining the first .1 mile of the Fire Road are easily visible from Highway 101 and elsewhere and have been a prominent landmark atop what is called San Rafael Ridge for more than 100 years.

Cemetery Fire Road runs parallel to Ridgewood to the left, then joins. Next, to the right, a path climbs very steeply to the top of Cardiac Hill (elevation 650 feet). It was named by the high school cross country runners who trained here.

Old fence posts left are believed to be original demarcations between the Cañada de Herrera and the Rancho San Pedro Santa Margarita y Las Gallinas Mexican land grants. The line of eucalyptus trees down (south) also marks the old boundary; today it divides Mt. Tamalpais Cemetery and San Anselmo's Sorich Ranch Open Space Park.

Views now shift to the south—Ross Valley, Bald Hill, and Mt. Tamalpais. The path from Cardiac Hill returns. Ridgewood F.R. rises to a three-way junction. Left is Tomahawk F.R., which rolls down to Tomahawk Drive in San Anselmo. Ridgewood F.R. descends right for another 250 yards. It ends at an MCOSD-signed gate atop Sleepy Hollow's Fawn Drive.

To connect to the Preserve's northern section, follow Fawn Drive down .3 miles to Fox Lane and veer right, or continue on Fawn to the MCOSD gate at Mission Pass.

SORICH PARK TRAIL (.31 miles)
From Sorich Ranch Park to Cemetery Fire Road

This is a relatively new trail, carved by the MCOSD in 1996 to replace a lower, rough path that crossed into the private property of Mt. Tamalpais Cemetery. Sorich Park Trail now provides a link between San Anselmo and San Rafael.

Sorich Park Trail sets off at an MCOSD signpost 100 yards behind the new (1998) parking lot cleared in San Anselmo's Sorich Ranch Park. The land at the head of the valley here was once the So-Rich Dairy, named for its milk products.

Sorich Park Trail skirts between the edge of San Anselmo's corporation yard to the right and a grassy hillside left. It then enters eucalyptus forest, where it remains.

The trees provide cooling shade, welcome on the hot days common here in summer and fall. The blue gum eucalyptuses here date from around the 1870's, when the trees were planted throughout the Bay Area as windbreaks, as an ornamental, and as a supposedly quick source of wood (the timber proved near worthless). Eucalpytuses, native to Australia, are high in volatile oils, earning them a reputation as a fire danger. They have also been called "widow makers," as they can shed limbs without warning. Removal efforts have proceeded in several Bay Area parks, such as Angel Island, and there has been some thinning here. Older trees carry evidence of the last major fire through here, in 1978.

A new footbridge brings the Trail over Irwin Creek, which flows underground along 5th Avenue to San Rafael Canal. The remaining section is more markedly uphill, aided by switchbacks.

Sorich Park Trail ends at Cemetery Fire Road. Immediately right is a gate at the boundary between MCOSD land and Mt. Tamalpais Cemetery (private) below. Left leads up to Ridgewood Fire Road.

SUN VALLEY TRAIL (.67 miles)
From Sun Valley School (5th Avenue, San Rafael) to Cemetery Fire Road
Note: Access is through Sun Valley School and beside a private parcel, so pass quietly

This is a relatively new Trail, carved and dedicated in 1991 soon after the District acquired the property. Switchbacks ease what had formerly been a very steep, more direct path.

Entry to the foot of the Trail is over an easement along the west edge of Sun Valley School property. The gate is open at all times, whether school is in session or not. Horses graze on the private property across the fence left. It is 150 yards from 5th Avenue to the Preserve boundary and the step barrier marking the true start of Sun Valley Trail.

The first of several sharp bends is at 100 yards, where an oak and a laurel grow out of a rock outcrop. By early summer, gilia, with dozens of blue flowers atop each head, dots the grassland. From August into November, masses of yellow tarweed provide late floral color.

Mt. Tamalpais Cemetery comes into view. The most prominent tombstone, a winged angel, marks the grave of John Joseph Reed, his wife Carlota, and son John Paul. John Joseph, eldest son of John Thomas Reed, the first land grantee in Marin, was born in Mill Valley in July, 1837, among the first of European stock born in the County.

Around the next bend, a glimpse of the Oakland skyline comes into view. Mt. Tamalpais is a striking presence due south.

Higher, coyote brush is expanding and will likely cover ever more of the grassy hillside. Still higher, the Trail encounters the eucalyptus trees that line the ridge.

A path right runs below Ridgewood Drive to Crestwood Drive. The Trail ends when it hits Cemetery F.R., which comes in left from Mt. Tamalpais Cemetery. To the right is another Crestwood Drive path entry and a connection to Ridgewood Fire Road.

TOMAHAWK FIRE ROAD (.37 miles)

From Tomahawk Drive (San Anselmo) to Ridgewood Fire Road
Intersection: Sorich F.R. (.22m)
Note: No parking west side of Tomahawk Drive, or in or above circle

From the turnaround atop San Anselmo's Tomahawk Drive, a public easement (marked by a blue MCOSD sign) crosses one-eighth mile of private land to Tomahawk Fire Road. Pass the two upper houses and a gate, then climb the pavement. Tomahawk Trail, a dead-end across private open space, veers left. Tomahawk F.R. begins above the water tank, at the MCOSD gate. Before the 12 houses of the Quarry Mountain development on upper Tomahawk Drive were built in the early 1990's, the Fire Road began at Miwok Drive. Public access through to the Preserve was a condition of the project's approval.

Left of the gate at the Fire Road's start is a long-time, private, horse ranch, accessed from Holstein Road. Horses can often be seen in the corral, or grazing outside it.

After a stiff but short climb, broad vistas to the south and east suddenly open. Continue up. A prominent chert boulder near the crest is popular among area residents as a stargazing site. The San Francisco and Oakland skylines are visible, along with a glimpse of the Golden Gate Bridge.

Tomahawk F.R. drops to a saddle. The boundary between San Anselmo's Sorich Ranch Park and the MCOSD Preserve passes through here. Extremely steep Sorich F.R. (unofficial name, narrow and outside the Preserve) departs right. It drops .4 miles to San Francisco Boulevard, the final yards over steps added in 1998.

In the saddle, a path branches right. It is used as a shortcut to Ridgewood Fire Road, but is muddy in winter and lined with poison oak.

Tomahawk closes with a final, very steep climb. Northern vistas open at the crest, where Tomahawk ends at its junction with Ridgewood F.R. Left is a drop to Fawn Drive in Sleepy Hollow and connection with the northern section of the Preserve. Right follows the ridge line to Ridgewood Drive in San Rafael.

NORTHERN SECTION

CHERRY HILL FIRE ROAD (.41 miles)
From Cherry Hill Drive to Cherry Hill
Notes: Dead-end

If the hill this Fire Road tops had an early name, it is not known. The short streets on its east flank, off Las Gallinas Avenue, all bear different "Hill" names; Twelve Oak, Clover, Pine, Maple, and Cherry. The latter now prevails because the route sets off at its end.

Deeply rutted Cherry Hill F.R. climbs steeply over grassland. Poppies are abundant. In 300 yards, a saddle (a pass or, in mountaineering jargon, a "col") is reached. Ahead is a path to the upper end of Canyon Oak Drive; other paths are blocked by residential fences. To the left, a very steep path rises to Park Ridge F.R. Veer right.

The first and highest (around 350 feet) of three crests along the Fire Road is at .2 miles. There are splendid 360-degree views, south to Mt. Tamalpais, west to the upper part of the Preserve, north to Big Rock Ridge, and east to Mt. Diablo. A very steep down is followed by another uphill and a second crest, at one-third mile. The pattern is repeated to a third, lower crest and the Fire Road's end. The continuing path left deteriorates and dead-ends, the one right drops steeply .1 mile to Cedar Hill Drive off Coast Oak Way.

DEL GANADO FIRE ROAD (.14 miles)
From Del Ganado Road to Terra Linda Ridge Fire Road
Intersection: Patricia F.R. (.02m)

This short fire road sets off from the upper end of Del Ganado Road. Less than 50 yards up, Patricia Fire Road branches off to the right, toward Patricia Way.

Water tanks—a round one left, a rectangular one right—catch flow from hillside springs above, as they have for decades. Invasive yellow and purple thistles border the way. Native tarweeds hold out, and add more yellow color in late summer and fall. There is evidence of erosion control work undertaken by the District.

Del Ganado F.R. ends at the next, three-way junction. Looming right is a 550-foot-high hill. Around it, Terra Linda Ridge F.R. descends right, to Lucas Valley Road. Left, Terra Linda Ridge F.R. climbs to circle Santa Margarita Valley.

FOX LANE TRAIL (.25 miles)

From Fox Lane (Sleepy Hollow) to Mission Pass
Note: Night parking restrictions on Fox Lane

This is a short but important Trail as it is part of the connection between the southern and northern sections of the Preserve. It begins at the end of Fox Lane, the only street intersecting upper Fawn Drive.

The Trail starts across the grass, then quickly descends into a pleasant oak and bay woodland. Poison oak is abundant; be alert.

The Trail drops out of the woods and ends where it meets paved Mission Pass. Three hundred yards right is the top of Freitas Parkway in Terra Linda. Fawn Drive is 100 yards below left. Rising straight ahead, as a paved road, is Terra Linda Ridge Fire Road.

IRVING FIRE ROAD (.63 miles)

From Irving Drive (Sleepy Hollow) to Terra Linda Ridge Fire Road

Irving Fire Road sets off from an MCOSD gate near the top of Irving Drive, the last right turn off Butterfield Road when heading up the valley. A turnout adjacent to the Trailhead has parking for a couple of cars but do not block the gate.

Irving Fire Road rises amidst a grassland sprinkled with oaks. Invasive star thistles are everywhere, virtually the only flowering plant by late summer. The Fire Road crosses a seep and enters a denser oak and bay grove. Above, the Fire Road levels, then descends.

At .28m, Irving Fire Road bends sharply left and up to climb Lang Hill. (The 180-yards fire road straight ahead, to Sleepy Hollow F.R., is considered a spur of Irving F.R.) The Lang Realty Corporation of San Francisco began erecting the first homes in the Sleepy Hollow tract in the early 1930's.

There are great views of Mt. Tamalpais awaiting those looking back. Irving F.R. then enters an oak grove. Just ahead is an intersection with a path right (Lang Hill Trail) climbing to the 655-foot summit of Lang Hill.

Irving Fire Road crests a few yards later. There is then a short drop to its end at Terra Linda Ridge F.R. Left leads toward Luiz Ranch Fire Road. Right circles Lang Hill.

The "Irving" of the street and Fire Road's name is New York writer Washington Irving (1783-1859). Street names in the Sleepy Hollow subdivision are taken from his short story *The Legend of Sleepy Hollow*.

LUIZ RANCH FIRE ROAD (.73 miles)

From Terra Linda Ridge Fire Road to Preserve's northwest boundary
Note: Separate from Luiz Fire Road in Lucas Valley Preserve

Luiz Ranch Fire Road rises off Terra Linda Ridge F.R. The junction is one-eighth mile beyond San Domenico F.R. when traveling from Sleepy Hollow and .4 miles beyond Del Ganado F.R when coming from Terra Linda.

Luiz climbs, steeply and steadily, along the grassy ridge line. In the 1960's, the Marin County Board of Supervisors and Caltrans planned to extend Highway 17 (now called Highway 580) from San Rafael to west Marin over this ridge. But the election of Peter Arrigoni to the County Board in 1968, ousting freeway advocate Ernest Kettenhofen, produced a 3-2 majority (with Michael Wornum and Arnold Baptiste) against the idea.

The views include San Francisco and the major peaks of Marin. Big Rock Ridge rises dramatically on the north side of Lucas Valley. The huge boulder of Big Rock itself, directly on Lucas Valley Road, can be discerned by sharp-eyed observers.

Luiz Ranch F.R. passes oaks charred in a 1997 fire. Just above is the fence and gate (make sure it is closed) marking the Preserve boundary with private Luiz Ranch beyond. At elevation 880 feet, this is the highest point in the Preserve, and the remotest. (The crest of the Fire Road itself, on private property, is 1,050 feet.)

Members of the Luiz family have operated dairy ranches on both sides of Lucas Valley Road for generations.

MISSION PASS ROAD (.23 miles)

From Fawn Drive (Sleepy Hollow) to top of
Manuel T. Freitas Parkway (Terra Linda)
Intersections: Terra Linda Ridge F.R. (.06m), Fox Lane Trail (.06m)
Note: Maintained by County Parks Department

Asphalt-covered Mission Pass was built as a bicycle path to connect the Santa Margarita (Terra Linda) and Sleepy Hollow valleys, and remains an important Central Marin bike and pedestrian connection. Plans have been periodically floated to widen the Pass and open it to auto traffic—a nearly 11-mile drive is now required to go between the two ends, less than a quarter-mile apart—but opposition is overwhelming.

The west entry gate is opposite 390 Fawn Drive, a half-mile up from Butterfield Road and just above Brookside School, Upper Campus (the former Hidden Valley School). There is some parking along Fawn Drive's east shoulder below the gate, but leave at least six feet clearance from the center of the roadway.

It is 100 yards, moderately steep, up to the true pass. At the crest, Terra Linda Ridge F.R. rises left. It too is paved, once a driveway to a Catholic priests' retreat just above. (The priests' home apparently led to the name "Mission Pass.") Other signs of the old house remain here as well. To the right is Fox Lane Trail, which rises to Fox Lane, a short street off upper Fawn Drive.

Begin the descent. The center line is for the many bicyclists who travel the Pass. There are fine views over Santa Margarita Valley, dairy grazing land until subdivision began in 1953.

Mission Pass Road ends at a barrier atop Manuel T. Freitas Parkway, where there is ample parking.

OLD LUCAS VALLEY ROAD (.62 miles)

From Canyon Oak Drive to Lucas Valley Road opposite Mt. Lassen Drive
Intersection: Water Tank F.R. (.27m)
Note: Paved

As the name indicates, this is the earlier routing of the main road through Lucas Valley. So it is not surprising to find it paved and striped down its center.

Trailheads at both ends have adequate parking. The route will be described from the eastern end, off Upper Oak Drive, also entry to San Rafael's Jerry R. Russom Memorial Park. In the early 1970's, the late Russom chaired the effort to form the Mont Marin Assessment District for acquiring the area as open space. He was later a member of the San Rafael City Council.

The old asphalt road sets off west. To the right is Miller Creek, born high on the slope of Big Rock Ridge and the only year-round creek in the Preserve. It still supports a modest steelhead salmon run. Willows line the bank. The creek was named for James Miller. He arrived in Marin in 1844 as co-leader of the first successful wagon train crossing of the Sierra, and became a prosperous rancher.

Fifty yards in, to the right, a planted fir tree carries a plaque reading, "In Memory of Fred Okey Jr., Dedicated September 23, 1979." Ahead are a bench and creekside picnic tables. To the left is an open field owned by the City of San Rafael. At 500 feet, on the near side of the MCOSD boundary sign, a path sets off left through the grassland.

The left side of Old Lucas Valley Road is now bordered by tree-covered hillside. With Miller Creek on the right, it makes for a pastoral scene, save for traffic noise from nearby Lucas Valley Road. Look along the creek for stately white alders (*Alnus rhombifolia*), hardly a rare tree in Marin but not particularly common within District preserves. Pendant male clusters are conspicuous by December. Then, in Howell's words in *Marin Flora*, "To see the green-gold of [alder's] blossoming crowns in January is one of the floral treats of the year."

The Road rolls gently, narrowed in places by slips into the creek and slides from the hill. Just past a quarter-mile is a junction with Water Tank F.R. It rises to a water tank, then on to the ridge top.

Old Lucas Valley Road exits on Lucas Valley Road opposite Mt. Lassen Drive. The gates bear the bicentennial dates of 1976 and 1996. The road up is a private drive.

PATRICIA FIRE ROAD (.61 miles)

From Del Ganado Fire Road to top of hill
Intersection: Patricia Way/Las Colindas Road access (.27m)
Note: Dead-end

Patricia Fire Road climbs to the highest point on the Preserve's northern ridge, where it dead-ends.

The Fire Road may be said to start 50 yards up Del Ganado F.R. from the Preserve gate, branching to the right. (It can also be considered as starting just ahead, at the Patricia Way entry). The Fire Road rises gently over the grassland, then drops slightly. A palm tree on the right and a water pipeline collecting spring flows are landmarks.

A quarter-mile in, the Fire Road bends sharply left. Straight ahead at the bend is the access route from both Patricia Way and Las Colindas Road. Patricia Way is closer (100 yards, veering right), hence the Fire Road's name.

Patricia F.R. now begins a steep, steady climb. Some 300 yards up, the Fire Road approaches the fenced, private driveway of a home high on the ridge. An unofficial path crosses that some visitors take right, along the fence, to Springs Hill Fire Road.

Twenty yards higher, Patricia F.R. bends left just before the driveway. The Fire Road is narrowed for about 100 feet. There is then a final one-sixth mile rise. Patricia Fire Road dead-ends on the summit knoll (called "Baldy" by local residents). The views are glorious, justifying the climb. An extremely steep path continues down to the Del Ganado F.R./Terra Linda Ridge F.R. intersection.

SLEEPY HOLLOW FIRE ROAD (.27 miles)

From top of Sleepy Hollow Drive to Terra Linda Ridge F.R.
Intersection: Irving F.R. spur (.18m)

Sleepy Hollow Fire Road starts from the MCOSD gate near the top of steep Sleepy Hollow Drive. Note that left of the gate is a private driveway.

The narrow Fire Road's lower yards are studded with oaks. In some 200 yards, a fine view of Mt. Tamalpais opens. You may hear the sounds of youngsters at Brookside School, Upper Campus; its playing field is soon visible as well. Vetches (genus *Vicia*), members of the pea family, color the grassland lavender-purple in late spring.

Sleepy Hollow F.R. meets the ridge line at its junction with a spur of Irving F.R. Left leads down to Irving Drive, another street off Butterfield Drive.

A 150-yard stretch around the east side of Lang Hill brings Sleepy Hollow Fire Road to its end at a three-way intersection. Left, Terra Linda Ridge F.R. heads toward Luiz Ranch Fire Road. Right, it drops a half-mile to Mission Pass.

Harvey Butterfield (1823-1903) leased a ranch covering today's Sleepy Hollow from Pedro Sais, son of the original land grantee. Peter Austin and Warren Dutton were the next owners, but Butterfield kept his lease. In 1887, the banker Ansel Hotaling foreclosed on Austin and Dutton's mortgage. Ansel's son Richard Hotaling then moved on to the ranch. He renamed it Sleepy Hollow, from the short story by Washington Irving, imported 200 Holsteins from Holland, and built an estate home just inside the present San Domenico School gate. In 1906, he leased the land to Sigmund Herzog.

A 19-hole golf course on the valley floor, with the old Hotaling mansion serving as clubhouse, opened in 1937. It closed two years later for lack of irrigation water. The Hotaling mansion burned in the 1950's but the foundations and steps are still evident.

During World War II, the Army maintained a secret ammunition storage depot in Sleepy Hollow, manned by 30 soldiers. Two anti-aircraft guns were deployed in the hills. Long-time residents recall the silo sirens sounding every New Year's Eve, until 1959.

The subdivision of Sleepy Hollow began in the 1930's, with street names taken from Irving stories. Choice acre-lots originally went for $1,000. The Sisters of St. Dominic bought the 550-acre parcel at the head of the valley and their San Domenico School relocated to it from San Rafael in 1965.

SPRINGS HILL FIRE ROAD (.89 miles)

Along ridge separating Terra Linda and Gallinas Valley
Intersections: Wintergreen Trail (.34m), Water Tank F.R. (.42m)

This is an odd fire road, dead-ending on both sides. Most people reach the Fire Road in the middle from the north (Gallinas Valley is widely called Lucas Valley, but the latter is actually to the west and drains towards Nicasio) on Water Tank Fire Road or from the south via Wintergreen Trail. But, for continuity, Springs Hill F.R. will be described from its eastern end.

A very steep path climbs from Corte San Benito off Park Ridge Road in the Mont Marin district. (Alternate names for the route are Park Ridge F.R. and Mont Marin F.R.) In 400 feet, the path meets the ridge and start of the narrow Fire Road.

The views are at once outstanding. The route rolls over the grassland, treeless save for a lone coast live oak. A very steep path right connects to Cherry Hill Fire Road. In a saddle, Wintergreen Trail, a very steep route down to Wintergreen Terrace in Terra Linda, enters on the left.

The Fire Road rises and passes some striking serpentine outcrops. It then drops to another saddle, where Water Tank Fire Road comes in on the right from Old Lucas Valley Road. Climbing resumes. A bench, placed in 1999, bears a plaque, "In Loving Memory of Ricky Tighlman Earle III, 7/23/78-3/1/97." It's a fine place to rest and enjoy the views.

The Fire Road slopes down as it approaches a private residence, served by a driveway up from Lucas Valley Road. The home was built in 1964 by Thomas Nunes, former owner of the Upper Ranch which covered this section of the Preserve (and across Gallinas Valley up Big Rock Ridge). A path skirts the fence to Patricia F.R.

Springs Hill Fire Road itself ends at the private fence line. It once continued down to Lucas Valley Road over part of the driveway and a now overgrown section.

Seventeen springs seep out of the serpentine band that underlies the hill's metamorphic rock upper layer. The flow from these springs was directed into a 75-foot reservoir at the top of today's Wintergreen Terrace, furnishing all the water for the old Freitas Home Ranch and its dairy operation.

TERRA LINDA RIDGE FIRE ROAD (1.94 miles)
From Mission Pass to Lucas Valley Road
Intersections: Sleepy Hollow F.R. (.45m), Irving F.R. (.80m), San Domenico F.R. (1.07m), Luiz Ranch F.R. (1.20m), Del Ganado F.R. (1.60m)

This well-traveled Fire Road begins, paved, to the west-northwest from the crest of Mission Pass. The short, steep, opening section is rewarded with striking Mt. Tamalpais views on the ridge line.

The pavement and ornamental landscaping, including fruit trees, relate to a building site once occupied by priests in the Passionist Fathers (Catholic) order. The house was torn down soon after the parcel was acquired by the District in 1973. There are remnants of the residence on the flattened area. There is much chert protruding here and an old chert quarry is still evident just ahead.

Terra Linda F.R. rolls, mostly up. Shortcut paths have been worn through the grassland. Soon, oaks border the way. Yellow star-thistle is pervasive.

At just under a half-mile, a plaque on the right marks the boundary of the former Lang property. The inscription reads:

SLEEPY HOLLOW OPEN SPACE, ACQUIRED THE SUMMER OF 1988,
THROUGH THE COOPERATIVE EFFORT OF
SLEEPY HOLLOW HOMES ASSOCIATION, MARIN COMMUNITY FOUNDATION,
MARIN COUNTY SUPERVISORS, AND MARIN OPEN SPACE DISTRICT
ENJOY—IT'S YOURS AND OURS IN PERPETUITY

A few yards beyond, the Fire Road meets the top of Sleepy Hollow F.R., which goes left down to Irving F.R., then Sleepy Hollow Drive. Veer right. The old fence across the Fire Road here was not removed until the 1990's.

The Fire Road climbs, shaded on both sides by oaks. Lang Hill is on the left. Views open right over the Santa Margarita Valley and well beyond. ("Santa Margarita" was a name applied to a broader area, including today's Terra Linda, in mission days.)

Soon after Terra Linda Ridge F.R. returns to grassland, Irving Fire Road departs left. It rises briefly on Lang Hill, then drops to Irving Drive in Sleepy Hollow. There are splendid views of Mt. Tam, White Hill, and Loma Alta.

Another old fence line is passed. Terra Linda Ridge F.R. crests, then begins a sharp descent. The softball field and stables area of San Domenico School become visible. San Domenico Fire Road (only the upper 100 yards are within the Preserve, so the route is not separately described) drops very steeply left to the school's stables. A path goes right.

The San Domenico campus covers nearly 550 acres from the valley floor up the canyon to the top of Lomita, just below the summit of Loma Alta. Much of it borders MCOSD land, in this and Loma Alta Preserve. San Domenico was founded as an all-girls school in Benicia by the Dominican Sisters in 1850, making it the oldest independent school in California. It moved first to San Rafael then to the present campus, formerly the Hotaling Dairy and later a golf course, in 1965. The school now educates boys and girls from pre-kindergarten through grade eight while its high school remains girls-only.

Terra Linda Ridge F.R. continues to descend sharply. It then levels before meeting Luiz Ranch Fire Road to the left. Luiz rises to the private property boundary at the western end of the Preserve.

The Fire Road now descends steadily. It passes a major slide repair project undertaken in 1999. Just below to the right is Santa Margarita Valley Park. There is an MCOSD gate across from the park, but no maintained trail.

The next intersection, last on the long route, is with Del Ganado Fire Road. It drops right one-sixth mile to the top of Del Ganado Drive.

There is now a pleasant descent through a shaded creek canyon. For a short while, one feels transported back to the Marin of the rancho era. Lower, the Fire Road passes close to a private horse barn and equestrian facility. Just beyond it, an abandoned old ranch road up right dead-ends at a private driveway.

Terra Linda Ridge F.R. ends at Lucas Valley Road, across from Mt. Muir Court. To the left are entries to two private ranches.

WATER TANK FIRE ROAD (.53 miles)
From Old Lucas Valley Road to Springs Hill Fire Road

This Fire Road has two halves, and two characters. The steeper lower section, on the north side of the ridge, is wooded, cooler, and wetter. The rolling upper section, above the water tank, is drier, shadeless, grassland.

Water Tank Fire Road rises from Old Lucas Valley Road one-quarter mile east of the Mt. Lassen gate. The utility pole at the junction is numbered "1363."

Early in the climb, look left for blue elderberry (*Sambucus mexicana*), one of the richer stands in the District. The elderberries here are generally 10-20 feet in height but are classified as shrubs because they lack a main trunk. The 3-9 deciduous leaflets per group are serrated, and elliptic to ovate in shape. But most distinctive are the clusters of blue fruits in fall (actually black when mature, with a whitish coating that makes them appear blue). Unfortunately, elderberries are toxic in quantity unless cooked. Miwoks brewed the berries into a tea and made clapper sticks and flutes from the stalks.

Bay trees prevail over oaks in the adjacent woodland, as they often do on the wetter north slopes of bay-oak forests. After a quarter-mile of steady climbing, the Fire Road meets the water tank. Veer around it to continue.

The route drops and there is a marked change in vegetation. The shrub baccharis is abundant in the grassland. A water pipe, which borders the Fire Road, meets a ditch on the right. Moisture-loving willows take advantage of the seepage.

The Fire Road now climbs to meet Springs Hill Fire Road atop the ridge. Mt. Tamalpais suddenly comes into view. Wintergreen Trail is 400 feet to the left. Right is a dead-end at a private home, in .6 miles.

WINTERGREEN TRAIL (.22 miles)
From Wintergreen Terrace to Springs Hill Fire Road

Steep Wintergreen Trail provides access from the south to the Springs Hill summit ridge. The route begins atop the short cul-de-sac of Wintergreen Terrace in Terra Linda. Here stood a cement-lined reservoir (70 feet long, 40 feet wide, 22 feet deep) that once collected water from the 17 springs on the hill above. The water was then piped across the valley to a smaller reservoir on a knoll above the Freitas Ranch buildings, which stood on the present site of St. Isabella's Church.

The Trail, deeply rutted, rises straight up the hillside. (A planned re-route will ease the steepness.) At .15 miles, Wintergreen Trail bends around a serpentine out-crop. There are striking views over Terra Linda to Mt. Tamalpais.

Wintergreen Trail ends at Springs Hill Fire Road on the ridge line. Sweeping vistas open to the north. It is .3 miles left to Water Tank Fire Road. Right, Springs Hill F.R. narrows and dead-ends.

Jean Starkweather, a long-time District volunteer, leads a walk in Terra Linda/Sleepy Hollow Divide Preserve.

TIBURON RIDGE

Size: 15.1 acres   Elevation range: 120-320 feet

*When I stand and face west on the upper slopes of this small
Preserve, the roar of traffic on 101 rings in my ears. North a few
hundred yards are new townhouses, south are old and new
condominiums and single-family homes. But turn around and
face east and you can see why this is the little Open Space that
could.*

*A great example of a green belt, this ridge separates the
communities of Mill Valley, Corte Madera, and Tiburon; keeping
nature where houses might have been. Connected by county and
city open space, the hillside leads to Ring Mountain, with all its
rare and wonderful biology.*

*As I walk east, the noise of the internal combustion engine
fades, replaced by the sounds of birds and insects, the whoosh of
wind across grass and brush. Oak woodlands reach up the hill to
the limit of their habitat and grassland spreads over the top
slopes. I remember these spectacular views of the Tiburon
Peninsula; the Bay and the expansive lands beyond will be there
for others when I am long gone.*

— Chris Bramham, Chief Ranger

AT JUST 15 ACRES, Tiburon Ridge is second smallest of the District's 32 Preserves. It
is also little visited, as it is unsigned and the one route through it has no public exit.
But, though few recognize it, Tiburon Ridge is one of the most visible Preserves,
adjacent to busy Highway 101 atop the hill that separates Mill Valley from Corte
Madera. Tiburon Ridge Preserve provides a permanent greenbelt on the east side of
the highway, as Alto Bowl/Horse Hill Preserve does directly across on the west side.

The Tiburon peninsula took its name from "Punta de Tiburon," Spanish for
"Shark Point." The Preserve, part of the former Koch property, was acquired by the
MCOSD through a development dedication.

The principal history of the Preserve area involved railroads. In 1871, the North
Pacific Coast Railroad Company was organized and hired Chinese laborers to build
a narrow gauge (three feet between rails) line north from Sausalito. It ultimately
stretched 85 miles to the Russian River in Sonoma County. The original impetus
was to haul redwoods out of western Marin and Sonoma.

The track began at a new Sausalito ferry terminal, at today's site. It hugged the
Sausalito shore, then crossed Richardson Bay to Strawberry Point over a 4,250-foot
bridge. The middle 50-feet of the bridge was movable to let boats pass.

The single track ran up the east shore of Strawberry Peninsula. It then made
its way up and over Corte Madera Ridge, a few yards south of today's Preserve, at a

crossing called Collins Summit. The line then ran through the Ross Valley, under White Hill (see Loma Alta Preserve), and on to west Marin and the Russian River.

The climb over 250-feet high Collins Summit was a slow, punishing one in both directions and an unwelcome feature of the route. When a rival line, Peter Donohue's San Francisco and North Pacific Railroad, began extending south to a new ferry terminal in Tiburon, the North Pacific Coast Railroad responded. In the early 1880's, they built a new line (part of which is now the Sausalito-Mill Valley Multi-Use Path (see Bothin Marsh Preserve) that reached Corte Madera through the new Alto Tunnel. When this faster route opened in 1884, the Collins Summit track was abandoned.

Donohue's standard gauge (three feet, six inches between tracks) line ran from downtown Tiburon along Richardson Bay, past stops called Hilarita and Reed's. It then went under a tunnel in the area between today's Tiburon Ridge and Ring Mountain Preserves, with the next stop north called Green Brae.

 Donohue's line was completed just six days after the North Pacific Coast's. Both charged fifty cents for a round-trip to San Francisco, including the ferry ride. The Tiburon terminus offered the world's largest ferry boat, the Ukiah, launched in 1891. It was 291 feet long, 78 feet wide, and capable of carrying 4,000 passengers and 16 loaded freight cars. Each of the competing railroads made the trip from San Rafael to the City (at the Ferry Building) in under an hour.

The two lines remained competitors until they were merged (along with other lines) in 1906 as the Northwestern Pacific (NWP) Railroad. The NWP ran all commuter passenger service on the Alto Tunnel route. But the line under the Tiburon Ridge Preserve tunnel remained active and busy for freight hauling. (Although there was one notorious, last passenger train. In 1934, mobster Al Capone and 52 other convicts rode through the tunnel, handcuffed in an armored car, on their way to becoming the first inmates of the new Federal prison on Alcatraz Island.) Freight service continued until September 25, 1967. The Tiburon section of track is now a popular multi-use path.

There is one route to and through the Preserve, a very steep fire road that has no public access to its base so is not separately described. The upper end of this fire road has two entries off the section of Ring Mountain F.R. over Town of Tiburon Open Space between the Ring Mountain Preserve boundary and the top of Via Los Altos. From its top, the fire road rolls, mostly steeply down, over grassland, through a eucalyptus grove, and exits onto private property of a residential development off Central Drive.

see map on page 194

VERISSIMO HILLS
Size: 109.55 acres   Elevation range: 200-520 feet

B.F.T. (Big Friendly Tree) comes to mind when I think of Verissimo Hills. As a new seasonal aide for Open Space in the early 1980's, one of my first projects was to build a rock wall along the (at the time) new Ravine Trail. In the middle of the summer the weather was hot and dry, and the slope faced south into the afternoon sun. I grew to appreciate the cool shade of a big Live Oak under which I worked for several days. When I hike the area I visit my wall, and give a friendly "Thanks" pat to that big oak for its help during that hot summer.   — Chris Bramham, Chief Ranger

JOHN TEIXEIRA VERISSIMO (1874-1929) came to Marin from the Azores Islands in the 1890's. He first worked on a ranch in Olema, where he met Theodora Bettencourt (1871-1949). They married in 1897 and had two daughters, Edith and Mae.

Around 1900, John leased the Connell Ranch off South Novato Boulevard. In 1913, he bought the E Ranch from the Bello and Souza families. He also acquired property in downtown Novato, where the family lived, first on Grant Avenue, then Machin Street. In 1914, he built the Verissimo Building on Grant.

Mae Verissimo married Joseph Sanchez in 1935. The couple lived in a house they built on the southwest corner of Novato Boulevard and Tamalpais Avenue, then later in another on Vineyard Road. They had no children. In 1960, they sold the part of E Ranch upon which today's Pleasant Valley sits. In 1978, they sold the property between Pleasant Valley and Vineyard Road, now called Verissimo Valle.

In 1985, Mae Verissimo and Joseph Sanchez donated Verissimo Hills to the District, and people of Marin. The Preserve was originally called Sanchez Hills but in 1988, Joseph requested the name to be changed to honor his wife's family. The Sanchez/Verissimo family also sold Little Mountain Preserve to the District.

OAK VALLEY TRAIL (.10 miles)
From Oak Valley Drive to Ravine Trail

Oak Valley Drive is a short street off Sutro Avenue, and Oak Valley Trail departs from an MCOSD gate at its top. The Trail passes between two of the new homes. A tangle of blackberry bushes abuts a seep.

Oak Valley Trail ends at Ravine Trail. Left leads down to Ravine Way off Vineyard Road and right up to Verissimo Hills Trail.

see map on page 147

RAVINE TRAIL (.28 miles)

From Ravine Way to Verissimo Hills Trail
Intersection: Oak Valley Trail (.10m)

Ravine Trail sets off from the top of Ravine Way (the paved road higher, to the left, is a private driveway). There is an MCOSD gate and, a few yards in, a trail sign.

The Trail immediately crosses boards over a culvert. It then sets off up the hillside. A boundary sign left reminds of adjacent private property. Just before 100 yards, the Trail enters a small grove of oaks and bays lining the watercourse.

At one-tenth mile, Ravine Trail meets Oak Valley Trail, which goes right .1 mile to Oak Valley Drive. Veer left and up. As the Trail rises over the grassland, broad views open. Mt. Diablo can be seen to the east. South are the redwoods atop Indian Tree Preserve.

Ravine Trail ends at Verissimo Hills Trail. Left leads to Sanchez Fire Road, then a climb to North Marin Water District lands. Right, Verissimo Hills Trail dead-ends high on the Preserve's ridge line.

SANCHEZ FIRE ROAD (.12 miles)

From Sanchez Way to Verissimo Hills Trail

Sanchez Fire Road offers entry into Verissimo Hills Preserve from the north. It is also one option (Stafford Lake Trail is another) for crossing between Little Mountain and Indian Tree Preserves.

Sanchez Fire Road climbs from the top of Sanchez Way, off Center Drive. The early going may be muddy from a spring flowing out of the hill. In September, a sea of tarweed flowers lines the way. There is also coyote brush.

Views open to Big Rock Ridge just before the Fire Road crests and ends at Verissimo Hills Trail. Right is a climb to the Preserve's boundary with North Marin Water District land. Just left, Ravine Trail departs Verissimo Hills Trail to Vineyard Road and access to Indian Tree Preserve.

VERISSIMO HILLS TRAIL (.70 miles)

From Preserve's west boundary to top of fourth crest
Intersections: Sanchez F.R. (.16m), Ravine Trail (.21m)
Note: Dead-end

This roller-coaster is the main route within the Preserve. Because it is a dead-end, the four hills encountered in each direction must be repeated, making for eight climbs per full round trip.

Many users access Verissimo Hills Trail from Sanchez Fire Road or Oak Valley or Ravine Trail, all of which rise from residential areas. But these routes join Verissimo Hills midway. To make the full journey, enter at the Preserve's west boundary gate, off Stafford Lake Trail.

Stafford Lake Trail runs 1.3 miles from Vineyard Road north to Center Road, an open-to-the-public route across North Marin Water District land. It is also part of the Bay Area Ridge Trail. The Verissimo Hills Trailhead is roughly equidistant between Center Road and Vineyard Road, at the ridge top. When approaching from Center Road (which is also the west end of Little Mountain Trail), you'll need to veer left toward the power poles and the fence line. When approaching from the south—Stafford Lake Trail sets off one-sixth mile beyond the end of the pavement on Vineyard Road—veer right up to the Verissimo Hills Preserve entry and Verissimo Hills Trail sign. Be sure to re-close the gate.

Splendid views begin immediately. Behind, is Indian Valley Golf Course and Stafford Lake, principal reservoir of the North Marin Water District (established 1948). Stafford Lake was created in 1950-51 with a dam across Novato Creek. It was named for Charles Stafford (1908-55), a Novato veterinarian and member of the NMWD board. The lake's western shore has been a Marin County Park since 1972; the entry is off Novato Boulevard. Beyond the lake are pastoral dairy lands of northern Marin. Near left is Little Mountain, then Mt. Burdell, both MCOSD Preserves. Right are the foothills up to Big Rock Ridge, lands holding other District Preserves. Straight ahead, east, views extend on clear days across San Pablo Bay to Mt. Diablo.

Verissimo Hills Trail starts with a plunge down through the grassland. By the base is the top of Sanchez Fire Road. It drops left to Sanchez Way, off Center Road, and can be taken as part of a loop with Stafford Lake Trail. Less than 100 yards later, on the right, is Ravine Trail. It leads to Ravine Way and to Oak Valley Trail. Likewise, Ravine Trail offers a loop option with Stafford Lake Trail via Vineyard Road.

Veer left and begin climbing. A path loops around the oaks at the first crest. There is a relatively easy down and up to the second crest. An appealing oak grove at the top invites a rest stop; bring a book!

Next is a steep plunge and equally steep, even longer, uphill. It leads to the third and highest of the crests (but lower than the Trail's start), elevation 475 feet. Three boulders are covered with colorful lichens. I've seen a kingsnake sunning here.

The broad Trail continues another 400 feet to a fourth, lower crest, where it is considered to end. The continuing path ahead abruptly narrows as it drops to the Preserve boundary.

WHITE HILL

Size: 390 acres   Elevation range: 320-1,430 feet

*On summer evenings I have on several occasions been very lucky
to observe a pair of red-tail hawks surfing atop the in-rushing
tide of cool air from the coast as it flows through the San
Geronimo Valley and surges up the western slope of White's Hill.
The hawks hang from outstretched wings, working their tail
feathers to tack back and forth above the grassy-blonde hillside
with heads down searching for rodents. As the sun disappears
behind Inverness Ridge, its rays glint off the incoming fog and
cast a warm orange glow on White's Hill, intensifying shadows
and seeming to coax the hawk's every feather to dance.*
— *Jason Hoorn, Ranger*

WHITE HILL has long been a barrier to east-west travel across Marin County. The
first wagon road over its flank was built by Jesse Colwell, using Chinese labor, in
1865. Marin historian Jack Mason wrote that the road "was so steep folks got down
and walked to give their horses a rest." That same year, a twice-a-week stage coach
was inaugurated "over the hill" to Olema.

In 1873, the North Pacific Coast Railroad undertook the tough task of crossing
White Hill for its new line (see Old Whites Hill Grade, Loma Alta Preserve). In 1903,
the North Shore Railroad, new owners of the line, began work on shortening the
slow, tough climb up White Hill by building a new, lower in elevation (but, therefore,
longer) tunnel. This tunnel and new routing opened a year later, cutting 4.7 miles of
climbing. The new tunnel was named for Henry Bothin, who owned the property
through which it passed. The tunnel was in use for 29 years; the last train passing
through July 31, 1933. Today's Bothin Access Fire Road is a surviving segment.

Meanwhile, the public road over the grade was originally posted as closed to
automobiles in the early years of the 20th century. The first successful driver over,
E.A. Langford in 1905, was arrested on his return trip and fined $10.

Sir Francis Drake Boulevard over White Hill has been plagued by subsidence
problems ever since it was graded in the late 1930's. In February 1940, the Bothin
Tunnel was temporarily re-opened to auto traffic, as a bypass to Drake during major road repair work. Asphalt is now added regularly and the County's Department
of Public Works estimates there is more than 30 feet of asphalt beneath the present
Drake surface.

All 390 acres of the Preserve had been part of the Boy Scouts' 880-acre Camp
Tamarancho. The initial 120 acre parcel, across Sir Francis Drake from Loma Alta
Preserve, was purchased in 1994 for $500,000. The second 270 acres was sold in two
phases, in 1997-98, for a total of $860,000.

The White Hill name comes from Lorenzo E. White, who raised livestock in
the San Geronimo Valley (called White's Valley on some old maps) from around

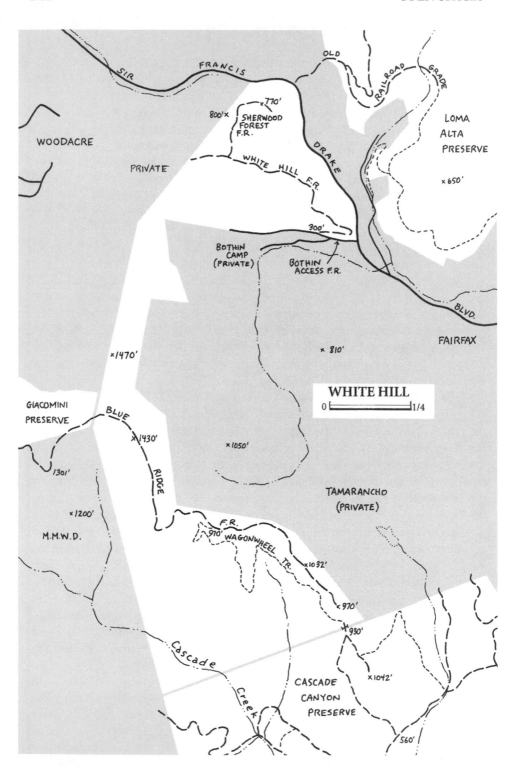

WOODACRE

PRIVATE

SIR   FRANCIS   DRAKE

OLD   RAILROAD   GRADE

LOMA
ALTA
PRESERVE

×650'

×770'
800'×
SHERWOOD
FOREST
F.R.

WHITE HILL F.R.

300'

BOTHIN
CAMP
(PRIVATE)

BOTHIN
ACCESS F.R.

BLVD.

FAIRFAX

×1470'

×810'

WHITE HILL
0 ⊢━━━━━━━⊣ 1/4

GIACOMINI
PRESERVE

BLUE

×1430'

RIDGE

×1050'

TAMARANCHO
(PRIVATE)

1301'

×1200'

M.M.W.D.

F.R.

970' WAGONWHEEL TR.

×1032'

×970'

×930'

Cascade

×1042'

Creek

CASCADE
CANYON
PRESERVE

560'

1850 to 1855. He was a true '49'er, arriving in California from Massachusetts in 1849 at age 21. After leaving Marin, he founded the L. E. White Lumber Company.

There remains a lively debate over whether the hill should be called Whites or White. ("White's," with apostrophe, although commonly used and found on several MCOSD signs and maps, is now generally considered archaic under U.S. Geological Survey naming conventions.) The 1880 Munro-Fraser *History of Marin County*, U.S. Geological Survey topographic maps, and most long-time San Geronimo Valley residents use "White Hill," so that name is adopted here.

Note that the upper (southwest) portion of White Hill F.R. is described in the Giacomini Preserve chapter and that the southern section of Blue Ridge F.R. is found in the Cascade Canyon Preserve chapter.

BLUE RIDGE FIRE ROAD/North (1.66 miles)
From Preserve/Camp Tamarancho boundary to White Hill Fire Road
Intersections: Wagon Wheel Trail & Saddle Cut F.R. (.50m)
Note: Southern section of Blue Ridge F.R., separated by private
Camp Tamarancho, is described in Cascade Canyon Preserve

The stunning northwest section of Blue Ridge Fire Road is one of the more isolated routes within the District, and only recently opened to the public. It crosses the summit of White Hill, with some of the most spectacular views in Marin.

From the Boy Scout's Camp Tamarancho property line at the southeast tip of White Hill Preserve, Blue Ridge Fire Road rolls northwest, up and down along the ridge, at around elevation 1,000 feet. There are some Douglas-fir and other trees, but mostly the route is lined with manzanita shrubs, permitting full enjoyment of the expansive views. White Hill beckons straight ahead. There are several bird houses from Boy Scout days. Wood rat nests also dot the edges.

A half-mile into the northern section, in a saddle, Blue Ridge F.R. meets a four-way junction. Left is the west end of Wagon Wheel Trail, the only official, public connection between the two halves of Blue Ridge F.R. and a loop option back for both hikers and bikers. Right is the top of Saddle Cut Fire Road, which drops 400 feet to the private Boy Scout property boundary, where there are continuing options for those holding a Friends of Tamaracho pass.

The next half-mile of Blue Ridge, to the White Hill summit ridge, is gruelingly steep. Treeless, the climb is even more testing in warm summer sunshine. Try visiting in other seasons. Winter brings the clearest air. In early spring, the grasses are still green and covered with wildflowers. In fall, yellow madias stand out even in the yellowing grasses.

Dig in and climb; the going actually steepens. But expanding views provide incentive and distraction. Attaining the first, and lowest, of three summit crests, dramatically opens vistas east and north. The third crest is slightly higher than the second and the knoll a few feet to its left is the true White Hill summit, at 1,430 feet. There are old metal and wood posts.

The views are spectacular. On the clearest of days, the snow-capped white peaks of the Sierra can be discerned. Nearer, most all of Marin between Mt. Tamalpais and Big Rock Ridge is spread out below. Both Bon Tempe Lake and higher Lake Lagunitas, and the dams that form them, are visible beyond the Meadow Club golf course. The pristine canyons of Cascade Creek drop immediately west.

Just down from the summit, at an old gate, is a historic boundary. Three of Marin's original Mexican land grants met here: Rancho Cañada de Herrera to the east, Rancho Tomales y Baulines south, and Rancho San Geronimo west. Blue Ridge F.R. briefly leaves the MCOSD into land of the MMWD. In spring, poppies and cream cups in abundance brighten the grassland. A path left leads to a splendid view knoll.

Blue Ridge F.R. ends at its junction with White Hill F.R., which drops right and rises left. This ridge is the watershed boundary between creeks emptying into the Pacific Ocean and those running down first to San Francisco Bay.

BOTHIN ACCESS FIRE ROAD (.08 miles)

From Sir Francis Drake Boulevard to White Hill Fire Road
Notes: No parking along paved entry road; use extreme care walking or riding on Sir Francis Drake Boulevard

Bothin Access F.R. is just under this book's minimum length requirement of .10 miles, but is too important (as entry to White Hill F.R.) and too rich in history to omit.

A paved driveway sets off from the "Henry E. Bothin Youth Center" sign at 3125 Sir Francis Drake Boulevard above Fairfax. Do not confuse this entry with the one to Camp Arequipa just lower on Drake; both are owned by the Girl Scouts. Proceed over the public easement to a fork. Left is private property, the driveway into the Youth Center. Right, behind the MCOSD gate, is the start of unpaved Bothin Access Fire Road.

The Fire Road is flat for good reason; it was once part of an 85-mile railroad route between Sausalito and Cazadero (Sonoma County). A wooded hillside borders the right edge. Left are glimpses into the buildings of what was once Hill Farm for sick, needy children, and now an active scouting camp. Just before a boundary fence, White Hill F.R. branches right. The barrier marks the Preserve boundary with private property.

The 3,190-foot tunnel through which trains passed under White Hill between the San Geronimo and Ross Valleys is a quarter-mile ahead, on private land and off limits. (The portal is still evident but the tunnel itself is well sealed.) The tunnel opened to traffic December 4, 1904. It replaced the original 1874 tunnel (see Old Whites Hill Grade, Loma Alta Preserve), which required a longer, more twisting climb. A huge trestle (remnants of which are still visible in Baywood Canyon) carried the track over the canyon to the east.

Henry Bothin (see Bothin Marsh Preserve) bought Phoebe Apperson Hearst's 1,230 acre ranch on White Hill in 1902, planning to build a grand hotel there. But a chance meeting with Elizabeth Ashe on the Sausalito ferry—she was carrying a sick child—changed his mind. Born to wealth, Ashe (1870-1954) devoted her life to caring for the sick and needy. She convinced Bothin to donate 122 acres on White Hill as a refuge for poor women and children from San Francisco. Called Hill Farm, it opened in 1905, then housed a massive influx after the '06 earthquake. Hill Farm closed soon after World War II, when it was leased to the Girl Scouts and renamed Henry E. Bothin Youth Center.

In 1910, also at Ashe's bequest, Bothin donated an additional 35 acres as site for the Arequipa Tuberculosis Sanitarium for Working Women. (The name was chosen by its medical director, Dr. Philip King Brown. Arequipa is a city high in Peru's Andes whose ancient name means "Place of Peace.") Arequipa opened September 4, 1911. Working women diagnosed with tuberculosis were charged one dollar a day for room and board, paid by their employers. They crafted pottery, hats, dresses, and baskets, which were then sold. The sanitarium closed in 1957. Since 1959, Arequipa has also been a Girl Scout camp.

In 1988, the Bothin Foundation tranferred ownership of both the Hill Farm and Arequipa sites to the Girl Scouts. A provision in the transfer states that should the scouts close the camp, the land will revert to the Open Space District.

SHERWOOD FOREST FIRE ROAD (.25 miles)
From White Hill Fire Road north
Note: Dead-end

About two-thirds of a mile up White Hill Fire Road from the Sir Francis Drake entry, Sherwood Forest Fire Road, the first and only intersection, departs to the right. A deep bay woodland borders the uppermost section of Sherwood Forest F.R. Then the route quickly drops to open grassland.

By .1 mile, the Fire Road faces Loma Alta. The Saddle Water Tanks in Loma Alta Preserve are a landmark. The fence left marks the boundary of privately owned Flanders Ranch. White-tailed kites, with distinctive black patches on both the underside and top of their wings, often hunt here, hovering about their rodent prey.

A short uphill brings the Fire Road onto a view knoll. Mt. Tamalpais is visible. Sherwood Forest F.R. then drops again and almost immediately becomes lined with coyote brush and even more abundant French broom. A few yards later, the route ends. The deep woodland below was dubbed Sherwood Forest (or Grove) by the Boys Scouts of Tamarancho, who once maintained a series of interpretive posts through it.

WAGON WHEEL TRAIL (1.32 miles)

Between Blue Ridge Fire Road
Note: Closed to horses

Wagon Wheel is one of the District's newest and loveliest Trails. It has also been the subject of controversy. In the mid-1990's, after the Marin Council of the Boy Scouts of America opened Camp Tamarancho to users paying an annual fee, mountain biking devotees helped build and maintain a number of trails on the property. One was Wagon Wheel Trail.

In 1997, the MCOSD purchased 270 acres of the western section of Tamarancho (thus linking Cascade Canyon Preserve with the new Gary Giacomini Preserve, and with Loma Alta Preserve across Sir Francis Drake Boulevard), including all of Wagon Wheel. The question arose: Should Wagon Wheel remain open to bikers, or conform to District policy of allowing bikes on fire roads only? After spirited discussion, Wagon Wheel was designated for dual bicycle and pedestrian travel (no horses). That, in turn, led to another brouhaha when some Fairfax residents near Tamarancho complained that too many bikers were passing on their way to Wagon Wheel. The County responded by hiring a consultant to prepare a management plan that would assure protection of the Preserve's resources and reach public consensus regarding trail use.

Wagon Wheel Trail can be approached from lower Cascade Canyon by either Blue Ridge F.R. or Burnt Tree Trail off Middle F.R. From the former, turn left at the summit ridge, from Burnt Tree, right. Wagon Wheel Trail is to the left by the several old and new property line markers. (Opposite, on Boy Scout property, is another trail open to both hikers and bikers holding Friends of Tamarancho permits.)

The Trail sets off downhill, and trends down over the first mile. But the grading is so gentle that the Trail appears all but level. Immediately, there are striking views over pristine Cascade Canyon and its ridges; they continue, even improve, the length of the journey.

The pattern of passing between low-lying chaparral shrubs (manzanita and chamise) and light woodland (oak, bay laurel, and madrone) is set early in the Trail and repeats itself throughout. There is a particularly striking, four-trunked madrone bordering the Trail's left margin at .4 miles.

Soon after, the chaparral begins giving way to a splendid grassland. The grasses are green in winter, colored by numerous wildflowers in spring, golden in summer, then yellow in early fall from abundant hayfield tarweed (*Hemizonia luzulaefolia*). The tarweed provides, in the words of botanist John Thomas Howell, "The floral effect of a second spring that lasts until the rains begin....[It] is the golden link that binds with flowers and verdure the end and beginning of successive rainy seasons."

Toyons become more common in the wooded stretches. Giant boulders sit amid a grove of laurels. Be alert to rattlesnakes warming themselves on rocks. There is a timeless feeling here, far from any road.

At just over one mile, two bridges are passed in rapid succession. Wagon Wheel now begins its winding climb back up to Blue Ridge Fire Road. The headwaters of

Cascade Creek, seeping out from White Hill, are crossed. The creek ultimately flows through the whole Ross Valley to San Francisco Bay at Larkspur Landing. Soon after, the Trail passes under a magnificent old oak, its huge limbs "resting" on the ground.

Wagon Wheel ends when it meets Blue Ridge F.R. at a four-way junction. Left, Blue Ridge climbs to the summit of White Hill, beckoning just above. Right, it returns to Wagon Wheel's start for a lovely loop. Directly across, Saddle Cut Fire Road drops onto private Boy Scout land.

The story is told that the Trail's builders unearthed a wooden wagon wheel during construction.

WHITE HILL FIRE ROAD/East (.78 miles)

From Bothin Access Fire Road to Preserve boundary
Intersection: Sherwood Forest F.R. (.64m)
Note: The upper, southwest section of White Hill F.R.
is described in the Giacomini Preserve chapter

Less than a decade ago, not a single foot of this more than three-mile Fire Road was over public land. Now most all of it is, within the District's new White Hill and Giacomini Preserves. There remain, however, three discontinuities in the middle section of White Hill F.R. across private property. For that reason, the description of White Hill F.R. is divided into two sections; the lower (east, or northeast) portion found below, and the upper (west, or southwest) section in the Giacomini Preserve chapter.

White Hill Fire Road rises from Bothin Access F.R., 400 feet in from the MCOSD gate and .2 miles from Sir Francis Drake Boulevard. The steep uphill begins at once, and rarely relents the entire first mile. The initial section heads directly back toward Sir Francis Drake, which is heard, then seen. Here too are the first of the vista points on the route, towards Loma Alta.

The Fire Road bends left and there is a view over the canyon to the White Hill summit. The Fire Road will climb to near the distant-looking ridge, then on to San Geronimo Ridge. There are glimpses of the pool and buildings in the girl scout camp.

At one-third mile, the Fire Road leaves the oak savanna for deeper woodland. Look back at the forest edge for a glimpse of the top of Tam's three peaks. First, madrones are prevalent. Then the Fire Road enters a redwood forest. A water pipeline runs below the Fire Road right and at .6 miles is its source, an old water tank.

One hundred yards above the tank is the first junction. Sherwood Forest F.R. descends to the right, a quarter-mile dead-end route.

Immediately beyond the intersection, White Hill F.R. levels and enters a glorious open area. The views are sweeping. First, they stretch east and south to include landmarks such as Red Hill in San Anselmo, Bald Hill, the Richmond-San Rafael Bridge, and out to Mt. Diablo. Then views open west over San Geronimo Valley to Barnabe Peak.

At .78 miles, White Hill Fire Road meets the fence marking the private property of the Flanders Ranch, the first of the three non-public discontinuities on the route. Some visitors follow a steep, unofficial, quarter-mile bypass on the Preserve side of the fence, which connects to White Hill Fire Road just above the upper Flanders Ranch gate, also signed "No Trespassing." The remote middle section of White Hill F.R. then runs one mile to the Giacomini Preserve line. It is more open, with some wooded sections, and has long fairly level stretches, even some downhills, for lovely travel. But it leaves public, District land twice more. The first is a stretch through the Boy Scout's Camp Tamarancho, then a section through other private property to the west. Description of White Hill F.R. resumes in the Giacomini Preserve chapter.

On the night of May 16, 1946, a B-17 "Flying Fortress," en route to Hamilton Air Force Base from Tucson, ran out of fuel and crashed into White Hill just six feet below the summit. The plane skidded, leaving marks still noticeable today. Wreckage was spread over 300 yards. The two pilots survived and walked out to get help for other crew members, two of whom died. (Courtesy Fairfax Historical Society)

SOME CAUTIONS

Travel over Preserve trails and fire roads is almost invariably a pleasurable experience. Still, much District land is truly wild and a few potential dangers do exist, and are discussed below.

Ticks and Lyme Disease

Ticks are wingless, eight-legged arachnids (not insects). They have long been a nuisance for open space travelers, and their dogs, with a danger of infection. This risk remains. But Lyme disease, only first described in 1975 from a case in Lyme, Connecticut, has made ticks more feared than ever. (Although new evidence shows the disease has been around at least 100 years, possibly much longer.) Even worse, the carrier of the bacterial spirochete that causes Lyme disease is the smallest of local ticks, the western black-legged (*Ixodes pacificus*). It is only 1/8-inch long as an adult and the size of a grain of sand in the even more dangerous nymph stage, so visible only upon close examination and rarely felt.

Ticks poise atop grasses and other brush. Then, attracted by the warmth of a mammal host brushing by, the tick climbs aboard. Males usually don't bite but the female can remain attached for days, enlarging to 200 times pre-meal body weight. The females then drop off, lay some 1,000 eggs to hatch in the following year's cycle, and die. While embedded, ticks may transfer Lyme disease spirochetes (*Borrelia burgdorferi,* not identified until 1983) into the host's blood supply. If left untreated, these bacteria can have a debilitating effect on the neuromuscular system.

On the positive side, only 1-4% of ticks in Marin carry the disease, far less than in eastern and midwestern states. (Recent research suggests that a protein in the blood of our abundant western fence lizards, a prime tick host, kills the bacteria.) Also, the tick usually needs to be embedded 24, possibly 48 hours, to transmit the disease. And now that Lyme disease has become well publicized, there are better diagnostic tests and at least one vaccine (LYMErix), introduced in 1999. Consult your physician.

The best precautions are avoiding cross-country travel through grassland and checking for ticks (or having a friend check) after an open space visit. Ticks tend to migrate to warm areas, such as armpits. Other tips include pulling socks over pant legs to cut off a common entry route, wearing light clothing that makes the black ticks more visible, and spraying with repellant.

If a tick is embedded, carefully remove it straight out with tweezers. You may want to save the tick for testing. If the tick's head breaks off and stays embedded, or if a circular rash develops around the site a few days later (a common but not invariable first sign of Lyme disease), see a physician.

Poison oak (*Toxicodendron diversilobum*)

All open space travelers need be familiar with poison oak, or suffer the consequences. The entire plant (save the pollen), in all seasons, contains urushiol, a toxin that produces a dermatitis in approximately 70 percent of those exposed to it for at least a second time. Urushiol is quick acting, begins to penetrate the skin within ten minutes, and can remain toxic on clothes hours or days after contact.

Adding to the problem, poison oak is common, likely the most abundant shrub within the District. There are huge tracts where poison oak is essentially unavoidable to those venturing off-trail. And the plant is highly variable, the species name "diversilobium" means varied-leaved. Responding to its environment, it can be a vine climbing fifty feet or more on tall trees, two-inches tall singly or in dense mats, a bush with stiff or pliant branches, or a small tree. It also grows in many habitats. On the positive side, the leaves redden in fall, adding color to the woodland.

Travelers who learn to recognize poison oak's distinctive three-leaved clusters, and exercise reasonable care on narrow sections of trails, need not worry. If you've been exposed, shower as soon as possible, scrubbing with a strong soap such as Fels Naptha. New preventive products, such as Tec-Nu, can be applied beforehand. Calamine and other lotions provide some relief. Nasty cases require medical attention. Do not burn poison oak; breathing the fumes can be a serious, even fatal, matter.

Rattlesnakes (*Crotalus viridus oreganus*)

Until the return of mountain lions a decade or so ago, rattlesnakes were the most feared denizens of Marin open space lands. Actually, they are uncommon, with Cascade Canyon and Indian Valley producing the most sightings. Years can pass without a single bite reported within District lands, and there has never been a fatality.

A rattlesnake's tail rattles (unless a juvenile) and broad, triangular head are diagnostic. A rattle segment is added each time the snake sheds its skin. Gopher snakes resemble rattlers, and even vibrate their tail when aroused, but are harmless, as are all the several other Marin County snakes.

Rattlesnakes are more likely seen in summer, when they are out in the heat, sunning on rocks. Although rattlers aren't aggressive, stay well clear. Most bites come from trying to handle or otherwise molest the snake. Bites require immediate medical attention. Some travelers carry venom removal suction pumps in their first aid kits.

Mountain lions (*Felis concolor*)

Mountain lions were probably never completely extirpated from Marin County, but reliable sightings in the post-World War II years were rare. Recently, possibly related to new Statewide protections against shooting mountain lions, sightings and encounters have increased, and have not been confined to the remotest areas. Now both the Golden Gate National Recreation Area and the Marin Municipal Water District post mountain lion warnings at trailheads. Still, no physical encounters in Marin between open space visitors and mountain lions have been reported and even most lifelong hikers have never seen one.

Mountain lions, also known as cougars and pumas, average 145 pounds for males, just under 100 pounds for females. They are about two feet tall at the shoulder. Their large size and long tail, two-thirds of body-length, clearly distinguish them from bobcats.

The closest most visitors ever get to secretive mountain lions is spotting their scat, an inch in diameter with different-length segments that are deeply constricted. Like other cats, mountain lions make some attempt at covering scat with nearby debris.

If a mountain lion is actually encountered, GGNRA warning signs read: "Remain calm—do not run; pick up small children immediately; stand upright—maintain eye contact; back away slowly; be assertive—if approached, wave your arms, speak firmly or shout, and throw sticks or rocks; if attacked, fight back aggressively."

Coyotes (*Canis latrans*)

Coyotes prowled Marin during Miwok days, then were basically extirpated as a varmint. But in recent decades, coyotes, perhaps drifting in from Sonoma County, have again established themselves and may be found in several Preserves.

The GGNRA recently became the first local land manager to post Coyote Advisory signs, as coyotes have been seen trailing visitors, particularly those with dogs. These signs suggest keeping children and dogs close and, in the event of an encounter, making loud noises, throwing rocks, standing upright, avoiding eye contact, backing away slowly (not running), and fighting any attack aggressively. Though nocturnal, coyotes may be out at any time.

Coyotes may be confused with domestic dogs; the two can and do interbreed. Coyotes, generally gray or rusty-gray, tend to have more pointed noses and bushier tails than domestic dogs and hold their tail down between their hind legs when running.

Mushrooms

Mushrooms are the reproductive structures of fungi, or, in a related meaning, a fungus that produces a fleshy, fruiting body. Hundreds of species of mushrooms grow throughout the District. They are most prominent in forests after fall and winter rains, but can be found in most any habitat at any time of year.

While only a few local mushroom species are poisonous, some are deadly so. For example, both Death Cap (*Amanita phalloides*) and Death Angel (*A. ocreata*) are common in Marin, and their names speak volumes. And some of the deadliest mushrooms look similar to some of the tastiest, so mistakes, often by foreigners not familiar with local species, are common. It is illegal to gather mushrooms within the Preserves.

Yellowjackets

Yellowjackets are a type of wasp (genus *Vespula*) that live in large colonies in paper nests. There are two common species In Marin, one that nests above ground (usually in trees or sometimes on buildings) and one that uses abandoned gopher or squirrel burrows. These animals are usually not aggressive when they are foraging, but may mount a fierce attack if they feel you are threatening their nest. Never linger near a burrow entrance from which wasps are emerging. Paper wasps are usually most aggressive near the end of summer when the queens (who will found the next year's colonies) are being produced.

While a yellowjacket sting is simply mildly painful to most people, it can be a serious, even life-threatening affair to others, requiring immediate medical attention.

Dehydration, Giardiasis

Since no fountains have been installed within any of the Preserves, visitors need to carry an adequate water supply. In summer, daytime temperatures of 90, even 100 degrees, are common in inland Preserves. Err on the safe side and bring more water than you think you'll need.

The protozoan *Giardia lamblia*, which causes the intestinal ailment of giardiasis, has not turned up in Marin County streams. Still, land managers throughout the County, including the MCOSD, caution against drinking untreated water.

Crime

While Preserves are the most crime-free areas in the County, problems do arise. Always lock your car at trailheads and don't leave valuables inside, certainly not visible. Report suspicious activity to the police (dial 911).

Fire hazard reduction

Although Marin's native plant and animal communities have adapted to fire—and in many instances benefit from it—the same cannot be said for humans. Thus, fire hazard is a concern throughout the County, particularly during the hot, dry months of summer and early fall. In response, the District includes the following tasks in its routine land management activities:

~ Creates fuel breaks at open space entrances and mows many miles of open space boundaries that adjoin homes

~ Maintains some 80 miles of open space fire protection roads

~ Cooperates with Marin's cities, towns, and other agencies to establish fuel management programs

~ Participates in the Mt. Tamalpais Vegetation Management Plan to reduce fuel loads on preserves in the Tam area

~ Offers open space neighbors the opportunity to supplement their own fire protection efforts by granting free permits to clear fuels on District lands adjacent to their homes

~ Closes certain Preserves during "red flag days," when a combination of temperature, humidity, winds, and fuel moisture content indicate a high fire danger

~ Enforces prohibitions on smoking (April 1-November 30), open fires, and possession of camp stoves, barbecues, gas lanterns, and other similar appliances.

SELECTED BIBLIOGRAPHY

The Crookedest Railroad in the World by Ted Wurm and Al Graves (Trans-Anglo Books,
    Los Angeles, 1983)
Early Marin by Jack Mason with Helen Van Cleave Park (Marin County Historical Society, 1971)
Hill Farm and Arequipa by Gunard Solberg (Fairfax Historical Society, 1997)
History of Marin County, California by J.P. Munro-Fraser (Alley, Bowen & Co., 1880,
    reprinted 1972)
The Jepson Manual, Higher Plants of California, edited by James C. Hickman (University of
    California Press, Berkeley, 1993)
Larkspur, Past & Present, A History & Walking Guide by the Larkspur Heritage (City of
    Larkspur, 1991)
The Making of Marin (1850-1975) by Jack Mason in collaboration with Helen Van Cleave Park
(North Shore Books, Inverness, 1975)
Marin Flora by John Thomas Howell (University of California Press, Berkeley, 1949, revised 1972)
Mount Tamalpais, A History by Lincoln Fairley (Scottwall Associates, San Francisco, 1987)
Movie Studios & Movie Theaters in Marin, A History Since 1898 by Lionel Ashcroft (Marin County
    Historical Society, 1998)
Narrow Gauge to the Redwoods by A. Bray Dickinson (Trans-Anglo Books, Los Angeles, 1967)
Novato Township, Land Grant to World War II by May Rodgers Ungemach (Novato Historical
    Guild, 1989)
Oaks of California by Bruce Pavlik, Pamela Muick, Sharon Johnston, and Marjorie Popper
    (Cachuma Press, Los Olivos, CA, 1991)
Old Marin With Love (Marin County American Revolution Bicentennial Commission, 1976)
Pictorial History of Tiburon, A California Railroad Town, Landmarks Society of Belvedere &
    Tiburon (Scottwall Associates, San Francisco, 1984)
Place Names of Marin by Louise Teather (Scottwall Associates, San Francisco, 1986)
Plant Communities of Marin County by W. David Shuford and Irene Timossi (California Native
    Plant Society, 1989)
Saving the Marin-Sonoma Coast by L. Martin Griffin (Sweetwater Springs Press, Healdsburg, 1998)

A great egret waiting for a meal.

The California Motion Picture Studio, on today's K Street between Forbes Avenue and Center Street, San Rafael, c. 1920. Behind is undeveloped Sun Valley and the southeast portion of what is now Terra Linda/Sleepy Hollow Divide Preserve.

The studio was built in 1915, not far from the base of today's Sun Valley Trail, and the grassy hills were used as backdrop in several movies. Many of the company's films featured Beatriz Michelena, a star in the silent film era who married the studio's director. The studio also was used by inventor Leon Douglass in producing one of the world's first color motion pictures, Cupid Angling, with cameo appearances by Mary Pickford and Douglas Fairbanks.

The studio, under various reincarnations, continued producing movies until 1929, after which the buildings were abandoned. All three million feet of highly flammable film archive stored inside were destroyed in a fire accidentally started by youngsters in a Fourth of July fireworks prank. (Courtesy, Marin County Historical Society)

INDEX OF TRAILS AND FIRE ROADS

Trail, Fire Road	Length*	Preserve	Page
Escalon F.R.	.67	Camino Alto	79
Evergreen F.R.	.23	Baltimore Canyon	55
Fieldstone Trail	1.16	Mt. Burdell	173
Fox Hollow Trail	.13	Loma Alta	149
Fox Lane Trail	.25	Terra Linda/North	230
Glen F.R.	.87	Blithedale Summit	64
Glen F.R.	.55	Loma Alta	150
Green Tank F.R.	.15	Ring Mountain	195
Gunshot F.R.	.75	Loma Alta	151
Halloween Trail	.73	Ignacio Valley	120
Happersberger Trail	.43	Cascade Canyon	93
Harry Allen Trail	.44*	Baltimore Canyon	55
Harvey Warne Trail	.18	Camino Alto	80
Heathcliff F.R.	.45	Old St. Hilary's	185
High Water Trail	.24	Cascade Canyon	94
Hill Ranch Trail	1.02	Indian Valley	134
H-Line F.R.	.89	Blithedale Summit	64
Hoo-Koo-E-Koo Trail	1.46*	Baltimore Canyon	56
Horse Hill F.R.	.34	Alto Bowl	46
Horse Hill Trail	.57	Alto Bowl	46
Horseshoe F.R.	.28	Blithedale Summit	65
Huckleberry Trail	.61	Blithedale Summit	66
Hunt Camp F.R.	.43	Giacomini	108
Indian Tree F.R.	1.98	Indian Tree	127
Indian Valley F.R.	.85	Indian Valley	135
Irving F.R.	.63	Terra Linda/North	230
Jack Burgi Trail	.56	Indian Valley	136
King Mountain Loop Trail	1.95*	King Mountain	144
Little Cat F.R.	.54	Pacheco Valle	190
Little Mountain Trail	.30*	Little Mountain	146
Little Tank F.R.	.14	Mt. Burdell	174
Lower Summit F.R.	.58	Camino Alto	81
Luiz F.R.	1.59	Lucas Valley	16
Luiz Ranch F.R.	.73*	Terra Linda/North	231
Lyford F.R.	.14	Old St. Hilary's	186
Manzanita F.R.	.46*	Giacomini	110
Marlin F.R.	.19	Camino Alto	82
Maytag Trail	.16*	Blithedale Summit	66
Meadow Trail	.23	Roy's Redwoods	205
Memorial Trail	.45	Terra Linda/South	225
Michako Trail	.50	Mt. Burdell	174
Middle F.R.	1.13	Cascade Canyon	94
Middle Burdell F.R.	2.00	Mt. Burdell	175
Middle Summit F.R.	.54	Camino Alto	82
Mill Valley-Sausalito Path	.75*	Bothin Marsh	76
Mission Pass Road	.23	Terra Linda/North	231
Montura F.R.	1.11*	Ignacio Valley	121
Myrtle Place Trail	.13*	Mt. Burdell	177

Trail, Fire Road	Length*	Preserve	Page
North Levee Trail	.22	Rush Creek	210
Oak Manor F.R.	.37*	Loma Alta	151
Oak Valley Trail	.10	Verissimo Hills	240
Octopus Access F.R.	.13	Camino Alto	83
Old Lucas Valley Road	.62*	Terra Linda/North	232
Old Quarry Trail	.98	Mt. Burdell	177
Old Railroad Grade	.62*	Blithedale Summit	67
Old Whites Hill Grade	2.02	Loma Alta	152
One Oh One Trail	.28	Rush Creek	210
Pacheco Creek Trail	.26	Pacheco Valle	191
Pacheco Pond F.R.	.39	Indian Valley	137
Pam's Blue Ridge Trail	.55	Cascade Canyon	95
Patricia F.R.	.61	Terra Linda/North	233
Pebble Beach F.R.	.92	Loma Verde	156
Phyllis Ellman Loop Trail	1.76	Ring Mountain	195
Pinheiro F.R.	1.67	Rush Creek	211
Ponti F.R.	1.40	Pacheco Valle	191
Posada del Sol F.R.	.34	Loma Verde	157
Ravine Trail	.28	Verissimo Hills	241
Reed Ranch F.R.	.32	Ring Mountain	198
Ridgewood F.R.	.86	Terra Linda/South	225
Ring Mountain F.R	.93*	Ring Mountain	199
Roy's Redwoods Loop Trail	2.48	Roy's Redwoods	205
Roy's Redwoods Nature Trail	.68	Roy's Redwoods	207
Rush Creek F.R.	.58	Rush Creek	212
Russell Antonio Trail	.12	Deer Island	104
Salt Lick F.R.	.59	Mt. Burdell	178
San Andreas F.R.	.73	Mt. Burdell	178
San Anselmo Creek Trail	.21	Cascade Canyon	97
San Carlos F.R.	.80	Mt. Burdell	179
San Geronimo Ridge F.R.	4.80*	Giacomini	111
San Marin F.R.	1.99	Mt. Burdell	180
San Pedro Ridge F.R.	1.12	San Pedro	219
Sanchez F.R.	.12	Verissimo Hills	241
Santa Margarita Loop Trail	.30	Santa Margarita	214
Santa Venetia Levee Trail	1.19	Santa Venetia	216
Schwindt Trail	.81	Indian Valley	131
Shepherd Way F.R.	.26*	Ring Mountain	200
Sherwood Forest F.R.	.25	White Hill	247
Ship's Mast Trail	.94	Indian Tree	129
Simmons Trail	.25	Mt. Burdell	181
Sleepy Hollow F.R.	.18	Terra Linda/North	233
Smith Ridge F.R.	1.77*	Loma Alta	155
Sorich Ranch Trail	.31	Terra Linda/South	227
Southern Marin Line F.R.	2.78	Baltimore Canyon	57
Springs Hill F.R.	.89	Terra Linda/North	234
Summit Drive F.R.	.22*	Giacomini	113
Sun Valley Trail	.67	Terra Linda/South	227
Susan Alexander Trail	.59	Indian Valley	138
Sylvestris F.R.	.95	Giacomini	114
Taylor Ridge Road.	.36*	Ring Mountain	201
Terra Linda Ridge F.R.	1.94	Terra Linda/North	235

A buckeye tree in Mt. Burdell Preserve, one of the few deciduous of the common native trees. (David Hansen)

Trail, Fire Road	Length*	Preserve	Page
Thorner Ridge Trail	.67	Maurice Thorner	162
Tomahawk F.R.	.37*	Terra Linda/South	228
Toyon F.R.	1.03	Cascade Canyon	98
Toyon Tanks F.R.	.33	Cascade Canyon	99
Upper Meadow Trail	.74*	Indian Tree	129
Verissimo Hills Trail	.70	Verissimo Hills	241
Via Escondida F.R.	.54	Loma Verde	158
Vistazo F.R.	.34	Old St. Hilary's	186
Wagon Wheel Trail	1.32	White Hill	248
Warner Canyon Trail	.48	Blithedale Summit	68
Water Tank F.R.	.53	Terra Linda/North	236
Waterfall Trail	1.63	Indian Valley	138
White Hill F.R. (East)	.78*	White Hill	249
White Hill F.R. (West)	1.49*	Giacomini	115
Wildcat Trail	.45	Indian Valley	140
Windy Ridge Trail	.45	Baltimore Canyon	58
Winged Foot F.R.	.32	Ignacio Valley	122
Wintergreen Trail	.22	Terra Linda/North	237
Woodoaks Trail	.98	San Pedro	220

*See individual descriptions for additional information on length outside MCOSD

John Alexander Roy (seated), second wife Barbara (seated beside him), and relatives on the veranda of the Roy home in Fairfax, c. 1900. In 1883, John Roy, a Vermont-born first cousin of the Roy brothers of San Geronimo Valley bought a 773-acre parcel on the south face of Loma Alta for $23,500. This acreage is now the heart of Loma Alta Preserve.

A year later, John built his ranch home. It burned in 1891, replaced by this one, on what is now lower Glen Drive. Though one of the stateliest in Fairfax, the house fell into disrepair and it was deliberately burned by the Fairfax Fire Department on November 17, 1973. Several old Monterey cypress trees, planted as a border, remain. A railroad stop here was also named Roy's. (Courtesy Fairfax Historical Society)

BARRY SPITZ has been exploring Marin County trails for nearly 30 years, and leading interpretive walks over them for 15 years. He is the author of *Tamalpais Trails*, the definitive guide to Marin's landmark mountain, *Mill Valley, The Early Years*, tracing 100 years of the town's history, and *Dipsea, The Greatest Race*, the story of the nation's oldest cross-country footrace. He served on the County's Open Space Trails Committee from 1989 to 1992. Spitz and wife Pamela live in San Anselmo with daughters Sally (9) and Lily (7).

The author, Barry Spitz, measuring distances in Giacomini Preserve.

Additional copies of this book, and the author's other titles, may be ordered by sending the price below, plus sales tax and $2 per book shipping (checks payable to Potrero Publishing Co.), to: Potrero Publishing, P.O. Box 3007, San Anselmo, CA 94979. Requests for autographs and other personal inscriptions will be honored.

Open Spaces, Lands of the Marin County Open Space District - $17.95
Tamalpais Trails - $18.95
Mill Valley, The Early Years - $35 (hardcover)
Dipsea, The Greatest Race - $27.95 (hardcover)